I0128086

Archibald Forbes

My Experiences of the War between France and Germany

Archibald Forbes

My Experiences of the War between France and Germany

ISBN/EAN: 9783742821898

Manufactured in Europe, USA, Canada, Australia, Japa

Cover: Foto ©Thomas Meinert / pixelio.de

Manufactured and distributed by brebook publishing software
(www.brebook.com)

Archibald Forbes

My Experiences of the War between France and Germany

COLLECTION

OF

BRITISH AUTHORS

TAUCHNITZ EDITION.

.

VOL. 1160.

MY EXPERIENCES OF
THE WAR BETWEEN FRANCE AND GERMANY
BY
ARCHIBALD FORBES.

IN TWO VOLUMES.
VOL. II.

MY EXPERIENCES

OF

THE WAR

BETWEEN

FRANCE AND GERMANY.

BY

ARCHIBALD FORBES,

ONE OF THE SPECIAL CORRESPONDENTS OF "THE DAILY NEWS."

IN TWO VOLUMES.

LEIPZIG

BERNHARD TAUCHNITZ

1871.

CONTENTS

OF VOLUME II.

___

PART III

PARIS.

		Page
CHAPTER I. To the great Sortie		7
— II. From the great Sortie to the New Year		117
— III From the New Year to the Armistice		220

PART IV.

THE CONQUERED AND THE CONQUERORS.

| CHAPTER I. The Conquered . . . . | | 303 |
| — II. The Conquerors . . . . | | 342 |

___

MY EXPERIENCES

OF THE

WAR BETWEEN FRANCE & GERMANY.

PART III.

PARIS.

CHAPTER I.

To the great Sortie.

Having returned to England for a few days after
quitting Metz, it became my duty to proceed to the
vicinity of Paris, to act as one of the watchers of the
terrible drama which was being slowly but steadily played
out with the beautiful metropolis as the centre of interest.
The siege of Paris may be said to have commenced on
the 21st of September, on which day the left flank of the
3rd army, and the right flank of the Maas army came
together round Paris like the closing claws of a crab,
and the grip was never relaxed till the preliminaries of
peace were accepted at Bordeaux. The armies, divisions,
brigades, and regiments dropped into their appointed
places, as you may see the bolts of a strong safe-lock
fall when the key is turned. The positions taken up on
the opening days of the siege were not materially altered
till the armistice. Temporarily and rarely an effort of
the French caused a slight bulging out of the circle of

environment, but the lost ground was always recovered. During the two months that had elapsed before I found myself before Paris there had been many skirmishes; one important sortie in force, that of the 21st October; and the capture and recapture of Le Bourget, the former event, characterised by no great shedding of blood, occurring on the 28th October, the latter, a desperate and bloody affair, taking place on the 31st October. A detailed account of the recapture of Le Bourget, gathered from the leading participators who had been left alive, will be found in the course of this chapter.

Choosing the road I knew best, I left Sedan at ten o'clock on the night of the 13th of November in the company of a Prussian courier bound for the head-quarters at Versailles, a favour for which I owe many acknowledgments to the distinguished personage through whose permission it was accorded. There was but very little interest attaching to a journey performed at full speed and without a halt, save for the purpose of changing horses at each stage. But one of its episodes may be worth narrating as an illustration of the watchful scrupulousness and sense of discipline animating German soldiers on sentry duty. My companion happened to be in civilian dress, not having expected to leave Belgium, and he therefore could not show the overt stamp of authenticity which the Feldjäger uniform confers. Thus at every turn he had laboriously to verify himself. Sedan was in a state of siege, the gates being shut at an early hour in the evening, and an order from the commandant had to be exhibited to the Landwehr under-officer at the gate before he would lower the drawbridge and make patent the way through the other defences. Just as we were outside, it occurred to my companion that he would not be likely to progress unless he had the watchword,

and he asked the under-officer of the gate guard to give
it to him. I believe this unyielding man, firm to the
letter of his orders to give the watchword to nobody,
would have refused it to Count Moltke himself, had he
been out of uniform. There was no help for it, but to
drive back to the commandant in the town, where the
courier duly got the watchword, accompanied by the
pleasing intelligence that it only held good for the garrison, and that he would probably encounter another
watchword before he had been a mile on his road. We
received confirmation of this when we reached the hamlet which forms a suburb of Donchery, on the south side
of the Meuse. To the "halt" of the Landwehr-man in
the road in front of the houses, we were able to give a
satisfactory response, and the watchword having passed,
we were told to pass likewise. But we had not gone
twenty yards when another hoarse challenge came sounding out of the darkness. It came from a post of regulars, who had a watchword of their own, which prevailed
throughout the brigade that occupied the territory as far
as Flize. The regulars refused to have any connection
with the gentlemen over the way, in the shape of the
Landwehr, and the Landwehr watchword was of as little
value as a brass sovereign at the counter of the Bank of
England. In vain did the Landwehr sentry represent to
his brother of the line that the travellers were all right,
his demand for a watchword having been responded to.
The sentry of the regulars would neither allow a passage
nor reveal the watchword. The courier had to dismount
and cross the bridge which leads over the Meuse into
Donchery, where he found an officer, and became possessed of the precious watchword. Precious it turned
out to be for only a very brief period. On the slope
between Dom and Flize we were challenged by a patrol

of two men, who in the accustomed manner demanded
the watchword. My companion gave that which he had
received at Donchery, but it seemed we were already out
of the region where it had efficacy. The men of the
patrol repudiated it, and looked gravely at each other.
Then they spoke in a low tone of the necessity for taking us back to Dom, to avert which fate my companion
produced copious legitimations, and at last contrived to
satisfy the patrol that he was really a person to be permitted to pass. They not only let us pass, but they gave
us the watchword which prevailed in the parts we were
about to traverse. With no small gratitude we accepted
the same, and went on our way rejoicing. Some distance
outside of Boulzicourt, on the summit of a little swell,
we were suddenly challenged in loud and stern tones.
The horses had a good deal of way on them, and the
driver could not pull them up quite within their own
length. Louder and sterner came the challenge repeated,
and we heard a couple of ominous clicks, as the sentries
on the double post cocked their needle-guns. Just at
the moment the moon flashed out, and there in the path
stood the two stalwart men, with their weapons at the
"charge," the bayonet points in very close proximity to
the noses of our team. The driver stopped his horses
just in time, and my companion, in the measured under-
tone in which this mystic communication is always made,
proceeded to enunciate the watchword. There was a
pause that was quite oppressive, till the sentry, instead of
the welcome "Pass," startled us by saying "No, there is
a mistake!" Of course there was nothing for it but that
we should be conducted to the guard as suspicious persons, who had attempted to pass with a wrong watchword. Here it became necessary for my companion to
descend and elaborately to vindicate his character by the

production of his papers seriatim. Then, and not till then, did the under-officer thaw, and communicate the information that our version of the watchword was wrong but by a single syllable. The patrol had blundered. I am certain the mistake was not ours—too much inconvenience was the sequence of an error for us to lapse into it through carelessness. At length we made a fresh start with the rectified watchword, which stood us in stead through several posts, and then came to an end as others had done. Two posts, however, consisting of single sentries, we contrived to satisfy without the watchword by the exhibition of legitimations, and drove on till interrupted by a challenge from a double post outside the village of Mondigny. The sentries demanded the watchword. There was no watchword forthcoming. "Why?" "Well, the road was horribly tantalising, every other mile there was a new watchword, and so difficult was it always to take up the new one that the attempt had to be given up." A grunt, in which there was assuredly incredulity, was the response, and then the sentries took post one on either side of the carriage, ported their arms, and gave the word to march. On reaching the guard the under-officer gradually became satisfied that my companion was neither a spy nor an unauthorised traveller, and gave us permission to proceed. The courier ventured to ask him for the watchword. Never shall I forget the look and accent of holy horror with which the honest fellow exclaimed "God forbid!" He would let us pass, to be dealt with by the tender mercies of the next post we should meet; but the watchword—that was his holy of holies, the palladium of his duty—not to be permitted unto King Wilhelm himself, unless he asked for it with the prescribed title to receive it. However, at Mondigny we had reached the left flank of the troops occupying

the valley of the Meuse and its vicinity, and had no more
trouble from scrupulous sentries as we journeyed on to
Rethel through the watches of the night.   Some may
imagine that it was an excess of caution thus to delay
the progress of a courier travelling with important despatches to head-quarters.   As the matter stood, the delay
no doubt was vexatious, and did not answer any good
purpose.   But there would have been no delay had the
courier been dressed in the distinctive uniform of his
corps, and he had to take the inevitable consequences of
not being so.   I confess that, looking at the matter from
a military point of view, I gloried in the rigorous discharge of their duties on the part of the trusty sentries,
looking as they did neither to the right nor to the left,
but straight forward along the definite line of their orders.
For once that this stern strictness may be slightly detrimental, as in the case of the courier, my companion, it
will ninety-nine times be of service in utterly preventing
the movements of suspicious or treacherous persons.   And
it was part and parcel of the rigorous discipline which
the journey illustrated, that my companion bore every
interruption, not indeed without a grumble, but without
a single remonstrance, accepting stoppage after stoppage
as if it was a decree of fate, against which there was no
use to rebel or even to get angry.   Nay, although, as I
say, human nature asserted itself, and he did grumble a
little, yet there was not wanting a tone of real national
pride, not to say exultation, in his comments on the state
of discipline which was the cause of his inconveniences.

At Meaux, being bound for Versailles, we wended
away to the south of Paris, using the Melun Chaussée for
some distance, and then entering upon a labyrinth of
side roads.   Between Boissy St. Leger and Limeil, on
the high ground overhanging the broad valley, the view

of Paris first burst on my sight. One must have looked
down on the beleaguered city from some one of the surrounding heights before the full impression of the reality
of the siege, and of the passing strangeness of that reality,
could actually come home to his mind. No reading, no
imagining, could produce the profound effect. There
lay, glistening in the peaceful afternoon sun, the great
expanse of white houses, alternated with towers and
spires. Notre Dame did not seem two miles distant; with
my glass I could trace the course of the Seine through
the city by the break in the bank of house tops. How
peaceful everything seemed! What prevented to turn the
horses' heads, and drive straight in to a dinner at Du-
rand's, and a bed in the Grand Hotel? How difficult to
realise the isolation among the white houses there of two
millions of human beings, to know of the seething ferment
that was ever going on in that dense, excitable mass of
humanity, cut off as it was from all communication with
the outer world.

Versailles. I found the Versailles that had been written
about *usque ad nauseam* for the two months before, a
dead stagnation with princes, correspondents, military
bands, representatives of the demi-monde, and the errant
wanderers of every country in Europe bobbing lazily on
the surface. No fighting, no real news, hardly even
gossip, unless scandal could by a stretch be called gossip;
and of that, of the most pitifully trivial kind, the crop
seemed plentiful enough. Undoubtedly, Versailles was
the place at which to see notabilities. What a place
would Versailles have been in those days for dear old
Pepys! How he would have bowed to the ground as he
sniffed the odour of exalted rank; how he would have
scuttled about from one back-stairs to another, from the
park to the table d'hôte and back again to the courtyard

in front of the King's residence in the Prefecture. It
struck me, even in the two days which was all the time
I had to spare to Versailles, that it was not wholly destitute of modern Pepyses, modified from the great original
but by circumstances.

As I sat writing in the Hôtel de France on the afternoon of my arrival in Versailles (I got there on the 16th
November) I heard the mournful wail of funeral music
out in the Place d'Armes. From out the Château, which
was one huge hospital, there came winding a long procession, headed by a military band. Behind the band
were three coffins, one covered by a black pall, the other
two by white palls, and all borne aloft on trestles on the
shoulders of soldiers. Behind the coffins marched the
mourners, consisting of a band of officers, and the rear
was brought up by a detachment of soldiers carrying their
arms. To the dirge-like strains the procession slowly
crossed the Place d'Armes, and wound through the streets
to the cemetery. There, in a corner, was the great grave
of the strangers, of those who are to be sojourners in a
strange land till the sounding of the last trumpet. Not a
few had already been buried below that raised parallelo-
gram of red earth, for there were many sick and wounded
in the vast halls of the palace; and the procession I witnessed was one of daily occurrence. Already tender hands
had been at work among the red clay. Headstones had
been set up and chrysanthemums planted. One grave,
that of a lieutenant, was already railed in. Around the
great open trench was collected a motley group—the
front tiers composed of the street boys of Versailles.
Behind them stood many women; in the background
were soldiers of all arms, who had come down to the
cemetery to pay the last mark of respect to their dead
comrades. Slowly the procession wound up to the grave's

mouth, and the band wheeling to one side continued to
sound its dismal moanings. The mourners took post on
either side, and the first coffin was moved up close to the
grave. Two French gravediggers seized it, bore it forward, placed it across the ropes, and lowered it down to
a third man in the bottom, who packed it away on one
side. There was no near relative there to lower the head
of the dead soldier into the grave; the real mourning for
him was yet to come in some quiet village of the Fatherland, when the Feldpostbrief should reach the simple
household announcing that its member with the army was
to return no more. The other two coffins were lowered
in like manner, the band still sounding its solemn strains,
the street boys standing in unwonted silence and stillness, hushed into awe. Then came forward Herr Pastor,
the chaplain of the division, in long black robes and
casket-like cap, his hands clasped over his breast. The
Germans have no set funeral service; it is left to the
clergyman to make the most of the occasion over the
open grave. Very much of the occasion did this most
eloquent chaplain make. He spoke of the dead there as
"our comrades, our friends, our brethren," of their death
in a righteous cause, of their having met their fate as
valiant soldiers fighting for their King and their Fatherland. Much more said he that would be out of place to
quote, and then stepping forward to the brink of the
grave, he strewed over the coffins a handful of mould,
with the solemn "dust to dust, ashes to ashes," words so
familiar to all, yet never heard without a new thrill. The
grey-haired Oberst on the mound of earth doffed his
helmet and bent his bare head. All followed his example.
To the "Amen" of the Pastor, joined in by all, there
succeeded a pause of dead silence, broken at length by
the still mournful music of the band. Then the Oberst

stooped, and, picking up a handful of mould, threw it on the coffins of his fellow soldiers lying dead there in the bottom of the deep grave. The other officers followed his example, and the soldiers standing all round threw in also their handfuls. The procession then reformed, and as soon as the gates of the cemetery were reached, the band struck up a merry march, as if to efface from recollection the memory of the mournful scene we had just witnessed.

It was arranged that, should I receive permission, I was to attach myself to the head-quarters of the Crown Prince of Saxony, who had commanded the Maas army ever since its formation after the battle of Gravelotte. The Prince had his head-quarters in Margency, a small village due north of Paris, and lying about two kilometres behind the well-known Montmorency. A journey round a section of the environment in the times I am writing of was a work of difficulty, and often of impossibility. Broken bridges, barricades, and stern sentries impeded the progress of the wayfarer; and if he was eager for a near cut, he had in many instances to make up his mind to chance being fired into by the French outposts. Anyone travelling between St. Germain and Argenteuil by the river route through Bezons had to face, not a chance, but a certainty of this dropping fire, and that not for a space across which he might gallop in a few minutes, but continuously for a distance of several miles. Discretion therefore prompted me on my journey to Margency to avoid the pontoon bridge below St. Germain, which led to the river, and to make a detour some distance down the Seine till I reached the railway bridge, a little beyond Le Mesnil. There was something almost oppressive in the utter solitude of the long drive through the forest of St. Germain. In the very heart of war as the forest was, the dead leaves

in its drives were not rustled by the tread of a single
living thing. One might have imagined oneself traversing
the New Forest, instead of driving through a spot that
was within, or at all events barely without, the range of
the guns of Mont Valérien. One of my most forcible
early impressions of the theatre of war around Metz had
been the comparative invisibility of the beleaguering force.
It was the same here. We know roughly how many thousand Germans there stood around Paris, ever ready for
action when the alarm was given. But where were they?
would have been the natural question for one who does
not know how compactly the Germans stow, and what
little show their hosts make when there is no occasion
for demonstration. The country all round is chequered
with villages and châteaux, in the vicinity of which was
visible an occasional spiked helmet. But let the alarm
have sounded, and see what a dense clump of spiked
helmets every village and château would have given up.
The railway bridge at Mesnil was not the most eligible
conceivable means of crossing a river; but it served its
turn. What between mud, rails, sleepers, and deep holes,
the springs of a carriage had need to be very tough indeed, and the horses dragging it need to be very strong.
One, however, was not disposed to be over critical when
he reflected how lucky it was that this means of crossing
was left to him at all. For not 200 yards down stream
were visible the shattered ruins of the road bridge. What
a deal of pains the French engineers must have expended
in utterly smashing up this structure. Hardly one stone
had been left upon another. The shattered stumps of
the piers stuck up out of the troubled waters, a swirling
rapid in which marked where the rest of the structure
lay in a rough heap on the bottom. It is inscrutable that

a little of the assiduity developed in the destruction of this bridge should not have been diverted towards rendering impassable the railway bridge, which now, for all practical purposes, supplied its place.

Mont Valérien is the Old Man of the Sea to the journeyer around this side of Paris. It is the most ubiquitous eminence imaginable. At St. Germain it is due east of you, and you think if you go a long way north, that you must presently leave it behind. But wherever you go there he rears his head, to all appearance ever in your path. After passing Argenteuil, however, I did contrive to give him a little the go by; but it was only in escaping from Scylla to fall into Charybdis. A little beyond Argenteuil my coachman turned boldly on the road, in a south-easterly direction, and passed on his left the village of St. Gratien, with a confidence which would have impressed the most distrustful that the man knew the road quite familiarly. At Epinay I was therefore greatly surprised to find us brought up all standing by a formidable entrenchment, beyond which there was no passing. From what the courteous officer who had charge of the post told me, I could not feel any great regret that we were thus brought to a halt, seeing that, as it was, we were all too close to the guns of the crown work of St. Briche to be pleasant, that fortification having a gay and festive habit of throwing shells into St. Gratien, which was considerably in our rear. Returning and passing through St. Gratien, Soisy was presently reached, where in a pleasant château were the head-quarters of the Fourth Army Corps, and a few kilometres further to the north-west I found the head-quarters of the Prince of Saxony, comfortably established in Margency. I have not words to express my sense of the frank and prompt heartiness with which my request for permission to be at-

tached to the Prince's staff was acceded to. Quarters
were at once assigned to me, cramped as the occupants
of the place were for room, and General von Schlotheim,
the chief of the staff of the Maas army, was good enough
to place at my disposal any information which I required.
Nothing could be imagined more dissimilar than the
head-quarters of the two armies which made up the besieging force around Paris. At Versailles there was royal
state and all the pomp and circumstance which the presence of Royalty implies. There was the King's staff,
with princes innumerable; and there was the Crown
Prince's staff, with ever so many more princes. There
was a large town. There were strangers of all countries,
of all classes, and with all sorts of business—not a few
with no business at all. Versailles was the centre of
political as well as military news, and of the deliberations
and gossip which tidings of both kinds generate. It was
dull enough, no doubt, to any one fond of action, but
then it presented lots of alteratives to dulness. There
was the casino, there were the cafés; to men of the Jeames
de la Pluche turn of mind, there was the great dining-
room of the Hôtel des Réservoirs, where Excellencies and
Serene Highnesses, and other kindred salt of the earth,
did so abound, that a couple of hours' inhalation of its
atmosphere might have made an imaginative Titmouse
believe for the time being that he, too, must surely have
some handle to his name. There were shops in Versailles. I met a gentleman who had got a dress coat
built in the place. There was champagne; little dinners
of a recherché (and expensive) character were possible,
and, in short, there was in Versailles a large infusion of
rosewater in the inevitably bitter decoction, the label on
which is horrid war.

Every item to which I have referred as characteristic

2 *

of Versailles was conspicuous by its absence at Margency.
The Crown Prince of Saxony's staff was of modest size,
and there was no sensational background to the quiet-
toned picture in the way of multitudinous princes. It
comprised about twenty-five officers, some of whom were
Saxon, the remainder Prussian and Würtemberger. The
staff dwelt together in a pleasant fraternal manner in the
big château and in a few smaller residences in the environs of the village. There was but one table kept—
that of his Royal Highness. The stranger coming to
Margency without the good fortune of establishing relations with the staff would have found himself in very
barren quarters indeed. A sign board afforded circumstantial evidence that there had been once an auberge in
the place, but it was now occupied by a marketender,
whose stock was at a very low ebb, and did not appear
likely to be speedily replenished. Except that the village
had no burnt houses, and that its gables were not smashed
by shells and pierced with loop-holes, it reminded me
forcibly of our deadly-lively dwelling-places around Metz.
But its environs were beautiful, and had sustained very
little injury at the hands of the troops. The gardens
were still full of fruit, and a salad, an article that could
not be achieved within a radius of ten miles of Metz for
weeks before the capitulation, was to be got with the utmost ease. Small as Margency was, the military occupants seemed determined to make the most of it in the
eyes of the world. Imitating the Parisians, they had rechristened the streets and had given names to alleys that
were nameless under the French régime. A practical
people, the Germans had gone largely into utility in their
nomenclature. Thus, we had "Ingenieur-street," where
the engineers of the staff resided; "Feldpost-street," which
explains itself; "Telegraph-street," where were the head-

quarters of the field telegraph train, and so on. "Albert-street" was the only departure from utilitarianism.

In the afternoon of the day of my arrival in Margency, a staff officer of engineers was good enough to be my guide to an eminence in the front, from which there was an excellent view of the positions of the besieged and the besiegers, all round the north-western segment of the operations. The ride was a very beautiful one. Skirting Montmorency and Soisy, we came upon the beautiful sheet of water lying to the west of Enghien-les-Bains—surrounded with its arabesque fencing, and with the weeping willows on the lawns of the châteaux, trailing their branches in the pellucid lake. The many hotels surrounding the water—pleasant places so well known to visitors to Paris—were now, without exception, occupied by troops, and the white-capped cook had resigned his office. The soldiers were enjoying their Sunday afternoon leisure in rowing about the lake in the pleasure boats, sharing the water amicably with the swans, which were not discerning enough to recognise in them the enemies of France. The largest of the many villas near the margin of the lake belongs to the Princess Mathilde Demidoff, and in accordance with orders from King Wilhelm, the château and grounds had been carefully respected by his soldiers. But subsequently the necessities of war interfered with this immunity, and on the night of the sortie on Epinay of the 30th November, the Château Demidoff had to be utilised as a lazarette. Bearing to the right through St. Gratien we crossed the road from Sannois to Epinay, and presently commenced the ascent of Mont d'Orgimont, the summit of which was our destination. When we reached the top, what a splendid panorama lay spread out before us! Almost at our feet flowed the Seine, on its way from the bend at St. Denis down to the other bend at

St. Germain.   But yesterday I had crossed the peninsula
held by the Germans, now I looked down on a peninsula
held by the French.   Looking due south I could track
the Seine as it emerged between Mont Valérien and the
Bois de Boulogne.   The latter, or such of it as might
have been left, lay too low to show distinctively; the
former asserted itself right boldly against the horizon,
with its two great barracks on the summit, and the white
puffs of smoke wreathing about its crest as its batteries
sent shot after shot across in the direction of St. Germain.
By the villages on its banks—Puteaux, Courbevoie, Asnières, and St. Ouen, one could trace the course of the
stream till it ran into the white houses and sombre groves
of St. Denis, and then it made the bend, and came down
towards us almost straight.   On one side of the stream
on the left was Epinay, not the pleasantest post in the
world when La Briche happened to be in a bad humour.
Down at our right lay Argenteuil, which had already been
the victim of very rough usage from the French guns in
what I may call the inner peninsula.   From where I stood
I could see no fewer than four destroyed bridges that had
once spanned the Seine.   The nearest was the railway
bridge on the Argenteuil link of the Northern line—it lay
now in the bottom of the river.   Lower down was the
bridge of Argenteuil, with four arches ruined.   Across the
two nearest to Argenteuil there stretched a slender tracery
which betokened that the engineers had been at work
endeavouring to repair them, but the operations were
suspended.   Lower down still was the Bridge of Bezons,
shattered almost to pieces; and nearer the bend towards
St. Germain there was visible the railway bridge on the
line leading to Rouen.   Looking across the peninsula it
was possible, with a good glass, to make out the *enceinte*
of Paris on the Monceaux and Batignolles face, and then

beyond lay the beleaguered city, the horizon closed in by
the Mamelon of Montmartre, with the towers of Notre-
Dame on our right of it; then the great mass of the Pan-
theon; and passing over a multitude of domes and spires,
the Arc de Triomphe far away on the right. The afternoon sun threw its bright rays on the glittering summits
and on the white houses. How difficult it was to realise
the idea that the city lying there so quiet and smiling
was girt by hostile troops and full of fighting men!

To come now to the peninsula lying more immediately
before us. Almost exactly in its centre was the village
of Gennevilliers—no doubt well defended by entrenchments, barricades, and stockades, but none of these were
visible from our position. Through the glass I could see
a sentry at intervals where the roads quit it—for the rest
it might have been a deserted village. On its left front,
and almost close to the Seine, was a small French earthwork, designed probably for a single battery. The earthwork seemed nearly if not altogether completed, but no
guns were in position, and the reason was not far to seek.
The Germans were both capable of preventing the guns
from being got into position, and of making the place
untenable were the guns already there. Near the right—
I speak always of our right and left—of Gennevilliers
was a much larger work, with a couple of bastions, and
evidently designed, when complete, to be a very formidable affair. But it was not nearly so far forward as the
smaller work I have just spoken of, and the same cause
which had arrested the progress of the one prevented the
other also from being further proceeded with. The earthwork lay there clumsy and nearly shapeless, without a
pioneer or a gun near it. In front of Courbevoie was
another French battery, on which the guns were actually
mounted, and long range pieces they were too, for they

had thrown projectiles across the peninsula on to the side
of the river on which is Mont d'Orgimont—a range of
8,500 paces.   Yet another and nearer battery was before
Charlebourg, mounted with guns of a smaller calibre.
This was the battery that had the special animosity against
Argenteuil.   And to conclude the peninsular defences, so
far as they were visible, there was a battery close behind
Nanterre, under the shadow of Mont Valérien—a battery
that in certain contingencies I could imagine not a little
troublesome.

Bang! whiz-z-z-z, came the long whistle of a big shell
through the air.   It struck and burst behind a lower
eminence about 150 yards to the east of where I stood.
Yet another, and another, and another. The shells came
from the big battery at St. Ouen right across the peninsula.   Not a shell came nearer us in our snug conceal-
ment in the observatory on the summit; the gunners of
St. Ouen had never yet got quite that length.   The mark
was a battery emplacement on the lower eminence, on
which were already mounted more than one gun of great
apparent size, and it was evident the French imagined a
position so commanding was being strengthened by working parties and room made for more guns.   I wonder
whether they would have fired so freely had they known
that there was not a man within three hundred yards of
the hillock, and that the threatening-looking big guns
were wooden "quakers" neatly constructed by the
pioneers.   The battery stood with its back to a big bank
of wood, with a church steeple on one side óf it and a
large white château on the other.   It mounted somewhere about twenty guns, which were 48-pounders, and
were believed to be naval guns.   Their range was estimated
at 7,300 paces.

One may write now freely of the forepost line of the

Maas army, a large section of which was visible to us
from the top of Mont d'Orgimont. All the way from
Chaton on the west to Epinay on the east the Seine formed
the narrow boundary line between besiegers and besieged.
At Epinay the forts of St. Denis compelled the abandonment of this natural line of demarcation, and the German
forepost cordon struck away from the river across the
plain in the segment of a circle, villages, châteaux, and
detached houses being carefully utilised as covers for the
strong *replis* which formed the supports of the venture-
some *Feldwachen* projected forward a little distance into
the plain. The line, quitting Epinay, rested first on the
village of Ormesson, then on the hamlet of La Barre, and
attained its most northerly point at the Château of La
Chevrette, in front of the village of Deuil. Thence it struck
eastward with but very little cover to the southern extremity of the village of Montmagny, with a debateable
ground in front consisting of a portion of the village of
Villanteneuse, which was scarcely perceptibly a distinct
village from Montmagny. This debateable ground was
wont to be taken up at night by a non-commissioned
officer's command, while the French held the rest of the
village, and the close proximity gave occasion sometimes
to fighting, sometimes to fraternisation, as the spirit moved.
Skirting the Paris-ward base of the height of Pierrefitte,
otherwise known as Richebourg, the line next touched
the village of Pierrefitte on the great northern chaussée,
and from Pierefitte audaciously struck south-eastward into
Stains, which is so close under the guns of the double
crown work of Fort du Nord, that the gunners could be
plainly seen with the naked eye, going about their business on the ramparts. Pierrefitte is only a little further
distant, not above a mile and a quarter from the town of
St. Denis behind the fortifications, and both villages must

be rebuilt before they will lose the traces of their proximity during the months of the siege, when hardly a day passed that St. Denis did not shell them with more or less acrimony. East of Stains the forepost line had no cover till it reached the Mill of Dugny, whence it passed athwart the front of the village of Dugny, and so following the road, the ditch of which gave some cover to the *Feldwachen*, into the village of Le Bourget. Of the latter section of the line, as well as of its prolongation on the eastern side of the environment, further details will be found on a subsequent page. I am writing now chiefly of so much of it as was visible from the top of Mont d'Orgimont. Had the French known how sedulously that eminence was used for purposes of observation, their artillery might have been more attentive to it than was the case.

The Maas army, as it was termed from the region in which on its formation after Gravelotte it was intended to operate, consisted when organised, and for some time after taking up its position before Paris, of three complete army corps, the 4th (Saxon province), under the command of General von Alvensleben; the Guards (Prussian), commanded by Prince August of Würtemberg; and the 12th (Royal Saxon), whose chief was Prince George of Saxony, the younger brother of the Crown Prince. The latter had commanded the army corps contributed by his father's subjects until the Maas army was formed, and Prince George had then commanded one of its two divisions (the 24th). After the siege was begun there had been added to the Maas army the Würtemberg contingent, consisting of one division under the command of General von Obernitz. It was by far the largest section of the environment which it fell to this Maas army so constituted to maintain. It kept the ground on the north, the east, and the south-east, all the way from

the Seine nearly to the Seine, from Sartrouville on the
west round to Bonneuil-sur-Marne at the bottom of the
horse-shoe, and occasionally with an extended front
approaching still nearer to the Seine. The 4th Army
Corps, with its head-quarters in Soisy, had the section on
the right to hold, as task of comparative ease because of
the natural obstruction which the river offered to an *Ausfall* along almost the whole of its front. It was generally
in Montmorency that its left flank touched, and indeed
blended with the right of the Guards. These splendid
soldiers, with their head-quarters in Gonesse, kept firm
and true the section of environment from Montmorency
as far east as Aulnay, although there were times when
the Guards had to extend to their left as far as Sevran,
and even to garrison Livry when the Saxons had to close
their front to make a denser obstruction to the enemy.
On the other hand there were occasions when the Guards
had to stand closer and closer and touch shoulder to
shoulder, and then the trim men of the Royal Saxon
Corps were to be seen in the wrecked skeleton-houses
of Aulnay. Give and take was the motto, so long as
there were no gaps uncovered by men with needle-guns
in their hands. On the left of the Guards lay the Royal
Saxons, the 12th Army Corps. Prince George had his
head-quarters in Le Vert Galant, a village in the rear of
Livry, and the kindly men of Saxonland confronted Forts
Rosny and Nogent, and before the great sortie of the
2nd December crossed the Marne, and held Champs and
Villiers. South of them lay the Würtembergers with
General Obernitz's head-quarters first in Le Peple, afterwards in Malnoue, extending their front through Champigny of the graves and away south by Chennevieres
and Ormesson, as far as Bonneuil, and sometimes further.
When the 2nd Corps came in on their left and took

part of their ground in that direction, then the Würtemberger kepi came to be seen in Villiers, Noisy-le-Grand,
and Champs, the right flank of the division touching the
Saxon left at the river. Give and take was the motto
here too, and there were no hard and fast lines. The
arduousness of the duty, and the assiduous efforts to
equalise it by interchanges of reliefs, made "dislocations"
very frequent, and if you saw a regiment one day, it
might be in Villiers, and coming back the next should
inquire for it, you might be told by men not only of a different regiment, but of a different corps and a different
nationality, that it had packed up and shifted to quarters
half-a-dozen miles in the rear.

Sights, incidents, and places connected with the prosecution of the siege naturally engrossed the largest share
of interest; but there came occasional lulls, fitful always
and often short, when one had leisure to realise the
wealth of historical and social-historical associations of
which there is so great a profuseness on the north side
of Paris. St. Denis, Montmorency, Aubervilliers, Argenteuil—there is not a name that is not eloquent of great
and stirring memories. Let us take one of those quiet
days, when the foreposts are lazily exchanging shots in
the crisp air of the morning—now and then a streak of
fire and then a jet of smoke flashing out from the steep
side of Mont Valérien—and climb in fancy to the top of
the Hill of Montmorency, whence we command the country
round about for miles in every direction. In that white
village out there in the middle of the peninsula—Gennevilliers is its name—there died some hundred and twenty
years ago a lady you may have heard of—one Mdlle. de
Launay. In Colombes, to the right, Rollin composed his
"Histoire Ancienne," and Bossuet pronounced that magni-
ficent funeral oration over the coffin of Henrietta Maria,

the young daughter of Henri Quatre, which serves as a pattern for many a man in the present day that would feel insulted if you questioned his claim to originality. That white house among the trees, between Colombes and Courbevoie—it has the battery for a background—is called la Garenne; it was the country house of the famous physician Comisart. Bring your eye round now to the shattered bridge of Argenteuil nearer you to the westward. There are other ruins thereabout than the bridge. See you that heap of stones among the trees at the bottom of the island? That is all that is left of the once famous Maison-Joli, the habitation of Watelet, whither about the middle of last century were wont to flock the litterateurs of Paris and the strangers of distinction who visited the capital. You may read not a little about the place in the Mémoires of Morellet and Suard—how it was the rival of Madame Necker's Château at St. Ouen, and of the mansion of Madame Helvetius at Auteuil.

Cross the stream with your eye, and it catches the roofs of the houses in the town of Argenteuil—roofs with holes in them in places, made by the shells from the battery over the way. If you ask a typical Parisian for what Argenteuil is famous, he will reply, "For the quantity rather than the quality of its wine." But Argenteuil has other claims to notice than its fecundity in the juice of the grape. There was a nunnery here once—if all tales are true it was an ugly scandal that caused it to be wound up—which had for one of its abbesses Theodrada, the daughter of Charlemagne, and for another the Eloise of whom our own Pope has sung. The church of Argenteuil is still to the fore. Under that long dead-coloured roof there is a relic, of which, were I a Catholic, I should speak with bated breath. Argenteuil shares, with Treves, Fribourg, and a score of other places for aught I know,

the repute of having in its church a piece of the seam-
less coat of our Lord—that garment of which Matthew
of Westminster wrote, "Mater ejus fecerat ei, et crevit
ipso crescendo." It is here now in a great massive chest
of bronze, designed by Cahier in the 12th century style,
after a series of adventures before which those of the
famous Scottish "Stone of Destiny" fade away into tame-
ness, resting quietly here within range of the shells, after
having escaped the machinations of Turks and Huguenots,
Saracens and Romans, Persians and Normans, after having been buried in a garden and its whereabouts
miraculously revealed to a nun in a dream, and after
having lain for a few centuries, more or less, in a crypt
in a city of Galatia. Look over the slates of Argenteuil
at that house among the trees, by the road between
Argenteuil and Bezons; that is the Château of Marais,
and it was there that Mirabeau dwelt during the stormy
times of the Revolution. Further on, and close to the
shattered bridge of Bezons, you come upon an old
memory in that smaller dwelling by the water side. This
was the château of Marshal Bezons, he who took Landau
in 1713.

If we look further westward we shall get confused by
distances, so let us turn sharp round and look south-
south-east toward St. Ouen. Here, 500 years ago, were
the head-quarters of the order of the Knights of the Star,
whose emblem was a star with the mystic legend,
"Monstrant regibus astra viam." Here Madame de Pom-
padour had a château. It was in this château that
Louis XVIII. halted irresolutely on his way to Paris in
May, 1814, and to it came Talleyrand at dead of night
with the draft of the proclamation, to consent to the
terms of which he found it so hard to persuade the conscientious but beetle-headed monarch. The château of

the Neckers, that once brilliant resort, is now partly in ruins; it may indeed be wholly destroyed, for the battery seems very near its site. Looking over St. Denis you can just see the spire of Aubervilliers or "The Virtues." It was as the Allies reached this spot on their march to Paris after Waterloo, stretched out in a weakened and elongated line, that Napoleon, eating out his heart in Malmaison, clutched at the idea that it was still possible to crush them by a desperate stroke. What an unquenchable energy the man had, how loath to believe that all was lost! Who will not own that there was something grand in the humility of his offer to make the attempt, not as Emperor, but as General, with the half-piteous, half-comical rider, that if he did not succeed he would forthwith take himself off to the United States?

And now we come to St. Denis. How the single word flashes out, as it were, with the limelight along the whole history of France! As one utters it he seems to hear the old war-cry, "Montjoie St. Denis!" so ready on the lips of the chivalry of France—he seems to see the oriflamme waving in the breeze of the battlefield. The last time they took the oriflamme out of the Cathedral was for Agincourt—would it do the men of Paris any service to revive the old institution, and bear it before them in their next sortie? Who cares to know that the old stones were first piled together by Catulla, knocked about by Sigebert, replaced by Chilperic, and dressed and squared by Dagobert? There is no sense of reality about such details as these; but, in the veritable history of the Cathedral, there is surely plenty. Why, if these Chassepots and cannon would only allow you, you might look on the receptacles that contain the dust of dynasty after dynasty of French monarchs. Surely there is reality enough about coffins. You might begin at the com-

mencement, with the baby of Chilperic and Fredegonde,
whose body was placed here in 580, and work systematically down, through the Merovingian dynasty, the Carlo-
vingian dynasty, the Capets, the Bourbons, and the
Orleans people. You would find no Napoleons in St.
Denis. We shall come to the tomb of some of them by
and by, in a more modern place, cheek by jowl with
other ex-royalties. It seems as if the old building would
have none of the parvenus. The First Napoleon built
himself a splendid vault there, and gave out by Imperial
decree that "St. Denis was to be the place of sepulture
of the Napoleonic dynasty," setting about repairing the
place, as was his energetic wont, after the ravages of
the Revolutionists. But the stones were more obstinate
than the Napoleons. Twice the repairs fell in with a
crash of remonstrance, and the late man gave up the
task, and devoted himself to the embellishment of the
interior. It was the merest luck in the world that the
bones of the kings were not made inextricable "pie" of.
When in 1793 Barrere proposed in the Convention to
celebrate the anniversary of the 10th of August by smashing the monuments and tombs of the Kings, he found
enthusiastic supporters. When the gay and festive icono-
clasts had polished off the marble, they took to the
demolition of the coffins, with all the heartier good will,
that the lead was found to make very good bullets. But
for the sagacious old Benedictine Father Poirier, the dust
of St. Louis might have been jumbled with the bones of
Charles Martel, and the Capets and Bourbons got
muddled irretrievably. But Poirier was equal to the hour
—quite a prototype of Dean Stanley. He had no difficulty, by their royal robes, in distinguishing Henry the
Second and Catherine de Medicis. He found Henri Quatre
"in a perfect state of preservation," with his moustache

neatly curled, and the mark quite plain of the knife of
Ravaillac. Louis the Fourteenth was recognisable easily
by "the traits of his visage," and one is not surprised to
hear that Louis the Fifteenth was found reduced to a
nasty mass of semiliquid putrefaction.

One is loath to leave off gossiping about St. Denis,
even at the risk of wearying the reader. Here it was
that Joan of Arc, after her wound, laid down her sword
and deposited her armour. How often has the open
space outside the carved arches of the door of the old
cathedral echoed to the shout of the multitude, "Le Roi
est mort, vive le Roi!" when a dead king of France had
been consigned to the grave of his fathers. I suppose
the Gardes Mobiles are in the old cathedral now, using
it as a barracks. There is less to wreck about it now,
if they are, than before 1793. Before then St. Denis
might have set up a score of ordinary cathedrals in the
way of relics. It could boast of three bodies—rather a
small share—out of the eleven thousand virgin martyrs
of Cologne; of the whole of St. Denis, and another odd
saint or two; of the ears of the Virgin, set in fleur de
lis of gold; of the head of St. Hilaire; of the rim of the
gridiron on which St. Laurent was roasted; of a bone of
the prophet Isaiah; of the sword of St. Louis, that he
wore on his campaign in the Holy Land; of a thorn
from the crown of torture; Charlemagne's sword and
spurs; Dagobert's bronze chair; the sword of Joan of
Arc; the old Royal crown and sceptre; and lots of other
"possibles" of the Wardour-street order. All these the
merry men of the First Revolution scattered to the winds.
But the Cathedral of St. Denis is still a cathedral. The
Abbey, once so rich that during a famine it kept alive
a large proportion of the inhabitants of Paris, has now
lost even its name. Madame de Maintenon diverted

a respectable slice of its revenues, in the shape of
100,000 francs of annual rent, and the First Napoleon
finished the work by rebuilding the old house, and de-
voting it as a *pensionnat* for the education of a number of
children, the offspring of members of the Legion of
Honour. The place is now known by the name of the
"Maison de la Légion d'Honneur." In St. Denis there
is one English association that occurs at the moment.
In La Paroisse, as the chapel of an ancient Carmelite
convent is called, in the Rue de la Briche, as you go out
to the fort of the same name, there lie the remains of
Henrietta of England.

Look down at these ridges at your feet, dotted all
over with villas and châteaux, that break the fall from
the height on which we stand into the flat plain, bounded
by the silvery Seine. This congeries of residences is
Montmorency, a name recalling memories of, perhaps,
the greatest family that France ever knew. It was from
this place that the Montmorencys took their title. Within
sight of his ancestral home, Anne de Montmorency, the
hero of a race of heroes, after a career rivalling that of
Bayard, fell on the field of St. Denis by the hand of
Robert Stuart, slaying his slayer, as he died, with a last
parting blow with the pommel of his sword. The "first
Christian barons," as the Montmorencys were called,
have no longer any foothold in this beautiful valley,
which once they owned from hill to hill; not a stone of
their original mansion near the Church now remains.
But the people will not let die the old glorious name.
Effort after effort has been made, without avail, to efface
its memory by changing the appellation of the locality.
One Louis made a decree that it should be thenceforth
known as Enghien, and another confirmed it. The
revolutionists tried their best to effect yet another change.

They rechristened the place Emile, moved thereunto by another association to which I shall presently allude. But it was all of no use: to this day the place is universally known by the name of Montmorency. Withdraw your mind from dwelling on the fights and highhanded statecraft of the Montmorencys, constables, barons, dukes, and what not, and look down at your feet on this little sequestered house on the fringe of the forest just outside the town of Montmorency. About a hundred years ago there came to dwell in this quiet cottage a man great in a sense, greater than all the Montmorencys —Jean Jacques Rousseau. It was professedly to a hermitage that this great man, so full of paltry littlenesses, came, on the invitation of Madame d'Epinay. Had he lived the life of a hermit it would have been better for his own reputation and for the peacefulness of that pleasant coterie of which the valley of Montmorency was the centre; or had he not been a cynic savage with a dash of lust—a double of Swift—he might have lived and died happily in the society he found ready to welcome him, comprising as it did Grimm, the graceful and spirited historian; the poet St. Lambert, none the less deserving the title of the "gentleman of the pen and the sword" because our Horace Walpole, in that sour way of his, called him a pretentious and lackadaisical jackanapes; the two sisters, Mesdames d'Houdetot and d'Epinay, and others, of whom it were tedious to write. But the cynic philosopher came like the apple of discord. He loved one sister and then abused her like a brute; he transferred his love, such as it was, to the other, who bore with his folly for the sake of his genius; then he packed up bag and baggage, and came across the slope to this other house further on the right —the cottage of Montlouis. It is, however, his first

3*

residence which is the original "Hermitage"—so long a
shrine of idolatry with the French Republicans. If you,
too, are a worshipper of Rousseau, you had better spare
your feelings by refraining from making a pilgrimage to
the Hermitage. There came to it after Rousseau left it
Grétry, the famous composer, and Grétry shares with
Rousseau the memorial trophies of the Hermitage. Indeed, Grétry has the bigger half of them, for he has a
bust on the front with bas reliefs, and a laudatory inscription; and Rousseau is but commemorated by a
painted notice calling attention to his chestnut tree, which,
by the way, is very rotten. You can buy the whole
concern if you like; for there is a notice nailed on the
chestnut tree, "This house to sell or let;" and the Second
Empire has clapped an unpoetical number on it; so that
the other name of the Hermitage is 47, Rue de St. Brice.
Inside it is a wreck, and it is the habitation presently of
a Corporalschaft of the 96th Regiment of Prussian infantry. Rousseau ended that unsociable discontented life
of his at Ermenonville, a village far away to the east,
and we are told when the Prussians under Blücher came
on to Paris, in 1814, hosts of them made pilgrimages
to the sage's tomb. The honest Teutons now in the
Hermitage don't appear to know anything about the
philosopher of Geneva, and, if firewood runs scarce, will
probably burn his chestnut tree. If you know Paris well,
sundry other memories of Montmorency will probably
occur to you, more closely connected with your physical
being than those to which I have been alluding. In
peace time the hotels of Montmorency are justly celebrated
for their cuisine. "Le Cheval Blanc" is quite an historical
hostelry. The Ledrus have been the proprietors of it for
three generations; the keen air gives one an appetite,
and a sight of the well-appointed *salle à manger* would

be right pleasant. Alas! now all that is left to the fore
of "Le Cheval Blanc" is the walls and the sign. That
sign, though, must not be passed over in the disappointment of finding Under-officer Schmidt sitting where
Madame Ledru, the smiling, was wont to sit. That white
horse up there on the creaking sign-board was painted by
the great Gerard, in liquidation of a score of 1,800 francs,
which he and a couple of gay and festive friends had
run up with Ledru the second in about three days. If
you are an epicure, don't turn your back on Montmorency and refuse to take interest in yet another cuisine
association. This villa near the church was the retreat
of the famous Véry, the

"César de la béchamel,
L'Alexandre du Rosbif."

who came out here in the evening of his days, like De
Fontaine's rat into the cheese. The Vérys now, however, have a habitation in Eaubonne, in a château adjacent to that occupied by the descendant of Mirabeau.
Other circumstances besides misfortune often make
strange bedfellows. It was in Eaubonne where Saint
Lambert lived to be conveniently near to Madame
d'Houdetot, whose château was in Sannois.

Nearer Mont d'Orgimont than Montmorency is
Enghien-les-Bains, with its lake and its sulphur springs.
The taps of the *thermes* have been knocked out of order
by the shells, and as you pass you smell the sulphur
strongly. The tragedian Talma died in this house close
to the baths. The French have made it a hotel, and the
other day their shells made it a skeleton. The road to
the left leads to Epinay. It is a very pretty spot, and
old Clovis was a sensible man to choose it as his country
residence. His example was followed by Dagobert (who
was not lucky in Epinay, for there he caught the

dysentery, of which he died), by Gabrielle d'Estrées, and
by Lacépède, artist, naturalist, and President of the First
Legislature in 1791. As we have followed the left road
leading to Epinay, it is only fair that we turn right for
one moment into St. Gratien, to recall the memory of
such a soldier as France would to-day be right glad of.
To this quiet retreat came the great soldier of fortune,
Marshal Catinat, declining titles, honours, and orders,
and cultivating a modest garden like a modern Cin-
cinnatus. It is a beautiful spot, and the soldier philosopher could have no more congenial home for his
meditations. Turn your back now on St. Denis, and
Paris, and Montmorency, and everything on which you
have been previously gazing, and cast your eye northward over Margency and Montlignon, to that church
spire which rises over the trees that crop out from the
forest into the valley. That is the church spire of the
village of Napoleon St. Leu, a place whose associations
are more recent, but certainly not less interesting than
those of any spot all round the horizon. On the slope
above the village, close to where there now stands the
beautiful residence of Lady Ashburton, there once stood
a much larger château. In the year 1814 this château
was inhabited by a queen without a throne, for she was
the wife of a monarch who had abdicated—and by her
two sons, the elder of whom was about eight years of
age. The Prussians and the Russians were in Paris.
Napoleon was already an exile in Elba. This queen's
château, undoubted Bonapartist as the lady was, somehow came to be looked upon as neutral ground. The
coterie in her drawing-rooms was sufficiently enticing.
She herself was a brilliant and beautiful woman. The
authoress of "Corinne," as she fondled the boys, sparkled
out ever and anon with some flash of wit. Mole, Lava-

lette, Flahaut, and Garnerey the painter, were constant
visitors. With the sour looks of the Parisians it was
dull times for the conquerors, and the great men among
them were right glad to mix in the sparkling society that
was open to them on the neutral ground in the Château
of St. Leu. Hither came once and again the Emperor
Alexander, with his minister Pozzo di Borgo. Blücher
cared more for a fight than a conversazione, but Prince
Augustus of Prussia would look in, and sometimes there
came with him a slip of a lad, in a lieutenant's uniform,
and with the down not yet budded on his lip. This
lad was then the younger son of the monarch of a second-
rate State. The down came, and gave place to the
heavy blonde moustache. The blonde is now snow-white,
and it hangs over the lip of one whose title to-day is
Wilhelm, Emperor of Germany, and who has come to
revive early memories at the head of half a million of
men. The mistress of the pleasant château was Hortense,
daughter of the Empress Josephine by her first marriage,
wife of Louis Napoleon, that Bonaparte who preferred
Lausanne and his library to the throne of Holland. The
elder of the two boys I speak of bore, too, the name of
Louis. A year after the time of which I write, his great
uncle was showing him, in the absence of the King of
Rome, to the cheering crowds of Paris from the balcony
of the Tuileries. After years of exile and imprisonment,
the people of Paris saw the same face again. The boy of
St. Leu was he who, till the other day, was Napoleon III.,
Emperor of the French.

The Germans lie between St. Leu and hot Republican
Paris, lusting to eradicate the vestiges of the Empire and
the Napoleons. The prefix which the name of St. Leu
got some twenty years ago still belongs to it without
question, but it may be taken for granted that the prefix

will go with the dynasty. I hope that when the Republicans sally forth to paint out the "Napoleon," they will respect the tomb of the Napoleons behind the altar of the Church. The ashes of this strange family have had as many vicissitudes as its members. The dust of the great Emperor has been excavated from below the willow tree in the shadow of St. Helena's rock. Of the rest of the family it may well be said—

> "Their graves are severed far and wide,
> By mountain, stream, and sea."

There are four Napoleons buried here in the Church of St. Leu—Napoleon Charles, the eldest son of Louis and Hortense, who died at the age of five; Napoleon Louis, Duke of Berg, then second son, who died in Italy in 1831; Louis himself, brought to St. Leu from Livorni, where he died in 1847; and the father of all the stock, old Charles Marie Napoleon of Corsica, who died at Montpellier in 1785. The last was the first of the Napoleons to lie in St. Leu; his son, the King of Holland, had his ashes transferred from Montpellier to a mausoleum in the park of the Château of St. Leu. When the little Prince Royal of Holland died he was buried beside his grandfather. But after the second restoration the château passed into the hands of the Duke of Bourbon, who disliked the presence in his park of the ashes of the relatives of him at whose instance the Duke of Enghien was shot. So he had them dug up, but considerately interposed no obstacle in the way of the curé when that worthy man would find a refuge for the outcasts in the vaults of the church—the burial-place of the Montmorencys. When Napoleon the Third got warm on the Imperial throne he had the church rebuilt at great expense, and a special vault constructed for the remains of the four members of the family who were already buried

in St. Leu, issuing at the same time a decree that this
vault was thenceforth to be regarded as the burial-place
of the dynasty. You may see the monument in the
recess behind the altar—three saints, one of whom is
"Saint Napoleon," painted above a big concern of white
marble, crowned by a life-size statue of Louis, the sensible
man who abdicated; and having niches in its front, containing busts of the other three occupants of the vault.
The Emperor and Empress presided with great state at
the inauguration of the new edifice in 1853. Strangely
enough that Duke of Bourbon, the last of the Condés,
who would not give the ashes of the Napoleons sleeping
room in his park, came in the end to mingle his own
with theirs. No doubt he was much disgusted at the
event of 1830. One morning in August of that year he
was found hanging against the window of his bed-room.
Somebody had gone about the business of strangulation
very systematically, and the two white neckcloths hanged
him most effectually. He was buried in the Church of
St. Leu, and you may see through the trees the column
which the Legitimists erected to his memory in the park.
It has engraved on it the inscription, "Hic cecidit,"
which is a misstatement. Had he fallen it might have
been the better for him; but the neckcloths and the
espagnolette held fast and prevented him. The park is
now broken up, and the château razed to the ground. It
is said that some of our countrymen, when the bricks
and mortar were being sold in lots, speculated in the lot
containing the fatal window, and that they did a good
stroke of business by selling as memorials at least four
"original windows."

There were several considerable outbursts of firing
during the night between November 20th and 21st, chiefly
from Mont Valérien; but the purport of these ebullitions,

if there was, indeed, any purport in them, was not apparent. On the foreposts down in the mist there went
on a desultory dropping fire entirely from the French
side. As the shooting men could not have seen an
object a hundred yards before them, they must either
have been working off superfluous energy, or emptying
their rifles of charges which the night air had damped.
In the absence of any occurrence of interest at head-
quarters, it struck me that a visit to the scene of the last
hard fighting on the north side, the village of Le Bourget,
might furnish matter likely to be of interest, and in the
afternoon, therefore, I started in that direction. My way
lay through Montmorency and St. Brice to Sarcelles, at
which village I obtained information as to the whereabouts of the Queen Elizabeth Regiment, with some of
the officers of which gallant regiment I had already an
acquaintance, and to whom I trusted, as the regiment
had borne the brunt of the fight at Le Bourget, for a
reliable cicerone to the scene of the action. The courteous major who commanded at Sarcelles informed me that
the Queen Elizabeths were in the neighbourhood of
Arnouville, or at all events there I should obtain definite
information respecting the position of the 1st battalion,
that of which I was in search. He added to his kindness a permission to ride along the direct road between
Sarcelles and Arnouville, by which I saved a considerable détour. This direct route was seldom used, as it
was close to the front, and, passing as it does over an
exposed table land, was within easy and tempting range
of the guns of Fort du Nord. However, Fort du Nord
was civil enough not to concern itself with a single
horseman, and I rode along in peace, enjoying the fine
prospect, in which the most prominent object was the
Cathedral of St. Denis, with the double crown work du

Nord lying down in the valley in front of it, a grim
proof that the aspiration, "Cedant arma togæ" had not
yet been realised. Along this road, after it crosses the
track of the Northern Railway, were the abandoned field-
barracks occupied by the Guards before they housed
themselves in the villages—pleasant habitations, no doubt,
in the fine weather, but now bearing a forlorn and
squalid appearance in the midst of the slushy fields.
Their construction, however, did great credit to the
troops, strengthened with earth banks as they were on
the front next Paris, so as to be practically bomb-proof.
At Arnouville I found the Emperor Alexander Regiment
represented, but the Queen Elizabeths were further on.
I had to turn my horse's head due Paris-ward, and jog
on the paved road till I reached the village of Garges.
Here, indeed, were Queen Elizabeths, but not of the
battalion I wanted. The latter, I was told, was in Dugny,
still further to the front—in fact, so far to the front, that
when there, there was nothing beyond save *Feldwachen*
and patrols. Through a miry byepath I took my way—
the regular route running along the front being too much
exposed to form an eligible means of transit—and
presently came upon a piece of road illustrating the
thoroughness with which the Germans do everything they
set themselves to do. The road must have been terribly
bad—too bad even for strong horses and resolute drivers
—seeing that its bottom was a quagmire. But the
pioneers had gone to work and fascined the track much
as the constructors of the Liverpool and Manchester Railway treated the quaking surface of Chat Moss. Over the
fascines had been laid a regular pavement of bricks, ar-
tistically beaten level with paviours' mallets, and the track
was sound enough for a road steamer. Crossing the
raised path through the inundations caused by the dams

on the river Morée I was brought up by a double post at
the entrance to the park of a château, and conducted to
the château itself by one of the sentries. Here I found
the Staff of one of the battalions of the Queen Elizabeth
Regiment—the battalion, too, which I wanted—and was
right hospitably welcomed by Hauptmann von Altrock,
who commanded the battalion, and by the junior officers
who shared the château with their chief. But the officers
of the Queen Elizabeth regiment were not in the same
blithe and buoyant spirits as when I had met them in
the early part of the war. Although frank and hearty as
of yore, a deep gloom hung over them, that could not
be dispelled by whatsoever exertion on their part. There
was a sternly good cause for the gloom. In the fight at
Le Bourget on the 31st October eight comrades had
fallen, to rise no more; twelve more had gone down
wounded. Of the whole fatal casualties to the regiment
that day, one-sixth part had consisted of officers. Among
the dead was Colonel von Zaluskowski, the father of his
regiment, a man beloved by all. The tears stood in
the eyes of his adjutant as he showed me the snuffbox
which the good Colonel had given him as a remembrance,
while he lay mortally wounded in the stable into which
they bore him out of the hail of lead that swept the
road.

While we sat at supper a detachment from the foreposts brought in a deserter who had come across from
the French lines. As regards the lower part of his person, he was a Garde Mobile; his trousers were uniform
trousers; but he wore the blouse and cap of the French
peasant. His appearance was sufficiently weird as he
was brought in—his face enveloped in the coloured
pocket-handkerchief of one of his escort. As soon as he
was uncased he eagerly asked for bread, and went at a

huge hunk which the Captain cut him with a vigour and resolution which, if displayed in warfare, would have made him a very tough customer. He had some disconnected and scrappy intelligence concerning an internal commotion which he averred had taken place within Paris in the afternoon; but he plainly knew very little about the matter. His information, however, in so far tallied with a report unofficially communicated by an officer on field watch, that he had heard during the afternoon firing, which seemed to him to be going on inside Paris. It was, however, so difficult to arrive at a correct conclusion whence came the sound of firing that did not take place on one's own immediate front, that the officer in question wisely refrained from giving a positive opinion on the subject.

Late in the evening some of the officers were good enough to escort me to a low bluff on the edge of the wooded grounds of a chateau—an elevation which, trivial as it is, commands the whole of the flat expanse, the defensive margin of which is formed by Forts du Nord, de l'Est, and Aubervilliers. Here was the plain seen by moonlight, and Paris by some other light also, whether gas, oil, or candles, I knew not. This plain was the first I had seen on the northern side of Paris, where the configuration of the ground admitted of a sortie in force. Here there was room for the deployment of a large army, and the evolution might have been performed under the great guns of the forts. It was this flat, between the Canal de l'Ourcq and the rising grounds to the west of St. Denis, which was the theatre of the battle by which Blücher terminated the campaign of 1814, and gained Paris. La Villette, Clichy, Rouvroy, and Aubervilliers, all localities on the plateau, occur again and again in the narratives of that engagement. Blücher would have

found some difficulty now in carrying the positions behind
these places as one day's work. It would have puzzled
Langeron to make a dash from St. Denis, and storm the
heights of Montmartre, as he did that afternoon of the
30th of March, 1814. The only defences then were the
entrenched lines across the face of Montmartre, stretching
over to the rising ground of Belleville. Now Blücher
would have found, as his countrymen were finding to-day,
the way stopped long before the ascent of Montmartre
begins, by the guns and works of that array of forts beginning with Du Nord and ending with Noisy. As a
vantage ground for battle the tables were turned. The
plateau was no longer an eligible space on which an
army could manœuvre itself into Paris, but a tempting
expanse on which an army defending Paris might come
out to do battle with the besieger. But this was only in
theory. The greenest military student knows what must
be the stamp of troops that will complete an effective
deployment under an enemy's fire, and advance to the
attack under the same. This was the imperative condition attached to a sortie on a large scale on this
plateau; and Trochu, who knew what manner of men in
the matter of discipline were his troops, was wise to
shun it. And the difficulty of which I speak was only
the difficulty on the threshold—the *pons asinorum* of an
offensive operation in force against the Prussian environment. How strong was the line which the besiegers
held athwart this plain is only to be realised by having
personally inspected it. Some details regarding it I will
enter into again; but it would be tedious to enter into
elaborate particularisation of every feature. It may be
said here that, held by the strong force which was wisely
judged requisite—a force consisting of the *élite* of the
Prussian soldiery, each position turned to the very best

account by the most careful and judicious engineering appliances, and with supports which were practically illimitable available at short notice, one with any knowledge of the subject could come to no other opinion than that the beleaguering line at this critical position could have resisted an assault of a more formidable character than any which the garrison of Paris, from what we knew of its character and appliances, could be judged capable of making. This is no *ex post facto* conclusion on my part, but one published long before events occurred to test and prove its correctness.

Each of these old-fashioned villages surrounding Paris is all but a fortress in itself. The walls are of great thickness, and there is so little woodwork that shells would not fire the houses. This Dugny, for instance, might be held by a handful of resolute men against all comers. Its streets—if streets the wall-bordered roads can be termed—are so many covered ways capable of affording safe passage even under a hot artillery fire. The farmhouses are built like citadels, walled in on all four sides, and with the windows looking inward. Some of them are even loopholed. A few judicious barricades were all that was needed as the complement of the defence. These, it is needless to say, the Guards had not neglected to erect. In Dugny were some of the most artistic barricades I have ever seen—in fact, barricade is hardly the term for them—constructed as they were of stones taken from the chaussée, faced with a deep slope of earth, and capable of protecting their defenders from the fire of the heaviest artillery. Their appreciation of the axiom that water is a better barrier than earth the Prussians had shown by effecting an extensive inundation between Dugny and Le Blanc Mesnil.

To return for a moment to the view from the fringe

of the grove.   Before us in the watery moonlight lay Le
Bourget, dark and silent, as if it were mourning for the
slaughter that had been wrought within it.   Across the
plain, and more to the right, the moon's rays fell upon
the great inundation which the French had made in front
of St. Denis, by damming the little river of Croud.   In
front of the water ran the chain of French watch-fires,
falling back towards the south-east on Aubervilliers.
There were bright lights in Forts du Nord and Aubervilliers.   Behind, there was a dark streak, presumably
caused by the *enceinte*, and then the bank of lights rose
in straggling tiers up to the top of Montmartre.   I could
trace no lines of street lamps defining the thoroughfare.
The lights I saw came exclusively from houses; and evidently there could then have been no great lack in Paris
of some means or other of "showing a light."   At times
it seemed as if we could see figures across the lights,
dulling their brightness momentarily.   Likely enough,
for as we stood we were within some five kilometres of
Paris.

Next morning, in the company of two officers present
at the recapture of Le Bourget on the 31st of October, I
went over the ground and carefully examined the village
itself, obtaining from my companions a detailed narrative
of the events of the day, and noting down also several
anecdotes of individual danger or courage.   On my return
to head-quarters, a staff officer, to whom the disposition
of important interests had been entrusted, was kind enough
to go over my notes, and add to them information only
to be obtained at head-quarters.   It may not be occupying space uselessly if I rapidly run over the incidents of
an action which was in its way certainly unique in the
late war, before describing the condition of the village as
I saw it.

The line of foreposts linking Le Bourget with Dugny has already been described. Le Bourget forms the apex of a tolerably acute triangle, having for its base a straight line drawn between Dugny and Le Blanc Mesnil. It stands out therefore in the plain detached and in front, so that the cursory observer might inquire of what use it was to hold it at all. But its value is easily apparent. In the first place, it stands on the great Lille chaussée, on which for some distance there was no such advantageous defensive position. In the second place, it acted as a kind of *tête du pont* to the inundations which protected the Prussian front in this locality. Had there been no Le Bourget, it would have mattered little to the German security; but there being a Le Bourget, it mattered much that it should not be occupied by the French, in whose hands it would have been constantly available as a nucleus for offensive operations. As a position of so much importance, it may be questioned to-day, with that *ex post facto* intelligence which is so suggestive, whether the Germans should not have held it with a stronger force than a single company standing in it, with orders to fall back if attacked in force. The explanation given me was that the post was so exposed that the fewer men in it the less the chance of casualties. It may be questioned, however, whether any probable number of casualties so occurring would have mounted up to the sum of those incurred on the 31st October.

Be this as it may, the expulsion, or rather the retreat, took place on the 28th, to be succeeded next by a German reconnaissance which showed the enemy in too great force to be assaulted without premeditated dispositions. While these were being deliberately made, during the days that elapsed between the French occupancy and the recapture, the German field artillery threw about 2,000 grenades into the place. An ordinary village would have been burnt over and over again, but Le Bourget does not seem even to have caught fire.

On the morning of the 31st, the three battalions of the Queen Elizabeth marched from Dugny, and by eight o'clock stood at Pont Iblon, on the Lille road, a point where there were temporary barracks for two battalions. In their front stood three batteries of the horse artillery of the Guard. Along with the Queen Elizabeths in Pont Iblon was one battalion (the Fusilier) of the Queen Augusta Regiment, commanded by the lamented Count Waldersee, and one company of Engineers. In Dugny (on the north of Pont Iblon, which may be described as the centre of the operations) there lay two battalions of the Emperor Franz Guard Regiment, under the command of Major Derenthall. I have already named the gallant officer commanding the Queen Elizabeths. At Le Blanc Mesnil on the east lay two battalions of the Kaiser Alexander Regiment, under Lieutenant-Colonel von Zeuner. Here also were two batteries foot artillery of the Guard, supported by three companies of the Schützen Guard Regiment. The reserve consisted of eight battalions, a cavalry regiment stood at Bonneuil, and a reserve force of artillery near Gonesse. All the attacking force belonged to the second division of the Guards. In all there were engaged about 6,000 bayonets. The French had eight battalions in Le Bourget—Gardes Mobiles and Impériales, besides Francs-tireurs. At Drancy, to the south rear, and almost opposite to Le Blanc Mesnil, they had a large force of reserves. Other reserves were seen in La Courneuve, but the artillery fire from the Prussian field-guns prevented any of the French reserves from taking part in the engagement. The Forts du Nord, de l'Est, Aubervilliers, Romainville, and Noisy, all poured

out a profuse fire on the Prussian troops, both in their
positions, and as soon as they began to advance, and a
battery of field-guns stood on the right of the village of
Le Bourget.

At eight o'clock the Kaiser Alexander Battalions
began their march, as they had the farthest distance to
traverse. Availing themselves skilfully of the course of
the little river Molleret and of the cutting on the Laon
Railway, they escaped with little loss the flanking fire
from Drancy and from the eastern forts, and by nine
o'clock they had captured and were holding the railway
station close to the chaussée at the south-western exit of
the village. Thus practically the French retreat was cut
off, and to appreciate the character of the resistance
offered by the French this important element must not
be lost sight of. At a quarter-past eight, the two battalions of the Emperor Franz Regiment quitted Dugny
and came on rapidly to Le Bourget by the road which
enters the village about midway in its length; while one
battalion fought its way in by the road and the houses
to the left, the other undertook to clear a large and
beautiful park flanking the village on the right of the
Dugny road. The three battalions of the Queen Elizabeth Regiment, with the accompanying Queen Augusta
Regiment, left Pont Iblon at the same hour as the Dugny
contingent, came on through the fire at the double, carried the barricade by storm, were inside by nine o'clock,
and finally, by hand-to-hand fighting from house to house,
cleared the village of Frenchmen, with the aid of the
other regiments, by half-past twelve o'clock. In the engagement there were killed and wounded 39 officers and
449 men. The French lost about 600, and 1,300 of
them were taken prisoners.

This much my companions related to me as we

4 *

walked down from Dugny to Le Bourget—it being forbidden to traverse the intervening space on horseback.
Bending to the left, so as to get on the chaussée, along
the sides of which the Queen Elizabeths had advanced,
we presently reached it about 500 yards from the village.
About the same distance on the other side stood a little
brick house at a slight bend in the road. "There was
where we got the order to double," cried big Lieutenant
von ——, "and didn't we pelt along!" "And didn't you
puff and blow?" slily asked our other companion; "anyhow," he added, turning to me, "von ——, big as he is,
was one of the first over the barricade."

At a glance, now that I was on the chaussée, I could
see what a tough place was this Le Bourget. It resembles
extremely those walled Indian villages on the road from
Cawnpore to Lucknow, through which Havelock had to
fight his way, and the loss in doing which made him
give up his first attempt to relieve the latter place. The
broad road formed its weak point. On either side had
extended, for a breadth of about 100 yards, a massive
wall, and this wall was continued longitudinally along the
backs of the houses. The place was a fortress. With
that strong entrenchment across the broad chaussée, I
think Prussian or British troops would have held it till
Christmas-time. But the French had made wofully little
use of the advantages to their hand. With the exception
of the single battery on the right of the village, they had
no artillery near it. A battery on the chaussée in front
of the entrenchment, another looking toward Dugny, and
another toward Le Blanc Mesnil, would have stiffened
the problem materially. And where had been the mitrailleuses? Here was just the place for their use; for a
street had to be traversed, and if the mitrailleuse has a
métier anywhere, it is in sweeping a street or a road.

There was, it is true, one mitrailleuse at the upper end of the village; but the capture of the railway station by the Kaiser Alexanders early made its position untenable. The big lieutenant told me how the Queen Elizabeths came on. They left the chaussée empty, and took to the fields on either side. On the right, in skirmishing order, came the 1st Company, with yellow-bearded Captain von Helldorff leading it on. On the left of the chaussée, in the same order, came the 2nd Company, commanded by Lieutenant von Buddenbrock. In the rear respectively of these two came the 3rd and 4th Companies (the four companies forming the 1st Battalion), in that columnar formation in which the Prussian company is wont to go into battle. Behind it came the 2nd Battalion; behind that again the Fusiliers. On the left were the Augustas. I could not wonder at the big lieutenant puffing and blowing. Through the deep potato-land the going must have been awfully heavy, and splashes of lead in the face did not contribute to lightening the way. All along the track were evidences of the latter hindrance —the accustomed relics of slaughter. Behind a friendly dungheap, the only cover in all the exposed rush of 1,500 yards, the wounded had crept, and there yet lay their blood-dabbled rags. The graves began at about 500 yards from the village. Just to the right of the now levelled entrenchment was one wherein lay three occupants. My companions owned how staunchly the French stood their ground here, fighting till the bigger men drove them back. Through the loop holes in the walls right and left of the entrenchment they kept their chassepots sticking, loading at the breech without withdrawal, and firing continuously. The officers, rushing up close to the wall, grappled with the weapons and dragged them from the hands of the men who plied

them.   The pioneers came up under the fire, and with
their crowbars stove gaps in the thick wall.   Nos.   1
and 2 companies, forming up from skirmishing order
right and left, inwards inclined and tumbled pell-mell on
the breast-high barricade.   The officers led till they fell.
One went down with a bullet from a revolver, another
got a bayonet right in the heart as he chested the stones
of the entrenchment.   As Helldorff dropped among the
Mobile Guards, one of them took off a part of his ear,
but fared considerably worse than Peter when he served
another fellow-creature in the same way.   The following
are the names of the officers of the Queen Elizabeths
who fell before reaching, or at the barricade:—Captain
von Renthe-Fink, Lieutenants von Merckel, von Schoenitz,
von Zedlitz, von Luks, and von Knobelsdorff.   The band
pushed up under cover of the wall on the right, and
placing itself there, played the troops past as they
stormed into the village—one air my informant remembered well—the "Pariser Einzugsmarsch."

Just on the left of the entrance to the village is a
small villa, which must have been the scene of a deadly
combat.   There were several graves on the tiny lawn: a
river god which had once adorned a fountain there was
knocked into splinters.   The house was riddled through
and through; it was new, and thinner than the houses of
the old construction.   There were bayonet marks on the
stairs leading to the cellar, and blood on the walls.   The
gable and front were pitted all over with bullet marks,
just as if the house had got a white small-pox.   In the
corresponding house on the right—a big old farmhouse—
the fight had been very warm. Here, storming in through
the breaches the pioneers had made, the Guardsmen had
fallen upon half a battalion of Frenchmen, and, after a
struggle, had captured 300 of them.   On the wall of this

house was chalked the words,—"*Prussiens du diable;
vous ne verrez pas vos femmes.*" The taunt stirred the
devil in the hearts of the Germans. There is a little bay
in the roadway a few paces further on formed by a projecting house. Here it was that Colonel von Zaluskowski
fell. He was carried into a stable to the right, and there
Dr. Schroeter found that he was shot through the liver
and fatally wounded. Hauptmann von Altrock was leading the advance, if the term could be applied to a desperate street fight in which every man's hand was for
himself. Count Kanitz, who commanded the 3rd Brigade, and Lieutenant-General von Budritzki, who directed
the operations of the day, entered the village with the
2nd Battalion of the Queen Elizabeths. From every
house, as the column pushed forward, poured down the
deadly hail; the French stuck to the houses as evicted
Irishmen stick to their cabins. The Grenadiers went
right and left into each individual house, and in each
house there was a fierce hand-to-hand fight on the stairs.
The Frenchmen fought on the landings—they fought in
the rooms. The Guardsmen had to carry the balustrades
at the bayonet point. Sometimes an obstinate Frenchman was pitchforked out of window on the bayonets—
for it was not a time to stand on ceremony. Others had
taken refuge in the cellars, and blazed away through the
flaps. In the cellars it was where most of the prisoners
were taken. But prisoners were not taken till the Frenchmen were utterly beaten out of defensive means; nay,
there were cases when, after these had "given out," the
stubborn Gauls still refused to yield. The smoke traces
were still visible against the entrance to one cellar, to
which fire had to be applied, and the occupants regularly
smoked out; they would not yield till the threatenings
of asphyxia became too strong. In the East-end of Lon-

don, just off the Mile-end Road, there is a spot known to and shunned by our metropolitan police. Its proper name is St. John's Place; its common acceptation is Jack's Hole. Hither it is that the blousy demi-monde of Ratcliffe Highway enveigle the sailor, who finds himself stripped and solitary when he escapes from his drunken sleep. The police despair of doing any good with Jack's Hole, it is so like a rabbit warren. You go in at one end, and you can go through, house by house, from one end to the other, without ever coming down out of the first floor. The labyrinth is useful when there is a hunt. As I saw it to-day Le Bourget, as regards thoroughness of communication, was a veritable Jack's Hole. So fierce had been the storm of fire in the street, that the pioneers had to break a passage from house to house through the dividing partitions. Thus it was possible to traverse along the upper floor of the houses nearly half the length of the village on either side of the chief (and indeed the only) street. And, in addition to the isolated fights in the gardens and outhouses in the rear of the houses fronting the street, there were actually, so to speak, three streams of combat going on in the place at one and the same time—that in the street, where men ducked their heads, and made a rush from shelter to shelter as they found it formed by the favouring projecting gables of houses, and those two going on on the upper floor of each row of houses. It was from a house, across the front of which is inscribed in large characters, "Pensionnat de Demoiselles," on the left-hand side of the way, that Colonel Zaluskowski was shot down. A party of his men made a dash forward, and carried the house with a rush. In the passage, which was densely packed with Frenchmen, the cry of "Pardon" was sent up, and the Grenadiers held the points of their bayonets

up as they crushed into the place and pushed their way
upstairs. In a room at the top of the stairs stood a
French officer, who shot down with his revolver the first
soldier who entered, and then, throwing his weapon on
the floor, appealed for quarter to an officer who was
among the first to enter. The officer would have granted
it, but for once the bonds of discipline were burst. The
men had heard the cry of "Pardon;" they saw their
comrade lying dead before them, and the fury of angry
revenge was stronger within them than the voice of their
officer could control. When the "*demoiselles*" come back
to the smashed and battered *pensionnal*, they will see
where the boards soaked in the blood of the French
officer. It was a little beyond this that Lieutenant
Paizeniki fell, shot dead on the spot as he was cheering
on his men. About half way up the village, on the right-
hand side as one goes towards Paris, is the church, a
building of considerable size, with a spire of some pre-
tensions. It stands slightly recessed from the street, and
in the little recess the Frenchmen made a desperate
stand, firing from the steps of the church and from behind the house that projects before one comes to it.
They were dislodged from this position by the Prussians
effecting a lodgment in the house, and from this point
of vantage firing down upon them. Then from a house
a little farther on upon the other side of the way, the
French, who had barricaded the windows and the roof,
opened a furious fire upon this house, occupied, as I have
said, by the Prussians. In its gable I counted two hundred dents of chassepot bullets, and then lost the tally.
At length the Prussians forced their foes to evacuate this
position, and got into the church. Hither they brought
their wounded to be companions to the French wounded,
who already littered the place. Even now the lower

end of the floor of the building had red coagulated cakes in the cavities of its pavement, where the blood had lain and thickened as it poured from the men lying there on the stones, waiting while Dr. Schroeter could overtake their injuries. His colleague was already *hors de combat* with a bullet through his shoulder. What a wan, dreary look that church had now! Its open door creaked dismally on the wind. As you entered there lay the bloody rags and the gouts that were the relics of the wounded. Shells had stove in portions of the roof, and the floor was strewed with fragments of ceiling. The light from the windows had been meant to be softened by pictured screens. These were all unfastened, and swinging in the wind. The Virgin had a bullet-hole through her heart; Our Lord had been shot right through the head. In the little side chapels the images and the alabaster candlesticks were unharmed, but the pale marble was spotted with blood. On the altar, dinted here and there with a bullet-hole, and with a blood-stained boot on its steps, there lay open the great psalter. Had the priest, I wondered, stood to his spiritual weapons to the last, as his countrymen had to the arm of the flesh? The book lay open at the 56th Psalm—"Miserere mei, Deus, miserere mei, Deu. Clamabo ad Deum altissimum." In the vestiary behind the altar lay a tangled heap of rich and sumptuous robes, such as would have delighted the heart of Mr. Mackonochie or Mr. Purchas—stoles and copes, velvet mantles with gold and green crosses embroidered on them, and a variety of decorated garments, the appellations of which are not within my secular knowledge.

Beyond the church the musketry fire seemed to have slackened slightly as the French became conscious of the hopelessness of the struggle. Still, every house afforded

evidence of the stubborn manner in which the fight was
maintained, in the shape of dents of chassepot bullets.
The swinging iron sign of the Cheval Rouge, the little
auberge of the village, was perforated by fourteen bullet-
holes.   The pioneers had to tear down the lower fronts
of some of the houses to let the men get at the pertinacious defenders.   When these did not back their way
upstairs, their usual "dernier ressort" was the cellar.   It
was out of the cellars that quite one-half of the prisoners
were excavated.   There were eloquent traces of hard
fighting in an enclosed row of houses which runs to the
left at right angles to the main street.   Here it was that
the Queen Augusta battalion came battling its way in,
having skirted the village thus far on the left.   Before
they cleared this clump of houses the Augustas lost six
officers.

Of all the desolate places I have ever seen this shattered village of Le Bourget was the most desolate.   Except its military occupants, who, in strength quite formidable enough to obviate any prospect of a repetition
of the occurrence of the 28th October, occupied a half-
detached portion of the village, there was not in the
whole of it a living thing, so far as I saw, save a forlorn
prowling cat that seemed to have inherited the spirit of
the French soldiers that once had been the occupants of
the place, and put her back up and spat at us veno-
mously, as if she were French to the core, and hated the
invader worse than she craved for food.   There was not
a house that had not been crashed into by several shells
—not a roof that had the remotest claim to be intact,
not a garden but what had nearly as many shell-holes as
it had plants, not a wall that was not breached, not a
window that was not shattered.   The chaussée was
strewed with the fragments of shells and with flattened

chassepot bullets.   In the entrance to the court-yards
were knapsacks, trousers, coats, shirts, blood-stained
bandages, and other *débris*.   The wind, as it whistled
mournfully along the deserted street, blew to and fro
fragments of soldiers' ledgers, scraps of Feldpost letters
with loving words on the yellow morsels of papers and
tattered leaves of pocket Bibles.   I think when Paris
may once again know the meaning of peace, .that her
wise men would do well to build a wall round this village, and keep it always as I saw it.   No better corrective
to a war mania could be imagined.   It is conveniently
near Paris, and when the unreasoning mob begins to
clamour it would be so easy to answer such a cry as
"A Berlin!" with the counter-shout of "A Le Bourget."
How near Le Bourget is to Paris is worth mentioning.
The stone that stands at the southern end of the village
record, "à Paris, 4 kil. 9"—not three miles from the
barriers.   We were a good deal nearer when we stood
behind the last barricade, and cautiously peeped over at
the French forepost across the chaussée in front of La
Courneuve some four hundred paces before us.

Returning to head-quarters in Margency on the 24th,
I found everything reported quiet on the north side, and
that tidings of the same tenour had been sent in from the
eastern section.   I may recall a conversation which on
the same evening I had with a distinguished officer of the
Crown Prince's staff, as tending to show how accurate
was the reckoning of the besiegers respecting the policy
to be pursued by the besieged.   My interlocutor told me
that there was no expectation, on the part of the German military leaders, of a sortie from Paris—that was
to say, of a sortie and nothing more.   Trochu, he argued,
was sensible enough to know that sorties, in themselves,
have very little effect in helping towards the raising of a

siege. But he had discrimination enough to perceive three things. First, that there were more troops in Paris than were wanted for its defence, now that it had been fortified to a pitch beyond which fortification could scarcely go; secondly, that as Metz had too forcibly illustrated, a superfluity of mouths, even if the mouths were the mouths of fighting men, was a source of weakness and of ultimate ruin to a city that had a limit to its powers of furnishing provisions; and, thirdly, that these superfluous fighting men might have a chance of effecting some good if outside the cordon of environment, and their character changed from that of a besieged army to that of an active field army, capable of co-operating with other forces, not cooped up behind walls and dykes. "Wherefore," continued my friend, "if we are not to continue in this state of utter stagnation till Paris has eaten its head off, and is forced by hunger to capitulate, we may expect an effort on a grand scale that will not be a sortie in the ordinary acceptation of the word, but an attempt in force to push a portion of the besieged force out through our lines into the comparatively open country beyond. On which side this effort will take place, if it takes place at all, there is no special basis on which to form a prognostication; but we may be sure of this, that on the side where the real effort is not made, on that side there will be a feigned attack in force, calculated to give the impression that it is no feint. The probability of such an effort depends materially, there can be no doubt, on the intelligence which may reach Paris as to the French forces outside, and what is the nature of their doings. The present quiet may be, and I am strongly inclined to think is, but the lull before a great storm. Should a real and heartily meant effort to break through be made, and fail (as fail it shall), and the failure be coupled with absence of news, or bad news, from outside, then surely the end cannot be far off."

The latter impression—I mean the impression that the siege could not last much longer—was very general in the German lines up to about the middle of December. There can be no doubt, I think, that Bismarck and von Moltke were deceived as to the store of provisions in the city.   The delusion was maintained by descriptions which from time to time were made public, written by persons inside of the beleaguered city, of the straits to which even people with plenty of money were already reduced.   If rats were selling for more than fowls were to be bought for in peace-time, and when donkey was a delicacy, surely a condition closely akin to famine was reached.   So it was argued; and it may be added to that, the besiegers utterly misjudged the power of Paris to face and endure continuously what, stripped of sensationalism, did intensify into a real and terrible pinch.   The miscalculation was not unjustifiable.   All that they, or that any body else, knew of the beautiful, sinful capital and its inhabitants was of a character to lead to the anticipation that Spartanism was an impossibility in frivolous, luxurious Paris.   Before the end came, the Germans frankly owned how far they had erred in their reckoning, and their respect for Paris grew in proportion to the duration of her resistance.   That resistance was the one break in the black cloud of humiliation that hung like a pall over French martialism when the peace was signed.

The world abused Bismarck for the dry matter-of-fact way in which he warned Paris that if it held out much longer it would incur a certainty of absolute starvation after the capitulation.   But, whatever sentiment might have had to say in the matter, and whether the German spoke from a single heart or not, it was unquestionable

that his warning would have proved but too true but for
the nobly prompt succour of Britain in the emergency.
The environs of Paris were stripped and depopulated.
In all the beautiful villages along this northern side,
there were but mere handfuls of resident population, and
they were all but starving. In the early days the Francs-
tireurs had overrun the district, frightening everybody
away either into Paris or off into the back country by
terrible stories of Prussian atrocities, and then, what the
people did not take with them, the Francs-tireurs looted.
The Prussians, on their arrival, travelled miles without
seeing a living thing. Now the people were beginning
to come back out of the back country, having heard by
report that the Germans had not teeth like boars, and
did not eat little children. But they came back destitute
to their forlorn homes. If they had money, they bought
some food of the marketenders; if they had not, they
lived on the vegetables which were still plentiful in the
fields (the German soldier does not understand the virtue
of salad), and on the bread the soldiers might spare from
their rations. Out of such a population and such a
country as this, Paris could not expect much to fill her
depleted magazines after the capitulation. You might
travel from St. Germain to Gonesse in the days I write
of without finding a place where you could get a dinner
by paying for it—a glass of wine or a feed of corn for
your horse. The Germans—provident fellows—had
cleared potato-fields of their produce, and stored them in
pits for winter consumption, in anticipation that they
should have to stay the winter before Paris. Out on the
foreposts under fire of the forts, there were still a few
fields where the tubers were yet in the earth. But what
is a potato-field to Paris? The French troops, by the
way, seemed inclined to risk more for their potatoes than

for anything else. At first they had come out potato-digging in large bodies—one batch using the spade while the other covered them. For a time the Germans had refrained from disturbing this industrial occupation; but the demonstration became too impudent, and the potato-parties were fired upon with the needle-gun. Now the tactics were different. The French came out in parties of three—two skirmishing assiduously, while the third dug with equal assiduity.

On the 26th of November, all being still reasonably quiet on the north side, I quitted Margency, with the intention to familiarise myself somewhat more with the positions of the Maas Army, by visiting at least a portion of the eastern side. On my way to Gonesse, which was my first halting-place, instead of taking the low-country route along the front, I crossed the summit of the hill of Montmorency and came down upon Ecouen, where in the beautiful and historical château—its style of architecture pure and veritable Renaissance—there was a large lazarette of the Guards, which I was desirous to inspect. It is impossible to imagine a building better calculated for an hospital than this château, standing as it does on an elevation which secures a fine prospect and a free current of air, with lofty halls for wards, wide staircases, hot and cold water on every floor, beds and bedding enough and to spare, commodious cooking apparatus, and a latrine system of an excellence very rare in France. With the introduction of a simple means of ventilation, such as that in so efficient operation in Middlesex Hospital, the place could hardly have been improved. It had been, till the invasion, a pensionnat for daughters of members of the Legion of Honour, who were cared for by a number of sisters or nuns, and the latter to the number of twenty still remained, and were indefatigable in their

attention to the ailing, although of another and a hostile
nation. Staff-Surgeon-Major Tegener seemed as efficient
as he certainly was a most solicitous chief, and he had a
sufficient number of able and zealous medical assistants.
The number of patients in the château at this time was
120, of whom two were Frenchmen, one an officer with
an amputation of the leg. The great bulk of the cases
were of sickness, the prevalent diseases being abdominal
typhus, typhoid and gastric fevers. There were but few
wounded, the proximity of typhus being detrimental to
recovery from wounds. Typhus supervening on a gun-
shot wound almost invariably, I believe, results in erysipelas. There had been one or two cases of *typhus ex-
anthematicus*—the "spotted typhus," which I had seen in
Metz—but those so attacked had recovered and been sent
home. A peregrination through typhus wards is never a
pleasant thing. Do what you may in the way of dis-
infection and ventilation, it is impossible to banish altogether the fever taint that haunts the air. And the taint
of typhus fever is, I think, worse than that of any other
sickness. At times it is so dense that you almost fancy
you can see it, and it sticks in your throat as if you had
tried to swallow a cobweb. I must say it was very
strong in the Château of Ecouen. The ventilation was
insufficient. Every military surgeon knows what a constant war he has to wage with his patients on the ventilation question, and the German military sick rebelled
against free air with exceptional stubbornness, because
the Germans, when well, seem to have but a rudimentary
conception of the meaning of ventilation. I knew a wily
old army surgeon who used to break by chance an upper
window or two in each ward, and always forgot to
schedule the breakages in the barrack damage-list. It
would have been no bad policy on Dr. Tegener's part to

have resorted to the same pious fraud. Matters were worse
than usual, because the sick were mostly in the smaller
rooms, the great hall—"Salle de Napoléon"—and the
other larger and loftier apartments having been emptied
for sweetening. The place had been used for some time
as an hospital. Before the Germans came the French had
so used it, and then it had been occupied as such also by
another army corps before the Guards came and adopted
it as their "2nd Lazarette." From time to time there
had been a good many wounded in it, and in the early
days, perhaps, not much attention to cleanliness. The
result had been that the place had in some measure become tainted with erysipelas, and, indeed, with gangrene.
How subtle, obscure, and persistent are these strange
place-infections there are few hospital surgeons who have
not had good cause to know. It was from a profound
conviction that not all the appliances of inlaid floors and
walls lined with glazed tiles sufficed to prevent the absorp-
tion and retention of the malaria that the late Sir James
Simpson was led to become so energetic an advocate for
cottage hospitals. Some years ago erysipelas got such a
grip of that admirably managed institution, King's College Hospital, that an indoor patient could not have an
abscess lanced that this disease did not almost inevitably
supervene. Certainly the empty wards in the Château of
Ecouen looked fresh and healthy enough now with their
scrubbed floors, their open windows, and their neat cots,
with the clean linen, the legacy bequeathed by the young
ladies who were the previous inhabitants. But he would
have been a rash man who would have been confident
that the demon had been exorcised out of them, especially
while it was still rampant in other parts of the building.
I saw one poor fellow dying in a corner, of hospital gangrene in its worst form; the part affected was bloated to

a great size, and the swarthy tint of the gangrene seemed
to fight for the mastery with the bright, glazed redness of
the adjacent flesh. His face had that ghastly, anxious
pallor which is the constant concurrent of gangrene. The
sad wistful eyes of the poor fellow are before me as I
write. In another ward were several cases of erysipelas,
chiefly as the sequent to typhus, from a low habit of
body. If this be a common result, I wonder the whole
crew were not down with erysipelas in a mass. Heaven
knew they had nothing to fetch them out of a low habit
of body. There was not a drop of port-wine in the place,
or indeed of any wine save a sour country trash that
would have given dysentery to a milestone. There was
no porter, no ale, no cognac, no Liebig, no milk extract,
none of those little comforts to which the heart of a sick
man turns when his gorge would rise at the food he eats
when well. Fancy men sick unto death of typhus having
a plate of lean boiled beef put before them. Chances of
recovery were incalculably lessened by their having to
live on this tough stuff or want; and when they should
have got round the corner, if they did round it, con-
valescence must have been materially retarded by this
unsuitable fare. Perhaps, however, the want of generous
wine was most severely felt. The poor fellow on whom
gangrene had fixed its fangs had at his bed-head a cup of
sour wine and water. I never was so thankful in my life
that I had a big and full flask in my pocket. Its contents were good sound cognac; we filled a great iron
tablespoon with the cordial and poured it down his
throat. He brightened visibly on the instant—not indeed
that cognac or anything else could have saved his life,
but material comforts help not a little to smooth the road
to the dark portals. The other fellows raised themselves
on their elbows from their fevered pillows, to gaze with

5*

eager eyes on the flask.   How I wished, as I poured out
its last drops, that it had the property of the widow's
cruise!

It may interest medical readers, should I have any,
to know that the cold-water treatment of typhus was tried
in the Ecouen Lazarette with considerable success.   I
saw several men snugly packed in the wet sheets, and
they expressed their sense of the grateful alterative which
the cold afforded them.   After all, the treatment differs
little in principle from that of applying ice to the shaved
head, which is in almost invariable use in delirium.   I
believe that here the treatment was resorted to in consequence of the want of physic, of which the stock was
exhausted.   The former occupants had a nice little apothecary's shop, which was still well stocked, but its use
was barred to the German doctors in consequence of the
difference in the two pharmacopœias.   It appeared the
premises were wanting for working the little question in
simple proportion which was all that seemed requisite.
Before leaving the château I wrote a letter to the chiefs
of the English Ambulance in St. Germain, laying the
facts of the case before them, and entreating them to send
a waggon-load of stores round to Ecouen with all haste.
How this request was acted on will presently appear.

It must be consistent with the experience of all who
had occasion to journey much among the German troops
during the war, that the Etappen Commandant* is a
being of a somewhat variable temperament.   Sometimes
he as good as tells you to go to the devil.   Again he is
fairly civil, but eminently unsatisfactory.   He is sorry,
but he has no quarters, you must bivouac.   An excellent
type of this variety was the Etappen Commandant at

---

* The Etappen Commandant was the military official (of rank proportionate
to the importance of the position) who acted as chief local administrator, seeing to
the billets, transport of troops, forwarding of stores, &c.

Corny, who consigned the English Ambulance to a muddy
bivouac in an open field, when a little trouble might have
enabled him to find them decent shelter. Again, your
Etappen Commandant is suspicious, and evidently would
like to stick a file of bayonets on either side of you, or
he is regularly and unmistakeably obtuse, and you leave
him empty, it is true, but with feelings of compassion
rather than of irritation. Sometimes you chance on a
prince of an Etappen Commandant, a gentleman who not
only puts himself out of the way to find you quarters, but
asks you to share his dinner into the bargain. Such a
paragon of Etappen Commandants was he of Gonesse.
When muddy and belated I called upon him, he made
me out a billet on the instant, and sent a man with me
to the same. It was not much of a place, it was true,
but it was as good as any other quarters in Gonesse. I
had my choice of four empty rooms on the first floor of
an abandoned apothecary's shop. On the floor of each
room was a mattress; the remaining furniture consisted
of a chair and the inevitable picture of the Napoleonic
dynasty—*the* Napoleon with an arm round that poor limp
son of his, and the other pointing towards the ex-Emperor,
who tries to look as like his uncle as possible, while he
pats his boy on the head. A man cropped up from
downstairs, and "took me in," as my servant for the
time being. A German soldier is always ready for any
job that will bring him in an honest penny, and is as
content with a five-groschen piece as an English servant
would be with half-a-crown. He told me of a misfortune
that had occurred the day before at Aulnay, illustrating
the danger of exposing lights on the foreposts within
range of the enemy's fire. A military chaplain and a
count, an officer in a cavalry regiment, shared the same
room in a château in that exposed village, and neglected

to close the shutters when they lit their lights. Presently a shell from Aubervilliers crashed into the room, and exploding killed them both.

I was now in the country of the Guards, whose general custom it is to establish a kind of regimental club, which they call a casino, wherever a regiment happens to be quartered. Head-quarters being in Gonesse, the casino there was both well appointed and well frequented; and on the invitation of the Etappen Commandant I spent there a right merry evening. While somebody was singing a comic song, an officer rushed in with the tidings that "Paris was open." The song ceased, and all sprang to their feet; but it turned out that our friend was only hoaxing us. Nevertheless there were symptoms that the authorities thought the end must have been near. Three days before Metz capitulated, the contractors of the army received orders to hold themselves in readiness at a moment's notice to pour forth into the surrendered city. In this particular the coming event cast a true shadow before; and one felt tempted, when he found the order now repeated, to draw a hopeful augury from it. On the night of the 26th of November the order was despatched by telegram to all the contractors supplying the army with food that, in anticipation of the early capitulation of Paris, they should be prepared to supply exceptional demands upon their stores. The order was urgent, and caused great animation among the contractors. The German troops consumed the extra rations, and rations for many days and weeks besides, before the wished-for day came at last.

It is an axiom of unquestionable truth that the strength of the whole is equal only to the strength of the weakest part. Sagacious men at home did not fail to perceive that there must have been weak points in an

environment of such a circuit as that with which the
Germans surrounded Paris, and the inference was tempting that a sortie at one or other of these weak points
might have an important if not a successful result. This
inference, natural enough for one at a distance, was dissi-
pated by actual inspection. As I have already remarked,
the weakest point of the siege on the north side of Paris
was unquestionably the level tract between the road from
Paris to Gonesse and the Forest of Bondy. While the
region due north is dominated by heights and complicated by water, while the *col* of Pierrefitte dominates
the flat on its left, at least as far as Stains, the space I
have referred to had no natural advantages ready to the
hand of the besiegers to meet the chances of a sortie in
force. But so careful and skilful had been the applica-
tion of military science that the position of the besiegers,
from being open and precarious, had been converted into
an elaborate entrenched camp, capable of being defended
by resolute men against any field force that could have
been brought against it. This line of defence had its
right on Dugny, which I have already described, and ran
east with a south-easterly bend through Pont Iblon, Le
Blanc Mesnil, Aulnay, and Sevran, to Livry, which is
the left of what was without it the weak joint in the
harness. The little river Moree ordinarily flows in an
insignificant channel scarcely capable of interposing an
obstacle to cavalry, the ground in its front is nearly level,
and for a great part of its extent is covered with a spur
of the Forest of Bondy. There is a slight swell behind
the little stream, but not enough to give any dominance
of value in hindering troops from crossing the stream.
The roads along which an attack would advance are
numerous and excellent. Finally, an attacking force
would have had the advantage of a covering fire from

the forts of Paris up to the very muzzles of the German needle-guns.

As I rode along this forepost line on the 27th of November, on my way from Gonesse to Le Vert Galant, I was much struck with the masterly manner in which these disadvantages had been negatived. From being the weakest point of the environment I question if this tract had not been changed into one of the strongest. By a succession of dams the waters of the Moree had been arrested, and formed a continuous inundation of considerable depth and breadth all the way from Sevran to Dugny. There were indeed two breaks in the continuity, one at Pont Iblon, the other at the village of Aulnay. At the former the chaussée alone waded, as it were, through the water; there was no dry land right or left. To protect this point, Le Bourget, a mile further on, was strongly occupied, and acted as a bridge-head. The Paris-ward end of the causeway was crossed by a regular earthwork of solid and substantial construction. On the German side, right and left, were two batteries, whose fire converged on the chaussée, and above these, again, two more, while further to the right and further to the left were other batteries whose united fire could have swept a gnat off the chaussée. All along to Le Blanc Mesnil there were substantial entrenchments for infantry, with frequent emplacements for batteries interspersed. The latter village sits astride of the Moree, and was the key of the whole position. It had been made a fortress of in a most elaborate and effectual fashion. An enemy trusting for a passage over the inundation to his ability to force Mesnil, would have been leaning on a broken reed. On his left the inundation again widened out, and the battery sites and infantry entrenchments sprang up again on the gentle slope and continued all

the way to Sevran. The water, and what would have
been behind it waiting for the attack, were designed as
the great obstacles to a sortie. Of course there was a
chain of foreposts in the forest beyond, but in the event
referred to it was their instructions to fall back and effect
the recrossing with all convenient speed. To have sent
supports, with a view to the retention of an advanced
position—in a wood though it were—with level ground
and great guns in its front, and deep water in its rear,
would have been bad tactics, and therefore unlikely to
have been put in practice by Germans. The line to be
held to was that of the entrenchments behind the water,
and a comparatively slender body of troops might have
held it, and did hold it, against all that the garrison of
Paris could do.

At Aulnay, going eastward, one first came among the
Royal Saxons of the 12th Army Corps. The Saxons occupying Aulnay were the 108th Regiment, the Schützen-
Regiment, a few days afterwards so cut up before Villiers,
clean-made, sprightly fellows, with much the style about
them of our Rifle Brigade, only that their uniform is a
little smarter. The German soldiers, Prussians, Saxons,
Bavarians, and Würtembergers, alike were fond of ex-
ercising a quaint wit in the matter of inscriptions. Sometimes it was grim, not to say profane, as witness a legend
I read at Noisseville, before Metz. The legend was on
a wooden cross, and the wooden cross seemed to be at
the head of a grave; but the grave was a dummy, and
was but a decoy to the mine that underlay it at the exposed corner of the *repli*. To complete the illusion, the
pioneer had painted in large characters the customary,
"Hier ruhen in Gott," and then added, in smaller letters,
"90 Pfund preussisches Pulver." Over a pump in Aulnay
here which was in a recess I noticed the mocking in-

scription, "Bier Salon;" a little further on there were two
bronze lions rampant on the pillars of a gateway. The
head of each was surmounted by the helmet of a French
cuirassier of the Guard, and from the embrace of the
fore paws there stuck a chassepot.

Prince George of Saxony seemed to rule his army
corps without much state or fussiness. I saw no liveries
in Le Vert Galant, only one gendarme and an aide-de-
camp going along at a walk. From the proximity of the
Forest of Bondy to the French lines the 12th Corps came
in for most of the first fruits of whatever oozed out from
Paris. At Prince George's head-quarters the staff got a
reading of the Paris newspapers before they were sent in
to Margency, and they had also the cream of the spies,
if such a sour-milk profession can be said to have any
cream. Le Vert Galant is a village bearing a considerable resemblance to Le Bourget, only it was not shattered,
and it has more châteaux in its neighbourhood. The
good people of Saxony seemed to look after their soldier
relatives with great attention. Just as I got into Le Vert
Galant, a convoy of Liebesgaben had arrived from Leipsic
under the charge of four representatives of the committee
of that city. Fifty waggons had been required to transport the consignment from Château Thierry; so it may be
conceived what a show the love-gifts made piled up in
the capacious shed. This was the second contribution,
too. There were spirits, wines, cigars, and tobacco, warm
woollen garments, soaps, matches, biscuits, pens, paper,
and that sweeping variety of odds and ends which the
word "sundries" comprehends.

"The German Organization." How much we have
heard of that lately from all sorts of different sources, its
excellence, its promptitude, how it never breaks down
under any strain. Among others, I have borne tribute to

its merits, but the most whimsical tribute I ever heard was exacted from a Briton who was with the head-quarters of Princè George of Saxony. I had the story from the gentleman himself. He had been dining with Prince George, and was on his way to his quarters along the causeway. On his road, he came upon a provision waggon, one of whose wheels had broken, and the concern was in the mud. Not for long though; presently the waggoner produced another wheel in a matter-of-fact way which seemed to convey that he had an unlimited quantity of extra wheels on hand. The new wheel was put on, and the waggon rolled. Our countryman, comparatively a new comer, had heard much of the German organization. Here, to his hand, as if he had ordered the rehearsal, was a specimen. Far away from a wheelwright, a waggon suddenly breaks a wheel at midnight; so thorough is the organization, that a new wheel is on and the vehicle is under way again in less than ten minutes. Our countryman followed Captain Cuttle's counsel by making a note of this illustration, intending, no doubt, after the manner of a Briton, to write about it to his newspaper. Before going into his house, he happened to look into a shed which had been allocated as the dwelling-house of a gig, in which he had a few days before invested. The wheel of his gig was gone. It was the wheel of his gig that he had seen stuck on to the proviant waggon. He went to bed, trying, as he might, to digest this last phase of his illustration of the "German organization."

Returning to Margency on the morning of the 29th, I learned that two posts of a line of telegraph wires between Argenteuil and Bezons, near the former place, had been felled during the night, evidently by malice. As it happened, the wires were on a French track which had not been utilised by the Germans, and therefore no actual harm had been done, except to Argenteuil, which, in accordance with the regulations in such cases made and provided, would have to pay severely for the folly of one of its inhabitants, who would have been hanged if he could have been found.   The French were reported to be still pottering over the construction of the materials intended for the repair of the bridge at Bezons, but in a dilettante way that indicated little heart.   On the previous morning intelligence had reached head-quarters that orders had been given for the gates of Paris to be closed, with intent that a sortie should be made by the troops outside the enceinte—a measure (the closure of the gates I mean, not the sortie) rendered necessary by reason of the crowds of spectators that insisted on witnessing every demonstration of the kind.

In the afternoon I rode westward in the direction of Bezons and Sartrouville.   On the front, immediately below head-quarters, things were comparatively quiet.   A tremendously heavy fire had been heard during the night, Valérien seemingly leading off the ball, and the direction whence came the sound appeared to indicate that the firing must have been taken up all along the southern side.   The din, I was informed, had been as sustained and continuous as that of the cannonade in a general engagement.   When I reached Argenteuil, it became evident that the Frenchmen over the way were in a powder-burning humour.   There was quite a lively little fusillade going on from the opposite bank in the orchards and gardens which slope down from Colombes to the waterside.   The guns from the batteries at Nanterre and before Courbevoie were booming away at measured intervals, sending their shells crashing into the lower part of Argenteuil, while the peasants worked placidly in the fields within easy range, with the courage either of despair or of obtuseness. Outside Argenteuil, on the Sartrouville road, a peasant hailed me in the road, and told me that the previous evening, about six o'clock, his wife had been wounded in one of the streets of Argenteuil, and now lay in a house a little above where we stood. Monsieur was not a Prussian militaire? No, I was not. And, pardon, but Monsieur is not then a *curé?* This peasant must have been a very cautious man, determined to make quite sure of his ground. Monsieur could with a clear consciousness disavow the clerical profession. Then for sure Monsieur must be a doctor. I am not aware that I am addicted to washing my hands with invisible soap and water, which I have been given to understand is the shibboleth of doctorhood; and I could not own the soft impeachment. But there is something fascinating in being taken for a doctor, whether the case is of a woman who has fainted in the streets, or one who has been wounded at the foreposts. I believe I did not repudiate M.D. ship with so much plainness as I had done the other professions. Monsieur must at least come and see the poor woman. To this, nobody with a spark of humanity could have had any objection. I found a woman of about fifty years of age sitting in a chair over a fire, in a state of considerable fever. The bullet had struck her forearm as it was stretched out in gesticulation, had, so far as I could make out, shattered both the bones below the elbow, then run up the bone into the shoulder, and finally lodged just on the lip of the shoulder-blade, where I could feel it quite easily, with nothing but the skin between it and daylight. I did what I could with pillows and other rough and ready appliances to make the poor creature somewhat more comfortable, and left her with the promise that I should send her a German

military surgeon from Argenteuil. She had fevered, and
it was sad to hear her half-delirious talk. She had a son
a soldier, inside Paris, and she seemed to have a morbid
fondness for brooding over the fanciful supposition that
it might have been a bullet fired by the son which struck
the mother. Strange war, of which such things were
among the possibilities.

Returning towards head-quarters, I was in time to see
the Crown Prince of Saxony pass in review two regiments
of Uhlans of the Guard, who had returned from the other
side of the Oise, having been replaced there by a larger
body of soldiery. The regiments were in a state of the
most thorough efficiency: men and horses alike were in
the very pink of condition. An opinion I observe prevailed in England that a Uhlan is a light-cavalry man,
and that his ubiquity is owing to his lightness. The fact
is, that the Uhlans are heavy cavalry, coming next in
ponderosity to the Cuirassiers. Roughly, the relations
between the German and the British cavalry may be said
to be the following:—German Cuirassiers equal to our
Household troops, but with an infusion of slightly
shorter men; Uhlans, equal to British heavy cavalry,
i. e., 1st and 2nd Dragoons and 4th and 5th Dragoon
Guards; Prussian Dragoons and Hussars, corresponding
to British intermediate cavalry (viz., the 1st, 2nd, 3rd,
6th, and 7th Dragoon Guards and the Enniskillens) and
the British Light Cavalry (Hussars and Lancers). The
Prussians have no cavalry the men of which are uniformly
so light as our distinctively light-cavalry regiments.

We were at a disadvantage in Margency as regarded
war news from outside the range of the Maas Army.
There came in the shape of speedy information only what
the Versailles people thought proper to transmit by telegraph; and as regards sortie-making not on our own

face of the siege, we had, at least for a day or so, to
trust to our ears and to our acuteness in speculation.
Our ears, too, did not have quite a fair chance in the
matter. All the sound of firing came to us, in whatever
quarter it might have been occurring, through one gap
—the narrow valley between the hill of Orgimont and
Sannois. Whether Romainville was speaking, or whether
it was Mont Valérien "*qui donnait,*" the distant din came
booming to us up through this gap. It was possible to
localise the firing somewhat by the exhaustive process.
If there were no communications from the right or left
of the Maas army, nor any telegrams, then we knew
there had been no attack upon any section of it. If
Mont Valérien was quiet, that was evidence that the work
was not on the west; and so by this process we got at
the fact that a cannonade under such circumstances must
be on the south.

Wednesday, Nov. 30th, marked the commencement
of an important epoch in the siege of Paris. The beleaguered city began its grand effort to break the cordon
which surrounded it. On our northern side demonstrations only were made—attempts successful enough to the
extent to which they probably aspired, that of keeping
the besiegers in play, and preventing reinforcements from
being hurried to the scene of the sortie that was really
meant. There raged a heavy and continuous cannonade
from all the forts, but it was only at one point on the
north side where the French infantry broke cover in imposing force. What occurred on the eastern side on the
30th I had not the opportunity of seeing, on account at
once of the distance and of the threatening aspect on
the northern side. Before, then, making any reference
thereto let me narrate just what I did see.

From a very early hour in the morning it was apparent

that there was hot work in the west. Mont Valérien was quite eruptive from the very smallest of the small hours, thundering away with a laudable impartiality as to the direction in which it sent its projectiles. Before daylight I had ridden forward to the top of Mont d'Orgimont, overhanging Argenteuil, and from this position had an excellent opportunity of observing this exceptional activity. It seemed to me that as day broke quite a battle must be in progress somewhere by Ville d'Avray, on the south side of Valérien, and directly in the track between it and Versailles. The crash of heavy guns was almost continuous, and when there was a brief interval in their deep bass the sharper sound of musketry firing came fainter on the morning wind. It struck me that while the cannonade was an all-round one in this direction, there was, besides the point somewhere about Ville d'Avray, another actual fight going on nearer me in the direction of Bougival. I could dimly distinguish down in the low ground in that direction columns of troops, and the frosty mist of the morning was made denser by the white smoke of the small arms. Closer to me, and in what I regarded as my own province, the work was very warm. From early morning shells from the batteries at Nanterre and Courbevoie had been crashing into Bezons and Argenteuil. The sheltered road behind the latter town was scored in many places with the deep ruts made by shells. The bank on the French side was lined by their infantry, who had kept up a pattering fire into the darkness. In the anticipation of an attempt to restore the bridge at Bezons, to which I have already referred, the troops occupying that town, Argenteuil, and the intermediate posts, had stood to their arms, but had made no effort to reply to a fire which seemed so purposeless, and was doing so little harm. On the eminence where I stood, the batteries on the other side kept up an unremitting fire. The shells ploughed its summit up in all directions, and the buildings which crown it were knocked about remorselessly. As day broke it became too dangerous a position, notwithstanding its great advantages as a point of outlook, and I was compelled to evacuate it, and retreat into the low ground beyond. It was out of the frying-pan into the fire. If I went east the shells from La Briche were tumbling into Epinay, St. Gratien, and Deuil. Montmagny and Stains were evidently having rough times of it at the hands of the Fort du Nord; further round Dugny and Le Bourget were receiving marks of the distinguished consideration of Fort de l'Est. Before returning to head-quarters, I went some distance to the west, to a point on the road westward from Argenteuil, which commands a view of Colombes and Courbevoie.

While I stood here, behind the angle of a wall, noting how alert the French sharpshooters on the opposite bank were in peppering at even a single man who exposed himself, I heard behind me the jingle of harness, and, looking round, beheld to my amazement the Union Jack waving in the wind. The old rag fluttered from a staff that was sticking in the front of a fourgon, and side by side with it waved the red cross flag. In front rode two gentlemen with the red cross brassard on their arm. The two gentlemen were Mr. J. S. Young (of the Army Control Department), superintending the English ambulance in St. Germain; and Captain Furley, a well-known and energetic member of the National Society. It was Mr. Young to whom I had written describing the condition of the lazarette in the Château Ecouen, and begging for some help for the poor fever-smitten fellows who lay there. Mr. Young immediately on the receipt of my

letter made his preparations with promptitude and zeal;
Captain Furley's invaluable co-operation was enlisted in
the cause, and here were the two with their waggon load
of good things behind them, jogging quietly through the
fire on their way to Ecouen. You can easily imagine
how delighted I was to see them, and how pleased I
was to know that, in consequence of my representations
relief was about to reach a spot where it was so badly
needed. It was thoroughly British—the cool quietude
with which the little procession pegged on steadily on
the path of duty, heedless of the chassepot bullets that
came singing past them from the Frenchmen over the
water. Here was the road; that was enough for our
countrymen. To reach Ecouen it had to be traversed,
and the dangers by the way were simply part of the
day's work. Further on, while passing between Montmorency and Sarcelles, the shells dropped profusely about
the waggon, but fortunately without any casualty. I accompanied Mr. Young and Captain Furley to the head-
quarters of the Crown Prince, at Margency, where they
met with a very warm reception from the gentlemen of
the staff. Of the reception they experienced at Ecouen
I shall speak presently.

From Margency I accompanied a staff officer through
Montmorency to Montmagny, and round to Gonesse on
the swell between Garges and Bonneuil, and Stains,
Pierrefitte, and Dugny. For the first time during the
siege Du Nord was throwing shells into Montmorency,
which was imagined out of range. It made one nervous
to hear them whizzing by us and bursting behind us in
Sarcelles, as we were cantering up the *chaussée* toward
Pierrefitte. I don't think the northern forts of Paris ever
squandered so much fire as on this day. It seemed to
me that they simply let drive in every direction, content

to know that a shell was off somewhere. We were just in time to witness from the ridge a sortie toward Stains, a village the exceptional position of which I explained in a recent letter. Three battalions came over the flat against it, supported by a close and sustained fire from Fort du Nord and the Lunette de Stains. The village was garrisoned by the 2nd regiment of the Guard and a battalion of the Queen Elizabeth's. The French troops, two battalions of Mobile Guards and one of the French line, came on with great resolution and in excellent order, notwithstanding that a German field battery in an emplacement to our left dropped shells among them with beautiful precision. But the German Guards were waiting for them, and received them with a steady fire at short range. The Frenchmen tried a rush; but the bullets met them in the teeth, and checked their impetus. After holding their ground for a little while, exchanging shots with the Guardsmen, the exposed position had the inevitable result, and a retrograde movement set in. The French, however, deserve great credit for the regular manner in which they effected their retreat.

There was another demonstration in the direction of Le Bourget at a later hour. Dense columns of French troops showed on the plain in front of Fort Aubervilliers, and advanced steadily in the direction of Le Bourget. But they lost heart before they got near the piquet in the railway station, and never came close enough to give the men behind the main barricade a chance at them. Le Bourget, however, already pounded with shells, had a fresh dose of the same physic all day; and when we were away in the east at Gonesse, the French had burst out of St. Denis, and had actually taken Epinay, although they were unable to hold it. The fire from La Briche had been all day so strong that it was necessary in Epinay

6 *

to huddle very close under cover; and no doubt the
battalion of the 71st, which was on duty in it, was in a
measure taken by surprise by the suddenness and fury
with which the French attacked. They burst out of St.
Denis at the double about half-past three P.M., and simultaneously a gunboat with a strong detachment of sailors
darted out from behind Fort La Briche, and came steam-
ing down the Seine. The vessel, as it came down stream,
swept the banks clear of the German outposts with its
fire, and landed its cargo at Epinay just as the troops
arrived that had come by *terra firma*. Of these there
were six battalions—four of linesmen, two of Mobiles.
The houses by the river-side and round to the west side
of the village were occupied, and the 71st at least half
surrounded before it had well realised the fact that it
was attacked. It had got so late that no sortie was anticipated. While the French were crossing the plain the
German batteries on the crest in front of Montmorency
played upon them with considerable effect. A lodgment
having been effected in the village by a force so immensely superior, nothing remained for the battalion of
the 71st but to extricate itself, with as much credit as
possible, from its awkward plight. It evacuated the village,
fighting as it retreated, and fell back toward St. Gratien.
Here it found immediate reinforcement. The French
utilised the time by barricading themselves in Epinay,
and making preparations to give a warm reception to the
force which should attempt to retake it. That force consisted of the whole of the 15th Brigade, the 71st and
31st Regiments, in all six battalions, with three companies
of the 26th Regiment lent by the 16th Brigade. The whole
belonged to the 8th Division, which was commanded by
General von Schöler. A rapid march was made on Epinay,
the ardour of which the French were unable to baulk, and

the place was retaken after having been held by the French not quite two hours. The loss of the Germans was very considerable, to be accounted for from the fact that they were the assailants in the second act of the piece. There were killed outright between forty and fifty men and five officers. The wounded were about 135 men and eight officers. It was at first believed the French were able to carry off no prisoners, although one officer and several men were reported missing; but it was thought likely they might be lying either killed or wounded in some of the unexplored houses. Although some were thus found, others could not be accounted for; and it was afterwards learned that six men were captured and taken back by the French into St. Denis. On the other hand, about forty French soldiers, chiefly linesmen, were taken prisoners by the Germans. I saw them in Montmorency next morning. They seemed in very good case, strong, fresh, and healthy, with no appearance of privation. It was a feature of this affair in Epinay that a party of the 71st, under the command of an Vicefeldwebel, held a house in the village during the whole time of the French occupation, and successfully resisted repeated efforts on the part of the French to drive them out. Their comrades thought them lost; and it was an agreeable surprise to find the staunch little garrison still holding their billet, and that without material loss. The wounded from Epinay were brought in the first instance to St. Gratien, where the chateau of Princess Demidoff was converted for the time into an hospital. The position, however, was too exposed, it being within easy range of St. Briche, and therefore the poor fellows were next morning removed further back— some to Montmorency, but the greater number to Eaubonne. Those who could bear the transport were sent to Germany as soon as possible.

The German loss in the sortie on Stains was inconsiderable. The Guards had only to defend the place; it was different with the French, who had to expose themselves in the plain on the way to the attack, and during its progress. Shells fell on the 30th November at a greater range than it had been believed the guns of the French forts were capable of carrying. Before then Montmorency had never been touched by a shell, and it was believed to be just out of range. But on the 30th the shells not only came crashing into Montmorency, but even fell behind it—a range of somewhere about 6300 metres. In all, seventy-two shells on the 30th fell in Montmorency. I heard of but one casualty from all this pounding: a line officer was wounded.

Dr. Tegener received the English ambulance with great enthusiasm. The tears were in his eyes as he shook hands with Mr. Young and Captain Furley. On my arrival at a later hour he fairly embraced me. The stores were carried into his own room, and as the box of sundries was unpacked it was glorious to watch the delight of the good old man. "Porter," "Ganz gut!" "Ale," "Ganz gut!" "Chloroform," "Ach Gott!" "Twelve hundred cigars," "Du lieber Gott!" and the hands and eyes went up in delight. The subscribers to the Society should have seen the sick men taking their first dose of the generous port, and smoking their first cigar. The sight would have been ample reward to Mr. Young and Captain Furley had they run greater risks than they did to bring the good things round. The woollen clothing must, I believe, have saved many lives. When convalescents are sent out from hospital to forepost-work, still weak and unseasoned, and thinly clad, they went down almost inevitably with rheumatism; but with the warm jackets and drawers of the Society they could brave with impunity the hardest weather. In the society of the Medical Staff we three Engländers spent a right pleasant evening over a bowl of punch, compounded by the joint efforts of the apothecaries, of materials not drawn from the stores for the sick. After supper Dr. Tegener asked everybody to dedicate a bumper to a toast which he was about to give, and then the good man made quite a little speech. Here is the purport of it:—"Gentlemen, —there are some people—we have indeed seen specimens of the species—who go about and make large and sweeping promises which are never fulfilled. What an example of the contrary we have now before us! There came here casually the other day *unser lieber* (the writer of these lines). He saw our state, and on the spot he wrote to his countryman, Mr. Young, at St. Germain, recounting what he had seen, and begging him to act. Mr. Young lets no red tape stand in his way. He and Captain Furley here put their heads together, and now this afternoon, without any bother, any previous correspondence, there comes jogging up our avenue a waggon bringing what is health—nay, what is life—to our poor sick. Here is the Engländer all over, gentlemen—the bulldog, that has no wind to spare in superfluous barking." Then the doctor went for a little down a side lane to prove that the English and the Germans were brethren, and that a mutual affection was natural; and wound up by calling for vociferous "Hochs" for the English ambulance. Captain Furley responded in a few graceful words, that were evidently not "from the teeth outward." Mr. Young contributed vocally to the harmony of the evening; and I, who could neither make a speech nor sing a song, had to concentrate my energies on the punch and cigars. And so passed our St. Andrew's night very merrily, for as yet we knew not that doings had been enacted in the

day-time that, had we known of them, would have made
mirth not only unseemly but impossible.

The great sortie on the south and south-east was to
have been essayed on the 29th November, and was arranged, as it appeared, to consist of a combined attack
on the parts of Generals Vinoy and Ducrot. Vinoy had
to deal with the southern section, his eruption taking
place from Villejuif and Vitry against Choisy-le-Roi and
up the valley of the Seine. Ducrot had the valley of the
Marne for his theatre of offensive operations. The combination failed, in consequence, as was afterwards ascertained, of a characteristic miscalculation, want of fore-
sight as to the length of pontooning required for bridging
the Marne, swollen as that stream was. The explanation
of the blunder was that an exceptional quantity of water
had been turned into the stream, either through neglect
of the sluice arrangements higher up, on the part of the
functionaries whose duty it was to attend to their manage-
ment, or through a cunning device of the Germans, who,
it was said, first dammed the water and then let out the
accumulation, with intent to hinder and hamper the
efforts of the French to bridge the stream lower down.
There was no foundation for the latter supposition: any
action of this kind on the part of the Germans would
have seriously inconvenienced themselves, as interfering
with the efficiency of their bridges at Chelles and Cournay;
in addition to which obvious fact, I had the positive assurance that nothing of the kind had been thought of.
The former is an absurdity on the face of it. The sluices
on the Marne are designed, not to regulate the quantity
of water in the river, but are in the nature of locks to
facilitate the passage of vessels going up stream over
shallows and rapids, which are ingeniously localised, so
that each lock suffices to neutralise a rapid, and conducts

from one long placid reach into another at a single step. The navigation on the stream having been suspended on account of the hostile occupation, these locks were simply left open: throughout the whole distance from Dormans to Chelles I never saw the gates of one closed. Thus the volume of water flowed without interruption, whether it was great or small; that it was greater than Ducrot's pontoneers had reckoned for was owing to freshets in the upper part of the valley. And under no hypothesis can it be disputed that one of the rudiments of the art of military bridge construction is to leave a margin for the contingency of a swollen stream, from whatever cause the increase might arise. In so far, then, as the failure in the arranged combination between Vinoy and Ducrot for the 29th was ascribable to the default in the bridge accommodation at the service of the army of the latter, the failure was utterly inexcusable, and reflects greater discredit on the military character of those at whose door it lies than any other episode in the defence of Paris. Vinoy's effort of the 29th against the 6th Army Corps failed utterly; and it fell to Ducrot to make his effort the day after, unassisted by the distraction which the former, according to the plan of action, was meant to afford, and which, but for the blunder referred to, it certainly would have afforded. It is a bad omen in such cases when a general has to begin offensive operations with the acknowledgment, *Perdidi diem.* It cannot be denied, however, that on the 30th he tried his best to make up for the lost time. By daybreak his troops, having for the most part crossed in the night, were pushing in the Würtemberg and Saxon outposts on the horseshoe-like peninsula, under cover of a heavy fire from Avron, Forts Nogent and Charenton, and the redoubts of La Faisanderie and Gravelle. I am writing now from

what I was able to learn of this affair after it was over,
for I did not reach the ground on which it took place
till the morning of the 2nd December.   On this account
I reserve topographical detail till I come to deal with
this latter event; nor, as not having been an eye-witness,
can I claim thorough accuracy as to the details of what
passed on the 30th.   The Würtembergers on the 29th
had occupied the whole of the line across the peninsula
as far as Noisy-le-Grand, which was the left flank post
of the Saxons, and were being partially replaced by the
Saxons, when the French attack was made.   A "dislocation," in fact, was in progress; and although in theory
an operation of this kind, instead of weakening a force
along the line where it is being performed, should indeed double the strength, since the relieved and relievers
should be on the ground at one and the same time, yet in
practice, especially if the line is somewhat attenuated by
its length, the force to be relieved not unfrequently an-
ticipates, partly at least, in its departure the advent of the
relief.   In such a case the temporary weakness must be
apparent; and in any case a "dislocation" is productive
inevitably of a certain amount of confusion.   Abraham
Lincoln's adage, "It is a bad time for changing horses
when fording a stream," is extremely applicable to relieving operations performed in the very teeth of an
attack by an enemy in force.   I think everything points
to the conclusion that the French, tardy as their movements were in losing the whole of the 29th, succeeded
to a great extent, after all, in surprising the Würtembergers and the Saxons in that daybreak attack of theirs
on the 30th.   Brie was soon in the hands of the French.
Then they spread out like a fan, their left threatening
Noisy, their centre looking straight at Villiers, their right,
in great strength, being already in possession of Cham-

pigny. They had hurled the Würtembergers back on
that village with a rush, while at the same time they had
taken it in flank on the south side; and although there
was some desperate fighting on the part of the South
Germans to hold the place, yet they were utterly over-
powered and driven back by sheer dint of superior
weight. Villiers was not so easily gained by the French.
It stands higher, has better defensive capacities, and they
had been more carefully utilised. Here I may state that
after the pinch on the south-east was over, and comparative quietude had been restored, I was informed on
authority which commanded attention that the Würtembergers had been somewhat lax as well as unskilful in
their attention to the artificial defences of the extreme
front of their position. It certainly seemed to one going
over the ground after the fighting was over that eligible
positions had not been utilised, and that there was a
want of that continuity and thoroughness of defensive
works noticeable in the front of the country of the Guards
and the Saxons. Confirmation of what I have alluded
to might seem to be found in the elaborate system of
defences the construction of which was set about as soon
as the French had fallen back from the positions they
had temporarily occupied. But to return to Villiers. A
Würtemberger battery stood in front of an emplacement
at the corner of the park in the village, and served for a
considerable time, supported as it was by the strenuous
efforts of an infantry force which was unfortunately but
too scanty, in staving off the rush of the French. It
suffered severely from the fire of Nogent, and ultimately
the infantry supports had withdrawn from it; but the
gunners stood to their guns with admirable persistence.
The French were no less obstinate in their assault, and
the spectacle was presented of a single unsupported

battery blazing into the teeth of a strong attacking force
with shrapnel shells at point-blank range of 300 yards.
When so small a distance separated the foes, the fire of
Nogent had to be suspended, and it seemed as if the
battery was holding its own; but at the critical moment
its ammunition was exhausted, and the gallant gunners,
in default of supplies, had no alternative but to fall back.
Then, with no inconsiderable amount of obstinate street-
fighting, Villiers fell into the hands of the French, and
the situation assumed a very alarming aspect.   Having
used Champigny as a kind of base of concentration, the
French had streamed up the slope of Mont Mesly beyond,
and actually were on its summit.   But further they could
not get.   Reitzenstein's brigade of Würtembergers (the
1st) held the heights beyond in force, along with all the
available artillery of the division; and this sufficed to stay
the advance of the French beyond Mont Mesly, removed
as they were from the covering fire of the forts.   They
were very stubborn, however, and it was not until late in
the afternoon that they relaxed their efforts to gain more
ground, and until the opportunity had arrived, in the
opinion of General Obernitz, for directing Reitzenstein
to alter his tactics and assume the counter-offensive.
Meanwhile three regiments (the 104th, 106th, and 107th)
of Nehrhoff's division of Saxons (24th) had got into
position behind Villiers, and covering Noisy.   Villiers
had cost the French so dear, that they were not prepared
immediately to pursue the offensive on their getting possession of that village, and, after a pause of some duration in the active operations on this section of the battle-
field, Nehrhoff availed himself of what seemed a good
opening for an attempt to retake the village.   The duty
was entrusted to the 47th Brigade, commanded by Colonel
von Abendroth, who had assumed the brigadier-general-

ship in succession to General von Schulz, who had been wounded at Sedan. In all the Saxon army there is no gallanter officer than the colonel of the 106th. He in person commanded the two battalions that made the assault on Villiers. The French had been utilising their occupancy, and already a barricade had been thrown up, which the Saxons carried at the point of the bayonet. The fighting was close, sustained, and desperate, all through the village street; but the Saxons stubbornly fought their way, and supports poured in behind the men in the forefront of the battle. I believe Abendroth succeeded in clearing the village. It is certain he took about 250 prisoners, chiefly in the houses at the end nearest the park. But this park was virtually part of the village, and till it was retaken the position could not be said to have been retrieved. Abendroth had gone down, his horse pierced with four bullets. His adjutant gave him a fresh mount, and the colonel was hardly in the saddle before it, too, was shot, and he on the ground. Scrambling up, as an eye-witness told me, the gallant old soldier headed the attack on foot, which was made on the park held so stubbornly by the French. The fighting was long and fierce in this neighbourhood, and the result I never could learn with that exactitude which was desirable. I was informed authoritatively, on the one hand, that on the night of the 30th the Saxons held Villiers, having recovered it by the attack of which I have been writing; but there was a want of explicit candour in communicating the details that was not altogether satisfactory. From other sources, and, indeed, from the men engaged, I gathered, on the other hand, that on the night of the 30th Villiers was only partly occupied by the Saxons, while the further end of it, including the park I have referred to, was beyond question in French occupation;

and French prisoners taken on the 2nd asserted un-
hesitatingly that on the night in question Villiers was
entirely in the hands of the French, they having recovered the place at nightfall, when Abendroth's men fell
back. I incline to place belief in the veracity of the
second of these three statements, and assume that Villiers
was only wholly evacuated in the course of the following
day (the 1st of December). But there can be no question
about Champigny, notwithstanding that great frankness
on the subject was not displayed by the head-quarter
staff of the 12th Army Corps. Close on nightfall Reitzenstein's Würtembergers had cleared the intervening ground,
and, well supported by field artillery, made a very
energetic attempt to retake the village; but it met with
a most stubborn resistance; and the Würtembergers not
only could get no foothold in the place, but the Mobiles
defending it succeeded in recovering some of the ground
they had lost in the direction of Mont Mesly, and they
employed the night in fortifying the position and in
throwing up earthworks outside the village, to render yet
more difficult another attempt on the part of the Würtembergers to recapture it.

The 1st of December was, as I take it, a day of forced
inaction on both sides. The Germans were certainly not
prepared to take the initiative on that day. During the
first half of it a kind of informal armistice existed for the
purpose of removing the wounded and burying the dead
—a task which neither side, so far as I could gather,
performed with the thoroughness which was desirable.
The French utilised the tranquillity by digging potatoes
on the blood-stained field, and in stripping the flesh off
the carcases of killed horses which strewed its surface.

The *rationale* of the French tactics on the 30th November is not far to seek. There was the sortie on the

west, one on the south against the 6th Army Corps,
other two at distinct points in the north, and yet another
threatened one in Le Bourget, all meant as feints and
distractions; and there was the great and seriously meant
one on the east, on to the horseshoe. It may surely be
safely assumed that the intention of the besieged was to
break through at the latter point, and at once relieve
Paris of superfluous mouths, and let loose a field army
to hang on the rear of the besiegers, and co-operate with
the army of the Loire. Had the attempt been successful, its success would have gone far to raise the siege of
Paris, at all events for a time. But the iron grip of the
German was too strong. The history of the siege of
Paris is the history of the siege of Metz over again. The
Germans threw their cordon round and round, they chose
their ground, they planted their feet firmly down upon
it, and held to it with a grim, quiet, terribly inflexible
tenacity. The French inside having lost the comparative chance open to them in the early days, while as yet
the German foot had not settled itself quite surely on the
ground, were now beating themselves furiously on the
stern barrier that surrounded them, all impotent, notwithstanding the unquestionable conduct and spirit which
they demonstrated, to hew a gap quite through that
barrier.

Such was the position on the 1st December. Would
the French gather heart for another effort? Would they
sulkily abide behind their ramparts till the last biscuit
was eaten; or would they let reason speak to them, and,
recognising the double fact that they could not raise the
siege, and that its maintenance inevitably entailed upon
them the horrors of starvation, would they avert that
misery by a timely and honourable capitulation? These
were the questions all were canvassing on the northern

side, while the Saxons and Würtembergers were drawing a long breath, and bracing themselves for the struggle that their eyes told them was close. The morrow brought at once the answer to the question and the renewal of the struggle.

After the storm of the 30th November came the calm —a short-lived one—of the 1st of December. On the former day, the air had throbbed and vibrated with the continuous din of the artillery; on the latter, not the sound of a single gun-shot came to break the stillness. The guns of the forts must have got very hot before the firing was over, somewhere about midnight. Their cooling had been helped during the night-watches by a keen frost, which hardened the ground and covered the ponds with a thin film of ice.

On the morning of the 1st Captain Furley and Mr. Young visited the railway station at Villers le Bel, to inspect the hospital train which was just on the point of starting for Berlin. I have read assertions that the Germans cared assiduously for the fighting-man so long as he was in a state to fight, but that when he became *hors de combat* the care ceased, and the useless man, rendered useless by wounds or sickness, was neglected. This train was in itself a conclusive reply to the calumny. It was a locomotive hospital. The beds were in two tiers along the sides of the carriages—beds furnished with every imaginable device for the comfort of the occupant. There was an apothecary-shop compartment, and another carriage which was a most convenient and admirably arranged kitchen. The train had its living cargo on board —men fit for the journey, culled from the field lazarettes all round the north and east sides of the besieging line. While the steam was getting up, there they were lapping their beef tea, made for them in the kitchen waggon, the hospital orderlies performing their duties just as in the hospital. One fellow told Captain Furley that he was so comfortable that he cared very little whether his journey lasted a week or a month. On their way back to St. Germain my countrymen picked up my female patient at Argenteuil, to transport her into a civil hospital in the former town. I cannot quit the subject of the English ambulance visit without bearing testimony to the promptness and efficiency of the performance. To travel to and fro some twenty-five miles either way in two days indicates a high state of efficiency; and it ought not to be forgotten that for quite half of this distance the road was under a very heavy fire. Between St. Brice and Sarcelles the men, horses, and waggon were twice spattered with a shower of earth caused by the explosion of shells in the field which they were skirting. I could not help being tickled at the sight of Captain Furley and Mr. Young coolly exchanging cigar-lights just at this interesting stage of the proceedings.

Between four and five o'clock on the morning of the 2nd, a good friend came to my bedside with sure information that at daybreak an attempt was to be commenced by the Saxons and Würtembergers to drive the French out of the villages of Brie and Champigny, which they had occupied since the day before but one. The strategical value to the besiegers of those villages was of only a negative kind, while Brie formed an eligible *tête du pont* for the French, and Champigny was invaluable to them as opening up the southern exit from the horseshoe. Under these circumstances, the intention, as resolved on at head-quarters, was not alone to drive the French out of the two villages, but burn them both, so that they should not in future be available as shelters or places from which to make head. I was in the saddle in half

an hour, and out on the long and weary road, eager to
be in time for what I knew was coming.

Past Montmorency, with its trim châteaux all silent,
its hill with the white house on its summit standing out
against the moonlit sky, with the lake of Enghien at my
feet, sleeping placidly in the flood of white light. Just
as I passed the now forlorn and abandoned dwelling that
was once the hermitage of Jean Jacques Rousseau—boom,
boom—there came five shells, one after the other, from
Fort Du Nord, as if Paris should say to the besiegers on
the north side, "Remember, although I mean hard fighting on the east, you are not to think that I am not
thoroughly on the alert all round; so don't attempt con-
centrations, if you are wise." Through the vineyards to
Sarcelles, and over behind Stains by the near cut, so
swept by the shells the day before but one; past Dugny,
where the Guardsmen were snoring in a full-nosed chorus,
trusting implicitly and with all safety, to the alertness of
their comrades on sentry. On across the *chaussée* before
Pont Iblon, whence the Queen Elizabeths sallied out for
that desperate rush of theirs to retake Le Bourget; past
the broad inundation on the left, across it into Aulnay,
with the brass helmets on the stone lions; on through
Sevran, and down into Livry, where I found the Kaiser
Franz Guardsmen occupying the old quarters of the
Saxon Schützen Regiment. Now a sweep to the right
into dangerous ground by Clichy, and forward through
the felled forest and the labyrinth of earthwork that crown
the summit of the Forest of Bondy above Montfermeil.
Before I had reached this spot the sombre music of the
cannon had begun to play. First came one sullen boom,
and a simultaneous flash through the morning twilight
from the lofty side of Fort Rosny, then a dull chaos of
noise, as from the guns on the newer works of Avron,

further to the south. After this overture, which was performed about seven o'clock, there was no intermission in
the din. The air seemed thick with the sound of the
terrible cannonade, and at times it was as if a gust struck
against one's face, when some huge gun emptied itself
into space. There was a sublimity in the roar, such as
could be produced by no bicker of mere field artillery.
From Montfermeil my way lay down between the two
heights into Chelles, where I found the Saxons in force
—the 103rd Regiment garrisoning the town, and ready
for anything that might take place on their immediate
front. But Chelles was not the theatre of action this
morning. The day before but one it had got a benefit
in the shape of some 200 shells, which represented simply
the waste of so much ammunition, since not a man was
hurt. Some special providence must surely have protected a field-watch commanded by Hauptmann von Zanthier, in the front of Chelles. The shells actually rained
about it, exploding in front, at the sides, and in the rear,
but never a one came into the little post where the Saxon
captain lay with his men.

On quitting Chelles I took the wrong road, following
the *chaussée* towards Neuilly, till convincing argument
proved to me that I was out of the track. Before this
road will be eligible again for traffic it will require to be
relaid with fresh blocks of granite. A heavy shell bursting on the hard causeway produces an absolutely dia-
bolical effect. Iron and stone fly in splinters together,
whole blocks are sent into the air, and hurtle outward
from the fiery centre as if projected from a gigantic
turbine. And it was not one shell that fell on this exposed *chaussée*, but many—so many that, when man and
horse were out of the solitude so infernally enlivened, I
thought both were lucky in the extreme. Crossing the

7*

river higher up at Gournay, I learned there that Prince
George of Saxony had shifted his head-quarters to Champs
on the previous evening, and I found a battle raging
fiercely on the tract of broken country to the south-west
of that village.

The Marne, beginning at Gournay, runs first nearly
due west to a little beyond Noisy-le-Grand, then makes a
sweep south, on the eastern bank of which sweep stands
the village of Brie, and then forms a couple of loops,
near the south of the broad neck of the most northerly
of which is the village of Champigny, and further north
and some distance to the east the larger village of Villiers-
sur-Marne.   It was in and around the three villages of
Brie, Villiers, and Champigny where had been enacted
the bloody drama of the 30th November.   When the
curtain had fallen on that drama the Saxons stood fast in
Villiers, spite of all that the French troops and the French
forts could do to dislodge them.   Brie and Champigny,
lying so close under the lee of Fort Nogent and the
strongly armed redoubt of Faisanderie, on the verge of
the Forest of Vincennes overhanging Joinville, remained
in the hands of the French, for whatever good they were.
What this advantage represented was simply this—that
Brie gave them a footing, so to speak, on the Saxon
mainland, while Champigny formed the key to the district behind the horseshoe formed by the loop of the
Marne. Whether the risk, nay the certainty, of the severe
loss entailed in an attempt to dislodge the French from
positions which may be fairly designated as outworks of
their fortifications, deserved to be weighed in the balance,
in a military sense, against the advantage to be gained
by beating the Frenchmen out of places so protected, is
a question the reply to which does not rest with me; but,
if it did, I would candidly give it as my opinion that the

objects of the besiegers would have been equally served by giving their forepost line on this face a wider and a safer sweep. A line drawn from Gournay to Chennevières presents a continuous defensive position of considerable strength, the complement of which might have been found in the utter destruction, by fire and crowbar, of the villages of Noisy, Villiers, and Champigny. Such a line would, at all events, have presented this advantage, that there need have been fewer earth mounds beneath which lie dead children of the Fatherland, beyond it on the side towards the French forts.

But speculations of this kind are as tedious as they must be purposeless. The object of the day on the side of the Germans was to dislodge the French from these villages—Brie and Champigny. To essay this task fell to the lot of Saxons, Würtembergers, and a brigade of the 2nd Army Corps. The Saxons engaged consisted of the second division of the Royal Saxon Army (the 24th division of the German host), under the command of General von Nehrhoff, and composed of the 104th, 105th, 106th, 107th, and 108th Regiments. This, taking each regiment at its full strength of three battalions, would represent fifteen battalions, or about 12,000 men; but as more than one battalion was naturally elsewhere engaged on forepost duty, it may be outside the exact figures to put down the Saxon force engaged at 10,000 men. Before the commencement of operations these splendid troops occupied positions in Noisy, Champs, Gournay, Villiers, and the vicinity. The division of the Würtembergers, the strength of which was considerably less than that of the Saxons, was commanded by General von Obernitz. Their previous positions had been Ormesson, Chennevières, La Queue, Noiseau, and the vicinity. I have spoken of a brigade of the 2nd Army Corps as co-operating, but I have reason to believe that this contingent was neither strictly a brigade nor did it amount to a division, but was made up of contributions from various portions of the Army Corps in question. It was commanded by General von Fransecki, who, in virtue of seniority, had the nominal direction of all the operations, which were, however, supervised generally as regarded the Saxons by Prince George in person, whose heedlessness of danger must sorely have tried the nerves of his staff. The contingent from the 2nd Army Corps supported and co-operated with the Würtembergers. The Saxons had no backing but their own resolute valour. In all, the German troops engaged and immediately supporting may have numbered about 22,000. The German programme was complicated more or less unexpectedly by a counter-offensive operation projected by the French against Villiers, no doubt with intentions of penetrating further, and of ultimately breaking through the cordon. Thus it fell out that as the Germans were pressing on to the attempt of driving the French out of Brie and Champigny, Messieurs the French were simultaneously pouring out with intent to take Villiers. When two bodies are going opposite ways in the same groove, it is a law of nature that a collision is the result. When the two bodies are armies, a fight is inevitable. Such events of that fight as came under my personal observation I shall endeavour to recount; but it is necessary first to give a brief description of the nature of the ground on which it took place. On the road to Noisy the south bank of the Marne is low, with a gradual rise, furrowed by inconsiderable rectangular depressions. As one reaches Noisy, which stands on the crest of the rise, and looks southward, he sees towards Villiers, and athwart the neck of the loop, a broad flat upland table-land, affording favour-

able scope for military evolutions. All along the front of
this table-land, on which Villiers stands, and which due
west of that village is projected some distance toward the
horseshoe, there is a continuous fall, in places shaggy and
abrupt, in others cultivated and more gradual, down into
the alluvial plain of which the major part of the horseshoe consists.

Toward Brie, which is nearly due east from Noisy, the
slope tumbles more rapidly than further to the south.
In front of Villiers is a château, inhabited by a courageous French lady, who remained at home throughout the
terrible scenes which were being enacted around her
habitation. The park around this château is girdled by
a wall, of the advantages of which the Saxons had made
the most, and in front of it again (I am writing always of
the side toward Paris as the front) there were still a few
fields and vineyards of level ground before the slope,
more gradual about here and to the southward, commenced to fall away down into the plain of the horseshoe.
The whole position, of which Villiers was the Hougomont,
although it was hampered by occasional broken ground,
hedges and brushwood, would have formed no bad stand-
point for offering resistance to a force which, having
deployed on the plain, was attempting to carry it, if it
were not that it was swept by a direct fire from Fort
Nogent and the Faisanderie redoubt, at easy range, and
enfiladed at longer range, but still effectually, from the
batteries on Mont Avron.

When I crossed the river the hour already was considerably past nine. It seemed to me that Noisy-le-Grand
was an eligible point from which to observe the operations,
and accordingly I directed my way thither. I never wish
to travel such a road again, nor to reach such a destination. The shells from Avron were coming very thick.

Now they fell with a great splash into the Marne at my
feet, starring the placid water as a stone stars a mirror;
now there was a great bang on the road, and a belch of
white smoke or a dull thud on the frosty ground above.
If the road was bad, Noisy itself was worse.   It seemed
as if the gunners in Avron and Nogent were determined
that not one stone of it should be left upon another.
Now it was a shower of slates, as a shell crashed through
a roof, rifting the solid rafters as if they had been laths.
Now half the side of a house went over bodily as a huge
projectile struck and crunched it.   In the shortness of the
range, strange to say, there was one element of safety.
The fire had to be direct, not plunging; and so massive
were the walls, that if one could only manage to get two
or three of them between him and the hostile guns, he
occupied a position of precarious safety.   Brie divided
with Noisy the attentions of the French batteries, and
Brie was still nearer them than Noisy.   I had been told
that the 107th Regiment had made a dash into Brie out
of Noisy early in the morning, and I wondered much how
it fared with them.   Hard enough, beyond doubt, but
could they hold the place under such a ding-dong pelting?   By ten o'clock the question was resolved.   First,
there came a drove of French prisoners, red-breeched
regulars, up towards Noisy, along the slight shelter
afforded by the use of the road.   Then came Saxon
soldiers, more prisoners, and finally the bulk of the 107th,
in very open order, and making the most of the few
opportunities for cover.   It was not a pleasant way to
traverse.   Nogent was firing heavily upon captors and
captured alike, and more than one Frenchman fell slain
by missiles hurled from French weapons.   As the struggling
columns came up I learned that the 107th, in its rapid
rush in the morning, had surprised the occupants of Brie;

some were asleep, others were composedly drinking their
coffee. There was but trifling resistance, and nearly five
hundred prisoners had been taken, including eight officers. The reason for the relinquishment of Brie on the
part of the 107th was not far to seek. The terrible and
persistent fire from the forts rendered it utterly untenable.
It would have been folly—sheer quixotry—to remain in
a place teeming with bursting shells. No good could
have been achieved by holding it under such conditions.
The troops, compelled, that they might escape annihila-
tion, to concentrate their attention solely on cover, could
not possibly have acted in any way on the offensive, in
the way of annoying the right flank of the enemy. As
this contingency must have been the sole purpose of the
continued occupancy, its impracticability simply nullified the position in a strategic sense, while the same
reasons prevented effectual steps being taken for firing it.
In a physical sense the shells were rapidly nullifying the
occupants.

The prisoners looked sturdy fellows, and anything
but ill fed. Their heart was good, too, if one might judge
from passing expressions. A sergeant bade me "bon
jour" as he went by, and told me cheerily that if anyone indulged the anticipation of the speedy capitulation
of Paris, he was extremely out in his reckoning. Food
was plentiful, he said, with a laugh, and the programme
was sorties every day in every direction. I believe it was
this laughing philosopher who afterwards gave up a proclamation of General Ducrot, dated the 28th ult., and
setting forth that he did not mean to re-enter Paris alive.
I dare swear he would not have done so had he chanced
about this time to fall into the hands of the Germans.
A drum-head court-martial and a volley from a firing-
party would assuredly have been his fate, and it would

have served him right.   There was found also, I learned,
on one of the prisoners a proclamation emanating from
General Trochu, that commander with "plan on the
brain," announcing that the time had now come for
making great sorties, since the German, or, as he called
it, the Prussian line had been greatly weakened (perhaps
by the fall of Metz), and that his plan was to peg away
at sorties till he had cut his way through.   The prisoners
were escorted back to Chelles, where, at a late period of
the day, I saw them penned in the yard of the Mairie.

As the procession from Brie had finished filing through
Noisy an ominous sight met my eye in another direction,
as I crept dodgingly forward further to the front.   There,
on the gradual slope of the further bank of the Marne,
under the wing of Fort Nogent and extending right and
left along the line of the Chaumont Railway, were dense
columns of French infantry.   How they came there I
knew not; it was as if the spectacle had sprung up by
magic.   Now they stood fast, closing up as the fronts of
the battalions halted; then there was a slow movement
forward, till the head of the column dipped out of sight
between the village of Nogent and the river.   Then there
seemed a final halt, and the dense masses stood there,
the bayonets glittering in the sun, as if the men who
carried them had come out to be spectators of the effects
of that shell fire which was cutting the air above their
heads.   But little by little there was a gradual trickling
off, as it appeared, down to the bight of the river
between Nogent and Brie.   Was there a bridge there?
There was the railway bridge, a lofty viaduct whose
arches also went across the flat, but there was a gap in
one of its river spans that rendered it useless.   Presently,
on the narrow level to the south of Brie there became
visible a knot of red breeches, that grew denser and

denser every moment. Simultaneously the whole plain sprang into life. From the farm-buildings about Le Tremblay, from Poulangis and Joinville, there poured out vast bodies of French troops, deploying at the double, as they came through under the arches, or showed on the slopes further to the south. The line seemed to extend right athwart the neck of the loop. What happened to Champigny I know not from personal observation; but I was afterwards informed that the Würtembergers, after some desperate fighting, had driven the French out of it not long after eight o'clock, to be in their turn subjected to a violent attack and partial expulsion by the right of the formation to which I have just referred. The tirailleurs dashed into the thickets lining the foot of the rise, and scrambled up through the vinebergs. The mass of troops behind them followed in serried columns. Whence had they come? Some of them had been bivouacking on the plain ever since the 30th. Others had crossed during the night, and occupied the loop by their bridges. Six of these were between Joinville and Nogent, and the nullification of Brie admitted the utilisation, at the later hour, of yet two more between that village and the railway viaduct.

Noisy seemed no place for a non-combatant. By a detour *viâ* La Haute Maison, I reached the house named Le Désert, in the immediate rear of Villiers, which evidently was the point for which the French advance was intended. That force—I refer exclusively to the section which threatened Villiers—must have been at least 20,000 strong. How large was the force with which the Würtembergers and their good friends of the 2nd Army Corps had to deal towards Champigny I had no means of even roughly estimating. Surely in those dense columns standing in support under Nogent there could

not have been less than 20,000 men.   But directly and
face to face it was with the 20,000 men of the left advance with whom the 10,000 Saxons had to cope.   Not
with them alone, but with those terrible projectiles also,
a storm of which incessantly clashed on to the upper
ground on which stands Villiers, and up to the table-
land between it and Noisy.

Had there been nothing else to do on the part of the
Saxons but to repulse an assault on Villiers, directed
solely and straightly against it, the task would have been
comparatively simple and not very bloody, notwithstanding the artillery fire.   But the French advance, threatening in its deployment as it did to sweep right on, over-
lapping Villiers, up the space between that village and
Noisy, and so to get through upon Champs, called for
other tactics.   Villiers could only serve as a position on
which to lean the Saxon left.   It became necessary to
meet the French in the open.   From behind Villiers the
several regiments came out to the right on to the brow
and under the shell fire.   As the French troops came up
the gentle acclivity, the guns of the forts continued to
play without interruption.   So narrow was the margin,
that I question much whether a shell or two did not find
its billet in the French ranks.   I stood by the 108th
Regiment as it quitted the position behind Le Désert
where it had found some shelter.   A couple of young
lieutenants gaily shook hands with a Hussar aide-de-
camp, who had just ridden up with an order, as they
passed him to go out into the battle.   On went the
regiments in their dense columns of companies, the shells
now crashing into the ranks, now exploding in the intervals.   Line was formed, the rear files pelting up at the
double, and in a twinkling less than fifty yards separated
the combatant lines.   Then came a volley, then a venom-

ous file-firing, and the French broke and gave ground. It was only to back a little in the dip of the ground to let the guns of the fort go to work again. . The Saxons had perforce to find what cover they might. When the 108th regiment came back—it had not been gone twenty minutes—thirty-six officers out of forty-five had gone down. Neither of the blithe lieutenants were to the fore. And now came a lull in the musketry fire, just as a few minutes before there had been a lull in the cannon fire. The Saxons failed to get their artillery into action with advantage. It was afterwards explained to me that the ground was unfavourable for its operations, but this, it must have been obvious from the description I have given of it, was incorrect. Although, exposed as the field-batteries would have been to a tremendous fire from the forts, it was in the nature of things that they should have suffered greatly; still, the time was one when loss was not to be considered, for the crisis was imminent. The artillery might have at least done something before being silenced, and God knows something was wanted to ease for the infantry the fierce brunt of the fray. While this was going on to the right of Villiers, the battle raged with continuous fury in front of the park of the château, but my position precluded me from seeing anything of it but the merest fringe on the right. How hot it was, however, the steady, heavy pattering of the musketry fire, interspersed with louder crashes that told now of whole volleys, now of bursting shells, sufficiently testified. If further testimony be required, let the ex-acting one go and look at the grave-mounds.

What I have been writing of took place before noon. After a little the artillery fire from the forts slackened considerably, and the French infantry made no demon-stration. On the German left, however, about Cham-

pigny, it was evident that hard fighting was going on.
About one the French made another advance, having,
as I believed, received considerable reinforcements, and
Avron and Nogent resumed the old fierceness of their
cannonade. The Saxon infantry confronted them on
the challenge, with the old result. But a different policy
was this time adopted. It was plain the only escape
from the terrible thunderbolts lay in getting to close
quarters with the French infantry, unless, indeed, the
position was to be abandoned, and that was not to be
thought of. So, when the French fell back, the Saxons
followed on, as if they wanted to settle the question with
the bayonet-point. It was the old motto, "*Vorwärts,
immer vorwärts.*" But the *vorwärts* was very slow.
What happened for the next hour I could only guess by
the constant crackling of the small arms. The forts confined themselves seemingly for the most part to firing
into and over Champigny, Villiers, and Noisy. But at
length the French were visible slowly and stubbornly
falling back across the north side of the neck, the Saxons
pushing them hard, the French ever and anon rallying.

On this portion of the slope and level south of Brie
there was a prolonged struggle. I understand the Saxons
were striving to get at and cut the obnoxious pontoon
bridge. But this was an impossibility, when Nogent went
to work again with the terrible accuracy of which the
short range admitted. The combatants parted about three
o'clock, both sides falling back. The fort fire continued
some little time longer. What shall I say of the result?
Not much did the Saxons gain—was there much to gain?
The Würtembergers held, I believe, at the close of the
fight, one end of Champigny. According to the information I received at night at head-quarters, Brie at night
stood empty and desolate—it might have been wounded

men were groaning in its cellars. There had been French
in it in the morning; later there had been Saxons. But
next morning I came to know that there were French in
it again after the Saxons quitted it, and they held it till
the general retreat across the Marne. The Germans had
gained the victory, in that they had not been beaten away
from their stand-point. The French had lost the day,
because Trochu did not sup in Lagny. And that is all
that can be said on the matter.

Here let me again observe that had it been possible
to hold and utilise the occupation of Brie, the French
advance would have been impossible. Its flanking fire
would have prohibited the breasting of the slope toward
Villiers. The French must have had mitrailleuses located
somewhere in the plain. I distinctly heard the horrible
whirr, which always set my teeth on edge.

At night I dined with the head-quarter staff of the
12th Army Corps, in the head-quarters in Champs. I
never sat down to a more sombre dinner-table. Men
spoke to each other in hushed, some in tremulous voices;
some ate nothing, for they had already supped full of
sorrow. The gloomy party broke into groups after dinner,
and what little talk there was was inexpressibly sad.
There were chairs empty at dinner-time that had been
occupied at the hurried breakfast. Not a man in the
room but had lost some dear friends; many had lost relatives, for there is much kinship in the little country
whence came those fighting-men. There were those in
the room who had brothers lying stark in the moonlight
by the park wall of Villiers. It chilled one's blood to hear
the scraps of question and answer. "What about——?"
"Todt." "And ——?" "Schwer verwundet." And
there were anxious thoughts about the morrow among the
chiefs. There was no talk about failure, but it was ob-

vious that the leaders comprehended how hard it had
gone with the linesmen in heading back the French.
Snow fell steadily all night. The frost came and nipped
the ground like a vice. It seemed, as I left the Prince's
château, that the dismal wintry wind brought on its wings
moans and groans from the miserable beings—rent with
double torture, the anguish of their wounds and the bitter
pinching of the fell cold—who lay there on the Schlacht-
feld up in our front. Lay there that night quite half the
wounded,—no longer, many of them, alive when the
morning sun broke through the frost fog; lay there some
for yet another night, and still lived when the Krankenträger found them.

On the forenoon of the fourth day there were found
eight poor wretches—four in the open field, four in a
house—who had survived the inclemency of two nights
of as hard frost as any we had during the hardest winter
on record for years. Some, if not all of them, lived at
least two days after they were found. On the morning
of the 6th I asked the question of a Würtemberg doctor
if his frost-bitten patients still lived, and he replied, with
a professional shrug of the shoulders, "Oh, yes, they are
a little alive." Two days after the battle two French officers were found skulking in a cellar unhurt, but half
frozen. No doubt it was their intention to escape away
into the landward parts of France. On being asked why
they did not fall back with the rest, their assertion
was that they were disgusted with the Army of Paris, it
was in such a state of disorder. They themselves—self-
constituted critics—were the best proofs of such a state
of things. I should have so liked to have seen the sneaks
handed over to Ducrot. There were corpses lying unburied for days after; for wounded had to be removed,
and dead had to be buried, under a steady relentless fire

from the forts. Under such circumstances the burial-
parties were not particular how deep they dug the graves.
Three months after, riding towards Paris across the fields
from the Imperial review of the Maas army, on the slope
before Villiers my horse suddenly shied with a great
frightened bound. Looking down, I saw a pair of human
legs sticking up out of the ground. Close by a ghastly
face showed up piecemeal through a broken sprinkling of
fat earth. The corpses of three French soldiers lay there,
side by side, buried so shallowly that the rain had washed
away the coating of earth that had covered them.

Complaints were rife as to the treacherous conduct of
French soldiers, and particularly of officers, in the field.
In the sortie at Epinay, two days previously, Count Keller
and another officer had been shot down by a body of
Frenchmen behind a barricade which they approached in
consequence of the hoisting of a white flag. On the 2nd
more than one incident of a similar nature was spoken
of. Unless strongly confirmed, I was loth to give credence
to stories of the kind; but the treachery towards Count
Keller was too well authenticated to be questioned. I
heard it alleged that Colonel Hausen, of the 13th Saxon
Jäger Bataillon, was fired on in this fashion. But this,
at least, may be contradicted. The colonel fancied that
a posse of Frenchmen who had halted, and were gesticulating after the French manner, had surrendered. He
rode forward to within a few paces of them, and demanded to know if this was the case. Somebody in their
ranks audaciously responded that, on the contrary, they
thought it was the Germans that had surrendered. Whereupon the colonel wheeled his horse and rode back. As
he went several bullets were fired at him, one of which
killed his horse, but he escaped.

The latest figures gave the Würtemberger loss at 40

officers and 1,500 rank and file killed, wounded, and missing, and the Saxon loss at 76 officers and 2,000 rank and file killed, wounded, and missing. "Missing" in such a case means "taken prisoner." Now it is certain that in the open the French took no prisoners, and I never could exact the confession that any were taken in the villages. A little mystery enveloped the doings there which it was not easy to penetrate, and one had to resort to collateral and circumstantial evidence, if he could find it. Prisoner-statistics are always a good test. If you choose to say that you evacuated a village because you found it untenable, the euphemism may be allowed to you; but if I learn that you had to leave behind you certain wounded men, which fell into the enemy's hands—and, it may be, sound men, who had to lay down their arms per force of circumstances—I am at liberty to put my own construction on your little periphrase. The loss in officers was unprecedented, even in a war in which the German officers poured out their blood like water, and fell in numbers far exceeding the usual proportion. I have already mentioned that the 108th (the Schützen) Regiment lost 36 officers out of 45. One battalion was taken out of action by a young lieutenant, a Hammerstein. The name must be familiar to everyone who has read the history of the King's German Legion, that splendid body of soldiers who did Britain service so staunch in the Peninsula and at Waterloo, and of whom Wellington had so high an opinion. He was the only officer left in the battalion that could stand, and he was wounded in two places.

Among the many officers whom the Würtembergers lost on the 2nd was one lieutenant, whose loss ought to have an interest for Englishmen, seeing that he, too, was an Englishman. His name was Knight. He had joined the Würtemberger Army in 1857, and when the war broke out was on a visit in England. He hastened back to rejoin his regiment, and served throughout the campaign scathless until this fight. It was in the storm of the barricade at Champigny that our gallant countryman went down, shot dead by a chassepot bullet. His comrades buried him by himself in Pontault, a village in the left rear of Champigny. It will be long ere an epitaph is necessary to prevent his memory from being forgotten at all events in the Würtemberg Army. The men of his regiment—the 2nd Jäger Battalion, in which· he was a premier lieutenant—spoke of him with tears in their eyes, and the officers told of him how he was beloved by all who knew him.

The fights of the 30th November and 2nd December call for but little comment; they furnish their own explanation. The French Army of Paris was never so near success as on the evening of the latter day, unless it were on the evening of the former. Had the Army of the Loire actually been in anything like proximity to the German rear, the environment must have inevitably been disrupted. Some pages back I quoted the expression of an opinion on the part of a staff officer that when the great effort came, it would be not simply a sortie, but an attempt to break out with a force sufficient to constitute a field army capable of co-operating with the Army of the Loire. The verification of his anticipation was found in the fact that in the knapsacks of the captive, wounded, and dead French soldiers were found full provisions for six days—bread, meat, rice, coffee, &c. The meat looked like horse, it is true, but there it was. The kit in the knapsacks almost exclusively consisted of provisions. The Saxons and Würtembergers, as it was, and with an enemy only in their front, were strained, perhaps more hardly than they cared to own, before they succeeded in balking the effort of the 30th, and, had the French renewed the fighting next day, the tension would have been still more strained.   But they were in no condition, seemingly, for such an undertaking, and the Germans were not idle in the interval fortunately allowed them.   Spite of the energetic exertions to repair damages, the links of the iron chain were again sorely tried on the 2nd, and the flaws that showed in places gave ominous warnings that made men tremble for the continuity.   But the links held till the strain relaxed at night, and then the cry was, "All hands to make good defects."   The French had enough of it; their general had not Grant's rugged doggedness to "fight it out in this line."   If Trochu, with his vast nominal army roll, could have swept to one side the troops out of whom two days' hard and unsuccessful fighting had taken the backbone, and could have substituted an equal force of good and fresh soldiers, well commanded, and full of resolution, he would be a rash man who would dare to define what might have been the result.   But what we now know entitles us to believe that he had nothing in hand on which he could rely, and that, in the despondent consciousness of the difficulties of the situation, he acted with a certain methodical discretion.   Whether in the circumstances he might not have done better to be reckless is a question on which it is useless to speculate.   As for the battle of the 2nd—and the same, no doubt, applies to that of the 30th—it was characterised by straightforward, slogging, hard hitting on both sides, and an utter absence of strategy.   If the Germans had elected to meet the French further back, they would have escaped the terrific hailstorm of shells from the forts that poured upon them with such steady fury, that the whole face of the battle-scene is studded over with craters as close as the pock-pits stud the face of a man who has had the small-pox. To one pressing this argument, their reply is that, had they taken up ground to hold further back, they would have given the French greater elbow-room in which to deploy their vast masses, while, with inferior numbers, their own front would have been extended to attenuation. It may be in its turn suggested, as a reply to this argument, that if on first selecting their positions, at the commencement of the siege, they had chosen some such defensive line as I have indicated further to the rear, they would have had leisure to strengthen it artificially,—that entrenchments, stockades, and batteries might have done service in lieu of the bare breasts of gallant men.

CHAPTER II.

From the great Sortie to the New Year.

ALL the livelong night between the 2nd and the 3rd of December, the movements of troops were going on. Artillery was being posted in cunning places. Strengthening drafts of soldiers, what the 23rd division dared to spare, were tramping over the upper Kriegs-brücke from the northern side of the Marne. The lower bridge at Gournay, that by which I had crossed in the morning, had been shot to splinters by Avron. Punctually at daybreak on the morning of the 3rd, did Nogent tender us his morning greeting, and soon after the cannonade became general. About seven I met one of Prince George's staff on the steps of the château. "Great God!" was his troubled greeting, "how is all this to end? Is it to be another hellish day, like yesterday? I shudder at the prospect." There seemed every likelihood of the fulfilment of his foreboding. The forts increased the fury of their fire. The roads and fields before Champs were covered with the dense masses of the reserves—reserves formed of troops that had been in action the day before. So sharp was the crisis thought, that a half-battalion of Bavarian Landwehr-men who had reached Lagny the day before, on their road to the south, were diverted through Torcy on toward Champs to help in case they should be wanted. The head-quarter column was on the road in the rear, ready for the contingency of the front being driven somewhat back; its heaviest fourgons had retired to Torcy; head-quarters themselves had no local habitation by name, but shifted about the field when Prince George moved backwards and forwards. Even the marketenders in Champs were packed up, and had fallen to the rear.

Soon after seven, the French showed in dense masses on the peninsula of the Marne, and took up their formation across its neck. Through the frosty fog their appearance was very imposing. A column quitted the main body and headed direct for Villiers, under cover of a heavy fire from the forts. Noisy and Villiers had been occupied by the Würtembergers during the previous evening. The occupants of Villiers showed a bold front, and the French did not seem inspired with the spirit that had actuated them the day before. By eight o'clock the column which had threatened an attack had fallen back among the mass, which to all appearance remained in position during the day. The forts continued their fire for some hours. The Würtembergers, in such exposed positions, naturally sustained some loss, probably a few dozens of wounded men. The head-quarters of the 12th Corps resettled itself in the château of Champs in the course of the day, and remained there till the 6th. On the morning of the return to the old location in Le Vert Galant, Avron got one gun or more guns into position of so great a range that several shells fell in the garden of the château, and two upon its roof. On the afternoon of·the 3rd the Crown Prince arrived from Margency, and immediately visited the battle-field along with his brother and the 12th Army Corps staff (the Crown Prince had with him but Count Vitzthum, his personal aide-de-camp), having several narrow escapes of shells from Fort Nogent. The Crown Prince, after a lengthened consultation with his brother, returned to Margency for the night, while Prince George remained in Champs; for the cloud had by no means drifted off the sky. So sullenly, indeed, although silently, did it still lower, that, as Count Vitzthum kindly whispered to me as he got into the carriage with the Crown Prince, it had been arranged that the head-quarters of the latter should come round on the morrow to the east, and take up a temporary location in Prince George's château in Le Vert Galant, to be at hand in case of need, till the storm should have blown off the peninsula of the Marne.

On learning that there were some symptoms of an attack in the neighbourhood of the advanced post of Ville Evrart, on the north of the Marne, on the left of that awkward part of the ring of environment of which Gagny, on the fringe of the Forest of Bondy, is the right, I rode over to Chelles after the Crown Prince had quitted Champs, and then walked out to Ville Evrart, horse-exercise being prohibited in that particular locality. There was no policeman to enforce the prohibition, but, nevertheless, I fancy it was very seldom infringed, Mont Avron having a playful way of potting at horsemen, or even at a single horseman, with little toys that had a tendency to break the skin. It was this *chaussée* along which I had been trotting the previous morning, on my road, as I fancied, to a bridge over the Marne, and it struck me that I must have come very near affording a practical illustration of the danger attending equitation in this exposed direction. Through the hazy drizzle, half snow half rain, there were visible in the fields to the north of Neuilly, and under the lee of Avron, moving bodies that looked as if they had military formation. They were soldiers covering potato-diggers, and Captain Hammerstein's Saxons were keeping up upon them a lively but intermittent fusillade. Whether the potato-diggers had filled their baskets or not, the whole body very soon vanished backward in the mist, there being a ghostliness about the whole incident that might remind one of a Fenian drill in the night. Captain Hammerstein, a cousin of the youngster of the same name I have already mentioned, was quartered with a company of his regiment (the 103rd) in a detached château, La Maison Blanche, to the north of Ville Evrart. This position here was such that every shot on its way from Avron to Noisy went high over his head, and he assured me that the fire of the latter had been more sustained that morning than even on the previous day. There had been hardly even a momentary respite, and often three of the great cannon crashed out their reports simultaneously. How the Würtembergers in Noisy suffered so little from such a fire is only to be explained by the thickness of the walls in the village.

Forty years ago there could have been few finer residences round Paris than La Maison Blanche. The railway came and infringed on its amenities, but not to any great extent, the noble old trees acting as a screen to the track. Later came the Germans, and they bedevilled the amenities far worse than the railway. War time is a bad season for trim grass-plots, painted staircases, and luxurious carpets. Then last of all came shells from Mont

Avron, over the way, and played old gooseberry with the amenities that still kept up a self-assertion in the face of the hostile occupation. The hour is midnight. A huge wood fire is blazing in the noble drawing-room of the mansion. In a comfortable armchair on one side of this fire sits a middle-aged Hauptmann, opposite him an individual in civilian attire. The two are drinking grog, and chatting as they drink. They are old friends. They knew each other a dozen years ago in Lüneburg, that dullest of all dull Hanoverian cities, when as yet King George, the pious, the blind, and the obstinate, reigned in Hanover, and annexation was only dimly apprehended by far-sighted people, who—such is the lot of the sapient —were put down as theorists and alarmists. The middle-aged Hauptmann had fought in six-and-sixty in the army of his monarch, and when the evil day came he, with some eighty comrades, had transferred his services to Saxony, in preference to remaining in an army which thenceforth was to be merely a Prussian army corps. The talk is of the old days in Lüneburg, of pleasant rides by the banks of the Ilmenau, of rowing excursions up to Rothensleuser, of naughty scampers to Hamburg, of those pretty English girls that stole the hearts of a couple of regiments of infantry, of the old Waterloo major that lived by the waterside, of certain sensational steeplechases and memorable mess dinners. Unto these two there enters Under-officer Schultz. Schultz is a Saxon, but utterly unlike the bulk of his countrymen. Schultz would make an excellent study for an artist anxious to limn a Cameronian or one of Cromwell's Ironsides. His name might be Praise-the-Lord-Barebones. Tall, gaunt, thin-flanked, and square-shouldered, with high cheek-bones, and a lofty, narrow forehead, Under-officer Schultz enters, and bringing his heels together with an audible clank, stands bolt upright and motionless. "Well, Schultz?" asks the Hauptmann. "Herr Hauptmann, the patrol is ready," replies Schultz, with solemn curtness. Herr Hauptmann bolts the heel-tap of his grog, rises, tightens his sword-belt, feels for his little friend the six-chambered revolver, puts on his cloak and helmet, pulls up his long boots, and is ready. The civilian's preparations are simpler, since he has no arms to see to. Out into the night air. "Der Teufel! what a beastly night." It had been hard frost all day, and now it rains a drizzly rain. The wet has mingled with the frost, and the ground is at once slippery and sticky. It will be dirty and heavy walking to-night, that is clear. There is a moon, but the sky seems as muddy as the earth, and her rays serve only to impart a dirty white tinge to the fine drizzling rain. The patrol—three sturdy Saxon soldiers—are standing motionless in the gloom, the red cigar tips showing dimly through the rime. "March!" says the Hauptmann. Schultz takes his place in front of the patrol, and behind the Hauptmann and his companion, and away goes the little party, slipping and stumbling down the tree-shadowed avenue. They traverse about half an English mile of flat country, crossed by numerous walls and fences, enclosing fields and the grounds surrounding châteaux. The way is winding and the road horrible. There is no life in this tract, till, lately, inhabited by wealthy Parisians. Somewhere about is a new château, not quite finished, belonging to the great French surgeon Nelaton. But the masons and carpenters have stopped their work, and are now in the Garde Mobile, and the doctor is certainly not at home. Presently the ground begins to rise. The party are climbing the slope of a hill. That hill is Mont Avron. There is no road, only a rough track through the copsewood,

interspersed with vineyards. At every second step somebody is on his hands and knees; now stumbling over a
stump, now losing his foothold in the mud with the
frost-hardened substratum. The vineyard track winds
and wriggles, but it is always upward, and that steeply
too in places, so that the breathing comes harder and
shorter. Suddenly there comes a smothered "Halt!"
from vigilant Under-officer Schultz, that curious pitch of
the voice in full development that is the characteristic
of Saxon-German, and that reminds one so much of
the "twang" of the fisher-folk in the villages on the
Moray Firth. Under-officer Schultz has not called "Halt!"
for nothing; his quick ear has detected coming footsteps.
"Dodge behind the thick brushwood there," is the sharp-
whispered order of Herr Hauptmann. The party is off
the track in a twinkling, hiding like a Fenimore Cooper's
Indian, the civilian, in particular, squatting like a rabbit.
The movement was not an instant too soon. The sound
of the footsteps and voices comes nearer and nearer.
There is a medley of jabber, everybody speaking together
in shrill French. "A patrol of Francs-tireurs," whispers
the Hauptmann. A nice patrol party truly, doing their
work with that silent vigilance and caution which the
duty essentially calls for. Pop! a gun goes off. Have
the jabberers spotted the lurkers in the wood? If so,
the pregnant thought occurs to one of them how a mer-
cenary life assurance office had "hung up" his policy
till he should return home in safety. Tut! any apprehension was ludicrous. One of the Francs-tireurs had
fired off his piece in mere lightness of heart. Probably
he shot into the air. Stern Under-officer Schultz gives a
snort of contempt, and mutters between his teeth,
"*dummer Kerl.*"

The Franc-tireur patrol has passed, and the squatters

get up from their muddy position, and stumble onward
and upward. They are near the top of the hill now. A
light is visible through the undergrowth of scrub, and
there is a halt. The light is the watch fire of a French
picket. There is a sentry posted, who has his back to
the forest and his face to the fire, such a position affording him full opportunities for the exercise of vigilance.
What is he doing now? Under-officer Schultz gives
another snort of contempt as the sentry props his piece·
against a tree, walks up to the fire, and has a drink,
taking a good long warm before he comes back. All the
picket are drinking. Some seem tolerably on toward
drunkenness, judging by the clatter of loud voices.
Above, on the flat summit of the hill, is the battery. It
is evident that there is another watchfire inside it. The
earthwork, whispers the Hauptmann, looks three ways,
and has six guns mounted on each face. It is the latest
construction of the besieged. It has only been in operation for about ten days, and it is an abominably mis-
chievous affair. There are no movements or signs of
movements in the vicinity. This ascertained, the patrol
takes its weary way back to the château. Getting down
the hill is worse than it was getting up. How welcome
is the wood fire in the drawing-room. Herr Hauptmann
and the civilian look at each other, and simultaneously
burst into a fit of laughter. They are plastered with
mud from head to foot. Under-officer Schultz, who is
muddier than either—for his nose seems to have been
rooting in red clay—stands by as solemn as a mute at a
funeral. He gets an order, goes right about face as by
machinery, and disappears. Grog and cigars in the arm-
chairs.

On the morning of the 4th, on my way from La
Maison Blanche to Le Vert Galant, I breakfasted in Chelles

with Major von Schönberg and the Staff of the 103rd
Regiment. While breakfast was proceeding it was suddenly announced that the whole 23rd Division, of which
the 103rd formed a part, was to cross the Marne. No
destination was announced. They might go to Noisy,
under the terrible fire; they might relieve the Würtembergers in the hardly less dangerous Villiers; or it might
be their lot to occupy the splendid château of the wealthy
soapboiler in Champs. Nobody knew, but the movement
looked like fighting. Before coffee was served, however,
there arrived a couple of lieutenants of the 108th Regiment, come to take up quarters for the regiment, and
bringing the announcement that the whole of the 24th
Division was under orders to take the positions of the
23rd on the North side of the Marne. The anticipations
of an immediate renewal of the combat subsided on this
intelligence—all that was in progress was merely an
outer change of quarters, and the relief of a division that
had suffered very much on the 2nd. But to return to
the two sprightly young lieutenants of the 108th, who
came there to choose quarters for their brother officers.
The youngest of them, a boy of about 19, had rare luck
on the 2nd. By the doctrine of chances he should have
been now on the look-out for a grave, not for quarters.
In the short skirts of his tunic were four bullet holes, his
left shoulder strap was severed and hung in fringes from
another bullet, and he had no knee on the left leg of his
overalls, the piece had been torn clean out by the fragment of a shell. The young rascal walked lame from
the latter casualty, but otherwise he was as sound as a
bell, and to see him tackle a yard of "wurst" was a
caution. While our young friends were talking with
Major von Schönberg about quarters, there dropped in
the representative of another regiment on the same

errand. I was an auditor of the interview. It was too good not to be narrated. Representative of incoming regiment: "You have here a beautiful place, Herr Major, with a fine *Speise-saal* and a grand piano. This will suit well our Herr Oberst." Herr Major Schönberg: "Oh, yes, and many grenades come into the garden. That will furnish a pleasant accompaniment to the piano." As if to confirm the Major's words, whizz—bang came a shell from Mont Avron, and lit right in front of the window, sending the pellets of half-frozen mud up against the glass. The Major grinned a dry grin. His sympathy had been enlisted as regards quarters in favour of the young lieutenants. The formal staff officer hesitated. Whizz, bang, another shell—this time on the roof. He looked still more undecided. Then up came the doctor of the 103rd, and recounted how the shells had interfered with him the day before. This was enough for our friend. He left the field to the young lieutenants, and went in search of quarters less exposed.

As I jogged out of Chelles, on the way to Montfermeil, I met the whole of the 1st Grenadier Guard Regiment. This was the *avant courier* of a whole brigade of the Guards, including its artillery, pressing on to occupy Chelles and the vicinity. The movement, and those movements along the whole line of which this was but a detail, did not augur anything more than a design to strengthen the position across the dangerous peninsula in such a manner as to negative whatever advantage the French might ostensibly derive from their occupation of Brie, Champigny, and the peninsula in the rear of these villages, which was still in their possession. As I rode out of Chelles, the shells—how similar are the two names —came pounding into it vigorously. The French must have seen the movement of the troops, and thought to

inconvenience it with their long-range artillery.   A German battery on a bluff between Chelles and Montfermeil
might have attempted a reply had the guns in it been
siege pieces instead of field guns, but as it was, Mont
Avron was allowed to have it all its own way.   The only
casualty, so far as I saw, which the fire produced was to
startle a pair of fine grey horses which, with a carriage
behind them, were coming down the steep slope out of
Montfermeil.   Off they tore at a furious gallop, kicking
the splinter bar to bits, and utterly ignoring the frantic
zeal with which the driver tugged at the reins.   They
dashed through a company of the Guards, routing with
ignominy a section which had taken up the road, bayonets
levelled, with intent to stop them.   The driver jumped
out here, and lit safely on the top of a soldier.   The
horses galloped on, strewing the road with portmanteaus,
cigar-boxes, a mattress, and other contents of the carriage,
which was rapidly going to pieces.   At length, still pur-
suing the same headlong pace, they vanished round a
corner, and their ultimate fate I know not.

On my arrival in Le Vert Galant I found that the
Crown Prince's head-quarters had already arrived, and
had occasioned a squeeze-royal in the little place.   Quarters, such as they were, were ultimately found for everybody without recourse being had to bivouac.   On the
5th the Crown Prince paid a second visit to his brother
in Champs, and an informal council of war was held, the
faces at which must have worn a much more cheerful
expression than those which had surrounded Prince
George's table on the night of the 2nd inst.   There was
reason for the good spirits.   The French had lost heart,
or had determined to concentrate their efforts in some
other direction.   On the morning of the 5th it was found
that they had not only evacuated Brie and Champigny,

but were engaged in abandoning the horseshoe also, and retiring beyond the Marne. This operation was performed under a very heavy fire from Mont Avron and Fort Nogent, which impeded the Würtembergers not a little in their occupation of the vacated villages. Several were killed and wounded in the course of the morning. There had been, indeed, a brisk little skirmish just in the neck of the peninsula. The Würtembergers, feeling their way ever onward to take up a forepost line aligning on Brie and Champigny, pushed on into a wood called Le Plaine. This same wood had been part of the French forepost line some twelve hours before, and it seemed that they resented the readiness with which on their abandonment of it the Würtembergers came to occupy it. The wood was an important post in the very throat of the peninsula, and on the south of the line of railway just where it bends to cross the river. The French thought it worth while to send a battalion to dispute its possession with the Würtembergers, and the little force was backed up by a fire from the big guns, but the Würtembergers pressing on steadily succeeded in occupying the wood and establishing their foreposts without exposing themselves much to the artillery fire, and without coming to close quarters with the French, who fell back on finding the wood occupied. The French did not wholly quit the peninsula. Although they destroyed their other bridges, they continued to retain at least one at Joinville, and held the few houses on the trans-Marne side of the stone bridge which spans the river opposite that village, while their outposts were stationed in the farm buildings of Poulangés. Here they were close under the lee of La Faisanderie and La Gravelle, on the ramparts of which were guns of long range and large calibre. Under the circumstances it was judged wise to leave them there in

peace. He who visits the spot now may see still traces
of the French bivouacs from the 30th November to the
5th December, and he will see another solemn relic of
this unfortunate expedition in a clay field on the river
side of the road.   The clay is dug out and piled up in
four or five long parallel ridges, like huge flat-topped
potato pits.   They are of unequal lengths, but two at
least are over fifty yards in length.   At either end of
each are rude crosses, and on one shapelier yet plain
wooden cross is painted the legend that here lie 800
corpses buried by the various ambulances.

On the 6th of December the Crown Prince returned
to Margency, and Prince George quitted Champs and
went back to his old quarters in Le Vert Galant.   The
whole of the officers belonging to the Crown Prince's
staff did not, however, accompany him on his return to
Margency.   The officers composing the engineer and artillery staffs of the Maas army, went to Champs instead,
and a hint which I received led me to think more might
be learnt as to the turn future operations were likely to
take by accompanying those gentlemen than by going
back to Margency.   Before leaving Le Vert Galant, in
the pleasant company of Lieutenant Hofmann, I was witness there of a scene full of pathos.   The 107th Regiment had marched in on the previous night and taken
up quarters.   In the morning came on, in a large waggon,
what the Feld-post had for the regiment.   The waggon
drew up at the battalion orderly room, and the bugle
sounded the rally.   It was a curious medley that streamed
out as the tail-board of the waggon was let down.   The
German Feld-post is an elastic institution, and I think if
you had chosen to send a soldier-friend out a box mangle,
or a live tiger in its cage, there would have been no
objections on the score of bulk.   There streamed down

cigar-boxes, wrapped in canvas, long shapeless rolls that
were eloquent of "wurst," flabby packets that one might
swear contained underclothing, and little boxes that
rolled as they fell, and evidently contained thalers. The
pile was made against the wall, the sergeant cleared a
space and commenced on the pile letter by letter, packet
by packet.

I made a note of the responses to the first six names,
and simply transcribe it:—"Schumann?" "Todt" (dead).
"Caspar?" "Verwundet." "Schultz?" "Weg." "Stol-
berg?" "Todt." "Schrader?" "In Paris." "Berg-
mann?" "In Lazareth." Thus proceeded the dreary
roll call. It was that of the 2nd battalion, which has
suffered most severely. Before the sergeant had done
there was quite a heap of packets which their owners
would never claim. The number of "Wegs" was surprising. "Weg" is a wide word. It may mean anything; prisoner, missing, unburied, deserted (but I never
heard of a German soldier deserting). The sum of it is
—not here, and Lord knows where he is. "In Paris,"
was not an uncommon response, but always with a little
ironical chuckle.

Whatever might have been the case with French people
in other quarters of France, there was no want of a certain kind of patriotism in those about this quarter. The
villagers on the wayside assailed the Würtembergers on
their way back to quarters on the 2nd inst., with cries of
"Deutsch nix courage," a piece of "pie" sufficiently intelligible. On our road to Champs we met a strange
gang, closely guarded by Saxon soldiers. These were
male peasants and female peasants, with year-old children
astraddle on their backs. It was clearly a case of going
wholesale into captivity. I had never seen anything of
the kind before, and I could not understand it. The

explanation was curt, but sufficiently easy to understand. The villagers—at least several of them—had been detected on the 2nd ult., signalling to their countrymen from the church tower and the top of the windmills. According to the regulations made and provided in the circumstances, the men should have been shot and the villages burnt. It was, it appeared, a merciful dispensation to substitute the temporary captivity of the whole population for the more rigorous measures. I must not be taken as expressing any opinion on a matter, the explanation of which I only received casually, and not upon authority. So far as I could make out, the whole gang would be set at liberty by-and-by, after they had got a good fright; indeed, the women seemed themselves to have discerned as much, for they did not look as if they believed that they were going to the slaughter, or even to captivity in Deutschland.

At Champs we shared the soap-boiler's château with the officers of a Würtemberger infantry regiment, and of a squadron of cavalry. It is heartily to be wished that some one had been present with the Würtembergers on the 30th of November and the 2nd of December who would have done justice to the conduct which it is unquestionable that they displayed. On the former day occurred the only cavalry charge on the part of the Germans which was made, so far as I am aware, during the siege of Paris. It was only a squadron that charged —a portion of the 3rd Würtemberg Dragoons, under the command of Graf von Kronsfeld. But everyone spoke of the gallant ardour which the handful of horsemen displayed, and of the service rendered by the charge in clearing the front, to enable the infantry to operate. From the officer named I had a story which illustrates a very genial trait in the character of the Crown Prince of

9*

Prussia. In the 3rd Würtemberg Dragoons was a certain Jacob ——, who had a father. The father had not heard from his son Jacob for an unconscionably long time, so the old man, in his rustic simplicity, sat down and wrote a letter to the Crown Prince, asking for information about Jacob. The old man knew he had been at Wörth, and also in the battle of Sédan, but nothing more. Wherefore he humbly prayed that his Royal Highness would make inquiry, and let him know at his earliest convenience whether Jacob was all right, and if not, what had befallen him. The Crown Prince, "of his own knowledge," as witnesses say, knew nothing about Jacob, but instead of putting the letter in the waste basket, he sent it round to the officer commanding the 3rd Würtembergers, with a request that the old man's mind should be set at ease. It is pleasant to be able to add that Jacob was not killed or wounded, but only a bad correspondent. How many are like Jacob!

The engineer and artillery staffs of the Maas Army went desperately hard to work as soon as they got to Champs—so unremittingly, that I felt myself *de trop*, and was wont to clear out on to the foreposts whenever I saw the maps and draughting paper produced. There were six of us in one room, and there were no other rooms empty. I felt that I ought not to listen while orders were being dictated about batteries, barricades, &c., not, I believe, that my gallant friends at all distrusted my discretion, but because it was obvious if anything were prematurely to leak out through another medium, both they and I might be compromised by mistake. But, although it was not a matter to be written about at the time, one behind the scenes could not refrain from being cognisant of the fact that the business which kept the artillery and engineer staff of the Maas Army in Champs was not wholly connected with the strengthening of the cordon across the horse-shoe. That it was true was their first work, but when the talk came to be of the ranges of siege guns, of the establishment of a park at Brou, a few kilomètres behind Chelles, of the construction of extra strong bridges capable of bearing heavy artillery, of the requisitioning of trains of cart transport for ammunition cases, of the wholesale manufacture of fascines and gabions, of the construction under cover of night of massive emplacements for great guns, of the time when Colonel Bartsch and his fortress artillerists should arrive, it was obvious that something else was in the wind. Three days after the fight of Villiers, I knew that the German tactics on the east side had been changed, and that Mont Avron was to be bombarded.

Visiting, on the 8th, the head-quarters of General Obernitz in Malnoue, I found there copies of the Paris papers containing General Trochu's reply to von Moltke's communication recounting the German victory at Orleans on the 4th, and offering a safe conduct to any officer whom the former might send out to verify the disastrous position. There was the ring of true metal in the note which the Paris Government appended to the Governor's letter. "This news," they said, "which reaches us through the enemy, supposing it to be accurate, does not deprive us of our right to rely on the great movement of France rushing to our relief. It changes nothing either in our resolutions or our duties. A single word sums them up—to fight! Long live France! Long live the Republic!" And so while one side set its teeth hard and resigned itself with gallant devotion to "ruin, disease, and death," the other in its masterful methodical way, went leisurely but thoroughly about its preparations for the bombardment. The same afternoon two French deserters were brought into the Würtemberg divisional head-quarters in Malnoue. They had come from Choisy-le-Roi, had dodged away northward, traversing the space between Fort Nogent and the Marne, and had crossed the river somewhere below Brie. They mentioned the construction on the slope in front of Nogent of a battery mounted with guns of twelve centimètre calibre, and stated that the vicinity was full of infantry. While riding next day, I met a Hamburg merchant driving full pelt to the railway at Lagny in a state of panic. He was full of a story that the siege of Paris was to be raised at once, in consequence of the interception of a balloon from Paris containing a despatch from Trochu, to the effect that he meant to gain Versailles at any cost. The King, according to the panic-stricken Hamburger, was off to Rheims that night with half the army, and the Crown Prince was to be left behind to fight his way out, covering His Majesty's retreat. Poor man! in the recesses of that deep waggon of his lay, it may be, a good deal of ill-gotten gear, and it might have been a troubled conscience which made his apprehensions so causelessly active. When I met this panic-stricken fugitive I was on my way to a large field Lazarette of wounded, which the Würtembergers had at Pontault, a place some distance to the south of Malnoue. Originally there were about 350 wounded brought thither; but, in pursuance of the usual policy, all had been evacuated towards Germany, with the exception of those cases which were too severe to bear removal. Of these there remained about 120, including a considerable number of amputations. It was the critical time with amputation cases—the third or fourth day—when the ligatures are prone to come away and great effusions of blood recur. In addition to the very bad cases, consisting of Würtembergers chiefly, with

a few Frenchmen and men of the 2nd Army Corps, there
were in the place about eighty Frenchmen, who had been
too severely wounded for the French to remove them from
the field, and had been brought in by the Würtemberger
ambulances.   The Mayor of Noiseau, a neighbouring
village, had volunteered to take these poor fellows off
the hands of the Würtemberger medical men, giving his
personal guarantee for them as prisoners of war. In most
of the cases the Mayor's guarantee was quite superfluous.
Unless the war had lasted far longer than it did, not
many of these could have been very formidable men for
many a day after its termination.   One word as to the
Würtemberger field ambulances, which are admirable vehicles for their purpose. The hinder end contains places
for wounded men on stretchers, which are run in from
the rear—two on the lower tier, two above.   The front
part is a kind of double coupé, comfortably padded and
seated for six men not so severely wounded as to necessitate a recumbent position.   The sides are well screened,
while at the same time free ventilation is secured.   The
body of the waggon is mounted on capital springs, and
four good horses, with mounted drivers, ensure rapid conveyance to the Lazarette. The Würtembergers had special
wounded trains of their own, which were employed in
despatching their men from Lagny to Würtemberg.   The
American construction of railway carriage is in use in
Würtemberg, and it is easy to conceive the facilities for
the conveyance of wounded afforded by this build.   I
learned from the Prince of Saxe-Weimar that one of those
trains had been inspected by our army medical representatives at the seat of war, Inspector-General Innes and
Dr. Becker. The representatives of another of our institutions, the British National Society, had put in a most
opportune appearance both at Pontault and Noisiel,

another large Lazarette in this neighbourhood. Four fourgons had arrived from Meaux on the 4th December,
under the direction of Captain Brackenbury; and Dr. Biberstein, the chief of the medical staff, spoke with enthusiasm of the business-like manner in which the British fourgons were able to fulfil his requisitions, which
he said were both large and various. The British Society
beat the Berliner Hülfsverein this journey. Active
men as the almoners of the latter were, they only
put in an appearance at Pontault on the day before my
visit.

While the doctor and myself were having a gossip
before making a tour of the Lazarette, the Prince of
Saxe-Weimar came to visit the wounded Würtembergers.
He is married to a daughter of the King of Würtemberg,
and had been commissioned by his parents-in-law to this
kindly duty. The Prince is a big man: all the Saxe-
Weimars run large, and he has a heart certainly big in
proportion to his corporal bulk. Sad as were the sights
the wards presented, it was a not unpleasant peregrination which I made round them in his company. The
Prince went round with a box of cigars under his arm.
With each man in turn he had a little conversation,
which always ended in the question, "Can you smoke?"
The affirmative response was all but universal. One or
two poor fellows there were who seemed past caring for
the cigar—past the power of speech, indeed. All that
they could do was to look grateful for the Prince's kindly
words. One bright-eyed young fellow replied so warmly,
"Ach, ja, eure Hoheit!" The doctor shook his head,
the boy was in the fever, and a cigar might not be the
best thing in the world for him. But he pleaded so
hard, that the good doctor relented, and let him have
the grateful weed. Another chap would have the Prince

see the piece of shell that had made a hole in him. "In
the cupboard" he directed the orderly.   The cupboard
was searched, but it could not be found, and the doctor
would have had the Prince pass on.   But he would not,
and by-and-by the bit of shell turned up in the wounded
man's waistcoat pocket.   There were two men who had
each lost a leg, with whom the Prince had specially interesting conversations.   One was a stalwart, hairy, under-
officer.   He was one of three brothers, and now all were
wounded in this war.   And was he married?   No; but
there was an old woman in some street or other in
Stuttgart, and now that all her sons were down it might
be bad times with her.   The other "amputated" was a
mere boy, handsome as a statue.   I don't know whether
it may have struck others as it did me, that there are a
great number of classically beautiful men among the
Würtembergers.   This lad was the only son of his
mother, and she was a widow.   In both cases the Prince's
hand went into his pocket, and came out with a gold
piece.   "Here, my man, send that to the mother, and
let her know it comes from the Queen."   In one ward
were two amputation cases—one was a Frenchman, the
other a Würtemberger.   Both had burst out bleeding,
and the orderlies were busy around them, pressing femoral
arteries, picking up veins, and applying ice.   The Frenchman was shrieking and yelling; the German lay silent,
the drops of cold sweat on his forehead, and the muscles
of his face working, but never a cry came from him.
The spectacle illustrated one of the differences between
the two nationalities.   As he quitted each room, the
Prince said a few simple words to the effect that he was
commissioned by the King and Queen of Würtemberg
to visit the wounded, and to thank them for their exertions on behalf of their country.   The words, I fancy,

and the visit did more good than any physic Dr. Biberstein could exhibit. All the occupants of this Lazarette
were wounded men; there had been a few cases of typhus,
but they had been sent to the rear. To quote the dry
professional remark of Dr. Biberstein, "We have no time
for typhus here."

A report was current in the Maas army on the 11th
December, of which, however, I could get no confirmation on my return to head-quarters in Margency on that
day, that Count Bismarck had transmitted an ultimatum
to the authorities in Paris, offering terms for acceptance
within a week. These terms were such as Paris might
have thought over before rejecting. Her citizens were
to be spared requisitions. No troops would be billeted
upon them. The thousand and one objects of fine art
in the Queen of Cities would be scrupulously respected.
The officers of the army would be treated with the fullest
consideration. There were other items in the rumoured
ultimatum of a decidedly tempting character, which, in
the absence of confirmation as to its authenticity, need
not be further alluded to.

On the 12th December the defenders of Paris, for
the first time since the 30th November, displayed some
activity on the northern face of the environment. Perhaps they were anxious to display to the chiefs of the
Maas Army their scornful repudiation of the ultimatum
which Bismarck was reported to have tendered. Early
in the morning Argenteuil the unfortunate was subjected
to a brisk cannonading from the batteries about Nanterre
and Courbevoie. The damage done was chiefly to stone
and lime. I heard of only one casualty among the
Germans, and an inhabitant was killed in his bed by the
bursting of a shell. There was a lull as the morning
advanced, but the firing was resumed about noon, and

was quite warm for a couple of hours. There was an unwonted amount of musketry fire between the posts on the opposite sides of the river all the way from Epinay down to Bezons. Accompanying a compatriot who had spent the night with me in Margency, I rode through Argenteuil about one o'clock, when one would almost have imagined that quite an engagement was going on close by, so heavy and continuous was the firing. Mont Valérien was speaking at intervals in its gruff tones, not, however, in our direction, but toward Bougival. It was evident as we rode along the bit of road outside Argenteuil, which commands so capital a view of the adjacent French positions on the peninsula, that the enemy were on the alert for something or other. One could see armed groups coming out from Colombes toward the left, and there was a continuous popping from the French posts among the poplar trees on the other side of the Seine. Presently the bugle began to sound, at first faintly and fitfully, but soon with a louder swell, and then the sound of a military band's music was borne towards us on the wintry wind. It was not easy to form a conjecture as to the nature of the French movements. Whatever they were the fire directed against Argenteuil and its vicinity was probably meant to cover them. Perhaps the French were massing troops on the peninsula, on which are the villages of Gennevilliers, Courbevoie, and Nanterre, and at the neck of which stands Mont Valérien, with a view to a sortie somewhere from it as a base after their failure on the other side of Paris. If this was their design, it was indispensable to its fulfilment that they should have established pontoon bridges over the river in the face of the German fire, and without so strong a support from their own fort guns as that under which they debouched over the Marne. There the crossing of the river was comparatively easy since they had never lost foothold on the further side; but in the direction to which I now refer, the Seine all the way to the Carrières above St. Germain marked the line of demarcation between French and Germans. I heard no more talk of the renewal of the once abandoned project, which had for its object getting over the river at Bezons. No further effort had been made by the French to repair the bridge there, and the boats which appeared designed to supplement the deficiencies in the means of crossing, had been to all appearance rendered useless by the German field artillery. The French fire lulled again for half an hour towards two o'clock; but was rather warmly renewed soon after that hour. It was then chiefly directed toward the base of Mont d'Orgimont, and between that eminence and Argenteuil. Before nightfall it fell away again.

There existed among the Germans a suspicion that Ducrot's proclamation after the battle of Villiers was meant as a ruse, and that he had not abandoned so fully as he protested his design of utilising for sortie purposes the foothold which he yet held on the other side of the Marne, at Joinville. Some colour seemed given to the suspicion by the unquestionable fact that French troops in great force were still lying around and under Fort Nogent, and towards Charenton. It seemed that the French on their side suspected that the Germans were finding the batteries on Mont Avron so inconvenient as to stimulate to efforts for effecting their silence, for the Mont remained garrisoned by a French force, guessed at not under 6,000 bayonets, which was assiduously engaged in the strengthening of their position in the neighbourhood, by enlarging existing defences and erecting others.

The 12th was the birthday of the King of Saxony,
and in the head-quarters of his eldest son the occasion
was warmly celebrated. The Crown Prince and his brother
at Le Vert Galant sent filial messages to Dresden, and a
congratulatory telegram in the name of the Saxon army
was also despatched. The reply which the King sent to
his eldest son was of a tenor creditable to our cousins
of Saxony. The King's birthday is usually celebrated
throughout his territory by great festivities, public feast-
ing, and other demonstrations which involve considerable
expenditure. The event in 1870, as one learned from
the Royal telegram, was not made an occasion for eating
and drinking. Those who lived at home did not make
merry while their brethren were standing with their face
to the foe, while the wounded groaned in the lazarettes,
and while the widows and children were weeping for
those who had found graves by Villiers and Brie. The
money that, under ordinary circumstances, would have
been spent in festivity, was diverted to a nobler use, to
add to the comforts of the wounded, and to help those
who have lost their bread-winners. But the loyal Saxons
in Margency managed to get up an illumination which
would have been creditable anywhere, but which was
positively wonderful in a region so barren of the materials
for such a purpose that if you wanted a candle you had
sometimes difficulty in getting one for money! As I
walked down to the Feldpost at night, I observed the
château on the left, inhabited by our pay-master, bril-
liantly lit up, and not only did stars and letters of fire
bedeck the front of his residence, but particoloured
Chinese lanterns hung from every tree in the garden. It
was the same in the grounds of the château in which
the Feldpost is located. I walked to the door up an
alley of illumination. On the night air floated the sounds

of vociferous "Hochs," which were calculated to suggest the idea that the King's health was being very warmly drunk in more than one Saxon gathering in this French village.

Perhaps the Parisians meant their activity of the 12th, on the northern side, as a complimentary salute to the King of Saxony. This, at least, is certain, that on the 13th, his birthday over, they were profoundly quiet again. It was not believed, however, that this quietude was anything more than a lull, and it seemed to be accepted as a matter of course about this time what we were to look for more fighting, and that the end was not yet at hand. I think it may be taken as a fact that the Germans had been quite out in their reckoning as to the food resources of Paris. According to the calculations and information on which they had based their inactive policy, Paris should by this time have begun to know the meaning of famine, and it was inexpressibly galling to them to find that she was not yet so far gone as to be wholly on salt meat rations. The miscalculation caused chagrin on several grounds. But for it, who can doubt that before this time there would have been a duel between the big guns of North Germany and those of the Paris forts? In that the error of reckoning as to the food resources of Paris had postponed this duel until now there was cause for self-reproach; but there was yet deeper cause for this in the fact that, so implicit had been the leaning on the broken reed of the miscalculation, that the indispensable preliminaries to a bombardment had been neglected. Thus, if it be assumed that now the eyes of the besiegers had been opened, and that they had seen it necessary to resort to this expedient, it was yet plain that they must perforce wait yet awhile; and it was irritating to reflect that the months which had elapsed had been in a great measure so much lost time. Now the work had to be gone about in earnest at the worst possible season of the year for such operations, when the roads were terribly heavy after the breaking of a hard frost and the thaw of a considerable fall of snow.

The eagerness with which the troops craved for what they considered the beginning of the end, in the shape of the bombardment, must have been known in headquarters at Versailles, and must have been taken as an element which could not well have been set aside. But, then, the troops, full of the belief that the bombardment had been now definitely resolved upon, used their discernment to wonder how it happened that so much time had to elapse before it were possible to act on the resolution, and the deduction could not fail to be unfavourable to the German prestige for forethought and a condition of preparedness for alternative events. Still it was safe to reckon that the thunder of the big guns, and the stir of a bombardment would do much to efface such an impression; and all that could now be done was to make up as fast as possible for lost time. There is no doubt that activity had become by this time the order of the day. To one quarter only, the south, had before the second week in the month, all the siege train been directed, and hence the delay elsewhere. Doubtless were the bombardment only to have been on this hand, it might have commenced earlier than it did; but then what of the east side, the side nearest the feeding railway line, and yet a side left utterly barren of siege artillery till the hour that the crisis in font of Villiers forced on the determination to resort to active measures in the shape of a bombardment?

Had guns been all that was required the delay would

not have been very long. But experience, if manifold, taught the error of beginning a bombardment without the means of sustaining it uninterruptedly for a considerable period. The reserve of ammunition must be large, and the commencement of the bombardment had to wait till that had been provided.

From the 13th to the 17th of December we lived in a state of quiet, presenting a strange contrast to the bustle and excitement of the early part of the month. To my daily question of the gentlemen of the Crown Prince's staff, "What news?" the reply was very curt, "None." "None!—do you mean that I am to know and to communicate, or really and actually none?" "Really and actually none," was the response. The French had seemingly taken to economise their ammunition. If you wanted to hear any shooting at all, it was necessary to go down into Argenteuil. There there was no cessation of the crackling fire across the river, but it was almost wholly musketry fire. The place was full of interest. It is a town of some size and it was not empty of people. The shops had re-opened, some of them, and a portion of the population having come back; the citizens, men, women, and children, were for ever in the streets gossiping with apparent cheerfulness and unconcern. Over their heads was the constant sing of the Chassepôt bullet, which they minded no more than they might the singing of a bird. When a shell came they ran into the houses, only to emerge when it had burst, to find out what damage it had done. There is a beautiful church in Argenteuil; its steeple made a good observatory. The market place is below it. In the steeple were several huge holes made by shells, and the roofs of the adjoining houses had been severely injured. But the people stood in the market place, the peasants brought in their carts, and sold poultry, butter, and cheese there with as much unconcern as if the French batteries and the German soldiers had been miles away. Some casualties occurred, but so far as I could learn they were very few. It almost seemed that the French sharp-shooters on the other bank had some occult means of discerning their countryfolk; I can at least testify to the briskness of their practice against those who were not their countrymen. One day, along with Mr. Sidney Hall, I went into a house which overlooked the esplanade on our bank of the river. The esplanade is about 100 feet wide; then comes the stream, and on the other side were the Frenchmen ever ready. I incautiously showed at the window for less than a minute, and drew quite a brisk fire, more than one of the bullets striking the walls of the house. When we went down into the street we found a French-man composedly posting up a proclamation issued by the commandant. There was nothing between him and the river but a loose barricade of timber. It turned out that it was his house in which we had been. Now how was it to be accounted for that he lived there without being shot, while we, wearing like him civilian clothes, could not show for half a minute at a window without being fired at?

Everywhere, as the winter progressed, the people came gradually back to their homes in the villages that were not on the foreposts. Their condition was very bad, yet not so utterly wretched as one might imagine. There must have been great stores of food in the villages around Paris; money would still procure almost anything. There was very little sickness among the native population, not-withstanding the hardships which most of them must have undergone in hiding in the woods, or huddling together in the backlying villages. The health of the

German troops was exceptionally good. Typhus fever
had nearly disappeared, and one hardly ever now heard
of dysentery. Rheumatism and bronchitis steadily sent
a proportion to the lazarettes, but in no great numbers,
and a large proportion of the cases recovered and returned to duty after a few days' lie-by. English ambulance
waggons from the depôt at Meaux frequently visited
the field lazarettes on the north and east sides during
the winter months, and distributed large quantities of
stores.

From other districts, too, came cheering tidings of
the good work done by other detachments of the "English Ambulance." It cannot be denied, nevertheless, that
there was in the late war a vast expenditure of British
money with disproportionately small return. Still, the
experience gained has been good, and will be found useful, let us hope, if another war should unfortunately call
for the services of another such organization. But there
are many difficulties in the way. A great one is in the
selection of qualified superintendents and organizers, in
view of the work to be done. What I saw and learned
impressed me with the conviction that to give a surgical
character to the ambulance organization, is a mistake in
many ways. If an army has not doctors enough of its
own, and appeals to neutral Powers for assistance of this
kind, it would be well were the organizations for medical
aid entirely separate from the ambulance, and that the
neutral doctors should work under the orders of the
medical authorities of the army to which they may be
attached. Squabbles about etiquette, personal tetchiness,
and professional jealousies did much to impair the useful-
ness of that organisation for which Britons so freely put
down their money. There ought to be a copious supply
of ambulance vehicles of the best patterns extant. These

might be horsed and furnished with all appliances, and then lent as they stand to the several Powers at war. No object is to be gained by the neutral State finding drivers and medical staff; and there are many embarrassments in the way. The adoption of this plan would leave the course clear for the concentration of the working staff on that part of the organization which concerns itself with the supply of stores to the lazarettes, a branch of the work which the experience of the war demonstrated, can be cultivated by far to the greatest advantage. The staff, from top to bottom, must consist of neutrals. The English ambulance drivers were chiefly Frenchmen, and the Germans looked upon them with great suspicion—not, I believe, invariably without cause. "English ambulance, sir," said a Prussian officer to me, speaking of the menagerie in St. Germains, "an infernal nest of French spies." Swiss drivers would be the best; they are more polyglot, and not such incorrigible jabberers as the Belgians, and Switzerland is in a condition of perpetual neutrality. Place at the head of the affair a strong man with a great command of temper, an entire absence of paltry self-seeking, some experience in kindred work, a man of promptitude, and without fussiness—one with self-respect, but without bristles, and give him the command—make him despotic. And make him responsible too, not only for efficiency, but for economy, and the prevention, or at least the check of malversation.

About this time, a large proportion of the Saxon cavalry left the front of Paris for the north, to strengthen the army under the command of General Manteuffel. I having indulged in a gossip about ambulances, let me ask permission for another about the German cavalry. All the Germans are excellent horsemasters—the Saxons, perhaps, best of any. The men must have taken immense pains with their horses, and that continually, to turn them out in such condition as those I saw march off northward—bright as stars, plump as in barracks. Rations were not very plentiful, nor were quarters always very eligible. Straw, especially, was short. But if a man caters assiduously for his horse, he can materially supplement the regularly issued rations, and this was what the German cavalry man did. The epoch of sore backs had now long passed. In the early days of the campaign there were many sore backs; ascribable partly to the bad pattern of some of the saddles, but more to the young-soldierhood of many of the men. Nothing teaches a dragoon solicitude for his horse's back and success in keeping it sound like a long march during a part of which he has had to walk while a chafe slowly healed. When will the "best-saddle controversy" be definitely decided? My own opinion is, that our cavalry never had a saddle like the old high-cantle and pommel saddle, with the thorough draught right under the tree, with the blanket instead of the numnah, and the cloak and valise well tightened up in the centre. The Germans have no valise, and the want has the result of increasing greatly the size and weight of the wallets. The strain on the withers that might result therefrom is prevented by placing the saddle farther back than with us, but with questionable advantage; and the valise is an article of immense use and convenience to the cavalry-man.

It may interest not alone military men when I note that the German cavalry have almost without exception betaken themselves to the practice of "jockeying" on the trot. We utterly prohibit jockeying, and a goodly proportion of troop defaultships have connection with addiction to the forbidden practice. The German officers and men alike assert that experience has convinced them

that to "jockey" in the trot is easier for the horse, spares
his back more, and averts his tiring, while it beyond
doubt is pleasanter for the horseman in a long journey.
We took our cavalry ménage from the Germans, including
the balance seat and bumping the saddle.   Shall we follow them into the abandonment of the latter?   I don't
think it matters much.   Lord Cardigan was perhaps the
strongest opponent of "jockeying" of his day, and when
he commanded the "cherry breeches" there were generally more sore backs among them than in any other
regiment in the service.   I believe that the legitimation of
"jockeying" would keep the dragoon longer sound.
After bumping the saddle for fourteen or sixteen years a
man's legs get strangely crooked, and if he has had a
succession of rough trotting mounts it is odds but that
he has palpitation of the heart and varicose veins.   But
the short service system diminishes the significance of
this consideration.

On the morning of the 18th, there occurred in our
neighbourhood an interesting little episode.   A little after
eleven o'clock two gunboats came out with a rush from
behind Fort La Briche.   One following the other, they
steamed rapidly down the Seine, puffing out vigorously
brown jets of smoke.   They never fired, although with
the glass one could make out the gunners standing by
the long gun in the bow of each, but held on their
steady way making for Epinay.   Presently there opened
fire on them our batteries on the slope in front of Montmorency, and as they got nearer, those recently prepared
on Mont D'Orgimont chimed in.   The shells splashed
into the water and burst on the banks, but still the gallant little craft held on their way.   When opposite Epinay
there was a stoppage, and it seemed that a landing was
contemplated from the vessels, but if so, the fire from

Mont D'Orgimont was too warm to make the undertaking
practicable. The boats, probably out of bravado, fired a
round or two at a necessarily high elevation toward Mont
D'Orgimont, and after a seemingly irresolute movement
or two, took their rapid course backward as they came.
There were troops on board the gunboats, but only a
comparative handful on both; however, amidships in one
there stood a group apart who seemed to be officers, and
it is conjectured, no doubt correctly, that the expedition
was a reconnaissance to spy out the condition of the
land in the direction of Epinay, which, it will be remembered, was the scene of one of the many sorties of the
30th of November. If this was the case, the recon-
noiterers could hardly have found grounds for much en-
couragement towards another attempt, for the positions
had been materially strengthened since the date of the
last attempt, and French troops would now have found
it very difficult to occupy Epinay by a *coup de main*.
The continuance of quietude on the front tempted
me on the 19th, to set out for a ride round to Lagny, a
little town on the east of Paris, some distance in the
rear, in order to see something as to the transmission
and condition of the wounded and the French prisoners
from the recent battle in the Orleans district. Lagny
was the terminus of the Eastern Railway, and thither
therefore, necessarily collected all and everything requiring transmission to Germany. "What a glorious thing it
would be for the newspapers if their war correspondents
were endowed with the gift of ubiquity," was the quaint
remark made to me by a young subaltern of the German
Guards who stood beside me in the lee of the white
house on the summit of the height overhanging Stains
and Villetaneuse, whither, leaving my horse in Groslay,
I had mounted for one last reassuring look at the front

and at Paris, before venturing out of range. I suppose
the multiplicity of objects of interest in the prospect before him prompted him to the reflection. The long
chimneys of the St. Denis factories were smoking as vigorously as if they had been Black Country chimneys
when a batch of urgent orders are in hand. What did
they smoke for? Was it machinery below them grinding
corn for the two million beleaguered ones? Were brawny
men at work in the forges below pouring molten iron
into moulds, hammering the outside of cannon barrels,
rifling the bores, filling the breeches, casting the projectiles which these cannon were designed to pitch among
the ranks of the enemy? Did they indicate powder manu-
factories? Perilous juxtaposition was not to be studied
in such a pinch as Paris was in now. Were they the
chimneys of bakeries, or of huge steam sausage-machines
for chopping up horseflesh? Whatever they represented
they were smoking away with a curious air of manufac-
turing prosperity that seemed utterly incompatible either
with a bloody siege, a close blockade, or threatened starvation. Were his companion ubiquitous, thought the
Guardsman, the puzzle—for to us, as to most, those factories were a puzzle—would cease to be so, nay, never
would have existed. Then there were those waspish-
looking, low, black little gunboats every now and then
showing their sharp snouts out from behind the crown
work of La Briche. What were they doing? Had they
any intention of another reconnaissance? Were they
acting as ferry-boats, or had they parties of ladies on
board, to whom these curious grasshopper-like motions
afforded pleasure? First, there comes out one—puffing
as if she were flapping her chest with her arms to raise
her courage. Out she comes bodily with a dash, and a
big gun from where I stand might cover even her stern.

Then she seems to lose heart again. You almost think
you hear the skipper crying "Ease her," "Stop her," and
then the word is "Turn astern." She goes back in a
droll pirouetting fashion, feeling, as it were, from side to
side with that huge antenna on her deck. I take it she
came out to see whether she could not find an eligible
object at which to discharge her gun. No reliefs are
crossing the plain, the officers in Epinay are at dinner,
men have learned to lie close in Deuil, Montmagny, and
Stains. So she has had her journey for nothing. A few
minutes after, two came out abreast, and, so far as we
could make out with the glass, there were groups on the
deck that seemed officers. Was yesterday's reconnaissance, then, not enough? Was there still a craving for an
attack upon Epinay, notwithstanding yesterday's lesson
from Mont d'Orgimont? Perhaps Trochu was himself
aboard, with Ducrot and Vinoy in the other craft, so
that the destinies of Paris might not be entrusted to one
fragile concern of tin-plates and maple pannelling. In
the green foreground of Gennevilliers we could dimly see
masses of men, now to all appearance swelling into
densely packed bodies, anon elongating into columns.
What was their purpose, or had they one? Were they
listening to a speech from Trochu, were they collecting
there to be ferried over by the gunboats upon Epinay, in
case these should make a rapid voyage in that direction;
or were they being marched away in the direction of
Bezons, in view of a contemplated renewal of the attempt
'o bridge the Seine at that point? Again the lieutenant's
remark as to ubiquity came home to me. But he had
his explanation ready about the shifting soldiers, whose
appearance was shaking my Lagny resolution. "They
are drilling the stupid fellows of Mobiles," was what he
had to say about it; being very anxious for Lagny, I ac-

cepted the explanation. Boom, and boom again, one gun from Du Nord, one from La Briche in momentary succession. With a far-off sough we heard the whistle of the shells through the air—that is a sound that carries far; but we heard not the dull clash that is the signal of the impact, nor the sharper crack that the explosion produces. Was the fire against Stains, or Le Bourget, or Epinay, or into miscellaneous space? Non-ubiquitous, we could not tell; but it was some consolation to know in this case that ubiquity of presence might have been accompanied with ubiquity of danger. Ten minutes more, and the same double salute; still another ten minutes, and the repetition with such clockwork regularity, that showed a mutual understanding by signal, telegraph, or otherwise, between the gunners of the two forts. A fourth double discharge, this time almost simultaneous and anticipatory of the expiry of the statutory ten minutes. That far-off sough comes nearer, nearer, nearer—cuts the air, as it seems, so close to our ears that I, at all events, swerve involuntarily. There is no mistake about the crash of the explosion this time—far too near to be pleasant. It is clear that we, and none other, were the marks for these two shells, at least. What keen dogs they must be behind those grim embrasures! Good afternoon, Herr Lieutenant, my winsome youngster, smiling there from ear to ear, as if gunpowder had been an amalgam of your mother's milk, and as if shells had been the *bon-bons* of your boyhood. I am not sufficiently acquainted with your domestic affairs to know if you have anybody whose livelihood depends on your existence otherwise than in little pieces—I have, so adieu to you, with all decent precipitation.

The shadows were falling as I rode through the Guardsmen in Sarcelles, Arnonville, and Gonesse, where

the men for forepost duty are turning out burdened with
wrappers of the strangest kinds.   Here is a man with a .
sheepskin door-mat lashed round him; and surely that is
a Brussels carpet that this big grenadier has over his
shoulders.   If you were to hear the alarm sound this
moment, down would go the wraps, and forward would
go their bearers, all the more supple because they understood how to keep themselves warm when the alarm was
not sounding.   When shall we learn that efficiency in the
field does not crucially depend on trimness on parade;
and when shall the adjutant of a British regiment understand that for a private to go on night guard with a comforter instead of a stock is not a fearful portent of the
end of the world?

Have the artillerymen in Sevran been fishing in the
Arctic Seas, and is that their catch of walruses that I see
on my left, as I ride through the little town? Synonymes
are often convenient, and this synonyme for a siege gun
we owe to the master of all of us in the profession of a
war correspondent.   The Sevran walruses have come
hither by train—preserved in ice, no doubt.   It is cold
weather, and a considerable number of them are allowed
to huddle together for the sake of warmth, but some of
them have been cut off from the "school"—that is the
technical word, I believe—and are located in smaller
groups farther to the front, placed in localities where, it
is true, they have a certain shelter consisting of earthen
embankments in front of them, but where that general
shelter is, to a great extent, nullified by the gaps cut in
their immediate front—gaps which those who have to do
with walrus fishing have a habit of calling embrasures.
· But cold though the unwieldy denizens of the Arctic re-
gions may be in such exposed positions, they are certainly not to be allowed to starve.   These streams of

waggons, drawn by teams of strong horses, and accompanied by men in uniform, are returning empty from the conveyance of food to the inhabitants of the deep. True they may have to hunger for their rations yet a while, but the meal will be all the heavier when it does come. What is the use of administering *hors d'œuvre* when the dinner is not ready? I was concerned, however, to notice that this catch of walruses ran smaller than one could wish.

I am bound for Le Vert Galant, and should turn away from the front at Livry; but let me go a little farther southward, through the *col* of Bondy, to see what that old *bête noire* Mont Avron is like in the thickening gloom. The place is true to its established character. From the range of the fringe of felled forest through which I have penetrated I can only faintly trace the familiar outlines, so rapidly has the darkness fallen. But—Flash! up goes the electric light from Nogent and Rosny, and bang comes the first shell—the "top of the evening" from Avron. What a humbug, to be sure, is that same electric light. The French were always using it. You saw it scintillating on the summit of Valérien and flashing out toward Le Bourget from Montmartre. To the defenders of Paris all it could do is to make darkness visible; to its besiegers, if they had only been in the mind, it would have been a gratis illumination that would be worth any money. In the foreground of the electric flashes from the forts before me, lies Avron as clear as if it were noonday. But Chelles, Montfermeil, Noisy, or Villiers might have been swallowed up in an earthquake, so utterly invisible are they. Oh for something else than the meagre walruses by the windmill and on the vineberg. Half-a-dozen hours pelting with real artillery on those impudent batteries on the verge and crest of the plateau so brilliant under the

rays of the electric light—then in the small hours a
storming party of one battalion of Saxons and another of
Guardsmen; a bayonet fight on the summit—and then
hurrah for the black, white, and red flag, to flaunt wherewithal the gunners of Nogent and Rosny. It would not
be a light cause for which the Saxons, having once got a
grip of the summit, would surrender it now. Well, let
us live in hope, in early hope. How long? How long?
I get angry as I look at the battery, made right in our
faces, but the other day comparatively harmless, and at
whose door, young as it is, lie the deaths of so many
stalwart Saxons, whose corpses will fertilise next year's
crops in the fatal horseshoe. I get angry and impatient
when I think that this place, which our ground dominates
so that not a gun could ever have been mounted but for
unaccountable *laissez faire*, should test the elasticity of
our forepost line in a direction that I am disgusted and
savage to have the knowledge of. The *laissez faire* days
were over; but there seldom comes an indulgence without a penalty, and on many graves around this side of
Paris, the pioneers might have substituted for the "Hier
ruhen in Gott," the words, "Here lie the consequences
of vacillation."

Making for Lagny on the morning of the 20th,
I was amusing myself, between Pomponne and my
destination, by noting the variety of railway lines
from which the carriages composing a single reserve
train had been drafted—Berg, Hanover, Taunus, Halle-
Cassel, Westfalen, Saxe, and half-a-dozen more, when
I observed a half troop of Blue Hussars on the other
side of the water coming at a trot down to the Kriegs-
brücke. The horsemen were followed by a string of
carriages, which were closed up by another half troop of
Dragoons. What could it mean? Was the King ful-

filling the frantic prognostications of the Hamburgh merchant, whose ravings I have chronicled, and flying to Rheims in twelve two-horse post-waggons? Had Trochu yielded himself up on the sly, and was he off to Wilhelmshöhe *via* Lagny and Bouillon, after the manner of his quondam royal master? Had the Crown Princess been on a flying visit to her royal and gallant husband, and warned out of Versailles by "Big Josceline?" How could I tell? None the more could I understand the *raison d'être* of the procession when the escort and the post-waggons came past me at a trot. I saw faces not wont to be seen on the war path—faces grave with thought, attenuated by long watching over the midnight lamp, civilian faces and dresses in every carriage. Although I did not express myself· audibly, I shared the sentiments of the honest Landwehrman in the gutter, who bluntly roared out to one of the postilions, "I wish you'd tell me who the devil you have there!" The man's quaint coolness reminded me of an Ost Preussen Marketender, who, passing during the memorable interview between the ex-Emperor and Bismarck after Sedan, bawled out lustily, "*Wo ist denn der Napoleon?*" The cortége whirled on, and I rode after it, but was accidentally so delayed that the waggons had discharged their freight in front of the Lagny-Railway-station some time before I got there. Very hungry, and with a trust in the chapter of accidents, begotten of some experience, to purvey somehow the information I needed, I turned aside to the 'officers' casino'—a modest eating-room, on the mess principle, established opposite the station. The place was full of the faces I had seen in the carriages. The owners of the· faces were hard at work—very. Sausage, ham, cold meat, were disappearing with creditable rapidity; the wine gurgled from the bottles, and

a silence reigned such as is wont to exist among very
hungry men. No wonder that they were hungry. The
thirty civilians I saw before me, in the fur coats, the fur
caps, and some, indeed, in fur boots; one man, with
white moustaches, many of them with bald heads, and
other signs and tokens of grave and reverend signiors,
were the deputation of the North German Reichstag, who
were on their way home from Versailles, after tendering
to King William the crown and title of Emperor of Germany, and they had not eaten since they left Versailles,
after a very early breakfast. It was a strange sight, no
bad emblem of a nation which loves peace, while it never
shuns righteous war. Here in the low-browed, narrow
room, waited on by soldiers in canvas undress, whose
straw beds were visible in the kitchen as the door stood
open, interspersed with officers in uniform—here a general,
there a lieutenant, the street in front crowded with the
wounded of two nations and half-a-dozen principalities,
its stones echoing to the din of galloping orderlies, to
the rattle of marketender carts, and the roll of tumbrils;
here sat the fathers in Israel, men wise in council; men
famous in literature; men whose names are a tower of
strength on every bourse in Europe. When has a Par-
liament been seen on campaign before? I can recal no
later instance than when the Council of the Covenant
went with the Covenanting fighting men into the field—
themselves, too, fighting men. Truly this modern Parlia-
ment on campaign took to the *rôle* very kindly, to judge
by the good knives and forks they played. Having had
the honour to be recognised by one of the members,
Baron Rothschild, I was most courteously requested to
take a seat at one of the tables. The Baron, in urbanity
and geniality, is a host in himself; at the same table sat
the following members of the deputations:—Präsident

Simson, Landrath von Cranach, Dr. Weigel, Herr Putt-
kamer, Baron Nordeck, Count Hompesch, Herr von Sybel,
and Herr Sombart. They told me, with much feeling,
how the tears had trickled down King Wilhelm's cheeks
when the grandest proffer of the age was made to him.
They expressed with hearty warmth their pleasure that
when the time came that Wilhelm's son should reign in
his stead, the Princess Royal of England should be
Empress of Germany; and before Herr Director came to
say that the train was ready, one toast was drunk, and
in that all the room joined with acclamation—"Prosperity
to Germany and England; may they ever be friendly."
Baron Nordeck it was who gave the toast. And then
"the house adjourned" into the snug first-class carriages,
"honourable members," not a few of them, showing
from their pockets what one might have taken to be the
muzzles of pistols, designed for protection against Francs-
tireurs, but which in reality were the necks of wine-
bottles. I could not help being amused at the gentleman
who was charged with the duty of settling the reckoning.
It was stiff, unquestionably—164 thalers for a simple
cold luncheon for thirty-one persons. No doubt the casino
keeper would have replied to a complaint to the same
effect as a Scotch change-house keeper is reported to
have used to James VI., "Ye dinna come this gate ilka
day, your Majesty." Certainly it is not often that a Lagny
marketender gets a chance of cutting into the purse of
the German Reichstag. The paymaster was disposed to
grumble, but I ventured to point out that it was all, so
to speak, in the family, since the man was a German,
and since Germany was paying the costs of the delegation—a view which the good deputy, perhaps, all the
readier adopted, because his colleagues, getting over before him, were picking up all the best seats in the train.

The deputation went the same night as far as Epernay, where, in its corporate capacity, it was to break up. I was forced to resist a very cordial invitation to accompany it as far as the city of champagne, but my duties called me elsewhere. Prince Carl's surgeon, who accompanied the delegation, had with him a cage containing a Paris carrier pigeon, which had been captured with its despatch, and which he was conveying home as a present to Princess Carl.

So pressing at the first strain were the needs, and so ghastly the misery, of the French prisoners passing through Lagny on their way from Orleans to captivity in Germany, that Captain Nevill, the chief representative in Meaux of the British National Society, had wisely thought it his duty for once to break through the trammels of rule and regulations, that the horrors of the situation might be alleviated. It would tax the vivid pen of MM. Erckmann-Chatrain to depict the sufferings of these poor wretches. I was told of one batch that came in so ravenous with hunger that the men grubbed in the gutter after turnip-tops and bones, and turned over dirt-heaps in search for stray crusts of bread. At Meaux, when the train containing these unfortunates passed through, the Society people threw hams into the carriages, which were seized and worried by the ravenous men, as dogs worry bones. Between wounded and prisoners, the German organization for the time broke down. It was little wonder. The average daily quota of prisoners from the 1st up to the 17th was 1000 men; the number of wounded averaged little less. Lagny did its best, but it is never a great place, and its resources had been severely taxed for months before. The cry of the great distress reached Meaux, and Captain Nevill and his colleagues could not withstand it. On the 17th December Mr.

Barrington Kennett came on to Lagny with twenty huge
cases of preserved meat; next day followed Captain Nevill
with 200 leviathan loaves.   Mr. Kennett was left at
Lagny in charge of the arrangements, and every one
spoke in terms of enthusiasm, as to the manner in which
he had accomplished what he set himself to do.   The
German organization had righted again—it was never
long in its broadside—and now the arrangement was in
force that every prisoner on his way through should
receive a lump of bacon and another of bread, while the
British Society, in case of another collapse, continued to
keep in reserve a store of preserved meat and bread for
administration in that event.   The horrors of Lagny
during December transcended all imagination.   Fancy an
average of 1000 wounded men pouring in day by day, a
fresh thousand every day, unfed, their wounds undressed,
bitter cold, and jolted almost to distraction.   There was
no hospital in the place.   No hospital, had it been as
big as new St. Thomas's twice over, would have sufficed.
Sheds, houses, railway vans, the lamp-room in the railway
station, the church, the Mairie, were turned into hospitals.
I saw one courtyard on which opened four or five squalid
rooms.   Into these eighty wounded Bavarians had perforce to be placed for the night, supperless, fireless—
hopeless, I should think, in their utter misery.   In one
day came 1800 wounded, nearly 100 of whom were
officers.   The men were put into the church; there was
no other place for them.   During the night a certain man
was wanted particularly for some reason.   Diligent search
was made for him among the masses of wounded men,
but it was like looking for a needle in a bundle of hay.
The search was unsuccessful.   As I walked about the
streets of Lagny, I continually met strange "mounted
men."   Now it was a man on the back of another, the

man carried having a leg swathed in bandages. Now
came a pair carrying a man in what boys call a king's
chair. All were on their way to the station, the platform
of which was continually littered with a kind of luggage
that made one's heart ache. There, at full length on the
litter lay the poor broken fellows, looking up at you with
their great, calm, patient eyes. I saw a clumsy fellow
stumble over one of the prostrate forms, and all the chiding
he received was a wan pinched smile. There was a lady
at Lagny whose name deserves to be written in letters of
gold wherever are recorded the names of devoted philan-
thropists; Madame Simon, the lady superintendent of the
Saxon ambulances. Day and night did this noble woman
wrestle with the torrent of human misery that had surged
upon Lagny since the beginning of the month. The
church of Lagny had come to strange uses; the previous
week, a refuge for 1700 wounded men; two nights before
my visit, the barracks for 1000 Bavarians—a new draft
pressing to the front; last night, the prison-house of some
1200 Frenchmen. I went among them into the stench
—stench and scene reminding me of the church of
Donchéry the day after Sedan. Most of the prisoners I
saw were boys, some the merest children, unable to carry
a gun, much less to use one. Their guards were very
kind and gentle with them, poor wretches; it would have
been difficult to be harsh with creatures so utterly down
and crushed.

At six o'clock, on the morning of the 21st, a good
friend routed me out of a comfortable bed in Lagny, with
the information that fighting was imminent. Taking at
once to horse, I heard nothing as I rode for the first two
miles, but had abundant confirmation everywhere that
my friend's intelligence was good. I overtook a pontoon
train going at a trot towards Chelles; the officer believed

that that was the point to be threatened, and the bridge might be useful to facilitate the passage of succours from the region of Champs, Malnoue, and Villiers. At Le Pin I found the three field batteries of the 24th Division quartered there, limbered up and taking the road. Their orders were likewise for Chelles, and I was tempted to accompany them. But as I spoke with the officers, there came down on the wind the sound of heavy firing from the direct front towards Clichy, and so I resisted the impulse to go to Chelles, where there was undoubtedly the most tempting district for an infantry attack, and headed up the slope to General Montbé's head-quarters in Clichy. The terrace of the château he inhabited commands a noble view of the whole country as far as Dugny and Gonesse, and this country was the theatre of the cannonade that lasted till the afternoon. By eight o'clock, when I arrived, the fire was continuous. The centre of the German position was that fortified camp between Sevran and Le Blanc Mesnil which I have already described, and around Aulnay, in the very middle of that stretch, were the batteries chiefly concentrated. The German force engaged there, so far as I could learn, was as follows:—Three batteries of the Guards Artillery, three batteries contributed by the 23rd Division of the 12th Army Corps, and three or four batteries of the Artillery Division of the 12th Army Corps. There were reserve batteries in addition to this, but those were not engaged. Infantry and cavalry supports were partly drawn out, partly standing ready in their quarters. The 103rd Regiment, the garrison of Clichy, were on the plateau of Raincy, to watch the French infantry that had been observed concentrating in Bondy.

The French artillery seemed engaged all round. Avron was firing over Villemonble at Clichy and Montfermeil;

11 *

and Forts Noisy and Romainville were vigorously following suit against Raincy, Gagny, and the German posts
in the forest of Bondy, which were also dividing the attention of Avron.   The batteries at Bondy and Drancy
were playing on Livry, Sevran, and Aulnay; and Aubervilliers, in combination with de l'Est, was throwing shells
into Le Bourget, Pont Iblon, and Dugny.   Du Nord was
bombarding Pierrefitte and Stains.   The French infantry
was concentrated between Bondy and Baubigny, one demonstration towards Clichy, and another toward Chelles,
having been arrested earlier in the morning.

About a quarter to nine Aubervilliers, de l'Est, and
St. Denis seemed to be concentrating their fire on Le
Bourget.   Six or eight French batteries had formed line
with their left on Drancy, and were partly firing obliquely
into Le Bourget at very short range, partly firing on the
German line behind the inundations.   I could see shells
bursting in Pont Iblon, also behind our batteries in Aulnay.   The French fire was quite furious, half a dozen
guns flashing out at once; but it seemed wild.   The German was regular as the beats of the pendulum of a clock.
An occasional shell from Avron was tumbling into Clichy.
At nine o'clock came a rattle of musketry on the wind.
It sounded from Le Bourget.   Were the French infantry
pressing on the battalion of Guards occupying it?   It
sounded like it.   It grew louder, and then there was a
lull.   It sprung up again nearer Pont Iblon.   "The
Guards must be in retreat towards Pont Iblon" was the
exclamation on our terrace.   The hellish shell fire concentrated on the place was enough of itself to drive them
out.   There were the shells bursting all along the road
towards Pont Iblon.   They must, mark, surely the line of
the retreating Guards,' the shells following as they fell
back.   Now it seemed as if they were safe behind Pont

Iblon, for the batteries above the causeway through the
inundations opened, their way seemingly free, since
friends were no longer in front of their muzzles.   It
afterwards turned out that we were wrong in the conclusion that the Guards had been wholly expelled from
Le Bourget.

The French, in the teeth of Pont Iblon's fire, had got
up batteries on the chaussée before Le Bourget, and
seemed to be exchanging shots with the Pont Iblon
batteries at point-blank range.   A German battery at
Sevran was beginning to speak in the direction of Bondy.
I could see the shells from Aulnay bursting in the middle
of the French batteries at Drancy, as the wind for the
moment blew the smoke away.   Still they held their
ground.   Fire seemed opening out towards us from Avron,
and now and then I heard the waspish sing of a chassepot bullet.   At half-past ten the French were brightening
up all round.   The forts were, without exception, firing
as hard as they could.   That white smoke I saw in the
far distance must have been the Lunette de Stains playing into the village of the same name.   Did the firing
go farther round towards Montmorency and Epinay?
I could not tell for certain; but the direction of the
noise and the smoke argued as much.   At eleven o'clock
both sides were at it ding-dong, without advantage on
either side.   Putting out of sight the forts, the French
had the greatest strength of artillery engaged.   I could
make out, as I reckoned, eighteen field batteries.   The
line of guns to the right of Drancy was lengthening.
How they did fire, to be sure!   Could they have been
aiming as they blazed away with such rapidity?   Splash
—splash—I saw now with the glass that most of their
shells were bursting in the inundation in front of our
position in Aulnay.   That could break no bones.   Why,

they had set the Forest of Bondy on fire, on their own side of the water! If they had meant to follow up with infantry, this would have inconvenienced them seriously. Kr-r-r-r, kr-r-r-r—one ought to know that sound if he ever heard it before. Where could they have got their mitrailleuses at work? That indicated close quarters. Had they got their infantry edged forward on the sly at some point we could not see from our position, and were they backed up by the mitrailleuse? Why, the sound was coming from two points at once. The glass explained the mystery. Near Drancy, and on to Sevran if it were not for the interruption, runs the Soissons railway. Below us, by Bondy, and so round to Villemomble and Gagny, runs the Strassburg line. There was a mitrailleuse train on each line. General Montbé saw it first—the locomotive puff-puffing out from behind the trees of Drancy, having the mitrailleuse waggons before it. There was the kr-r-r-r again. The concern was playing dodging tactics—it came out to fire, and scuttled back to load. Another mitrailleuse train was at the same game on our direct front—on the Strassburg line—that was the song of some of the bullets. I wondered how von Schönberg and Hammerstein, and the rest of the 103rd fellows on Raincy were relished their closer contiguity. At twelve an orderly rode in with the information that in the direction of Noisy-le-Grand French infantry were pushing forward, and that a battery had been established and opened fire in the same place, up the valley against Chelles; also that all the batteries south of Avron were at work playing on the horseshoe. This bad a serious meaning. The artillery in the neighbourhood of Chelles would be able to honour none of our drafts now, if we should want them. It looked as if we might need them. The fire was as hot as ever, the

French activity seeming unabated. Our guns were pounding away in a steady, business-like way—they would not spurt. Artillery spurts never pay—infantry spurts sometimes, but not so often as is generally thought. The "walrusses" by Sevran were asleep; it was evident we were not firing a gun that was not a field one. At a quarter to one there came a 24th Division battery past Clichy toward Sevran. It was one of those that had left Le Pin in the morning. This was reassuring as to the state of things to our south by Chelles and the horseshoe. The battery could not well have been spared if it had been very hot there. A shell—it must have come from Fort Noisy—burst in the battery as it traverses the space at our feet between Clichy and Livry; one horse —a detachment beast—was down, that was all. They had got the range from Avron now pretty closely. Where we were standing was hot quarters now. Bang. General, you are not hurt, are you? A close shave, in all conscience; a 24lb. shell came right in among us, alighting among the stacked arms of a picquet, and sending the needle-guns flying right and left, and, for that matter, the men too; not a soul hurt, but all smothered with gravel and mud. At one o'clock it was evident our fire was beginning to tell. The batteries flanking Le Bourget were shutting up. They were beginning to retreat. What was that burst of black smoke behind them? The French must have been trying to burn Le Bourget. They had succeeded so far; there was a jet of fire, but the place must have been washed, surely, in the composition ballet girls use for their skirts; it would not take to burning kindly. I supposed it was the wet straw that raised so dense a smoke. At half-past one there was a lull. The French were changing position. The lull was only on their side, ours was pegging away as if driven by steam.

There were the Le Bourget batteries at work again, but
farther behind; they must have limbered up and been
falling back, and suddenly unlimbered again. There was
a gap in the line of batteries on the right of Drancy before another quarter of an hour had passed. The centre
batteries seemed to have dropped out. What is the artillery word of command? If it had been cavalry I should
say they were retiring by columns of troops from the
centre. The front batteries had wakened up again as hot as
ever to cover the movement of the others no doubt. By
half-past two the French artillery was all but silenced,
and in full retreat. All the firing we now saw was our
guns milling away steadily as if paid by the piece, and
the French forts of De l'Est, Du Nord, and Aubervilliers.
In the distance, under the hill of Ecouen, which shuts
in the horizon, I saw smoke rising. Perhaps Dugny or
Garges might have been fired. Perhaps a shell had
lodged in a straw stack. By three o'clock hardly anything was audible to our north front. Noise still came
from the direction of Montfermeil, Chelles, and the south.
The neighbourhood of Clichy, for the time, seemed to be
attracting exceptionally hot fire. Shells were falling on
the slope below us with disagreeable frequency.

Although in other parts of the line, at least to the
northward, the firing seemed to be dying away as the
early winter twilight came on, shells continued to be
thrown toward Clichy, with perhaps greater frequency
than in the earlier part of the afternoon. About five
o'clock the fire from the German guns about Aulnay,
which had been dying away as it ceased to evoke a
response, suddenly flared up again, and continued very
brisk for about a quarter of an hour. It appeared to me
as if the French were disposed to halt at least some of
their batteries for the night in advance of the position

out of which they had come in the morning, and that
the warm fire of their opponents was intended to prevent
the execution of this design. The French guns, which
had been utterly silent for half an hour, could not refrain
from replying to this fire, however feebly, and they were
unlimbered—a couple of batteries, in the flat some distance to the north-east of Baubigny. It was very pretty,
in the all but darkness, to watch the rapid flashes, and
the shells bursting in the air, like a comet that has knocked
out its brains against some aërial rock. But the pyro-
technic display was not of long continuance. The German fire was too steady and rapid to admit of a lengthened
interlude of the illumination of the inundation waters on
the part of the French by the bursting shells on its margin.
All grew silent and dark again over against Baubigny, and
it was as if the French array—the forts, whose grey embrasures had been visible in the daylight, the serried batteries of artillery which had maintained their share of the
day's din with so much spirit, and the dense battalions
of infantry men which had done nothing all day but hold
themselves in reserve—as if all these were blotted off the
black face of the night. But not for long. From the
far-off firing platform of Fort de l'Est suddenly flashed
out the electric light, followed by a flash that heralded
the dull thud which, as it seemed quite a minute after,
struck the ear. At what De l'Est was firing we could not
tell—if indeed at anything, and not in pursuance of that
Gascon custom to which the Paris forts were addicted, of
having the "last word" in every affair, no matter what its
issue. Presently there rose against the sky another light
farther south—directly between Clichy and Paris, a whole
chain of lights so numerous that they blended as in one
great fire, and made the heavens bright above them.
These were the bivouac fires of the French camping in

the open in the position they had taken up on the previous
night, their right resting on Bondy, their left on La
Courneuve. There they lay—foiled indeed in whatever
they contemplated to-day, if it was of an actively offensive nature, but still stubbornly refusing to relinquish it.
They were at hand for anything. To-morrow their infantry might be raging against the needle-guns of the
Saxons lying before us on Raincy. To-morrow their field
artillery, changing its direction, and backed by Avron,
might be pounding inconveniently into Montfermeil. To-
morrow, changing its front, the Bondy-Baubigny force
might be supporting a division farther to the south or a
heavy attack towards Chelles; we could not tell. There
they lay, at all events, the object of an undefined uneasiness, in which there was no trepidation, but something of nervousness. Ah, well, sufficient for the day is
the evil thereof.

What was the *raison d'être* of this great powder-
burning demonstration? It could hardly have been intended as an attempt to break through. Speculations in
the early part of the day had been various. It might,
thought some, be a reconnaissance in force to discover
by drawing their fire whether the besiegers had any heavy
artillery mounted on the works between Sevran and Pont
Iblon, with future intentions towards the forts. It might
be, thought others, that, in the knowledge of the rail-
ways being in use as far as Gonesse and Sevran, the
speculation might have been ventured by the French that
to these termini were centreing the siege guns, and that
under a heavy artillery fire the infantry might get the
chance of making a dash in an exploring and destroying
expedition.' But in my opinion the cue was given to the
motive of the day's work in the terms of a communication
made by General von Montbé, at his hospitable dinner-

table.   All day long heavy columns of French infantry massed on and about the slope of Avron, and as far forward as Neuilly, had been threatening the gap of Chelles. This alluvial tract presented several obvious advantages for a sortie.   It is quite flat, is open in the physical sense all the way to Lagny—all the way to Chalons for that matter —and the French holding Neuilly as they did, already sat astride of the flat country, and could make their dispositions without annoyance or exposure on the same level as their succeeding operations.   Then there was no river to cross.   But for that somewhat sturdy obstacle, the Saxons, there would have been a straight run home unobstructed by water or broken ground all the way, as I have said, to Lagny; and behind a sallying force there stood up the formidable Avron, a most judicious bottle holder, and something more.   No doubt there were disadvantages to set against all these advantages. This world is a vale of crosses, and nobody can expect to have it all his own way.   The bluff of Montfermeil would have enfiladed a force coming up the flat toward Chelles as soon as it had shown out from Neuilly.   The height behind Chelles looked nearly direct in the face of any such force; and the Germans had batteries of field-guns both on the bluff of Montfermeil and the heights around Chelles. Those heights, too, narrow the fair way considerably, and from the outset it is the reverse of too large.   Still I had wondered that the French, who had essayed ground far less eligible in a physical sense for a sortie, should not have tried this.   It was clear that I was not alone in my opinion, for Chelles was the line taken by the 24th Division Artillery in the morning from Le Pin.   The French columns —a whole division it was known—were waiting under and around Nogent opposite the gap, ready to throw themselves into it.   But they knew of old the results of a concentration at any point of the deadly field artillery of the Germans. Had they come on directly, and with no diversion, what would have hindered it, but that the Saxon batteries from the Marne to the inundations, the Guards batteries from Livry to Gonesse, should have been waiting there for them across the throat of the gap at Chelles, and on the crest of Montfermeil? Wherefore was made a great artillery demonstration, supported with infantry, to look in earnest on the north-eastern face, in the hopes to draw off the artillery from the Chelles positions, and leave the coast comparatively clear for an attack. The plan might have succeeded with a weaker artillery than that possessed by the Germans—that, as it was, it was not partially successful, I am not quite prepared to assert. Any how, the French division about two o'clock thought itself justified in advancing to the attack up the northern bank of the Marne.

What followed, General von Montbé had not learned when I left Clichy. But when I came on to the headquarters of the 12th Army Corps in Le Vert Galant, I found that Ville Evrart and La Maison Blanche, the two keys to the Prussian outpost line athwart the alluvial plain, had been taken in the afternoon by the French, and that the staff were waiting for information concerning the result of an attempt which had been ordered to recover those positions under cover of the darkness. The attempt was successful. At six o'clock in the evening the whole of the 106th Saxon Regiment simultaneously fell upon Ville Evrart and La Maison Blanche. The latter, a minor detached post, was first taken, the capture including a major and five officers, the former of whom must have been making the rounds, and about fifty men. Ville Evrart followed, and it contained 500 or more defenders, who were all made prisoners. Some of the outlying enclosures on the western side of Ville Evrart still remained for the night in the hands of the French; but in the morning the Saxons got possession of them also. The French made hardly any resistance in either of the two places. They had settled down comfortably for the night, and when the Saxons burst in upon them, were utterly panic-stricken. The prisoners said that everybody believed the Saxons had been lying in ambush in the cellars, and had rushed out on a given signal. The major protested against his capture with comical lugubriousness. "It was not gentlemanly warfare," he argued, "to take a man at advantage when he had his boots off and was thinking about supper. He understood there was some kind of tacit pact that there was to be no fighting after sundown, and of this the surprise was a reprehensible infraction." He could not, however, argue either his liberty back or the Saxons out of La Maison Blanche.

The chief loss of the day was sustained by the 1st Battalion of the Queen Elizabeth Regiment, old friends and good friends of mine. The battalion, which the reader may remember, had headed the attack which re-took Le Bourget on the 31st of October, had again terrible reason to remember that village. Of its remnant of officers left, five more went down on the 21st of December, 117 men were killed and wounded, and some sixty were taken prisoners. The chief, Hauptmann von Altrock, seemed to bear a charmed life. He had on the 31st of October fourteen bullet holes through his loose mackintosh, and not a single wound. On this sortie of the 21st December his officers fell around him, but he never was touched. A severe mishap befell a very dear friend of mine, young Freiherr von Brockdorff, a lieutenant in the Kaiser Franz Regiment, and the nephew of General von Moltke. He was shot through the chest

near the close of the action, while occupying, with a
portion of his battalion, an exposed line of barricades
closing in the village of Le Blanc Mesnil. A brighter lad
I never knew. He was a student at college, in Berlin,
when the war broke out, and joined the army at once.
He had won his commission and the iron cross. Now
the war had brought him something else. I saw him in
one of the Gonesse lazarettes the next day but one. He
was lying nearly comatose, and very weak. He believed
it was the splinter of a shell that drilled the jagged hole
in his side; but the surgeons were certain it must have
been a stray chassepot bullet, or one of the mitrailleuse
balls which the cuirassed train sent over. His elder
brother, a lieutenant in the Thuringian Uhlan regiment,
had been sent round by General von Moltke to see how
fared it with the lad. The tidings which he took back
were the reverse of good; but the fresh-constitutioned
youngster pulled through ultimately, and by this time is
no doubt a healthy veteran, proud of his scars. ·

Many circumstances occurred during this campaign,
tending to imperil the continued existence of the Geneva
Convention. One abuse of its stipulations occurred on
the night of this artillery duel. The French had collected their wounded in the village of Bondy—fearfully
wounded most of them must have been, for shell-splinters
do not make neat holes in men. Bondy being in a line
with the front of their position, and one of the keys to
it in the event of that position being assaulted, they had
run up the red cross, and doubtless there would have
been the cry of "brutes and barbarians" if that cross had
not been respected. It had not been fired on, but none
the less was it a flagrant abuse of the terms of the Convention, which stipulates expressly that no Feld Lazarette
shall be erected in a position too near the front or of

value in a military sense. Neither side adhered closely
to this definition, and the consequence was that each
had stories of asserted atrocities to narrate against the
other. Speaking of wounded, our losses at Clichy during
the day consisted of a field-postman's foot damaged, a
soldier severely wounded by a splinter and a *Krankenträger* cut in two by a shell. In all from 500 to 600 prisoners were captured, chiefly when Le Bourget was retaken
after its partial occupation by the French, headed by their
gallant corps of sailors. Several of these were among
the prisoners, but most had died as they had charged,
with an implacable fury that disdained quarter. On the
morning of the 22nd the French looked very threatening
for a time; they sent forward about a brigade of infantry
against Chelles, which coalesced with the troops yet remaining in Ville Evrart. But a hot fire from Noisy-le-
Grand and the opposite bank of the river between it and
Cournay was enough to cause a retreat with some precipitation.

The air was clearer on the 22nd December than on
any day within my recollection since I had come to the
scene of operations before Paris. From the advanced
forepost in the Forest of Bondy, from which I looked out
upon the beautiful panorama, Montmartre did not seem
two miles off. I could discern the sun-glints on the
windows of the Cathedral of St. Denis far round on the
right front. Bondy, directly in our front, seemed so
close that you might almost have sent a stone the length
of its church steeple, and yet the French were in it,
although they kept very quiet and out of sight. Still,
occasionally a few were to be seen prowling about, and
the smoke which hung in the air behind Bondy marked
their camp fires. On the left front was the abrupt rise
of the long ridge crowned by Forts Noisy and Rosny—

right between us and the latter was the lower blunt-
headed summit which we had learned to detest under
the name of Mont Avron. Noisy at intervals was wreathing itself in white smoke, which showed out in fine contrast against the blue horizon. As I watched it and the
whole picture spread out before me in its loveliness, it
was difficult indeed to realise that the foreground was
full of fighting men, and that the smoke was the signal
that a deadly missile had been sent hurtling through the
air. But here comes something to remind one that smiles
and peace are not synonymous. Carry him gently over
the rough ground—ah! I fear from the look of him he
will not long feel whether he is handled roughly or
tenderly. That shell you heard explode in the foreground
tore half his hip away as he stood leaning against the
wall; he is quivering with incipient tetanus, and the blood
is dripping on to the ground as it soaks through the
canvas of the stretcher. How tenderly Colonel Dietrich
speaks to the poor fellow. Ah, colonel, no wonder that
you sigh and turn away at that faint reply to your question—"Landwehrmann, Herr Oberst." In that word
"Landwehrmann," uttered by that poor bleeding soldier,
is a volume of meaning. It means a widow and orphans,
a shattered home, the breadwinner of a family struck
down. There were gay lads standing about, brisk young
regulars, and eighteen year old volunteers; but the shell
spared them and whizzed straight on to the man who
has mouths to fill. How one feels to hate war, as the
Krankenträger carries the man out of our sight!

The whole regiment—the 103rd—is on the foreposts
to watch the French, and there is a squeeze in the little
huts which have been run up to shelter the men. Strange
dog holes they are! The men are lying so close that it
seems in places they are in layers among the straw. The

officers have a separate place which is nearly as full as are the huts of the men. There is a stove, but it smokes; so does everybody in the place, and you cannot discern clearly the features of the man sitting opposite to you. Faintly it is apparent that he is eating sausage with a pocket knife. Yes, that is a tumblerful of neat rum which he is tendering you. It is so strong that it would bring the water to your eyes, only that the wood smoke has done so long ago. Somebody is asleep—at least vociferous snoring ought to be an indication of sleep. He must have tried very hard to sleep, else he could not have been successful in the din. But, then, remember that this regiment has been on this forepost duty without a break for three whole days, and your wonder will not be that one can sleep, but that the whole are not asleep.

Here comes the orderly with the welcome order that the relief is coming, and we shall get to dinner in Major von Schönberg's château. The good major is in great fettle. He has a wife in Saxonland, a lady for whom I have an intense respect, although I do not know her. I respect her for two reasons; first, because she is the major's wife; secondly, because she has had the thoughtfulness to send her husband—by the field post of course —a couple of barrels of Bairisch beer. These barrels are ever in the major's mind and on his tongue. He shouts, "Hurrah for the barrels!" when the orderly brings the tidings of the relief. While waiting for the relief I went with an officer into the batteries of siege guns, which had been surreptitiously preparing for days before with a single eye to the discomfiture of Mont Avron. The guns were already in their places,—fell tigers lurking in the jungle. Their ambush was complete. In front of the batteries stood intact a fringe of that close undergrowth which pervades everywhere the forest of Bondy,

intermingled with tall trees with bushy tops. There was
a substantiality and trimness about the works that spoke
of skill and method—the parapets solid and well defined, the covers for the supporting infantry elaborately
finished, even to the dainty flattening of the slope of the
banquette. The magazines were already about half full,
but not a shot was to be fired till the complements should
have been made up. No signs of exertion towards this
result were visible in the broad sunlight; but had I
waited by the batteries till twilight, I would have seen,
coming slowly rumbling through the glades of the forest,
long trains of carts driven by peasants escorted by cavalry,
and each loaded up with ammunition-boxes. There was
a quiet power about the whole scene which was very im-
pressive.

The relief arrived, we returned to the château, and
spent a delightful evening. The beer turned out per-
fection. There was a lack of beds in the château, which,
however, as regarded myself was supplemented with
characteristic Saxon courtesy. A captain gave up to me
his bed, and slept himself on the straw on the floor.
About four in the morning I was awakened by a shake
on the shoulder. As, half awake, I looked up, there
stood over me, looming very large, an Uhlan, with his
throat wrapt up in many and preternaturally-complicated
folds of comforter. He handed me a paper, and shoved
a candle under my nose. What could the man mean?
Was this an order for my immediate execution, or had
that rich 93rd cousin died and left me his heir? I
sleepily read over the paper, and found it was an order
to turn out at once and march my company, with the
rest of the brigade, to the neighbourhood of Sevran.
Where was my company? Who had a right to order
me—a free-born British Christian, and a neutral—thus

peremptorily to turn out in so cold a morning?   All at
once I remembered I was in the captain's bed, and the
sagacious idea occurred to me that the order must be
intended for him.   So it turned out, and the captain did
the same.   There was a general turn out in the early
morning of the 23rd.   The 2nd brigade of the 23rd
division consists of the 102nd and 103rd Regiments, and
there being, it seemed, symptoms that the restless French
contemplated another attack on Le Bourget, this brigade
was ordered to march to Sevran, to stand there in reserve
in case they should be wanted.   On we went, through
the fiercely cold morning air—the breaths freezing into
spangles on the beards, and little icicles forming on the
tips of the moustaches.   Everything seemed quiet.   In
Livry we met the Saxon Schützen Regiment going on to
strengthen the Bondy foreposts.   How well their black
plumes looked in the gray light of the early morning.
Livry save for them was empty.   A couple of forlorn
turkeys, ready plucked for Christmas, hung mournfully in
a marketender's window.   The customers had gone away,
and might never come back.   When the brigade reached
the halting ground all was still quiet.   There was nothing
to be seen, and therefore I rode forward through Sevran
and Aulnay.   Between these villages the emplacements
for the field guns were all appropriately occupied, and
the gunners stood at their posts; no infantry was to be
seen.   But as soon as I cleared Aulnay and got up the
gentle rise on the top of which runs the great Lille road,
which passes through Le Bourget, it was apparent how
thorough were the preparations.   There were in position
six or eight batteries of artillery all along the rear of the
inundations, and on the slope rising behind Le Blanc
Mesnil and Pont Iblon.   Farther back stood other battalions in reserve.   The great road itself was clear; I

12*

could see along it right into Le Bourget, a mile and a
half to the front.   But right and left of it stood the battalions of infantry, eleven of them, the whole of the 2nd
division of the Guards.   Here stood the pink and pride
of the Prussian army—the Kaiser Franz, Kaiser Alexander,
Königin Elizabeth, and Königin Augusta regiments.   The
Elizabeths had one battalion away out to the front there,
holding Le Bourget, and have only two battalions on the
ground here.   The artillery consisted of that belonging
to the 2nd division, and also of the artillery division of
the Guard Army Corps.   At the cross-roads, as I rode
on, there met me a quaint little figure with a knot of
officers behind him.   His head seemed literally "in a
bag," one could see nothing but a pair of keen eyes and
a pair of white moustaches.   Don't laugh at the funny-
looking old man; you see before you a soldier than whom
there is not a gallanter in all the German hosts; one
who, though a general, ever lusts to be in the thick of
the fray, fighting with his own good sword.   The owner
of the white moustache is General von Budritzki, the
Commander of the 2nd Division of the Guards, the
general with whom rested the dispositions of the day.
He told me, as I halted for a gossip with his staff, that
he *feared* there would be no fighting to-day.   It was
clear he was longing for a brush with the troops who
gave him so much trouble on the 31st of October, when
it fell to him to retake Le Bourget.   That same Le
Bourget—out to the front on the farther side of the inundation—seemed to stand strangely isolated.   If the
Queen Elizabeths occupying it were looking behind—a
custom they were not addicted to—it must have had a
tendency to make them nervous that there was nothing
in the way of supports all the way back to Pont Iblon.
But behind Pont Iblon there were supports enough in all

conscience.   Depend on it, the Elizabeths would stick to
Le Bourget as long as they could, and if they had to
fall back they would only entice the French forward into
the half-burnt, half-shattered man-trap. A French occupation of Le Bourget, always temporary, simply meant so
many French prisoners.

It was now one o'clock, and looking across towards
Drancy, I could see no move on the part of the French,
whose fires were smoking in front of Baubigny.   Behind
us, in Pont Iblon, there stood the Guards, waiting in the
cold for whatever might turn up. It struck me, for my
own part, that nothing would turn up, and that we should
all go home to dinner. I knew Major von Schönberg
was thinking of the beer again as he stood in that breezy
meadow beside Sevran.

My anticipations of a quiet afternoon and a peaceable
return to dinner were not realised. I was the solitary
occupant of the officers' casino in Gonesse, when Aubervilliers fired a gun which seemed to be a signal, and
a furious cannonade almost at once began. Le Bourget
—poor battered Le Bourget—with my friends of the
Queen Elizabeth Regiment, was again in receipt of all
the punishment. Instead of returning to my post of the
morning at Sevran, which was ineligible as a view point,
I made for the high ground above Bonneuil, from which
the whole scene lay spread before me like a map, in the
clear afternoon air. In a long column, with its left resting
on a clump of houses, a little in front of la Courneuve,
right athwart the plain behind Drancy, and on as far as
Baubigny—farther, perhaps, only I could not see it—
stood the French infantry. There must have been 30,000
of them at least.   On the left flank of the infantry,
in front of la Courneuve, were two batteries of field
artillery continually firing; there was another near the

farm of Groslay, and at least two more in front of the
village of Drancy itself. Then the forts were all hard at
work from du Nord away in the north, the lunette of
Stains, its covered way running across the inundation,
de l'Est flashing out its discharges so close to the water's
edge that the smoke might have been taken for jets of
steam—Aubervilliers, the grey and grim, squatting there
like a gigantic toad in the middle of the green plain—
and Romainville on the farther brink of the canal; while
the puff and curl of smoke which ever and anon hung
round the lofty summit of Noisy, far away on the top
of the ridge, and standing bluffly up against the horizon,
told that again to-day Clichy was experiencing its tender
mercies. But this was the only diversion; everything else
concentrated itself doggedly on Le Bourget, if I except
Mont Valérien, which away far to the right in the eye
of the declining sun had also his mantle of white smoke
about his shoulders, betokening annoyance to St. Cloud
or Bougival. La Briche alone was quiet, lying there by
the north bank of the Seine, looking as sulky as might
be, as if out of temper at being debarred from joining
in the mêlée. And a right boisterous mêlée it was, yet
for the most part one-sided. The Guards' field artillery
between Gonesse and Aulnay was profoundly silent; I
suppose the French infantry were beyond range, and the
forts, of course, yet more so. On the tract between
Aulnay and Sevran the batteries of the 12th Army Corps
were very brisk, firing steadily across into Drancy and
the line toward Bondy, but making comparatively a poor
show in comparison with the profuse fire of the French
bursting out from so many points simultaneously. I
was almost certain that I heard the crashing of the
shells into Le Bourget; every moment I saw the flash
and smoke of their explosion. With hardly an exception,

every gun had the range well, and how it was possible
for anything to live in the place passed my comprehension. But certain it is that there was in it von Altrock's
battalion of the Queen Elizabeths, in the cellars it might
be, or behind the thick walls, but there sure enough,
as the French infantry would have found out had they
ventured on the attack. Several times it seemed as if
this was coming. Once three battalions threw themselves into as many columns—just to the right of la
Courneuve, and made a start. I could see the officers
out in the front. There was one man on a white horse
—it might have been Ducrot himself—who was ubiquitous, now cantering right out beyond everything, now
wheeling and halting, as if making a speech to encourage
the advance. They came on very steadily for about a
quarter of a mile, then they slowed, and finally halted.
The officer on the white horse seemed to go frantic; he
dashed hither and thither with desperate energy. Once
or twice he rode right into one battalion, then came
scouring round the rear, no doubt to stay the tailing
off. But all was of no use. He could not get his fellows'
steam up. A few shells came flying over Le Bourget and
burst under their noses. There was one sharp bicker of
musketry out from behind a barricade by Le Bourget
railway station. That was von Altrock giving tongue,
and when the Queen Elizabeths barked they also bit.
The battalions went about, the white horseman bringing
up the rear at a slow walk, as if marching to the funeral
of his honour; and they blended again with the long
fixed line. At a later hour I saw less distinctly another
threatened assault from Drancy, but it made no head,
and I could not distinguish its strength or character.

How brisk the French were everywhere behind this
long line of theirs! The whole plain between la Cour-

neuve and Baubigny was alive. I could distinctly see the red-cross flag flying on the ambulances as they stood by Maison des Ponceaux, in the southern rear of la Courneuve. The Soissons Railway line was extensively utilised. Half a dozen locomotives were puffing on it at once, each drawing a train of three or four carriages. When the train got to the end of its tether, about 500 yards beyond la Courneuve, it halted, and disembarked its freight—always soldiers. Reinforcements kept being drafted up till the very close—a circumstance auguring ill for peace the morrow. At the improvised railway terminus stood fast a locomotive, with a couple of carriages in front of it—no doubt those famous pieces of workmanship of Cail's, the cuirassed mitrailleuse waggons. They were, however, never called into action to-day. I never saw the locomotive move, but it had its steam up.

Riding along the front to the edge of the terrace of Montmorency, I came on the artillery officers stationed here, looking out on the scene through a huge telescope—a very powerful instrument. Bending it across to Montmartre, I could distinctly see the Parisians packed in dense masses on and around the top of the hill. Behind the round column of Solferino, now used as an observatory, there stood the largest group—men, women, and children. I wonder what they thought of the scene, such a contrast to scenes Parisians wot of which these once-quiet villages in the foreground had seen. By four o'clock the fire was burning out; only the embers still smouldered in the shape of a sullen gun from De l'Est or Aubervilliers. The smoke from our artillery away at Sevran was still banking up in large clouds, and we could just hear the sharp cracks of the field pieces. By five the forts had left off, and although the field batteries

in front of la Courneuve brightened up again, it was but
a momentary spurt—the usual "last word."   Before I
turned my horse's head towards Margency, the watch
fires were burning up brightly in the crisp darkness of
the frosty night, and all was quiet.   My last view of
Montmartre as I looked back going down the slope
showed me the electric light flashing out from it across
the plain in a great weird streak.

In describing, a few pages back, the manner in which
the Germans had thrown up works across the naturally
weak tract which lies on either side the Canal d'Ourcq,
and northward to Gonesse, I expressed a conviction that
they had made this section strong enough to turn any
French force that might assail it.   The events of the 21st
and the 22nd December fully proved the correctness of
the first anticipation, and inspired me with all the fuller
confidence that any future effort must share the issue of
those operations.   Why, so far from carrying the "entrenched camp," the French had not been able to take
and hold Le Bourget, its mere incidental advance post.

Yet another *dies iræ* was the 24th.   The French
seemed determined on fighting it out on this same Le
Bourget line even to the bitter end.   What the measure-
ment of bitterness that end might represent it was impossible then to foretell; surely the intermediate stages
must have been bitter enough for them, in bloody
bivouacs, with the temperature twelve degrees below
freezing point.   I left them on the previous afternoon
still standing in position there athwart the plain from la
Courneuve to Bondy, with the setting sun on their backs,
and Le Bourget the untaken in their front, the guns of
the forts still hot from hurling the projectiles high over
the heads of the immobile soldiery.   The evening lapsed
into the long hours, and the lull still continued, and one

thought, for sure, the guns would at least be given a few
hours to cool. But at midnight just as, after three rough
and terrible nights, I was preparing to turn in between
the luxury of a pair of sheets, the dreadful din commenced again. There was no roll of proviant columns
or artillery tumbrils to deaden it—every bomb smote the
ear as it were with a blow. Then, as the gunners warmed
to their work, the separate and individual booms merged
in a concatenation of hellish noise. I can sleep through
most things; but I could not sleep through the fierce
sound-clashing of this night, hard as I tried. There
was nothing for it but to lie awake till one got nervous
—and cannon fire produces inevitably this result in the
strongest nerved—or to get up and go and watch the
scene. Choosing the latter alternative, I soon found myself in the emplacement on front of Montmorency, where,
in the cold, there stood a couple of artillery officers,
watching the scene professionally. It was, indeed, a
strikingly beautiful scene, if one could have eliminated
from it its deadly nature. The night was so black that
you almost fancied you could cut the solid darkness
with a blow of your stick. From out the pitchiness there
flashed the straight jets of fire, widening out like the
mouth of a trumpet. Then away through the air went
the projectile, recalling the memories of the old nursery
alphabet, "C was a comet, with a fiery tail." Perhaps
it burst in mid-air, as if it had brained itself on one of
the rocks forming the foundation of heaven. Then the
living fire flew in coruscations in all directions, the sparks
gradually growing dull as the principle of specific gravity
asserted itself. Or the bolt after its flight struck the
ground, and striking burst, sending into the air an upward centrifugal illumination, as if it had stabbed the
subterranean reservoir of a volcano. On the intermediate

ground was the long serrated and irregular line of the
French watch fires. We could see them one after another burn red and dull as the fuel got low, and then
flash up with long-streaked tongues of flame as the
watchers heaped on the wood. Hour after hour we
gazed at the strangely weird scene, heedless that the
bitter frost caught the breath on beards and moustaches,
and matted them with ice tangles. There was a resist-
less fascination in the scene, under the spell of which
one forgot even to smoke. But towards five o'clock,
through the air troubled with the bellow of the firing,
one could detect another sound—the rumble of artillery
wheels in the rear. The Fourth Army Corps was contributing its quota to the resistance of the expected on-
slaught. Six batteries were on the road from Franconville
to Gonesse, on the ground beyond which they would
be in position before the darkness lifted. Then silent
Montmorency burst out into life and candlelight. A
brigade of the 7th Division was under orders to back up
the sturdy Guardsmen, and the men of Anhalt-Dessau,
the square-built soldiers of the Ludwig-Franz regiment
—the 93rd of the North German line—were turning out
of château and cabin, of desolated restaurant and apartments, no longer *meublés*, and heading for the front.
Then it was time for me to go back to Margency, to get
to horse; for the Crown Prince and his staff were bound
for Gonesse before daybreak, and there were all the
symptoms of a wild day's work.

The explanation of the persistence of the French in
their efforts on this face was believed by the staff to lie
in this—that they had received intelligence of the Army
of the North having made some head, and that they were
battling on ever in the expectation of hearing its answering cannon from the woods of Chantilly or the slopes of

Dammartin. They did not know what we knew, how
the day before Manteuffel, the grim, the curt, the astute
diplomatist and able general, had sent Faidherbe reeling
back with a facer, from which it would take him some
time to recover. But who could help honouring them
for their pertinacious endurance—that passive valour not
reckoned an attribute of the French character in the
traditional estimate? Just think, British reader, as you
read this with feet in slippers in a cosy arm-chair, with a
bright coal fire curling the edges of the boards of the
volume, what it must have been to lie on the ground,
badly clad, for three, aye four nights, with the glass
several degrees below freezing-point! To do this at
night, and to stand all day with faces to the foe! I protest
I was filled with admiration, respect, and heartfelt compassion for the men whom I saw before me doing this
—doing it too, it might be, on scanty rations, and without the spur and the backbone which the prestige of
conquest ever gives. Those men out in the plain there
must have been soldiers, and they must have had men
to lead them who were worthy to command troops that
could suffer privations so great. Not indeed soldiers in
the highest sense of the word, since they manifested
evident reluctance to come on to close quarters; but one
knew not the circumstances under which they seemed to
hang back, and if one had been among them he might
have found their *élan* on a par with their endurance.

Gonesse was reached by eight o'clock, just as the
sun rose. Again the Guardsmen of the 2nd Division
were out waiting for the foe that never came, gallant old
Budritzki impatiently pulling his white moustache as he
stamped up and down the road. The whole line was
"alarmed," that is, ready to turn out and fight in anything but alarm. On the further side were the Royal

Saxons of the 12th Corps in reserve; on the hither side
the Prussian-Province Saxons of the 4th Corps, also in
reserve.   The forts thundered continuously—hapless Le
Bourget still their target.   Major Kuene, of the Staff, had
been in that village the day before, to know how it fared
with its garrison of Guards, and he told me that in all
his experience he had never seen anything to give him
power to realize that such a rain of shells was possible.
Yet the case of Le Bourget only bears out all previous
experience regarding the comparatively little harm to life
and limb which a shelling, however severe, causes to a
place in which there are houses of tolerably strong construction.   The Guards had sustained no great loss—less
than they would have done in half an hour's skirmish in
the open.

Hour after hour passed monotonously as we stood
listening to the artillery fire.   It would only have been
wasting ammunition to attempt a reply with field guns;
for the French infantry stood out of range, and concentrated their fire on Gonesse, considerably to our front;
their artillery had no occasion to come so far forward as
to give the Germans a chance of silencing it, while on
the other hand had the latter been pushed forward, it
would have to no purpose come within the range of the
heavy metal of the forts.   So there was nothing to do
but stand watching the pounding of Le Bourget, and a
terrible pounding that La Haye Sainte of our position
got.   But it became evident by one o'clock that the
French contemplated no active forward movement, and
the Crown Prince took the homeward road to Margency.
The artillery and infantry of the 4th Army Corps followed him, leaving the Guards to the enjoyment of the
Christmas-eve concert alone.   In very deep bass that
concert still continued long after the Ludwig-Franz men

were cooking their Erbswurst in their billets in Montmorency.   It was still making the air pulsate when I left
the position there, as the shadows of the twilight were
coming down.   But there were signs that Christmas-day
—the day sacred to associations of peace on earth and
goodwill among men — was not to have its hallowed
character desecrated by bloodshed.   True, instead of the
chimes of the bells that you heard in merry England, we
might hear the hoarse-throated roar of the cannon from
Du Nord and De l'Est.   True, instead of wreaths of
mistletoe, we might have wreaths of white smoke, beautiful, indeed, to look at against the clear blue sky, but the
evil sign, nevertheless, of a terrible missile having been
sent out into space; but there would to all appearance
be no fighting.   The French infantry, so far as I could
judge, were breaking up their bivouacs, and falling back.
The railway trains were brisk as ever in the afternoon,
but they were, as it seemed, going out empty, and coming
in full.   Trochu was giving his poor fellows a chance to
thaw—they must have been frozen stiff after so much
exposure.

    It was Christmas morning.   Where shall we dine?   I
know where I should have liked to dine; but the obstinate Parisians came between one and "the old folks
at home," and the young ones as well.   I had no need
to complain of want of Christmas invitations; it was in
their very number that the bewilderment lay.   I refrain
from more than an allusion to one kind invitation from.
one who was ever kind.   Then there was that genial one
from compatriots in Versailles.   Good old Dr. Tegener,
of the Ecouen Hospital, had sent round another with a
postscript to the note in the shape of the single word
"Punch."   Some merry lads in Epinay wished me to go
down there, and be jovial under the shadow of La Briche;

a battery of artillery would be glad of my company—at
least they said so—at Napoléon-St.-Leu; a battalion of
Würtembergers in Champs had half booked me more
than a fortnight ago; and the list ended with the genial
and cordial invitation of good Major von Schönberg, and
his officers of the 2nd Battalion of the 103rd Saxon Regiment. It was the battalion's turn on Christmas night
for duty on certain far outlying foreposts in front of the
village of Raincy. The officers I knew to be right hearty
fellows; then there was Frau Majorin's Bavarian Beer (per
Feldpost). Yes, I said done and done again with the
major. ·It was a long ride, with the temperature, too,
below freezing point, and things over on the French side
were not altogether tranquil, but the way I was going
would bring me to the right spot, if that sluggish firing
from the forts should warm up and cover a sortie; and
there was something in all likelihood to be got by a
gossip at the officers' casino in Gonesse. The latter anticipation was realized even better than usual.

Among the men of the Queen Elizabeth taken prisoners in Le Bourget on the 21st, was an ambulance
assistant, whom the French had sent back the next day,
in terms of the Geneva Convention, and, having been
sent for by his captain to the casino, he gave me some
interesting details of what he saw during his brief captivity. The prisoners were taken into St. Denis, and
temporarily placed in a house with sentries over them.
.They were treated with the greatest humanity, amply
supplied with coffee, sugar, wine, and bread. There was
also given them abundance of flesh, but it was candidly
owned that the meat was horseflesh. The French officers
came among the Prussian prisoners, and asked them with
great solicitude whether they had any cigars. An exchange was effected, the Germans giving cigars for cognac,

of which there seemed to be great plenty. A party of ladies, dressed with the utmost elegance, came also to see the prisoners, and bound also, besides the gratification of their curiosity, on an acquisitive errand. "Had Messieurs les Prussiens any bacon in their knapsacks?" If so, the ladies would be glad to buy it of them. Only two fellows had any, and they gallantly made a present of it to the fair inquirers, who became very complimentary then as to the personal appearance of the captives. "What great, huge fine men these Prussians are to be sure," remarked one lady. "Yes, and just compare them with our little morsels of fellows," added another, pointing to the five feet nothing sentry who was on duty over the stalwart Guardsmen. Not unnaturally, as I think, the "little morsel" in question felt aggrieved at this observation, and his irritation took the form of turning the ladies out. My informant saw nothing of any privations during his sojourn in St. Denis; but then he was there only for a few hours, and owned his opportunities had not been great.

In the officers' casino there was sitting a dragoon officer who had come thither on an errand worth mentioning to English readers. His men, quartered in a village a considerable distance to the rear, had heard that there was in Gonesse a colporteur of the English Bible Society with his waggon, and they had asked the officer to come and ask the colporteur either to visit or to part with a few parcels of his tracts. I should have mentioned that on the road between Gonesse and Aulnay, on the morning of the 23rd, a road which two hours after was a very via dolorosa of exploding shells, I met this same colporteur coolly jogging forward with intent to distribute his wares among the battalions standing on the slope there waiting for the battle to commence. "It was a good time," according to the expressed views of this simple, brave Christian man, "for the men to read good words when they were standing there with nothing to do, and with the shadow of death hanging over them." There are few who will disagree with him, but there are not many who would have proceeded so practically to give effect to his convictions. I regret much that I lost the card on which I had written down the name of this brave colporteur, but he came from Carlsruhe, he told me.

Here is a story of valour of another kind, but not of a higher character. In the 1st battalion of the Queen Elizabeths there was a boy-lieutenant, with a swarthy face and bright black eyes, whose name was von Schramm. When I knew him he could not have been more than eighteen: had he been an English lad, he would have been at Eton. A German lad, he had done with the schools, passed his examinations, got his commission, won the iron cross, and was the adjutant of his battalion. When Major von Altrock (Le Bourget, if it had made bullet holes in his mantle, had brought him, too, a step in rank)—when Major von Altrock led his battalion into Le Bourget, on the 20th, little von Schramm was left behind sick in Aulnay. The gun fire on the 21st knocked the sickness out of him; his regiment was fighting, and he not there. He jumped on his horse, crossed the inundation at Le Blanc Mesnil, and rode into Le Bourget athwart the artillery fire from Drancy. The Queen Elizabeths, however, were already driven far down the street; and he, striking the village street half way up, found himself in the crowd of the Frenchmen. To leap from his horse and dash into a house was the work of an instant—if he could get out at the back door he might yet escape. But there was no back door—the pursuers were

hot on his heels, and von Schramm was a prisoner. His
captors asked him for his parole, but he refused to give
it, and they proceeded to conduct him towards St. Denis
—a convoy of two officers and two men. In going
through the park of Le Bourget, a beautiful spot in which
there is a lake and many thickets, the musketry fire from
the retreating guardsmen came very close and fast. The
officer who carried von Schramm's sword was shot, and
fell. Von Schramm made a dash at his own sword, got
his hand inside the hilt, cut down the other officer, took
to the water like a duck, dodged the bullets of the
soldiers as he swam across, and finally joined his regiment after all—rather damp it is true, as a man will be
who takes to swimming with his clothes on, but extremely
jolly. And the best of it was that the ducking cured
his sickness. At least one was entitled, I think, to say
so after having seen him demolish a massive dinner and
two bottles of beer.

It is a long weary stretch from Gonesse to Aulnay.
There is no intervening village, and not a single house
by the wayside. It was a curious proof of that masterly
consciousness of ability to concentrate, and absence of
fussy demonstration on the part of the Germans, that not
a single soldier nor a single gun was visible on this expanse on which the day before there had stood an army.
The men were in the villages on the alert, it is true, and
ready for action at a moment's notice; but they were not
needlessly brought from under cover.

I arrive at the château in Clichy, and put up my horse
there, going out to the advanced foreposts before the day
fades. As I reach the garden opening into the forest, a
discouraging sight meets the eye. Four soldiers are carrying on their shoulders a motionless form, lying on a
stretcher and covered with a bloody blanket. "Wounded?"

The solemn "Dead" comes from the mouth of the accompanying under-officer. It is a corpse they are carrying up into the village. This was Private Jeskow's last Christmas morning. He was making his coffee in a house behind outpost Nr. 8, when a shell burst under the window. His sergeant told him he was in dangerous quarters, but the coffee was near the boil. Before it boiled, another shell had come and burst in the room; a fragment struck Jeskow in the back, and killed him.

Forward down a slope through a solitary wood of dense underwood, mingled with goodly trees. On the pathway are numerous craters of shells. There is a little rise, and then I emerge on to a belt of heathy clearing in the wood. Everywhere the wood has been full of barricades, of *chevaux de frise* of all kinds of appliances for arresting an enemy. On this cleared belt are works of greater pretension—parallels, entrenchments, strong stockades, trenches, enfiladed approaches, and what not. A few soldiers were visible about it. There are more among the huts to the right. What a glorious sky is that which lies over the faint gossamer-like smoke of Paris. The sun is going down, not in human blood this Christmas afternoon, but in blood-like hues of his own creation. All the firmament is rippled in crimson wavelets, and the light comes ruddy on the earth as if it fell through stained-glass windows. Five minutes brings one across the clearing into more scrub, and then into a village of châteaux nestling in the scrub. Forest, clearance, and village all reminded me very much of the neighbourhood of Chislehurst in Kent. There is the same ruggedness, and still the same appearance of vicinity to the metropolis in the physical aspect of the scene. On the cross-roads, in the centre of this collection of villages, I meet the officers in command of the two battalions waiting to be relieved. The men are massed behind the walls. They are sauntering up and down on the exposed road. Any news? None. Perhaps a little. At ten o'clock this morning two French brigades had deployed in parade order before Bondy in two long lines. Then it seemed as if the troops marched past a general and formed a hollow square, in which they stood for nearly an hour, after which one brigade went back to quarters, while the other marched on to the foreposts. It was conjectured that a religious service was being performed while the troops stood there in hollow square. If so, Du Nord and De l'Est furnished the responses, for they were firing at that hour. About the same hour three brigades were visible, marching in the front of Aubervilliers, and the Observatory officer reported that he had seen two naval batteries arrive by train at Bondy, and immediately push forward, as if to take up position. This would seem to argue that there were to be heavy batteries so near as Bondy, which must, it seemed, in the event of their not being shut up by our still, grim, silent friends that sulked behind the parapets in our rear, have the inevitable result of widening the circle of our forepost environment.

Tramp, tramp, tramp, here comes the 103rd. There is the major in front talking earnestly with the field-officer he is going to relieve. Here comes Hammerstein, unrecognisable by reason of wraps, and only to be discerned and greeted by his voice. He has got on a pair of fur boots, that seem a legacy from an Esquimaux, and here is his big brother-in-law, Kirchbach, and von Zanthier, and the whole lot of them. Now comes the relieving of the foreposts—a ticklish duty, for the relief must be in full possession before the relieved dare to come out. As each company goes on to its post, it is met by a trusty non-commissioned officer of the depart-

ing outpost, who acts as its cicerone. Then the sergeant
and the lieutenant go out and change the sentries, and,
with a cheery "Good night," off stumps the "old guard."
Glad enough to go, beyond doubt. The duty here just
now is one night on, one night off; but when, as has
occurred for the last three days, the day and night "off"
are spent standing on the alert, there is not much relaxation. Two battalions, instead of one, are now detailed
for the outposts, owing to the necessity for dry-nursing
in this way the babes in the wood, who have not yet
begun to squall; and this makes the duty all the harder.

The relieving duty over, we reach our home for the
night out beyond the villas. Let me describe it. It is
a long, low wooden hut, such as you may see squatters
and gipsies occupying on the debateable ground between
Peckham, Lewisham, and Nunhead Cemetery. Its loftiest
part is about six feet high, the roof sloping till, at the
back, the height is about four feet. The erection is
wholly of wood—chiefly, as it appears, of château doors.
There is one window in the place; it is sashed and taste-
fully curtained. There is a wooden floor. One—the lower-
roofed side of the room—is lined with spring mattresses,
that have evidently also come out of the châteaux. On
the walls are pictures—aye, and mirrors—to be ascribed
to the same origin; and between the window and the
beds is a range of good massive mahogany tables, that
were not made by the pioneers. The chairs are a study.
They are here of all styles. The fauteuil, the ottoman,
the American rocking-chair, the high straight-backed
Elizabethan, the Louis Quatorze settee, and the humble
wicker-bottom. There is a pleasant fire burning in the
little stove, and you cannot well imagine how cheerful,
with the bright lamp burning and the sparkle of the fire,
the little nest looked—if you could only forget that the

French were not 1000 yards off, and that you were in so
ludicrously easy range of their guns.

But we did forget these facts somehow. The quarters
were those of a Hauptmann, he in whose charge was the
uttermost forepost. But by common consent the officers
from the other positions further back—the *repli*, where
the major had his post, and the captains from the right
and left rear, came dropping in to eat their Christmas
dinner with the English guest and comrade. The kitchen
was a part of the hut partitioned off, and we had the
battalion cook there—a resplendent being in a white cap
and apron. Before dinner he entered in state and lit the
candles on the Christmas tree, a goodly sprout, from
every bough of which dangled cakes and comfits. The
cloth—we had a cloth, never mind about its colour—was
laid, the plates and wine were warmed, and we drew
around the social board. I am in a position to present
the reader with the Christmas menu of the 2nd battalion
of the 103rd Regiment on the foreposts: Soup—Liebig's
extract. Fish—sardines, caviare. Entrées—goose sausage,
ham sausage, a variety of undistinguishable sausage.
Pièces de résistance—boiled beef and maccaroni, roast
mutton, and potato-salad. Divertissements—Schinken,
compot of pears, ditto of apples, preserved sour-krout.
Cheese, fresh butter, fruit, nuts, biscuits, tarts, &c. The
potables were as follows:—One barrel of Frau Majorin's
beer still· to the good, the other a dead marine; very
good red wine, champagne iced—a little too much in
fact. The caterer had stuck the bottles outside on his
first arrival, and it seemed as if the wine had frozen in a
solid mass. When it came to be poured out, it would
not run. A proposition was made that the bottles should
be broken, a hatchet fetched, and a portion of champagne-
ice be served out to each person; but an officer of an

inquiring turn of mind, who had been pricking the ice on the surface of one bottle with a skewer, found that it was only about half an inch thick, and that below there lay a limpid pint of liquid champagne. We pricked all the bottles with the skewer, and got on beautifully.

After dinner there were but two toasts: One was "The King of Saxony;" the other "Frau Majorin von Schönberg." Both were drunk with enthusiasm; the latter—in her beer—with positive effusion. Then we got to song-singing. A Degenfähnrich came to the front in this line—the young Baron von Zehmen. Instrumental accompaniments were forbidden on account of the proximity of the enemy, but the choruses were loud enough to raise the dead, let alone the Frenchmen. Let me give a list of a few of the songs; they deserve popularity in England.

> "Stehe ich in finsterer Mitternacht."
> (Standing in the dark night.)
>
> "Wer will unter die Soldaten?"
> (Who'll be a soldier?)

The beautiful and plaintive

> "I hatte einen Cameraden
> Einen besseren findest du nicht."
>
> (I had a comrade,
> A better one ne'er you'd find.)

I seem to have a hazy notion that somebody tried "Bonny Dundee," and failed ignominiously.

About ten o'clock a deserter was brought in—a decidedly unfavourable specimen of the French line. He was very dirty, and he had no buttons anywhere—rather a common want I have noticed with French soldiers. He said he was hungry and thirsty. The major gave him something to eat and the run of a bottle of brandy, while we listened to the rascal's lies. When he had finished

his rigmarole, which consisted of all sorts of canards, it
was too late discovered that he was as drunk as David's
sow.   He insisted on singing the Marseillaise, and when
that was done, roared *"A bas les Prussiens!"*   What was
to be done with the wretch?   If he were turned out of
doors he would go to sleep in the ditch, and freeze so
hard before morning that you could chip pieces off him.
Ultimately he was relegated to the stable by the *repli*,
where stood the battalion horses, and was borne away
shoulder high, roaring *Vive la république!*

Enter Under-officer Schultz, wooden as ever, a little
woodener perhaps on account of the hard frost.   Under-
officer Schultz came to read the orders.   Ordinarily he
would have read them dry and gone away dry, but this
was Christmas time, and kindliness prompted the wetting
of Under-officer Schultz's throat.   "Champagne, red wine,
or cognac, Schultz?"   "Cognac, Herr Hauptmann," came
woodenly from the lips of Schultz.   Schultz bolted a big
glass of cognac, and then read the orders.   I think the
cognac gave him unction to roll out sonorously the sentences of King Wilhelm's address to his troops, which was
in the orders for the night.   Then he went about with a
wooden click of his heels, and disappeared.

Continually there was a circulation of officers as we
sat by the board in the wooden house.   The major and
myself were the only sedentaries.   Duty called, and men
obeyed it.   About midnight Hauptmann von Zanthier rose
and buckled on his sword.   He was going round with
the patrol; would I go with him?   Certainly.   There were
the officer, three men, and myself.   Out we went into
the brushwood beyond any of our posts.   There were the
French outposts—not 500 yards off.   We could see the
fires lit by the watches.   Could a neutral go across and
have a chat with them?   Well, not exactly; there were

two or three obstacles. Here is a noise in the brush-wood; somebody is coming down the path; there are three men. A voice says, "*Venez, Messieurs!*" It is a French patrol, and the officer thinks our patrol is French too. Von Zanthier and his men accept the invitation. I stand fast. Presently he comes back with three prisoners —a Mobile officer and two men. The officer is a thorough gentleman. On our way back to the Feldwacht he has an immense deal to say, *de omnibus rebus et quibusdam aliis*. When we get back we find that that wonderful man in the white cap has made egg-flip for us. The Mobile officer joins us heartily in a caulker, and does not need to be pressed to take a little supper. He is a jewel of a man. He tells me he once had a moor in Scotland. He laughs at the notion of Paris capitulating. The Mobiles alone are capable of averting that fate. They certainly are not very brilliant specimens, the two he has met with; but then, as he says, "they were selected promiscuously." More egg-flip, and then the spring mattresses.

The bombardment of Mont Avron—that event which had for days past formed the chief topic of discussion and for anticipation—commenced on the morning of the 27th of December. For many nights before, indeed ever since the change of policy which I noted as having taken place immediately after the great sortie at Champigny and Villiers, the woods which covered the German advanced positions before Montfermeil and Clichy had been full of life. First, working parties toiled in the dark, or by moonlight; then came the heavy roll of the siege artillery, and of the tumbrels weighted with the heavy ammunition. About half the guns arrived direct by the Soissons Railway to the last available station on the foreposts, and were almost immediately placed in position on the batteries. The rest came *viâ* Lagny, and were des-

tined for the more southerly batteries. Most of the guns
were from Spandau, and had already done more or less
service in the sieges of Strassburg, Toul, La Fère, and
Soissons. The batteries began on the south on the
further side of the Marne in close proximity to Noisy-le-
Grand. There was a gap across the valley of Chelles,
but they began again in front where the height of Montfermeil juts out into the plain, and continued at intervals
with a slight sweep, of which the convexity was toward
Avron, further to the north than, and in front of, the village of Raincy. There were in all thirteen batteries, but
only 76 instead of 78 guns, one of the batteries at Maison
Guyot, before Montfermeil, being two guns short of its
complement. Batteries, Nos. 1, 2, 3, and 4 (24 guns in
all), were in front of Raincy; batteries, Nos. 5, 6, 7, and
8 (22 guns in all), were at Maison Guyot, above Gagny,
and in front of Montfermeil; batteries, 9, and 10 (12 guns),
were above the bridge at Cournay on the south side; and
batteries, 11, 12, 13 (18 guns), were on the low bluffs,
at Noisy-le-Grand. Ten of the batteries consisted of
Krupp's steel 24-pounders; the other three were armed
with 12-pounder rifled cannon, adapted from smooth
bores. As must be almost universally known by this time,
the poundage of the German guns refers only to round
shot, not a single specimen of which I saw round Paris.
All the guns threw shells of a weight more than double
their nominal capacity, the relative proportion being, I
believe, as 6 to 14. Thus, the piece known as a 24-
pounder threw a shell of about 56 pounds weight. I do
not trouble the reader with the fractional figures, involved
in a calculation allowing for the trivial difference between
the German and the English pound. The French on
their part had been working hard on and around Avron
ever since the 2nd: indeed before it. It was understood

that in all, standing opposite the German batteries, and in a position to reply to them, there were about 60 cannon, exclusive, of course, of those on the forts.   These were chiefly, if not altogether, naval guns, of recent construction and considerable calibre—say 64-pounders.   A few were heavier.   The German batteries had, according to this computation, a numerical advantage, with the advantage of greater precision—a notable feature of German artillery *in se*, and backed by special shooting accuracy on the part of the siege gunners, who were not drawn from the field artillery, but had been specially imported from the fortresses, and were thoroughly conversant with the handling of those huge arms of precision.   The design and construction of the batteries for the reception of the guns had been the work of Colonel Bartsch, the famous artillery officer who had already proved his skill in not a few of the earlier sieges of the war, Colonel Oppermann, Chief of the Engineer Staff of the Maas Army, and Colonel Himpe, Chief of the Artillery Staff; and I am satisfied that the most experienced judges, if conversant with the positions, would admit that all that skill and knowledge, both practical and theoretical, could effect, had been bestowed on the duty.

If the French had ears to hear, it was simply bewildering that they should have remained ignorant of the fact, that something exceptional must have been going on for nights before behind the sheltering fringe of trees. We know that they were so, so blind and deaf were they in their reckless confidence; but at the time this seemed so incredible that some of us had the fanciful notion that they knew all about it, and, like a boxer who disdains to hit his antagonist till he has "peeled," that they refrained from disturbing the operation.   Night after night the electric light flashed across where the working parties

were working; as its rays went dancing round the line of
environment, ·like a grotesque gigantic will of the wisp,
the spademen held their hands, the raised pick fell not,
the tumbrils halted as if the flash had been a ray from
the eye of the Gorgon; but the precautions, although wise,
were probably superfluous.   What is the use of light, if
there are not eyes to use it?   Will thistles yield grapes?
No lime-light, or electric flash, or other fancy expedient
that ever was invented, is to be named in the same week
with the good to be achieved by a system of linx-eyed
piquets and patrols, and by small reconnaissances, pushed
home with a daring that would be reckless but for their
skill and tact.   The extraordinary fact stands that it was
not till the night which preceded the commencement of
the bombardment that the French batteries seemed to
awake to the position.   All night long the Saxon pioneers
were hard at work with their keen axes cutting down, un-
gratefully but necessarily, the friendly trees which had
sheltered their previous labours.   It is the way of the
world—to the devil with a friend when you have no
further need for him.   Among the Saxon woodmen who
did not spare those trees came not a few shells during
the night, not only to their discomfort, but to that of the
battalions who, ever since the guns had been placed in
position, were sent on to the foreposts nightly to double
the usual guards for the protection of the big toys in
the front.
    It was originally intended that the firing should begin
at seven o'clock.   Half an hour before I was out on the
plateau of Raincy, midway between the batteries in the
park of Raincy and those at the Maison Guyot, listening
in the cold morning air for the first booming report, the
emblem and herald, as it would be, of a new phase of
the war, and, as we hoped, of a cogent argument towards

its early termination. Seven passed, and all was still silent—for the French had left off their firing. Eight came, and the keenness of expectancy became absolutely painful. Was the whole thing after all a snare and a feint? Were these "quakers," whose cold sides I had leaned against a few days before, and were the ammunition cases in the magazines so many "dummies"? No; the evidences of one's senses contradicted this. Was, then, the day postponed yet once again? No, only the hour. At exactly half-past eight the first gun crashed its report below me from the Maison Guyot battery, and I could hear its angry whiz as it cut the air in crossing the intervening space. In three minutes more the air was full of a din of deep diapason. There was nothing to see, and I saw it—such may serve as a summary of my morning's work. At daylight the snow had begun to fall —not heavily and in big flakes, but in feathery particles, which filled and whitened the air, making obstacles invisible a quarter of a mile off. Of course the gunners had got their sights and ranges the day before, and their shot must have been "there or thereabouts," but Avron was as invisible as if it had been on the further side of the North Pole. The work gave one the idea of fighting with knives in a dark room. At first it seemed as if the French artillerymen were taken by surprise. It was not till nine o'clock that Avron sent back the first instalment of its reply. When it did begin, though, it went to work with a will, but rather wildly, the shells flying about promiscuously in a fashion that impaired the safety of any given point. By ten, this duel in the dark was in full sway, the air incessantly lacerated and tortured by the whistle of the projectiles, so that one might have imagined himself in a calm at sea, with the rush of a coming squall bearing down upon him. The German

fire was like clock-work; the French fire came more in
spurts and gusts, and then was silent for some half a
minute. When in full blaze, it was so rapid as to be
continuous, and not admit of being timed itself, or of
one timing the German fire. About eleven the batteries
at Bondy—as well as I could judge by the direction of
the sound—took up their parable, and were replied to
by the extreme right flank of the German position, which
had been designed amiably looking toward the said Bondy,
with a view to such a demonstration. All day long the
fire continued, with no great variation to speak of. Perhaps it was heaviest from twelve till two. After that
hour the French fire seemed to slacken visibly. There
were longer intervals between the spurts, and the spurts
were not so animated. The forts of Rosny, Nogent, and
Noisy, however, chimed in occasionally, covering the
slackness of Avron's efforts. About sundown there was
a marked weakness in the enemy's fire, the German fire
continuing meanwhile in a steady, slogging, stolid fashion.
By nine o'clock at night both sides had partially suspended operations.

The regulation night-fire from the German batteries
was one shot per hour from each gun. All day long the
troops on the eastern side stood in quarters, ready for
anything that might turn up, and some batteries of guard
field artillery were actually out in the cold behind Pont
Iblon, but there was no hostile demonstration. At an
early hour in the morning Prince George of Saxony went
to Chelles, with the design of witnessing the commencement of the bombardment, but the snow in the air hid
everything, and hearing was the only sense called into
requisition.

The firing continued sluggishly during the night of the
27th, and on the morning of the 28th the French ability

to reply, measured, at all events, by their reply, was so feeble as to admit of a considerable further relaxation on the part of the Germans. During the day their firing was continued at the rate of about five to eight shots per minute, chiefly from the guns on the right-hand batteries in front of Rancy. Those batteries had been, in the words of Mr. Swiveller, a "staggerer" to Mont Avron. The French batteries on that commanding position, although it is true that they looked all three ways, were not quite impartial, and they had been constructed so that the most dangerous direction of their gaze was towards the valley of the Marne. Thus they could cope face to face with our batteries at Noisy-le-Grand, they could sweep the "horseshoe," they could pound into Chelles, till a man was thankful when he was out of it, and they could send their missiles into Montfermeil; but on the country further north than Raincy fewer and less powerful guns were trained, and consequently our batteries further north, in front of Raincy, actually enfiladed the batteries and parallels of Mont Avron, throwing in a flanking fire, against which, when the north-eastern battery was silenced, neither retaliation nor defence was possible. Of course a short time would have remedied this defect; even in frosty weather, a battery can nearly as soon alter its face as can a hypocrite his; but just as the mask fails the hypocrite in extremis, so it becomes impossible for the battery to change its front in the teeth of a heavy and unremitting fire. This circumstance accounts for the collapse of the Avron batteries earlier than any of us in the German lines had allowed ourselves to anticipate. There could be no question as to the collapse; so early as the afternoon of the 28th the fire from Avron was all but extinguished, and the four battalions of French infantry which were supporting the gunners

when the firing began on the previous morning were believed to have fallen back off the table-land with considerable loss.   Our casualties from the fire of the 27th
were twenty-three killed and wounded.   I was surprised
that it should have been so heavy, spite of the unquestionably heavy fire, looking at the strength and height of the
protecting parapets, and the short range, which gave little
scope to a plunging fire.

The easy and speedy silencing of Mont Avron sent a
shock of surprise—I can find no other expression—
through the Maas army.   Men themselves who, the moment they took up a position, set about strengthening it
to the utmost of time and power, if they were to evacuate
it but next morning, the Germans could not realise how
a mass of persons calling themselves soldiers should not,
during an occupation lasting for a month, deal so with
a position like Avron as to make it something else than
a mere noisy blustering bully—awkward till somebody
tackles him, but doubling up with ludicrous promptitude
as soon as a good man stands up to him.   The pessimists
shook their heads, and hinted at a ruse to draw on an as-
saulting party; sanguine men, on the other hand, spoke
of seeing on the ofternoon of the morrow the Krupps
from Raincy in position on Avron, and hammering away
at Rosny, Nogent, and Noisy.

Other results had been attained by the two days' work
besides the silencing of Mont Avron.   The German batteries did not all face that eminence.   They "set to
partners," with a view to other contingencies than the
mere silencing of Mont Avron.   The 22-gun battery
farthest to the right had two fronts.   Its left portion
looked to Avron; then, by the formation of a very obtuse
agle, its right flank was thrown back and faced, across
the level, on Bondy and Baubigny.   This arrangement

was devised to admit of the engaging of the French batteries in front of Bondy. There had been a feeble fire
from that quarter on both the 27th and 28th, but of a
character calculated to give the impression that the batteries which had been believed to be there were elsewhere. The French, although the large force of four
divisions, if not more, which they maintained on the
Bondy-Baubigny-Courneuve line for three days—commencing with the 21st Dec., had partially dispersed and
fallen back, still maintained, it was believed, quite a
division, with its right on Bondy, and its left retired on
the railway station at Baubigny. The camp occupied by
this body had been broken up, no doubt in consequence
of the fire directed toward the positions named. That
same railway station at Baubigny (on the Strassburg line)
was of immense utility to the French in many obvious
ways. If the German fire of the two days had not convinced the French of the inadvisability of using the line
so far for the future, the fact of its being commanded
by the Raincy batteries could not fail to be of incalcul-
able importance to the Germans in the event of any
renewal of the French attempt to break out or extend
their ground in the Le Bourget direction. There were in-
dications that the idea of efforts in that direction had not
wholly been abandoned. They had constructed—I don't
know, indeed, that they were ever finished—no fewer
than six batteries at intervals across the plain between
la Courneuve and Drancy, pretty much on the line on
which I described their infantry as standing on the afternoon of the 23rd. These could only have been intended
to support an attack on Le Bourget by dealing more
formidably than could field artillery either without emplacements or in emplacements hastily thrown up, with
the German artillery, that was ready at a moment's notice

to take up the Pont Iblon-Aulnay-Sevran line behind the
inundations—that position which I have ventured to
describe as virtually an entrenched camp. It was on
this line that the German artillery had stood on the 21st,
and where, although unable to prevent the partial storm
of Le Bourget by the French, it had paralysed their succeeding efforts, and covered effectually the successful
effort of the Guards for its recapture. That we should,
therefore, have had warm work again in that quarter before the end, I have little doubt, but for the arguments
of the siege-gun batteries between Aulnay and Dugny;
the sites which had already been pegged out before Avron
had been evacuated.

That event had, in my judgment at the time, this
important effect, it made an *Ausfall* of any other proportions than a demonstration, and occurring anywhere between Chennevieres and St. Germains, not, indeed, as
an utter impossibility physically, but as being impossible
in a military sense, because certain, on the face of things,
to be utterly disastrous in its results. The nullification
of Avron as hostile, supplied the wanting link in the im-
pregnability of the German cordon. But this condition,
valuable as it was, was but passively useful in contributing
to the end for which the German army stood round Paris.
In the recognition of the fact by men craving at once for
victory, for peace, and home, the anxiety for a general
bombardment as appearing to tend toward the accele-
rated realisation of their ardent aspirations, became very
intense.

Before the bombardment began I expressed my doubts
whether the Germans would be able to do any great
things by a systematic bombardment of the forts, and the
forts alone. Remember how many days of bombardment
it cost us, and what pyramids of projectiles we threw

before we rendered the Malakoff untenable. And we were close to the sea-board; yet, nevertheless, we had to pause again and again for supplies of ammunition. Every projectile thrown by the Germans represented arduous and long-continued toil to bring it to the cannon's mouth. They had to lay their account with the certainty that the Parisians would strain every nerve to return the fire and to repair the damage it causes. It would then appear, as it seemed to me, that to operate against the forts successfully would require both a stronger artillery, whether in calibre or in number, than that possessed by the French, and a large and continuous supply of ammunition. But a comparatively small array of artillery—of such weapons of precision as the German artillery consists of, and with the dexterous German artillerymen, would suffice, as it seemed, to keep the guns of the forts in play, so that they could divert none of their attention; while a few guns of longer range were meanwhile negativing the forts altogether, and pounding directly into Paris. The adoption of this expedient, supposing it successful, had the obvious advantage that it would save the carriage of the vast quantities of ammunition which a lengthened bombardment of the forts would necessitate. I readily and cheerfully own that in believing that a very short duration of such home-practice would suffice to end the siege, I did injustice to the enduring fortitude of the Parisians; but there were no precedents, and I think that if what we knew of the Parisians led us to misjudge them, what they must have known of themselves must have surprised them with a greater surprise than even outsiders felt—that heroism should be extant in Paris in 1870-71. And, further, I do not think that anyone who was in Paris in the early days of the armistice, could fail to gather that the shells which had fallen into Paris had an appreciable effect in

14*

hastening the end which was otherwise inevitable. I do
not say that the bursting of shells in the street daunted
the Parisians, but it produced a vague, uneasy nervousness, the revulsion from which had not yet taken place
when I got inside, and aided the logical perception of
the fact that further resistance was utter madness as, in
a few days, it would have been impossible from famine.

But to return to Mont Avron, definitely shut up by
the German batteries on the afternoon of the 28th December. It was "dead," in the expressive German phrase.
For the first time for several weeks its slopes were
cautiously traversed by German patrols, who saw or heard
nothing indicative of life, and the conviction gained
ground in the morning that men and guns had alike
cleared off it. Perhaps it was just as well, both for the men
and guns, for it consists with my information that certain Saxon infantrymen had been looking to the contents
of their ammunition pouches and the setting of their
bayonets, and that certain artillerymen had been handling
long nails, which a not very vivid imagination might conjecture were intended for spiking purposes.

One or two slender day-patrols had in the course of
the afternoon of the 29th groped their way up the sides
of Mont Avron, and brought back word that, so far as
they could discern, there were no Frenchmen in the
vicinity. But the night had fallen, and the young moon
had risen, before Hauptmann von Zanthier, of the 2nd
battalion of the 103rd Regiment, stepped out on to the
platform of the Raincy-Villemomble station, where his
company had its outpost quarters for the night, and
summoned to turn out the first four corporalschafts.
Out tumbled the sturdy fellows, shaking off them the
straw, as hens do the loose feathers, and falling into their
places with that rapid, silent method that speaks of real

discipline. When the sergeant reported "all right," the little band, eighty in number, marched off the platform, and took its steady way through the scattered village of Villemomble. Outside it we came—for I was an unattached companion of the gallant Hauptmann—on detached châteaux, standing in their grounds on the plain —residences that had been beautiful once, but which were now ghastly in their utter ruin. Straight on went the road, till one began to feel the gradual rise. We were on the slope of Avron. Then it bent to the left, for the hill was too steep for the road to climb direct, and in the bend we came among the trees and brush, out of the middle of which were dug clearings, on which châteaux stood, looking out over the plain to the northeast. About half-way up the ascent we came on the line of French piquet-posts. The French had certainly been very fond of Avron. What between barricades, entrenchments, rifle-pits, and loopholed houses, many a stout Teuton would have gone down before that position could have been forcibly carried over which we passed so peaceably in the silent moonlight. Working always round to the left, we reached the crest of the hill on that face of the plateau which looks out on Montfermeil, and where the summit was marked by the largest batteries. Once inside them, there met our eyes one of the weirdest scenes that imagination could conjure up. Ground ploughed with shells, embrasures stove in, parallels all but obliterated, and yet seemingly not a single cannon left behind. But if the French had removed their cannon, they had left their dead. One slid and stumbled over a little ice puddle. The ice blushed up red in his face —it was frozen human blood. Behind the batteries and inside the breastworks the dead lay thick. Dead! No man who long followed this war but must have become

so familiar with the aspect of slain men, that the original
thrill and turn of the blood at the sight had faded into
a memory of the past, at which he all but smiled when
it dimly recurred to him; but the terrible ghastliness of
those dead transcended anything I had ever seen, or
even dreamt of, in the shuddering nightmare after my
first battle-field. Remember how they had been slain.
Not with the nimble bullet of the needle-gun, that drills
a minute hole through a man and leaves him undis-
figured, unless it has chanced to strike his face; not with
the trenchant sabre-cut of the dragoon, not with the
sharp stab of the bayonet, but slaughtered with missiles
of terrible weight, shattered into fragments by explosions
of many pounds of powder, mangled and torn by massive fragments of iron. There lay behind one of the
embrasures a form utterly headless. I suppose the shell
had struck the hapless being full in the face, and carried head and throat before it in its fierce rush. The
guillotine could not have performed the operation more
cleanly.

But what need to dwell in detail on such a topic?
Let it suffice that there lay the unburied and abandoned
dead among the snow stained with their blood, and with
the depressions in those ghastly faces turned up to the
calm moonlight, drifted up by the snowflakes which had
fallen since they had been shot down. When would
they be buried? When would those wan faces cease to
look up into the eyes of the moon, in silent but eloquent
protestation against the institution called war? When
would the stray human fragments over which one stumbled
as he went be gathered together, and their ghastliness
be hidden beneath friendly earth? Not yet. Men will
not dig graves in war time as if they were blasting
tunnels, and the earth was as hard as the bowels of

Mont Cenis. The corpses on Mont Avron had to lie there till the thaw came. That gruesome group in the camp here who had been sitting round the fire when the shells came and burst in it, and blew one and all of them into the other world, had to remain as it was—a horrible mockery of conviviality, for a time at least. To look at the group from a little distance, one would conclude that its members, lying or seated in a circle, were hobnobbing genially round a common pot, or eating out of one dish. Come nearer, and look inside that ring of squatting men, or what once were men. I care not how inured you are to sights of horror, you will turn away sick and scared from that circle of carnage. Great God! that man should be able so to mangle his fellow-man made in thine image!

Behind the batteries, besides the relics I have alluded to, were found many evidences of the precipitation with which the French had evacuated the position. There were lots of wine—we drank some of it standing there among the dead—and piles of loaves—which the Saxon soldiers skewered on their bayonets. There were blankets, too, and military saddles, one of which, an officer's, Hauptmann von Zanthier philosophically annexed. Both in and about the camp lying farther back there was a considerable quantity of rice, and also many blankets, shoes, and soldiers' knapsacks. Lumps of horse-flesh lay about or hung on cross-sticks. Investigations amongst the tents and mud huts brought to light bottles of rum and bags of peas. The ground was strewn with chassepots, and behind the batteries, as well as in the battery magazines, were gunpowder bags containing each a charge, and many projectiles. The camp, and indeed the whole of the plateau, bore numerous traces of lengthened occupation. The French are the beastliest campers in the world, and they seemed to have been exceptionally beastly in Mont Avron. Behind the camp lay the little straggling village of Avron, still smoking from the fire that had raged in it during the morning; whether kindled by a German shell or by the last Frenchman I do not know. There was not a sign of life on all the plateau, except a lurching cur who gnawed something under a waggon; what it was I did not care to investigate too closely. The greater part of the plateau had been occupied with vineyards, which were now, of course, trodden down and ruined. Stumbling through the stumps of the vines, I crossed the plateau, and looked down over its farther verge. Below me lay the village of Rosny, easily to be distinguished by its lights. Above it was the horizon line, with Forts Rosny and Noisy standing up against the sky; and there were visible in their neighbourhood lights which seemed to indicate the new outpost line taken up by the French. Then across again to the south-eastern edge, and there lay the Marne, silvered to whiteness in the moonlight; and Chelles, with its bright cottages, and Montfermeil, with its swarthy hanging woods, and the horse-shoe farther to the south. How often during the month so nearly closed had I looked up at Avron from these spots—at Avron hostile and dangerous; and now, here I looked down upon them from that very Avron, with its fangs drawn, and not a Frenchman near its summit.

It surprised me much, looking at the abundant evidences of precipitation visible, that the French should have removed all their cannon except two (one dismounted, the other abandoned in transitu); and still more so, looking at the evidences of the German fire, that they should have been able to do so. It is about as easy to transport a big ship about the country as it is to

move a big gun after it has been dismounted; none of
the French guns could have been dismounted, with the
single exception just noted, else we should have found
both gun and carriage where the damage was done.   It
seemed to me that the infantry men must have skedaddled
in a panic, and that the artillerymen, fearing an assault
from infantry which they had no means of resisting,
had removed their guns before an absolute necessity existed for evacuation from the strength of the German
fire.   They were wise, if this was their reckoning.

During the 29th, the German batteries continued in
full work against Forts Rosny, Noisy, and Nogent, which
by no means allowed the transaction to be a one-sided
one.   Each had its satellites in the shape of detached
auxiliary batteries, and they chiefly have devoted themselves to the reply.   It was believed that the forts had
in a great measure denuded themselves of artillery for
the furnishing of these.   Conspicuous already among
those auxiliary batteries was the Redoubt de la Boissière,
on the slope of the bluff behind the village of Merdan.
The German batteries also found leisure for an occasional salutation in the direction of Bondy and Grand
Drancy.

A deserter was brought into Gonesse on the 29th,
who reported that Ducrot had been living in Drancy ever
since the 21st.   Ducrot, he further reported, had been
assiduously engaged in strengthening his offensive position, and constructing works, with a view to dominate
Le Bourget, Le Blanc Mesnil, Aulnay, and Pont Iblon.
According to the deserter, there were now in and around
Drancy four batteries of naval guns of heavy calibre,
three batteries of long 12-pounders, and two batteries of
mitrailleuses.   Three days before such tidings as these
would have made one devoutly wish that the inundations

were longer, broader, and deeper, and that there were
no bridges. But now they could be listened to with
equanimity, for operations were rapidly approaching com-
pletion, that would enable the besieging force to reply
no longer with field artillery, but with batteries of siege
guns of a power and range calculated to render it advisable for Ducrot, if he still held to his doughty resolve
not to re-enter Paris alive, to look for safer quarters than
Drancy would then afford.

During the 30th, a languid fire was maintained against
Fort Rosny, which appeared to be replying with only
two guns. On the same day, Lieutenant Hoffmann, of
the Engineer Staff of the Maas Army, visited Mont
Avron, for the purpose of taking careful drawings of the
plateau, and tracings of the positions which had been
occupied by the French batteries. He was joined by
Colonel Bartsch, and the conclusion was arrived at, that
while the forts and redoubts remained capable of sweeping the exposed summit of Avron, it would be unwise
to attempt the utilisation of the position for bombarding
purposes. It was determined, then, to continue the steady
bombardment of the eastern forts and of the adjacent
villages, which continued to be occupied by French
troops, both from the existing batteries and those in
other positions whose construction was already far advanced. No doubt Avron would have afforded a splendid
position for the German artillery, had it been easily
tenable, and in a strait, I doubt not, it would have been
utilised. Without this advantage, however, the result of
the three days' firing had been something to be com-
placent about. Avron was "dead," and the Saxons had
a night-watch on its summit. Villemomble had once
again in its wrecked houses men wearing spiked helmets.
Neuilly sur Marne, which the French had continuously

held from the beginning of the siege, they held now no
longer, and the German patrols perambulated it during
the night. It was too near Nogent, while as yet Nogent's
teeth were unblunted, to be occupied regularly as a
post; but there was a good time coming. Launay was
also German once more, and Gagny, which conventionally had never been utterly lost, was again Saxon
beyond all question. The outpost line had made a real
stride in the right direction.

On the 31st I went to Brou, a village a few kilometres
in the rear of Chelles, to spend the New Year's Day with
my friends of the Artillery and Engineer Staff of the
Maas Army, who had been quartered there for some
time. The *Belagerungspark* for the eastern side had
been formed there, as it was convenient for railway purposes, the ammunition and gun cars being run on through
Lagny up to Brou, where the line skirted the park. Here
all was activity. A whole battalion of the 105th regiment
was engaged in filling the powder into shells, which had
come empty and harmless from Germany. Huge siege
guns on massive carriages were ranged in long rows,
handled delicately by gunners who seemed to have a
real tenderness for the grim monsters. There were sheds
adjacent for the horses of the miserable peasants who,
with their teams, had been requisitioned to cart first
fascines and gabions, and then munitions from the park
into the batteries. I don't know how it fared with the
poor *habitants* themselves in the matter of shelter; I saw
none specially provided. They had got past the grum-
bling stage into a kind of equanimity of misery; what
worse could befal them? They belonged to villages and
country places in the rear, and had been provided by
the Maires on requisition. Would M. Maire ever pay
them for the ungracious work on which they were per-

force engaged? Who would compensate the owners of
the horses whose carcases lay about—fifteen in one
group—dead of sheer cold before the sheds had been
run up? When you asked them about their plight, all
you could get from them was, "*Ah, Monsieur, c'est la
guerre*," and that—so crushed were they—without the
shrug of the shoulders, which I had believed a Frenchman would give when the doctor announced to him that
he must surely die. It appeared to me that the miser-
ables lived chiefly on *eau-de-vie;* I never saw one eating,
and they were as gaunt as scaffold-poles. Clad in the
everlasting blouse, they must have suffered fearfully from
cold, and as you passed a train of them, their coughing
drowned the rumbling of their wheels. I saw one man
trudging along without stockings, his bare feet stuck in
a pair of sabots. I don't exactly remember how many
degrees below freezing point the temperature was that
day, but I remember that on coming in-doors, I had to
thaw my moustache at the fire before I could open my
mouth to get a cigar between my lips.

CHAPTER III.
From the New Year to the Armistice.

THE New Year was celebrated very quietly by the
Maas Army. I saw it in with a goodly company of frank
comrades in a château at Vaires, where the pontooneer
company of the Guard Engineers had their head-quarters,
and with whom, as belonging to the same branch of the
service, the head-quarter engineer staff, whose guest I
was, messed during their sojourn in the adjacent village
of Brou. Returning to Brou in the small hours of the
morning, we heard still the sounds of conviviality from
sundry apartments in the great château there; but one

by one the revellers sank into slumber. The latest
roisterer was a Frenchman; who he was or where he had
got drunk, I have not the remotest conception; but about
four o'clock I heard some one tumbling about in the
passage, *sacré*-ing most vigorously through a bad fit of
hiccough. Ultimately he rolled into the chamber, on
the floor of which I lay, and even in his drink he was
civil. With profuse *pardons* he asked for a light, but
forgot what he had asked for the next moment, and
staggered out again into the passage. A quarter of an
hour afterwards I heard him making a speech to the
sentry, and what ultimately befell him I know not.

On New Year's morning Colonel Bartsch, who was
also quartered in Brou, received a very flattering souvenir
in the shape of the Iron Cross of the first class, in token
of the success which had attended the efforts of the
Artillery under his command. The Colonel had a good
right to be gratified at a distinction which is comparatively rare. The bearer of the Iron Cross of the first
class wears it on his left breast, while he also wears the
cross of the second class attached to his buttonhole. On
the same occasion Captain Reinsdorff, the adjutant of the
Artillery Staff of the Maas Army, received the Iron Cross
for his share of the work that resulted in the French
abandonment of Mont Avron, and soon after the same
honour was conferred on Lieutenant Hoffmann of the
Engineer Staff. Colonel Bartsch had brought so many
fortresses to reason with those grim toys of his that one
might have expected to see in him a formidable personage, smelling of gunpowder, with a frown like the
sombre mouth of a 24-pounder, and a voice like its
report. You could not well imagine a stronger contrast.
He was a gay, dapper little man, as merry as a grig,
with a fine open forehead, good-humoured smile, and a

close-cropped black beard. You would not imagine that it could enter into his heart to hurt a fly, and there was something quite boyish in the unaffected delight with which he sported his first-class Iron Cross for the first time on this New Year's morning. Young ladies would call him a "dear little man." Ask Strassburg, Toul, La Fère, Verdun, and a few other fortresses what they thought of him as seen from a distance; they might indeed reckon him a "dear" man, but in another sense.

On the afternoon of New Year's Day we had not, indeed, a "midnight meeting," but I was present at a very interesting religious service by candle-light. The scene was the fine old church of Chelles, one of the most venerable religious edifices around Paris, with massive stone pillars, old Norman arches, much stained glass, carved oaken work, and Popish decoration generally. The service was for the whole of the 24th division (Saxons). As we drove from Brou in the moonlight, we passed large groups hastening on the Chelles. It must be remembered that the service was an entirely voluntary one. There was no command laid upon the men that they should turn out of warm billets and walk four or five miles in one of the coldest nights of the year. Nevertheless, the old church, I venture to say, never had within its hoary walls so numerous a congregation. The officers whom I accompanied were unable to struggle their way up to the inclosure in front of the altar, and we were glad to find seats among the men by the side of one of the pillars. There was something indescribably affecting in the music. An harmonium close to the altar led; the strain was taken up by a military band in the balcony, and the two thousand men present joined in with one accord. There was no discord, but the church was too small for the volume of sound; yet one would not have wished it more slender. Then the divisional chaplain, standing on the steps of the altar, not occupying the pulpit, delivered what was something between a sermon, an address, and a prayer. He had the natural gift of eloquence; his words came from the heart, and they went to the heart. As he spoke of the night this time last year, in the happy homes of Germany, and contrasted it with the melancholy that now assuredly reigned in these households, in so many of which there was a vacancy, right many were the bowed heads and the moist eyes. Then the speaker struck a new key. The war had, indeed, made a sombre New Year in the Fatherland; it came upon many a household desolated by its ravages. "Aye, out there on those slopes across the river," he broke out with raised arm and flushed face, "there lie beneath the foreign sod many and many of our dear comrades and brethren never to rise again till the last trumpet sounds. But though each grave mound there is the sad emblem of so much misery, this New Year's Day, of broken home circles, of sorrowing parents, of weeping wives, of fatherless children, yet—" and here the arm swept round the head as if there was a sword in the hand's grasp—"yet we know our brothers died in a good cause. They fell *für König und Vaterland*, and surely they are *mit Gott*. And the war, sad and solemn episode in our history as it is in one sense, has had yet another glorious result. It has made our Fatherland not a name, but a reality. Already one race, one people, we are now one nation—Saxon, Prussian, Mecklenburger, Badener, Bavarian, we are all now children of the great German Empire."

The speaker paused, and through the dead silence of the moment there came the faint boom of the cannon on the batteries in the front. The sound gave him a new

cue. "Listen to the sound of the German cannon—a
sound now, as ever, heralding the victory to our arms.
To that sound you have listened on many a battle-field
—you may hear it on yet other battle-fields before you
re-cross the Rhine. But, oh! remember ever in its midst
that it speaks the tidings for you, 'Death is near; prepare
to meet your God.' The good soldier is always ready
when the battle-bugle sounds—he falls into the ranks
with needle-gun and ammunition ready for action; but
there is something else for which he must ever be ready
too—death, and that which follows death. His peace
with God must ever be part, and the chief part for himself, of his battle equipment."

This will give an idea of the strain in which was
couched what was certainly a most powerful and telling
address. When it had finished, the instrumental music
did not at once commence, but the vocalists of the band,
under the conductorship of an under-officer, struck up
Luther's "New Year's Hymn," the difficult part singing
of which they accomplished with real beauty and feeling.
Then another burst of instrumental and vocal music, that
seemed to make the roof vibrate—the blessing—and the
quiet dispersal of the great throng. As I walked to our
carriage, we passed twos and threes of the soldiery talking earnestly of the words they had heard. Yet let me
be candid. Their tone was rather that of connoisseurs
than of Christians. "It was very beautiful," "His words
were like fire," "I could have listened to him ever so
much longer," and so forth—that was the tone of the
comments. It was, as regarded the religious sentiment
of the address, much the same tone in which men speak
of an actor's performance, of a prima donna's singing, of
a horse's galloping—not as if the matter were one of the
deepest personal import to each one of them.

The New Year ushered in a period of quietude after the turbulence and excitement that had prevailed in the latter days of the old year. When I speak of quietude I must be understood as using the term relatively. The distant sound of firing was ever in our ears. The batteries that had driven the French off Mont Avron were still firing steadily against the eastern forts and redoubts, and I did not learn that there was any perceptible decrease in the sluggish steadiness of the reply. From no position on this face of the environment were French infantry visible in any direction. Snow to the depth of two inches lay on the plains of Courneuve and Baubigny. The Seine was frozen over in places, but the ice was not reliable enough to furnish a natural bridge for the passage of troops, much less of artillery.

Highly creditable to the German besiegers were the friendly, and indeed cordial terms which they had contrived to establish with the villagers around Paris. These, indeed, were mostly of the humbler classes, either labouring folk or the servants left in the villas, and nothing could have exceeded the kindliness with which they were treated by those whom circumstances had so strangely placed among them, while they, for their part, appeared to feel and appreciate this kindliness. They were all gradually picking up some little German, while the German soldiers were by this time becoming quite proficient in a guttural broken French. In the early days, by Sedan and by Metz, it seemed as if the French summarised the whole German language in an emphatic "nix," but now they had begun to go deeper into the mysteries of the language. I had a Frenchman in Margency, who was a fund of recurrent amusement to me. He was the gardener of the château in which I had rooms, and he and his wife had remained behind in

charge of the place. I casually discovered how handy
and obliging were the pair, and how much better I should
be waited on by the same than by the willing but clumsy
German *Diener*. I was rather a transitory resident in
Margency, but each time I came back, honest Auguste
had a surprise for me in the acquisitions of German
which he had made during my absence. Apart from
what may be called "household words," the French peasant's acquisition of German chiefly developed itself in
the direction of ability to put questions as to the state of
the war and the probable period of its termination. On
the other hand, the first French that a German learnt
was invariably the numerals and the appellations and
values of the current coins. If every German soldier
about Paris was not a master of Mr. Goschen's "Theory
of Foreign Exchanges," he was, at all events, thoroughly
at home in the relative values of French and German
money, and when you now priced a thing with a German
merchant or marketender, it was as likely as not that
he named the cost in francs and sous instead of thalers
and groschen.

The inclemency of the weather and the hardness of
the recent service were making the inevitable impression
on the health of the German troops on the eastern side
of the circle. There were not, indeed, so many serious
cases of illness in proportion as there had been around
Metz in September and October. One seldom heard of
dysentery; and typhus, except in lazarettes where there
were many wounded, had all but died out. The chief
diseases were of the bronchial and rheumatic type.
Neither were very serious in the majority of cases, but
both incapacitated the sufferers from present duty, and
pro tanto weakened the field force. Then aggravated
forms of inflammation of the lungs and rheumatic fever

had become not at all uncommon, and the man who had
gone down with either could not be expected to be fit
for a resumption of duty while the winter campaign
lasted. Illness would have been more prevalent than it
was were it not for the now copious supply of warm
clothing and blankets. Every soldier now had his thick
double blanket, and at Christmas-time the *Liebesgaben*
and home presents poured into the army in a steady and
copious stream. A very wholesome regulation had been
adopted in shortening the term of sentry duty from two
hours to one. This did not necessitate a stronger guard,
but only involved shorter periods of relief. Instead of
the relative periods being "two hours on and four off," a
phrase familiar to every soldier, they were now one hour
on and two off, in the twenty-four hours, the duty being
exactly the same, viz., eight hours on sentry and sixteen
in the guard-room, or whatever might correspond to that
shelter. The German soldiers had learned to go to sleep
at a moment's notice, so that the shortening of the un-
broken period for rest did not affect them injuriously,
while the shortening of the spell of duty was much to
their advantage. In very inclement weather I have known
the one hour system adopted in home garrisons in Britain.
In Canada, during the winter, it is invariable.

On the 2nd of January 7 new batteries had been
completed on the east of Paris, flanking both on the
north and south those already in existence, and fire from
their guns began to be delivered on the following day.
There were 13 batteries originally, the 7 new ones of
course made the number up to 20, the new ones numbering from 14 to 20. Nos. 14 and 15 were close to the
old batteries at Raincy, but faced directly toward Bondy
and Drancy; Nos. 16 and 17 were in front of Chenevières, to the south of the horseshoe and close to the

15*

bank of the Marne; No. 18 was behind Le Blanc Mesnil,
No. 19 at Pont Iblon, and No. 20 on the slope between
Garges and Dugny.   When there had been 13 batteries,
there had been 76 guns; now there were 20 batteries and
yet no more than 82 guns.   How arm 7 more batteries
with only 6 more guns?   The seeming puzzle admits of an
easy explanation.   The abandonment of Avron permitted
the utilisation elsewhere of some of the guns that had
been doing service in the old batteries at Raincy, Gagny,
and Cournay.

Visiting St. Germain on the 4th of January, late
business compelled me to stay there over-night.

Before ten o'clock on the morning of the 5th, the air,
thick with fog, was burdened also with a sound to which
one could not well give a name.   It was not loud—at
times it died away altogether, then it came again with a
sustained song, as if of wind moaning through a keyhole.
What could it be but the sound of distant firing far
away round to the south?   Was this then the day of
days—the day so long waited for, so anxiously hoped
for?   It might be or not the commencement of the
bombardment on the southern side, hopes and speculations as to which had been on every tongue for a fortnight before.   There were some in St. Germain who
laughed at the idea, while the din was all in the distance.
"Do you think," asked they, with scorn in their accents,
"that it can be the bombardment, when no sound comes
up out of the immediate foreground in the south—when
the tongues of Valérien are still?"   I could not profess
to arbitrate in the question, for Valérien and St. Germain
were not within the ring fence of my hunting-ground
with the Maas Army, and I had no acquaintance with
the ground to justify me in even making up my own
mind.   So I took horse while as yet the question was

undecided, and made the best of my way home toward
Margency by the much-vexed Argenteuil and the dangerous
gap behind Mont d'Orgimont. Before I had reached
Sartrouville the noise had swelled to a much louder
volume. As I rode through the woods of Bezons the
clash of artillery sounded so near and so full that for the
moment it struck me that the Frenchmen must be making
a real effort at this point of the peninsula, and that they
were trying to get over the Seine under cover of a heavy
cannonade from Courbevoie and Nanterre. I looked forward to the open high bit of road between the forest
and Argenteuil, with no small interest. It was never a
safe road to travel, individuals of a bloodthirsty temperament making it a point to pot continually at the peaceful wayfarer from the farther side of the river. But
when I got out upon it I found two French boys and an
old woman placidly discussing the attributes of a very
aged white horse, which stood meditatively listening to
the criticisms passed upon it. Then there was no storm
of shells tearing across the exposed bit of road, as would
have been the case had the batteries at Nanterre and
Colombes been demonstrating. Argenteuil was even undergoing a temporary respite from its peppering. But
still, full, close, and continuous, came the steady roar of
big guns from the south. I was on my own ground
now—my foot on my native heath—and at liberty to
think for myself. There was little thinking required.
In the nature of things what I listened to, what made the
aspen leaves tremble as the air throbbed to the crashes,
could be nothing else but The Bombardment. It was
with a real sense of relief, with that frame of mind which
I may designate a relative cheerfulness, that I turned
away from facing the sound, and struck towards Margency.
Everywhere I passed there was a brightness in the faces

that looked up at me on the road and in the villages. The sentries, stern duty men, prone to demand inspection of "legitimations," men wont to halt to ponder ere they returned your greeting, gave me "'Morgen" with a ready heartiness that betokened how welcome was the sound that filled the air. "Bombardment" was the first word in everyone's mouth everywhere. At Margency Herr Secretair in the Feldpost bureau was so full of the subject, complicated as its discussion was by the dinner he was eating, that he actually forgot to charge me two groschen marked on one of my letters. Head-quarters beamed radiantly, and I almost expected to see the paymaster, who was given to such ebullitions, blossom forth into a night illumination.

We had a little English colony not far from Margency, in the village of Napoléon-St. Leu. They were humble folks, it is true, but what little I have to say of one of the families may perchance interest the reader. They were the servants left behind in Lady Ashburton's château, and I had taken some interest from time to time in ascertaining that they were comfortable, and not subjected to annoyance. This they certainly were not. Two artillery officers lived in the château, and its owner, if she has already returned, has doubtless found it totally uninjured, even to the cover of a book. On my return to Margency on the 5th, there came to me the old housesteward with a sad story, told in a broken voice. He had a daughter who was shut up in Paris, and the girl had contrived to send her parents a letter by balloonpost. It had arrived on New Year's morning, and the anxious mother sat down to read it with avidity. The letter killed her on the spot. With it in her hand—containing as it did a recital of privation and misery which I refrain from giving in detail—the poor woman fell

dead to the ground. Her husband had buried her the
day before I saw him, and now he came to me to ask
whether I could do anything to get the girl out of her
trouble, and also whether I could send certain letters to
England. The latter request it gave me great pleasure
to comply with; I was forced to tell the old man that
his first desire was not to be thought of. He, for one,
we may be sure, was praying God to shorten every hour
till the capitulation. It is pleasant to add that the German officers showed him the most solicitous consideration in his trouble, and smoothed every difficulty for him
with genuine kindliness.

The morning of the 6th presented a remarkable contrast in every respect to that of the preceding day. The
latter had been cold to chilling of the marrow of the
bones, and so thick that nothing was to be seen half a
mile away. The former was clear, bright, and warm as a
morning in the end of March. Yesterday the air was
charged with sound; to-day there reigned the stillness of
an Arcadia that knows not war. Men looked at each
other in blank amazement. Had Paris, forts, big guns,
bombardment, and the no-bombardment on the eastern
side alike been spirited away? Had the French reply
shut up our pretty Spandau toys in one day? Or, on the
contrary, had those pieces of finished mechanism stove
in the forts and batteries bodily? and if we were going
up to Montmorency, should we see the white flag on the
top of Montmartre in token that all was over? Men were
reticent in expressing speculation, but at the corners of
the straggling lanes of Margency I heard the words,
"Capitulation," "Parlementaire," muttered as the Feld-
gensdarmes and the orderly-men gossiped in little groups.
Making the best of my way to head-quarters, I found
head-quarters in ignorance and suspense. Nobody could

interpret this strange, ghostly silence. There had come from Versailles on the previous night a telegram stating that the King was well pleased with the results which the day's bombardment had achieved. So it was plain the silence was not on our part due to coercion. "Negotiations, then?" I suggested to my friendly interlocutor. "No, that cannot well be," was the reply, "since in that case we should have received instant instructions to silence our Maas Army batteries, and this has not been the case." "Are they firing, then?" I asked, for it might be that I had been struck with sudden deafness. "No, it would seem not; I can hear nothing. The silence is a puzzler, but we are sure to hear all about it within a few hours." Determining to anticipate by personal investigation the information which was kindly promised me, I rode off to the front of Montmorency, whence there lay spread before the eye the wide panorama of the north side of Paris. Still all was silent as the grave. There was the white foreground, the ice-bound river and the St. Denis chimneys smoking lustily according to their wont. Neither from the east nor the west came there the slightest sound of any firing. A slight haze bank hung over Le Bourget, which might have been snow fog or the filmy smoke of a cannonade; but if the latter it must have surely been audible. There I found three mounted officers, and we had a little talk about the position. They inclined to the armistice-negotiations theory, more especially as they had not heard a single shot since morning. As we spoke there came a white jet of smoke out of the grey side of La Briche. No sound—for all the noise made it might have been an escape of steam. But in a second or two we did hear something, the close swish of the shell, and then the explosion about fifty yards to the right. La Briche could not resist the temptation of the group. "No negotiations, then, that is certain," was the remark as we broke up and went our several ways.

This action of La Briche rather intensified the puzzle, because it seemed to knock away the only explanation. I could not go to the south, but I could visit the batteries about Pont Iblon, and get at the root of the matter. As I rode through Sarcelles I overtook the "Lady-birds" from Groslay. The "Lady-birds" are the Guard Fusilier Regiment, called by this familiar name by the good folks of Berlin from the circumstance that they pass through that capital, changing quarters from Spandau to Potsdam, every year in the month of May, the lady-birds' month. Dainty lady-birds are the Fusilier, to be sure; huge, hulking, six-foot chields, with broad shoulders and great stalwart limbs. Glad, though, would they have been, if they could, to accept the pretty little one's adjuration to their tiny namesake, "Lady-bird, lady-bird, fly away home," for nostalgia was a disease from which more or less they all seemed suffering. They formed part of an intended demonstration, to consist of the bulk of the 1st, Guard Division, that had been ordered to be made in the region behind Le Bourget, and to be synchronous with the commencement of the bombardment in the south. Events in the latter direction had anticipated this arrangement, but the demonstration had not yet been countermanded, and I had a pleasant hour's ride with the officers of the Lady-birds. They told me how friendly the French foreposts were getting between Groslay and Villanteneuse, and how greedily they craved for Erbswurst, offering for a modicum of the same to pledge themselves not to fire for ever so long. Now and then the Frenchmen handed over a paper. A captain had *La Nouvelle France*, two days old, in his pocket. Among other details it mentioned that the force on Avron had been commanded by Colonel Stoffel, so long the French military attaché at the Court of Berlin, who if this were true, seems certainly to have been wiser in precept than in practice.

At Villers-le-Bel came the countermand for the demonstration, and I came on to Gonesse alone. What was my surprise to find all the German batteries from Gonesse to Sevran firing away vigorously! They had been at it since eight in the morning. In Gonesse I learned that the firing on the south side was believed to have recommenced at the same hour, and was certainly going on. Yet, at Margency and Montmorency we could not hear a sound. It was all owing to the air; it was to-day as non-conducting of sound as it had been the reverse yesterday. Even in Gonesse we could not hear the guns that were thundering, so to speak, at our elbows.

Afterwards I rode along the chaussée behind the batteries. There was firing from right and left of Pont Iblon, from Le Blanc Mesnil, and to its right, and also from an old field artillery emplacement between Le Blanc Mesnil and Aulnay. The fire was not very brisk, but it was ever so much brisker than the reply. It was chiefly directed against Forts De l'Est and Du Nord, and the redoubt at la Courneuve, but the leftmost battery also fired into Drancy, where the French still must have had some kind of lodgment, since they had fired a few guns from it in the morning. I remained for about an hour behind the batteries, and the French only fired three shots in reply during that period. Their shells were well aimed; one of the three came on to the chaussée, just behind one of the batteries; another exploded on the outward face of the parapet, and the third fell in the field a few yards to its front.

On this day (the 6th) there was a considerable moving
of troops. The 2nd Division of the Guards evacuated
Sevran and Aulnay, and came farther up to the north-
east. The Saxons came northward in their room, unfold-
ing again into the old positions occupied before Mont
Avron forced the Saxons to stand four or five deep on
their ground, instead of the ordinary three, and thus to
narrow their front. The movement extended all round,
and among other things it relieved the tension of the
4th Army Corps, which covered an immense front, although not a dangerous one. The "dislocation" had a
feature that from one aspect was ludicrous, and from the
other sad. Who could refrain from laughing when he
passed a battalion, half the men of which carried chairs,
while there was a string of carts behind, laden with mattresses, sofas, tables, washhand-stands, crockeryware, and
an endless assortment of the contents of a furnishing
warehouse? I passed detached groups laden with the
oddest articles. One man had a bird-cage with a canary
in it; another had a picture lashed in front, and another
on his back, in the sandwich fashion of our street ad-
vertisement men. There was pretty well everything belonging to domestic economy, with the exception of a
cradle, and that useful adjunct to married joys I confess
I did not observe. A stalwart "Sheep"—the Second
Guard Regiment goes by the name of "Muttons," on account of some old recondite tradition or other—staggered
along with a great glass shade on his back, inside which
was a massive ormolu clock, supported by a pair of extremely badly-clad angels in brass. I asked him whether
the clock was his. "*Ach nein*," grunted he in reply, "the
cursed thing belongs to the battalion bureau." Not exactly the *spolia opima* were the mattresses and chairs of
the inhabitants of the villages around Paris, but the be-

siegers had come, with a kind of naturalness begotten of all but necessity, to regard them not as spoils at all, but as fairly their own property, at least for the time being. War blunts sadly the moral sense. In the eyes of none of the "Sheep" were the chairs and mattresses stolen, and yet when one comes to look into the question as a non-belligerent, what else were they? This much else at all events, that they made up a very laughable procession. You could not keep from laughing, although you must sigh the moment after, when you thought of the inhabitants of the villages coming home after the evacuation and finding what terribly sad havoc the German occupation had caused. After all though the doctrine of averages came in as some consolation. If one regiment carried out of Dugny and Bonneuil a given quantity of furniture, the marching in regiment bore with it also a certain quantity which was roughly an equivalent. I don't think any of the beds or chairs have gone back to Deutschland, and if the inhabitants when they came home did not find their own furniture in their houses, they found somebody else's.

Staying overnight in Le Vert Galant, I went forward to Ville Evrart on the 7th, in hopes of learning something about the state of Fort Nogent, from the holders of a position so close under its wing. The frost had given on the previous night, and left us to the full enjoyment of the first day of rain for many weeks. For siege work, frost, bitter cold as it is when it was so strong as we had had it, is infinitely preferable to wet weather. It was terrible work to man the foreposts on such a day as this, when men got muddy to the waist before they reached their posts, and when the wet and muddy clothes dried, if they dried at all, on the persons of the wearers. Fine time for rheumatism and catarrh, and other affections of the same kind, was such weather as this, when the warmth opened the pores just to let the raw dampness come in. In Ville Evrart we had not mud but water. The place was all but flooded out. There was a partial block of ice in the Seine, lower down, and the river had overflowed its banks, and spread out on the always juicy plain. Nogent was utterly invisible in the drizzle, although to do it justice, it was occasionally audible in reply to the steady but slow firing of our batteries. Ville Evrart was a bad find in the way of information, but outside were rain, water and mud; inside friendliness, a good fire, and a sofa, which with a chair at its foot to eke out the length, made a decent bed. So I stayed the night with the Saxon lieutenant who commanded the post. And my ride to Ville Evrart had not been wholly barren after all; I had picked up by the way a little nugget all the way from Chelsea. Thomas Carlyle on the foreposts! The "sage of Chelsea" among the besiegers of Paris! Yea, verily, not indeed in the actual flesh and Scotch plaid, but represented by certain written words, the authorship of which no one could doubt, even if he were not familiar with the handwriting. In the German armies are many who know how to wield the pen as well as the sword. One of these ambidextrous men now in the Saxon Army before Paris here had sent a little book of his to Chelsea, sure that the matter of it would find sympathy there, and as I rode through the village in which Herr Waldmüller was quartered, he brought me the letter which Mr. Carlyle had sent him in acknowledgment. With the permission of the recipient I transcribed it, and here is the copy:—

"5, Cheyne Row, Chelsea, Dec. 27, 1870.

"Sir,—Three nights ago there came to me from

Dresden a beautiful little blue book, 'Die tausendjährige
Eiche in Elsass,' which—especially as coupled with your
kind inscription on the cover of it, bearing date 'vor
Paris'—I read with very great interest. It is in itself
truly a beautiful little book, put together with a great
deal of art, and betokening in the writer a delicate, affec-
tionate, poetic, and gifted human brother, well skilled in
literary composition—not to speak of still higher things.
Nowhere have I seen a more ingenious arrangement of
whatever was bright and human in an antiquarian study
into a really living and artistic form than this of Elsass
and its 'Thousand Years' Oak!' That a soul capable of
such work should now date to me from 'Le Vert Galant,'
and the heart of a great and terrible World-event, supremely beneficent and yet supremely terrible, upon which
all Europe is waiting with abated breath, is another circumstance which adds immensely to the interest of the
kind gift for me; and I may well keep the little book in
careful preservation as a memorial to me of what will be
memorable to all the world for another 'thousand years.'
I wished much to convey some hint of my feeling to
you, as at once a writer of such a piece, and the worker
and fighter in such a world; and I try to contrive some
way of doing so. Alas! my wishes can do little for you
or for your valiant comrades, nobly fronting the storms
of war and of winter; but if this ever reach you, let it be
an assurance that I do in my heart praise you (and might
even in a sort, if I were a German and still young, envy
you), and that no man, in Germany or out of it, more
deeply applauds the heroic, invincible bearing of your
comrades and you, or more entirely wishes and augurs a
glorious result to it at the appointed hour. My faith is
that a good genius does guide you, that Heaven itself
approves what you are doing, that in the end Victory is

sure to you. Accept an old man's blessing; continue to quit yourselves like men, and in that case expect that a good issue is beyond the reach of Fortune and her inconstancies. God be with you, dear sir, with you and your brave brethren in arms.

"Yours sincerely,

"T. CARLYLE."

About the second week of January, when the new batteries had lost their novelty, and were found not to realise the sanguine expectations of thôse who had anticipated a speedy reduction of the eastern forts through their instrumentality, we seemed in a state of puzzlement for the time. Were we utterly knocking the French into a cocked hat? Were they squatting in their casemates, watches in hand, counting the hours and the minutes before the time should come when the defence should have reached the climax of heroism, and when, without spoiling their claim to deserve well of posterity, they could send the parlementaire out to the Prefecture of Versailles? On the other hand, were they silent and quiet as they were on some plan or other? were they striving to make us think it was all over with them, and that we had extinguished them, only to turn upon us presently and make a harder attempt than ever to rend us? It was a curious crisis. Day after day, hour after hour, our batteries, all the way from Chenevières to Gonesse, were steadily pelting away at something or other in the nature of hostile positions. On the night of the 7th for instance we began to think we had done a great deal. Rosny and Nogent had not fired a shot all day. Drancy had been a dumb dog. Du Nord, de l'Est, and Aubervilliers had just done enough to let us understand that their pipe was not utterly put out—no more. Then we got com-placent, not to say triumphant. We had "silenced" Rosny and Nogent, that was beyond question. Somebody of a sanguine disposition intimated his conviction that Rosny had but one gun on its ramparts, and that it had been dismounted. Another gentleman, whose forte was saturnine wit, suggested that Ducrot did not want a fire to keep himself warm in Drancy, and, indeed, that he must have some time before found the quarters too hot for him. We did not let ourselves be led away exactly into buncombe, but we were very anxious for the end, and everybody knows how much the wish is father to the thought. Well, the morning came laden with its eventualities. What were they? The white flag, general silence of the forts, Ducrot's coat-tails visible to the mind's eye fluttering behind him as he skedaddled, a triumphantly pious telegram from Versailles, and a general gaudeamus? All the other way. Rosny and Nogent the "silenced" were firing just enough to show that each had more than one gun, and that nothing was farther off than a condition of "dismount;" Drancy, the despised, absolutely flared up, and gave us back quite a warm cannonade, regardless of our speculations as to Ducrot's coat-tails. But the day before we had thought Drancy not only silenced, but abandoned. Abandoned batteries don't, as a rule, fire three or four rounds a minute. No doubt Drancy must have been undergoing a heavy punishment, but it came up for it like a glutton, and seemed to have an unlimited capacity. I imagine a good deal of pains had been taken with the place. Although it looked detached, and although our fire could converge on it from several points, there had been time to improve its few natural advantages, and it might perhaps be best described as a kind of informal outwork of Aubervilliers. My information led me to believe that from that fort to it there ex-

tended across the plain a more or less regularly constructed protected way with a continuous entrenchment
and strong earthworks supported by batteries at intervals.
It was curious, not to say suggestive, how the French
clung to this position out on the plain, when they had
given ground everywhere else on the east side.   In itself
it was not worth a second thought strategically—it must
have had some relative value in their eyes, else why should
they have continued to hold it now that, instead of being
aligned with other forepost positions of theirs, it was not
indeed altogether detached, but the pharos on the end
of a pier running out into an ocean, raked wholly by
German artillery? It is unquestionable, I think, that they
continued thus limpetlike to hold on Drancy because of its
value as a base of operations against Le Bourget, the key
to the easiest natural road out of Paris, nor do I believe
that till Colonel Bartsch's guns opened their thunder
against St. Denis, the idea was definitely abandoned of
an eruption by this face.

January the 9th presented still abominable drizzle of
fast-falling minute snow flakes, coupled with intense frost,
that made the atmosphere as thick as pea-soup, and the
roads as impassable as if they had been made of glass
lubricated with grease.   A bombardment in such weather
could not be brisk.   Still, the German guns had been
pegging away with a measured steadiness, and, to judge
by the faint sounds that came to us from the south, there
was no want of activity there. Preparations were steadily
going on for increasing the din on the north side. Colonel
Bartsch had moved to Villers-le-Bel, along with Colonel
Himpe, and a park of artillery, brought down from Mezières,
had been established there with all its accompaniments
of mud, grenade-filling, trains of country carts, and

miserable peasants. St. Denis, its forts and town, were
to be subjected to a systematic bombardment. The scientific men had been over the ground and chosen the positions for the batteries, the which I shall presently describe in detail; then had come staff-sergeants of engineers with tape and pegs; and now the working parties
were toiling by night and sleeping by day. Long before,
in case of need, vast quantities of fascines and gabions
had been woven together in the forest of Montmorency
and the wood of Arnouville, and those had now found a
use and were being carted under cover of fog and darkness to the places where they were to be utilised. The
loading-up depôt for the Montmorency was the lawn in
front of Rousseau's hermitage. Forts Rosny, Noisy, and
Nogent still preserved their strange silence, with the
blinds down or the shutters up, whichever expression
may be most applicable. No liberties were, however,
taken with them, for the mask of silence was distrusted.
The Redoubt de la Boissière above Merdan was the only
French work on the east side that continued to mani-
fest any activity, and its fire was steady, although very
sluggish.

When visiting Soisy, to have speech with some French
deserters, I saw General Manteuffel as he halted in that
village to dine with General Alvensleben, on his way to
Versailles, prior to taking up his new command—that of
the 5th Army. He had left General von Göben with
the 1st and 8th Army Corps and Kummer's Landwehr
Division, forming the 1st Army, to dominate the North,
and keep Faidherbe in check. He himself was to take
command of the 2nd, 7th, and 14th Army Corps, to
form a separate army, which was already on its march
to support von Werder, and baulk Bourbaki's attempt.
General Manteuffel was confident that von Göben was

left quite strong enough to stamp out Faidherbe, and keep the North in order.

It was quite in accordance with German forethought that before the middle of January the dispositions had been all arranged that should follow the capitulation of Paris, should hostilities still continue to be maintained in the provinces. These dispositions certainly did not comprehend, as some reported, a retirement on certain provinces of France, leaving meanwhile isolated garrisons in the strong places outside these districts. Nothing could have been madder than that policy. It would have involved a forepost line to which the circle around Paris was a bagatelle; armies standing ever ready, waiting for the concentrated attack of French armies, choosing their own place and their own time. A French success in such circumstances needed only a pushing General to make an invasion of Germany practicable. Three or four days' forced marches from the line fancy dictated to rumour-mongers would have brought the red breeches again on to the Exercise Platz above Saarbrück. There would have been no "masterly inactivity" in such a policy; it would have been pure fatuity. No; if the French had obstinately refused to throw up the sponge and own to the loss of the stakes, the punishment, sickening as it was, was perforce to go on. Manteuffel's duty, after foiling Bourbaki, was to bring to reason Lyons and the south-west. Two days before the formal capitulation of Metz, the 2nd Army Corps, it may be remembered, took the road for action elsewhere. That corps was now once again on the march—this time eastward; and I know that other orders of readiness had been already issued before the 10th of January, that all the dispositions had been made, and that all that was being waited for was the right time in the judgment of the

16*

244 THE WAR BETWEEN FRANCE AND GERMANY.

military authorities. In the event of the continuance of the war after the capitulation of Paris, the Maas Army was to have been broken up, and its commander, the Crown Prince of Saxony, with the 4th Army Corps and the Guards, was to have gone away northward, with the duty of subjugating right to the water's edge the whole of France lying to the northward of Paris. This arrangement would not have superseded General von Göben even nominally; he would still have retained the command of the 1st Army. Paris, of course, was to have been occupied militarily, and its garrison was to have consisted of the Bavarians, Saxons, Würtembergers, and Mecklenburgers. Further details with which I became acquainted have ceased to interest since the contingency to which they related was happily averted.

Till the 10th of January I had occupied very comfortable quarters in a château in Margency, known familiarly in the head-quarters of the Maas army as the "Guesthouse." But the "Guesthouse" filled up so that there was scant accommodation for guests. There came to head-quarters for a day's visit a certain Russian Prince, and what was to be done for him in the shape of quarters? There came unto me Hauptmann von Wurmb, our quartermaster, full of polite regrets to disturb, but with a request that I would make room for the Prince. There was a château of great beauty and comfort in Andilly, he said, close by, to which he would be glad to escort me, and which I was free to consider my own. Andilly is a hamlet a little higher up the hill of Montmorency, about five minutes' walk from the head-quarter château. It was added, with great geniality, that I was not entitled to reside in the "Guesthouse," since I was no longer to be considered a guest, but "one of ourselves." The objurgation which I felt inclined to launch

against the Russian Prince, I repressed when I saw my
new dwelling-place. Talk of the hardships of war! Why,
as the result of the change I became the sole occupant
of a château, in which there were gorgeously-furnished
public rooms, a billiard table, a library, ever so many
snug bedrooms, a hot-air apparatus, carpets, blankets,
sheets, a good cellar of wine, everything, in short,
"suited," as the advertisements say, "for the occupation
of a nobleman or gentleman of position." The place
had not been injured so much as by the breaking of a
glass. There was a French gatekeeper and his wife, and
a French gardener and his wife, and the quartette had
nothing to do but wait on "Monsieur." If any lady of
my acquaintance had desired a camellia for her hair, she
would only have had to send a "trusted courier" across
to Andilly, and she should have been accommodated
punctually. For there were in "my grounds" a hot-
house, a special camellia-house, and an orangery. I
quailed in sight of the luxury, dreading lest it might
prove my Capua, and tempt me from braving the chances
of casual quarters with a shake-down or a heap of straw
for a bed.

This same village of Andilly was less eloquent of
war time than any other place in the neighbourhood.
Nearly all the inhabitants had come back who had left
—numbers never had quitted their homes. You saw
children playing in the street; and as I passed to the
Feldpost in the morning, I could hear them hum over
their lessons in the "École Primaire," in the Mairie. The
village was strongly anti-Republican. It would have been
heartily glad to see the Emperor back; or, if that were
impossible, it would have been delighted to be ruled over
by the Orleanists—which of the two was quite immaterial,
only please, "for the love of God, no Republic." I must

add that the village was very drunken, at least its male
population was. You see they had nothing to do but
chop firewood and wait for the surrender. There was
no want of money, as most were gentlemen's servants,
or hangers-on of some kind to the neighbouring *propriétaires*,
who had all fled. And there were two wine shops where
very bad brandy was retailed, and which were ever
full of chattering, gesticulating individuals in blue blouses
and wooden shoes, who seemed to get the more civil in
the same ratio as they got the more drunk.

The 11th of January brought little perceptible change
on the eastern and northern aspects of the siege. Drancy
had been seemingly definitely silenced, if not abandoned.
The three easternmost forts were silent and blinded, but
this was no synonyme for "silenced," and that they were
distrusted was evident from the avoidal to occupy the
plateau of Mont Avron. The Redoubt de la Boissière
continued firing. Aubervilliers fired very heavily and
continuously for some hours against the batteries at Le
Blanc Mesnil and Pont Iblon. The new batteries in
front of Chenevières had produced more appreciable
effects than any of the others. It seemed to have driven
the French out of St. Maur, and, in conjunction with the
guns at Noisy, to have greatly quelled the firing of the
continuous work above Joinville, which had Gravelle and
La Faissanderie for its flanks. The importance of having
cleared the peninsula formed by the most southerly bend
of the Marne, and at the throat of which is St. Maur,
must be obvious by a glance at the map. The gunboats
were lying, with their steam up, in the reach of the river
that skirts the flank of Fort La Briche. They had, four
or five of them, and more than once, made short raids
out to fire a shot towards Epinay. Fort La Briche itself
had been comparatively silent lately, but on the 11th it

and the double crown work Du Nord fired with some
persistency into Epinay, St. Gratien, Ormesson, La Barre,
La Chevrette, Deuil, and Montmagny, in fact all round
our forepost line to the north-west and north. I am not
aware that any shells have fallen in Pierrefitte, but it is
likely enough. It was noticeable that the projectiles
thrown by La Briche were of inferior calibre to the large
shells it had been wont to fire, and it was thought
probable that that fort had been at least partially denuded
of its' bigger guns, with their ammunition, for the
strengthening of the southern positions. The signs which
I have narrated were not uncommon portents heralding
a sortie, and, in anticipation of any effort of the kind, I
made the circuit of the forepost line, extending from
Epinay, where the line of the Seine was quitted out of
respect to Fort La Briche, around the half-moon in the
plain, the other horn of which rested on Stains. Epinay,
once the most beautiful of all the beautiful villages on
this north side of Paris, was a shattered wreck. Its church
was smashed, riddled with shells; its population had long
fled, and its aspect was unutterably desolate. The gunboats were pounding into it as I was being civilly enter-
tained by the officer of the 31st Regiment who commanded for the day. What had been once one of the
finest houses in the environs belonged to a brother of
M. Crémieux, of the Provisional Government. Between
French shells and German "belligerent rights," the place
was wrecked utterly. The floors of the deserted rooms,
in which the wind whistled gustily through the shattered
windows and the shell-holes, were littered with mouldy
papers. There were layers of cancelled cheques drawn by
Levy, Crémieux, and Co. on the Bank of France, nearly
all for large sums. The road was very much exposed
between the villages, and collisions between the patrols

were of nightly occurrence. There had been quite a little
fight outside Ormesson on the previous night, upwards of
forty shots having been fired, at random no doubt, for
I heard of no casualties. In this village, which is not
an English mile from the guns of La Briche, and which
had by no means escaped its tender mercies, it was
strange, and indeed affecting, still to see inhabitants
clinging, poor precarious wretches, to what had been
once prosperous homes. The château of La Chevrette,
once the residence of Madame d'Epinay, Rousseau's
friend, had escaped with wonderfully little damage from
shell-fire, although it would hardly have been an eligible
residence. The walk across the open in front of Deuil,
from La Chevrette to Villanteneuse, is not one exactly to
be prescribed as a pleasant relaxation for a holiday; but
then its disagreeables and dangers disappeared in the
knowledge that one was going to Villanteneuse, a village
which till the morning I had believed to be still, as regarded one end of it, in the French hands. It seemed,
however, that the Germans had quietly got possession of
it a few nights before, and certainly there they certainly
were occupying the place as far as the church, which is
at the St. Denis end of the village. Then there is a bit
of open ground, and presently, about 150 or 200 yards
away, are the walls surrounding the grounds of the château of the same name as the village, where the French
were still located. If the sun rose or set in the south,
the place is so near St. Denis that the long shadows of
the chimney stalks would all but reach it. You heard of
fraternising hobnobbing over the contents of flasks between the sentries under cover of the night, of requests
made and granted for lumps of sausage and pipefuls of
tobacco, and really nothing seemed to be more natural.
The sentries did not need to bawl to each other to

ascertain mutual friendliness. The grey-coated gentleman yonder, who now and then showed little bits of himself, I could have conversed with in quite an ordinary tone. On the heights above Pierrefitte the batteries, being constructed for the edification of St. Denis, were already far advanced; the one on the Villanteneuse side of the height was, indeed, ready for the guns; the Stains batteries were also progressing rapidly. A careful inspection of St. Denis and its surroundings from the closest accessible point did not impress me with the idea that any preparations for an *Ausfall* were going on, and no troops were visible on the other side of the inundations, in the vicinity of La Courneuve. Returning *viâ* Montmorency, I paused as well on the terrace for a last look southwards; and lo! huge clouds of black smoke were rising away over the western shoulder of Montmartre, just about the place where in a very clear day one could see the towers of Notre Dame. The smoke evidently rose from a burning area of no small magnitude, and it was continuous, rolling away on the wind in great swarthy folds. The fire that caused the smoke must have been far behind Montmartre, although it was over its shoulder that I saw it, and there was too much of it to have been caused by the burning of a single house. Of course, the connection between German shells and a big fire in Paris was not conclusive; but the coincidence of bombardment and fire had a certain suggestiveness. The smoke continued to thicken during the half-hour we stood watching it. When darkness came on no flames were visible, but the cloud became lurid as if the fire lay too low behind Montmartre to be itself visible, while it threw its reflection upward.

One beautiful autumn afternoon—it was the 7th of October, although now it seems years ago—I witnessed

the Landwehrmen of the Division Kummer falling in their
ranks as they stood, rather than give ground before the
furious assault that burst out upon them from the works
to the north of Metz.   In earlier pages of these volumes
I have tried to describe what I witnessed and what I felt
—inadequately, I am conscious, for there are certain
feelings that will not somehow go into writing, strive
how you may to give them expression.   In the course of
my daily duty it fell to me to write of what I had seen,
in the columns of the newspaper, as whose representative
I was on the field.   In no long time there came to me
the first of a series of very pitiful letters—letters that
made me shudder when I saw the under-officer with the
bundle from the Feld post, although I knew that the
packet was sure to contain letters from loved ones over
the water.   But with these there came with some frequency others.   It so happened that what I had written
in the *Daily News* found its way into most of the German papers, and not a few were the Landwehrwomen—
alas! that so many were in truth widows—who, in their
simple reasoning, concluded that he who penned it must
have a soft spot in his heart, and would try hard to answer the questions they asked as to how it had fared
with the fathers of their children.   That I did what I
could in this way, under difficulties that must occur to
any reader, I believe not a few humble families in the
Fatherland would bear ready testimony.   The sad stream
flowed toward me again while I abode before Paris, this
time from Saxon-land.   God help us—no man feels war
till it comes home to him in some such way as this.
Morning after morning, that smiling secretary at the field-
post in the park handed me over letters, which, were I
to copy a few of them, would bring the water into the
eyes of every reader.   Some were from friends asking

after friends—these were generally wordy and occasionally inflated, although always doubtless genuine.   But
brothers wrote simple questionings about brothers.   Fathers wanted to know about sons, wives about husbands.
Oftener still, mothers were the questioners.   Poor creatures, how precise were the details! Regiment, battalion,
company, aye, and a personal description now and then
besides.   "Tall, slender, with bright blue eyes and curly
auburn hair, very small hands, and a greenstone ring on
one of the fingers of the right hand, and his ears pierced."
This minuteness, it was explained, should I happen on
Fusilier ——— lying on a battle-field.   Ah, fond mother!
there would have been little brightness in the blue eyes
in that case, and I should have had to look a long time
before I found the "greenstone ring on one of the fingers
of the right hand."   There comes a lump in my throat
when, looking over the packet, the most touching souvenir
man could have of the war, I light upon a tear-blurred
epistle from a poor woman in Kamenz, who, it seemed,
had seen some extracts from my correspondence in some
Saxon paper.   She wrote that she "was sure I must be a
father, and would not spare, therefore, a little trouble to
get information for a mother about her sons."   She had
given two hostages to the Fatherland—in what guise
could the Fatherland redeem the pledge? Was it easy to
tell her, think you, that one of her sons lay behind Brie
with twenty inches of frozen French earth on his breast,
and comrades unto the death—comrades in the grave—
right and left of him? That I had seen the other in a
ward in the Noisiel lazarette, contemplating with a philo-
sophy that seemed begotten of a cigar, the stump of one
of his legs that the doctors had stripped for dressing?
Strike up the martial music, ring the joy bells; fire the
salutes! Let the cities illuminate, and the mob roar itself

hoarse at the news of victories! God knows all these counterdins are needed to drown the groans from hearts wrung by war.

The 13th of January was a day of dense fog and equally dense dullness. From the east we heard the lazy thud of a big gun now and then fired in protest of total inactivity. Sometimes there came a faint sough from the south that might have been a cart-load of stones emptied in Epinay, or might have been the attenuated noise of the southern bombardment. I saw a regimental officer this day, who had come from Versailles, bringing the tattle and gossip of the second "Staffel" of little big men located in the Hôtel des Reservoirs. His report was that, unofficial or semi-official, Versailles was not at all pleased with the results of the bombardment, so far as it had gone, and especially was disgusted because some 200 shells said to have been projected into Paris had not produced the effect of a capitulation. I ventured to interpret this news according to my own lights. I know that the dukes and princes of the Reservoirs did not wish for the bombardment at all, and had been therefore not indisposed to cry it down. Now that it had commenced, however, there was a not unnatural, although very mistaken, impulse to weigh its effect against the effects of former bombardments by German siege guns. "No fortress has stood our breaching artillery over three days except Strassburg, and that for little longer." "Avron was swept clean in thirty-six hours." "We have been pounding away at these eastern forts now ever so long, and for not a few days at the southern, and yet who can see the holes in them that a serene Pumpernickel could walk in at?" The worthy Pumpernickels of the Reservoirs forgot what these forts surrounding Paris were. Avron was a thing by itself; the most stupendous blunder that

a garrison containing a corporal of engineers ever perpe-
trated. But Mézières, Phalsburg, Toul, Verdun, Strassburg
—one and all of them fell either of starvation or because
the population of the towns around which the fortifications were built were being burnt and bombarded out. I
believe, trusting to memory, that in this war Strassburg
was the only town in the fortifications of which were
battered practicable breaches. The forts round Paris had
no internal population; no houses to be burnt; no children to be blown up as they played in the gutter; no
closure of their supplies either of food or ammunition.
They had to be battered to bits on their own merits; and
you don't batter to bits in a day, works built and protected as they were.   There seemed no reason that, bar
assault and bar panic, the bombardment of the Paris
forts might not last as long as the food inside Paris. But
there is starvation and starvation.   There are few com-
munities that would not arrive all the sooner at the conclusion that starvation pitch has been reached, when a
bombardment is going on around them, and occasionally
into them, than if hunger pinched them in peace.   Why
did Paris hold out? Scarcely, surely, with the forlornest
hope that it could ultimately escape the doom of capitulation; but to deserve well of the country of which it is
the capital—to give time, by engaging the attention of
so many of the enemy, for the provinces to resuscitate
themselves—to earn for itself a name for enduring heroism to last unto all posterity.   But Paris must have
been surely all but hopeless for itself before the middle
of January.   And nobody can deny that the defence of
Paris, had Paris capitulated then, would still have been
one of the grandest episodes of modern warfare.   How
much more then when she bore the terrible strain yet
fifteen days longer?

It would not have been pleasant for such French officers as had broken their parole to have been re-caught by the Germans; still their plight would probably have been preferable to that of officers who had deserted to the enemy, and who might have been given up or re-taken. A message was sent to St. Denis, to acquaint the French chiefs with the fact of the apprehension of three deserting officers who had lately come over the Seine. Trochu sent back a grim and curt message:—"I am already acquainted with the disgraceful fact, and it would be a great kindness if you would send the scoundrels back into Paris, or if there are obstacles to that, if you would yourselves shoot them."

It was observable about this time that drunkenness was on the increase in the German army besieging Paris. In the active campaign preceding the siege you would hardly ever have seen a man drunk; now hiccoughing gentlemen making a staggering exit from the shop tenanted by a marketender were far from uncommon. There were more causes than one for this. The men in a siege get inexpressibly *ennuyé*, and somebody has said that the climax of *ennui* is delirium tremens or suicide. Perhaps even a stronger cause was the want of beer, and the consequent necessity, if a man drank at all, to take glass after glass of rot-gut rum, schnapps, or arrack. If you give a German plenty of beer, you seldom see him actively drunk. He may be passively muzzy, but with thirty or forty glasses inside him he will go through his facings so as to satisfy the sharpest sergeant in the service; but spirits double him up, unless he be an East Prussian or a Pole. The former can take a stint about equal, I reckon, to a seasoned Scotch Highlander; the latter reckon brandy no more than water. I marched, in the early part of the war, for two days with a company of

the 63rd Regiment of von Tümpling's Army Corps. They
were all Poles; half of them spoke no intelligible German,
and the raw spirits that they put out of sight without so
much as winking struck me with abject amazement. We
had little or no beer around Paris. A beer-lover myself,
I knew all the "sure finds" on the northern and eastern
sides, and they did not number half a dozen. Now and
then a few stray casks came to what may be called the
out-quarters of beer. One day in Margency I saw on a
marketender's shutter the label "Bier!!" conspicuously
displayed. This was in the morning; in the afternoon
the ticket had disappeared; the beer was drunk out, and
disappointed men who had come in from the neighbourhood on the strength of the winged report were turning
away, muttering speeches the reverse of soft.

Up till the night of the 13th January, it might fairly
have been said of the defenders of Paris that their actions
were good, if one had regard to the Scriptural explanation
why certain people loved the darkness rather than the
light. The French certainly had never manifested any
love for the darkness for any other purpose than that of
wasting the ammunition of great guns. They had never
snatched the opportunity of a dark night to make a dash
on an exposed German forepost; never marshalled their
forces under cover of the night, that they might be ready
for the assault and surprise with the peep of dawn.
That comical major of Mobiles, who, when he was surprised at his dinner after dark in Ville Evrart, grumbled
most furiously that such tactics were in violation of
civilised warfare, and that there was a tacit understanding that after sundown fighting should cease, expressed,
I take it, pretty closely the general opinion on the subject of the defenders of Paris. They were not even prone
to take advantage of fogs. Nay, Trochu had referred

to fogs as standing in the way of his exertions, although
most men would be inclined to think a fog was just the
thing he would have fervently prayed for. But the night
of the 13th witnessed the double revolution. On that
night—to make a bull—the moon did not rise till the
morning; the night was as dark as a wolf's mouth, and
the fog besides was so thick that in getting along you
had almost to lean against it and press it out of your
path. I was thinking about bed, after quitting the Feld
post-office in Margency, when I heard a sudden burst of
heavy and close firing. As I stood listening, report after
report came up the valley, that could only have proceeded from the big throats of the guns of the forts of
St. Denis. Then there was a spurt of faint musketry
fire, then a louder burst, the din between artillery and
musketry gradually becoming continuous. It happened
that in the afternoon I had been having a discussion
with a staff officer as to the likelihood of a sortie out of
St. Denis, either towards Stains and Pierrefitte or toward
Epinay and Enghien. He took the view that the French,
not being rank maniacs, would make no such attempt; I
contended that, a sortie in any direction being now an
indication of mania, if seriously expected to succeed,
there was, to the perception of the besieged, rather less
insanity in coming out in this direction than any other.
Was this sudden firing, I asked myself, my triumph over
my friend of the staff? It looked very like it from where
I stood; but Margency was a deceptive place as regards
sounds. So I took to horse, and set off for Montmorency
as fast as I could.

Montmorency was "alarmed," but not turned out.
The opinion of those with whom I spoke there was that
Stains and Dugny were the objects of the attack, the noise
of which was swelling louder and louder. There was no

guide by eyesight. The fog was so dense, that one could not have seen a shell burst 100 yards in front of him. Anyhow, whatever was going on was farther east than Montmorency, and the great guns of the St. Denis forts were in full swing. The way to Stains, if a man had any reasonable desire to get there whole when the forts were firing, was to go to Arnouville, and bend backward again by the road leading through Stains into Paris. When I got to Arnouville I had, therefore, overshot Stains, and still the noise of the musketry was south, a little east. It was not Dugny; that was too near. Was it possible that it could be that unfortunate Le Bourget again in trouble? A passing orderly from Gonesse gave me the "office" opportunely. It was Le Bourget, and the French out of Drancy had been pitching into it ever since ten o'clock—it was now eleven. He did not know the dimensions of the attack, but judged it to be considerable from the noise it made. Well, I had ears of my own. "Was he carrying the alarm?" "Nay, Gott bewahr!" and he jogged on contentedly. I made the near cut through Dugny, and got into Le Bourget about half-past eleven o'clock. I cannot say it was a strange scene, for you could see hardly anything; but there was sufficient to engross other senses. Behind walls and in the shelter of the court-yards and their entrances stood the men of the 1st battalion of the Queen Augusta Regiment, which had just been hurried up from Pont Iblon. They were in reserve, for they were not wanted. Shells were crashing in the already smashed and battered houses, and the rattle of musketry was incessant from the end of the village. I took it for granted that the old bone of contention, the railway station outside the village, and close to the Lille road, was what was being fought for, and cautiously adventured in that direction, intend-

ing to go as far as the barricade across the road. In the
darkness I ran up against an officer standing out in the
open coolly smoking a cigar. The officer was Major
von Thümmel, commanding the 2nd battalion of the
Queen Elizabeths, which formed the garrison of Le
Bourget for the night. But there was no fighting for
the railway station, for the unanswerable reason, as the
Major explained, that no railway station existed now.
It had been pounded to splinters in December, and, no
longer affording any cover, the Guards had utterly demolished it, and had used the available wood to make
their fires wherewithal. The Queen Elisabeths thus held
the barricades on the roads, three of which diverge near
the Paris end of the village, certain loopholed shelter
afforded by garden walls, and sundry detached houses of
great strength, which form a kind of suburb on the Paris
side of the little brook Molleret, which passes through
the village at right angles to its principal, and indeed
only, street. They were mostly concentrated in these,
one company, however, being in the houses farther back,
to keep up the communication with the Augustas. The
outermost posts were held by a company of the Guard
Schützen Regiment, these extending away in exposed
field watches on the margin of the Molleret; to the left
of Le Bourget, as one looks toward Paris.

There was a lull in the firing presently, as regarded
musketry at least, and so Major von Thümmel condescended
to enter the doorway wherein I was only too glad to shelter
myself, and give me the history of the evening. It was not
very eventful after all. Our outposts, it seems, as early as
eight o'clock, had heard significant sounds in Drancy, which
the French still obstinately refuse to vacate. There were
bugle-calls and the tread of mustering men, and (so near
were the positions) there had been heard also the tramp of

men being marched across from la Courneuve into Drancy.
I must mention, by the way, that this space, naturally a
level plain, almost bare of houses, had been furrowed by
the French with three successive continuous lines of entrenchments.   One interpretation of this operation was,
that they had so far sapped up toward Le Bourget; another was, that they had thus triplicated the defences
of a tract they might have judged to have been exposed.
Anyhow, the farther parallel touched with its left the la
Courneuve road at a point in advance of that village;
came with a slight sweep to the Lille road at a place
where there are two or three houses; and was continued
with a little more bend to the end of Drancy nearest Le
Bourget.   The second line had its left on la Courneuve
itself, and its right on the farm of Drancy, in the rear
of the village of the same name.   The *repli* line was the
road from la Courneuve to Baubigny.   It was inside one
of these lines that our foreposts had heard the Frenchmen
coming over into Drancy, to act as supports probably.
A little before ten the guns—first of Aubervilliers, then
of de l'Est, du Nord, and, last of all, of Romainville—
had begun to shell Le Bourget furiously.   Then two field
batteries in the first French line between the Lille road
and Drancy had got to work, and suddenly, just after
nine, came a splash of musketry fire out of the thick mist
and darkness.   The Queen Elizabeths knew what was
coming.   Their patrols had been out feeling the interval
between Le Bourget and Drancy, and the advance of a
strong body of French troops had been notified.   Every
man was under cover; every man had finger on trigger
and muzzle out to the front.   So, when the French fire
came, the Elizabeths gave it back steadily and with interest; not acting so foolishly as to rush out to close
quarters in the open, but lying snugly behind their stout

17*

barricades and the strong walls of the houses, and firing
in the direction whence came the French fire. It seemed no
Frenchmen were visible. They were within a hundred yards,
but came no farther. After firing they stood for awhile,
then gave ground and fell back towards Drancy. Yet,
again, about eleven, they had come on; much the same
features characterising this attempt as the last. And now
had they got enough, did I think? asked the Major; or
did I think they were gluttons, and would come at it
once more?

They answered his question, not I. Just as he spoke
came the "Steady, men!" from the officer by the barricade. There was a dull sound of tramping, sharpened
by a few isolated shots, and then a confused belch of
musketry fire. I heard the officer by the barricades order
—"*Schnellfeuer!*" and *schnell* was, beyond a doubt, that
same *Feuer*. Nor were the French behind-hand in their
reply. One could hear the bullets pattering on the walls
on both sides of the road, as if the fog had burst out
into big hailstones. This steady firing lasted some five
minutes, then the French musketry fell away. In the
comparative silence from the front there were audible,
easily, the shouts of the officers, "*En avant!*" "*En
avant!*" One officer—judging by the direction whence
came the firing, he must have commanded the right—
had a very shrill voice, and as he screamed rather than
shouted a wretched dog, close by, began to bark in
opposition; whereat the Queen Elizabeths laughed con-
sumedly behind their cover. Another officer—how I pitied
the poor gallant fellows—ranged from wrath to sorrow
in his desperate efforts to make his men charge. "*En
avant*," he began, and repeated once or twice. "*Sacré
nom de Dieu, en avant, canaille!*" And then he was ever
so much nearer us, and must have dashed out to the

front alone—"*Pour l'amour de Dieu en avant, mes enfans!*"
But the *enfans* didn't see it. Indeed, they did not see
the pleasure of staying where they were. I heard no
command of retreat given, but the firing dropped away
to a distance, and intermittingly, and then ceased altogether. At a quarter to one there was an advance on
the other side from la Courneuve, but enfiladed in the
way as the troops composing it were by the guard field
watches on the Dugny road, they never got so close as
the assailants from Drancy, nor did they hold their ground
so stubbornly. Till three o'clock the forts continued their
fire; then all was silent again. And so ended this sortie
—if you can call it a sortie—against Le Bourget. German
loss: one man of the Queen Augustas; two, of the Queen
Elizabeths severely wounded. The Augusta man had his
shoulder smashed by a shell: three men of the Queen
Elizabeths, slightly wounded. No officer touched. But
surely there must have been ever so many Frenchmen
killed and wounded? the reader is entitled to ask? Perhaps there were—indeed, I don't see how it is possible
that they should not have suffered considerably. But they
left nothing behind them, except here and there a red
patch of blood on the snow-covered ground. Patrols of
the Guards were beating the front all night, as well to
ensure security as to pick up any wounded men they
might fall in with. They found none. The French had
carried off their dead and wounded.

On the 14th the guns of our batteries, 18, 19, and
20, continued firing heavily into Drancy, and there came
a boom through the thick air from the southward that
spoke of the gunners of Raincy, Gagny, and Noisy-le-
Grand being busy likewise. There was no renewal of
the attack on the part of the French, and the forts of
St. Denis were almost wholly silent.

During the latter part of my residence in Margency
I received a considerable number of letters both from
England and from various parts of the continent, sent
me by English families who had residences in the northern
and eastern suburbs of Paris, and who were anxious to
learn what fate had befallen their houses and furniture.
Many of these it was impossible to answer on account of
the difficulty of definitely recognising the places inquired
for.   But there were certain general facts capable of ap-
plication to individual cases.   In any village or district
that was not in the immediate forepost line, the property
of neutrals had been as much as possible respected. The
property of French residents had been treated with equal
deference, in cases where either the owners themselves
had remained, or where they had left responsible servants
to represent them. Such a course was obviously necessary
also for neutrals, such as English people. It did not
suffice to stick up the Union Jack, lock one's doors, and
clear out, trusting to the talismanic influence of the bunting.
But as, for instance, in Lady Ashburton's château at St.
Leu, and in Madame Sapey's residence in Andilly, in
which latter I was now located, leaving behind the servants
had secured total immunity from any injury whatever; and
these may be taken as illustrative cases. There were other
instances where servants had abandoned their master's
houses, after being left in charge of them, with the result
that they were pillaged by mauraders and by Francs-
tireurs before the Germans threw their grapple round
Paris. Such was the plight of a once pretty house in
Montfermeil, concerning which its owner, an Englishman,
wrote to me from Nice. When the Saxons came they
found it already a wreck internally. Had it been spared
by the Francs-tireurs it would probably have been occupied
by officers, and so escaped material hurt. But there being

no furniture left when the German occupation took place
it had been relegated to the soldiers, and was usually inhabited by a Corporalschaft of a Saxon regiment.   Still
no material injury had been done to the house.   A painter
and glazier might cure all the hurt the Germans had done
it.   The upholstery work necessary must go to the débit
of the Francs-tireurs.   Around Montmorency, St. Brice,
Ecouen, Clichy, Montfermeil, &c., this may be taken as
a typical condition of the habitations.   Farther to the
front again, the wreck was more thorough, because there,
the shells from the French forts had a voice in the matter.
An English lady of the name, I believe, of Stephens, had
a beautiful residence in Pierrefitte, with a fine picture
gallery.   There was a shell hole through the biggest of
the pictures, and the château had been otherwise extensively ventilated by similar masterful expedients.   Respecting this mansion, I afterwards learned, that one of
the last thrown from Du Nord in reply to the bombardment had fired it.   There was a beautiful mansion belonging to an English family on the verge of the Forest
of Bondy before Raincy, and to the right rear of the
Villemomble station.   If that family has yet come back
to what was once their home, they must have recognised
the need, not alone for the painter and glazier, but for
the mason also.   The place was occupied by the Saxons
for about a month as Outpost No. 5, and Mont Avron
refused to respect its neutrality under such circumstances.
It was as nearly as possible laid in ruins.

The fog was not so thick on the 14th; but there was
a bright sunshine and a fall of small snow.   Either the
air was in an exceptionally good condition for conducting
sound, or there was an exceptionally big din somewhere,
for the noise of distant heavy firing came ever and anon
in a very discomposing way.   Nothing in the siege opera-

tions was calculated to make a conscientious man more nervous than this undefined and indefinable sound of remote firing. If he disregarded it and stopped at home, induced thereunto by bitter inclemency outside and by comfortable quarters inside, he could not quit himself, as every wind-puff brought the noise toward him, of the dread that he might be missing something of importance; and if he kicked off the slippers and drew on the long boots, what, oftener than not, had he for his pains? Many a time did I chase this same sound much as a man hunts a Will-of-the-wisp, ever thinking that the next crest would bring me in sight of the work, only to be disappointed, and be farther off the nucleus of the sound than when I started. On this occasion I hardened my heart sedulously against the temptation, because there were reasons why one should not be out of the way of head-quarters even from hour to hour; but it is impossible to convey to a home reader how uncomfortable this constant distant unexplained booming made one. One consolation was that head-quarters had no cognisance of anything abnormal going on; and the sound was philosophically set down, by those whose duty it was to know, as emanating from the southern and eastern bombardment.

But about four o'clock in the afternoon the firing became so hot that one could stand the uncertainty no longer. After all, when I got to Montmorency, it turned out to be nothing very serious. The northern forts had noticed something—it must have been very dimly—that they did not like in the neighbourhood of the heights above Montmagny and Pierrefitte, and were pegging away very furiously at these seemingly solitary slopes. Solitary, however, they were not, for the working parties were taking advantage of the fog (which had thickened since

morning) to expedite by a spell of day work the com-
pletion of the siege-batteries getting ready for St. Denis.
All round the forepost semicircle from Epinay to Pierrefitte there was a tolerably brisk musketry fire, but it was
at long range, and no positive attacks fell to be repelled.
Argenteuil had been full of noise all day, fuller than
usual. I think there is a chance of lead mines being discovered in the vicinity of this town in some future age.

Before going to Soisy, where I had an engagement
for the evening, I made a detour into Epinay, from which
direction the sound of the musketry fire came the most
strongly, to ascertain for myself what was doing. That
there were French sharpshooters on the long island in
the Seine, the crackling intermittent fire therefrom seemed
to prove, although the gentlemen themselves were invisible in the fog; while the German posts on the Epinay
bank now and then drew a bow at a very wild random
venture. When in Epinay this afternoon I saw handled
for the first time a weapon which I learned was coming
into considerable use along the northern foreposts. It
was called the *wallbüchse;* it was of the needle pattern,
but the balls were of iron, and the calibre was at least
three times greater than that of the ordinary needle-gun,
while the range of the weapon was considerably longer.
It carried 2,000 mètres, and sent a ball right through a
fascine stuffed in a battery. It was, however, a cumbrous
weapon, requiring to work it properly two men, one to
hold it on the shoulder, one to serve the breech-loading
apparatus. The recoil was so strong, that it required a
spring coil in the stock to counteract it. The forepost
men were much fonder of the chassepot with which they
were supplied in considerable quantities; and were thus
able to meet the French sharpshooters on about equal
terms.

In Soisy in the evening I was present at the opening of a packet sent from home to a young lieutenant of the 66th Regiment, with whose Company I had been dining. The worthy people, his parents in Magdeburg, understood pretty well what were the wants before Paris. Here is the inventory:—One box of very good cigars; a selection of wurst; a bottle of mustard, unfortunately broken; a warm woollen comforter; a glorious piece of flannel for the chest; a piece of German cheese; two pair of cork soles; two pair of long thick woollen stockings; a pair of wadded goloshes; fur gloves, photographs, a letter. The transmission of the whole cost about 9d. Verily the Feld post is a great institution!

The 16th brought a total change of weather. Frost and snow were alike gone, and we had a high wind from the south, bringing frequent splashes of rain on its wings. It brought something else besides rain—the bellow of the bombardment in the south, which dinged steadily from morn till night. There was a curious regularity in the sound. It did not come in casual and fitful gusts, but with a regular beat and stroke just like the working of a steam-engine. The mist was gone, and although the squalls, when they came, dimmed the prospect for the time, in the intervals the air was very clear, and one could see long distances. I sat at my window half the day, watching the southern bombardment. Strange as it may appear, I could see it with the utmost distinctness, owing to the elevated position of my habitation, half-way up the hill of Montmorency. In the foreground was Enghien and St. Gratien; then, across the Seine, Gennevilliers, Asnières, and the other villages on the peninsula; then Paris itself, looking absurdly near. With the glass I could see every detail in the structure of the Arc de Triomphe; and the dome of the Invalides and

the tower on Montmartre were equally plain.   Right
across Paris, on its farther margin, there was first a continuous streak of white smoke.   This was from the guns
on the *enceinte*.   Farther away, in the middle of the
rising background, were three distinct patches of white
smoke.   These must have been Forts Issy, Vanvres, and
Montrouge.   To judge by the smoke, it was clear enough
that they were not silenced, nor anything near it.   Still
farther away and close to—in some cases on—the horizon,
were more patches of white smoke, and these were the
German batteries.   Much nearer to us, and farther to
the right, Mont Valérien had got his nightcap on, and
certainly was snoring in his sleep very heavily.   Let
anybody try to look in this way across smoky London,
and see what a failure it would be.   At all times the
atmosphere of Paris is clear; it was clearer than ever
now when fuel is so scarce.   If shells, as was reported,
were regularly coming into Paris, they were not firing
the city.

I heard many expressions of pain and indignation
among the members of head-quarters staff of the Maas
Army, on account of an utterly gratuitous falsehood put
in circulation by the *Wiener Fremdenblatt*, to the effect
that disagreements had occurred between the King of
Prussia and the Crown Prince of Saxony, and the King
of Saxony was coming to Versailles with intent to solder
up the unpleasantness.   The falsehood was too apparent
to merit anything but contempt.   Throughout the siege
there never was anything but the utmost cordiality between Versailles and Margency, and nobody could live
long in familiar relations with the latter head-quarters
without becoming aware how genuine and hearty was this
cordiality as regarded the chiefs of the Maas Army; and
—judging from every appearance—how reciprocal was

the good feeling. Ever since I became acquainted with
the composition of the Maas Army head-quarters staff, it
had impressed me strongly as being a really valuable and
successful auxiliary in the actual and virtual unification
of Germany. Here we had Saxon officers, Würtemberger
officers, Prussian officers, officers of the late Hanoverian
Army, all working together in the most enthusiastic and
genial manner, living together in the same quarters,
associating round the same board, taking their daily
rides together, and, in fine, blending so thoroughly, that
the differences, of what can scarcely with truth be called
diverse nationality, were utterly invisible.   The same
thorough blending was apparent right down the ladder
till it reached to the private soldiers; among whom it
was as marked as higher up.   Saxons, Guardsmen, and
Würtembergers, had stood to one another like men—like
Germans—in more than two or three bloody tussles with
the common enemy.   They had shared the same bivouac;
drank out of the same bottle; and they were, in the
words of the old song, "brethren all."   A large share of
this thorough blending that had welded the Maas Army
into a consistent whole, from the staff to the field watch,
was due to the personal influence and personal attributes
of the Crown Prince of Saxony himself, the commander
of that army ever since it was first formed.   The soldiers
who were the subjects of his father spoke of their Prince
with a personal love and admiration which was right
pleasant to listen to.   "He is a gallant soldier and a
true man," said to me that wooden under-officer Schultz,
his woodenness disappearing for the moment when he
came to talk of his Prince.   And Prince Albert had likewise won the personal liking and respect of the whole of
his army, besides that portion of it which came out of
Saxony proper.   The explanation is simple enough.   He

is a plain, frank, manly soldier; too fearless for the heir-
apparent to a kingdom; utterly unskilled in Machiavel-
lianism, and, likely enough, quite blind to the advantages it may possess. His *métier* was to command the
Maas Army, and he did so with credit and distinction.
My own estimate of his soldierly frankness and straight-
forwardness of purpose carried me on to this conviction
—that if on any point there ever occurred any misunder-
standing between him and those at Versailles, he was
just the man to get into his little oak-painted carriage,
start off for Versailles without an escort—there never
was a more unassuming Prince in such respects—drop
into the Prefecture, have a quiet talk over the trouble
with the King—who is a man of much the same straightforward soldierly type as himself—put everything straight
by that great institution, "word of mouth," and drive
back again to dinner in Margency, nobody a whit the
wiser; except, perhaps, his sagacious chief of the staff
General von Schlotheim.   But it was all but impossible
to conceive how a conjuncture demanding any such visit
could arise.

On the night of the 16th inst. there rendezvoused
in Margency the officers, under-officers, and privates
from the Guards and Saxons—one of each rank from
every regiment—who had been selected as representatives to be present at the assumption of the Imperial
dignity by King Wilhelm. My "humble roof" was called
upon to afford accommodation for the sixteen officers.
It is a little curious how thus fortuitously I should have
come into close contact with the military deputation after
having casually hit upon the civil one at Lagny in its
way home from Versailles. Monsieur Bourgeois, at the
corner, had some very good cognac; and among Madame
Sapey's goods and chattels, of which I was the temporary

beneficiary holder, was a jolly big punch-bowl. I rather think we made a night of it, but M. Jules, Madame's serving-man, was equal to the occasion with a continuous flow of boiling water. Jules' personal opinion was, that *Messieurs les Prussiens* were *bons garçons*.

My guests, especially the sprightly young Guardsmen, were curiously cynical about the event of the morrow, in which they were to be participators. A studied abstention from the display of any emotion is fashionable among other Guards besides our own, but I should not have cared to be the man to chime in with this tone of the Prussian Guardsmen. One can take a good many liberties with the German if one only goes the right way about it; but there are topics on which one is sure to put his foot in it, if not very careful. I remember one day in the early part of the war, as I lay under a hedge near Vouziers, in the Ardennes, a train-man, with his short sword drawn, rode by me, hectoring a Frenchman, whose horse he wished to requisition, and he turned to me with a humorous grumble about the hardship of his duties. Taking up his tone, I asked him banteringly what he carried his "bread-knife" thus exposed for? Heaven and earth! you should have seen the man's face change. He called me a pig-dog; he swore he would split me up from thigh to throat for insulting the Prussian arms; and he looked uncommonly like as if he would carry his threat into execution. The more I tried to throw oil on the water the fiercer he got, and I really began to fear that I should have to recall old defensive memories with my walking-stick, when an officer opportunely turned up. I have no doubt these Guardsmen would have taken seriously amiss any chiming in with the tone in which they thought it *comme il faut* to adopt regarding their mission.

Next morning (the 17th) the deputation waited on the Crown Prince of Saxony, and received his cordial congratulations as to the object of their mission; and then they took the road for Versailles, whither His Royal Highness, and the leading members of his staff, followed them.   Versailles was off my beat, so I set my face eastward with intent to see what was doing among the batteries in that direction; and on a whisper—not on authority—that there might be a chance of seeing some more active operations than the besiegers had lately been indulging in on the eastern face.   My road lay along the top of the ridge between Sarcelles and Bonneuil, whence a wide and sweeping view is commanded.   The day, atmospherically, was one by itself—one of those dull, surly, yet semi-clear days, that are commoner in summer when thunder is in the air than in mid-winter.   Under such circumstances, the aspect which Paris presented was weirdly unique.   There is a town in the south of Scotland around which lingers to this day a ghastly memory of, which the elders shudder when they speak, and of which the young ones are thankful that they had no personal experience.   Dumfries stands in the bottom of a cup, the edges of which are formed by hills.   At no time is there much circulation of air. . When fogs prevail, or when there is a stagnation of the wind, the stillness is positively painful.   In 1832 the cholera raged in Britain, and it fastened its fell fangs on Dumfries.   For days, for weeks, for months, it claimed its victims, till one-eighth of the population had been heaved into the pits in the churchyard, and till the ill report of the pestilential place was so strong that never a vendor dared enter it with his wares.   And all these days—days when the pest stalked abroad relentless—there hung over the cup, in the bottom of which stands the town, a dull, heavy film—not dense, indeed, but mystically altering the sun-rays from bright gold to a lurid orange, and mantling the whole place with its evil shadow, as if some foul and persistent ogre of death were spreading his pinions over the place. As men walked the streets they felt to smell the cholera-breath, so stagnant and rotten was the air, and they went home and wanted graves ere morning. Let any man who would realise how a death-pall like this can hang over a city, read in Macdowall's "History of Dumfries" the chapter where the author describes the ghastly features of this visitation. As I looked down on Paris to-day there came vividly before me the description I had read of Dumfries in '32. All round it, save on the north side, surged up the foam of the white smoke of the bombardment. Over it hung the dull brown pall of the smoke thrown up by the exploding shells and the casual conflagrations, not large but frequent, which they occasioned. Underneath—below this brooding demon of brown smoke—the city showed out wondrous clear and plain. At times the sun's rays struggled through the black clouds that underlay the heavens; fell on the brown pall; battled through the crannies in it; and kissed lovingly some white house or metal roof in the beautiful city. Never can I forget the strangely beautiful and yet almost ghastly and utterly abnormal effect.

The eastern batteries had taken to volley firing. Instead of timing their shots so that you might have counted a patient's pulse thereby, they now loaded almost simultaneously and fired almost simultaneously. The two batteries between Pont Iblon and Dugny were at work with great energy as I passed behind them, firing towards St. Denis, but, as I take it, chiefly dropping their projectiles into Courneuve. The Blanc Mesnil and Aulnay batteries were pegging away at Drancy, which looked forlorn enough to move the bowels of their compassion, if they had any. There had been no return fire for some hours, as I was assured by the under-officer when I halted in the little battery for a while. Our shells were falling and exploding all about the place, but never a shell came back. Now, it is easy enough, if a shell happens to come to hand to you, to know whether over against you on the enemy's side it is a shell that has exploded or a gun that has been fired, but if you don't hear the whizz and see (or feel) the splinters, it is rather bothersome to distinguish the difference. The sergeant and I agreed for a quarter of an hour that Drancy was silent, and that the explosions in its vicinity were the shells he was projecting, but suddenly there came a jet of smoke, not upwards and umbrella-shaped, but forwards and then upwards, in shape like a series of bed-pillows, and I ventured to express my opinion that these appearances betokened a shot. He differed in opinion—he was a "yearling"— but he owned up to his mistake like a man when the shell came whizzing over the parapet and exploded in the field, about one hundred yards behind the battery. This is the only evidence I saw that any battery on the east side of Paris was alive, with the exception of La Boissière, which was firing very steadily in reply to the Raincy batteries.

I had my ride to Clichy for next to nothing. And yet it was not for nothing. My eastward trip satisfied me that there was no immediate prospect of any attempt to establish batteries on Mont Avron or to assault any of the eastern forts, as I had vaguely heard was in contemplation. The *status quo* of steady slogging at the forts and batteries of junction was steadily maintained, without much apparent effect; but the people working them seemed satisfied, and it was not for outsiders to grumble.

There was a rumour about guns having had what is vulgarly known as a "skinful" of work, and having to be allowed to rest; but if this was the case, certainly the other pieces were made to work double tides. The silent sulkiness of the forts was still preserved, with the exception of Aubervilliers, which was given to losing its temper now and then, and let drive in some direction or other. The St. Denis forts were very quiet on the 18th; their calm trustfulness in a peaceful future was touching, but, as they discovered by-and-by, fallacious. Argenteuil was vexed on the same day by much musketry fire; but Argenteuil was ever a barking dog, and the bite was never reported.

All the northern side the Maas army made merry on the 18th in honour of the event which on that day occurred in Versailles. Champagne was the first tipple to give out in the officers' casino in Gonesse. But when the champagne was done, the fellows philosophically took to beer, and when that in its turn was drunk out, they tackled the red wine without an apprehension as to the intestine commotion the heterogeneous mixture seemed calculated to produce. Weak stomachs are luxuries not to be indulged in by campaigners.

After a sulky, lowering, gloomy morning on the 19th, there came a clearance of the weather in the forenoon, and with it tidings of an important sortie to the southwest and west. No part of the Maas army was engaged, with the exception of the artillery division of the 4th Army Corps, generally quartered in Sannois. The batteries to the northward of Valérien, at Nanterre, Courbevoie, &c., and the big fort itself became eruptive about ten A.M.; and it soon became apparent that they were firing to cover the advance of French infantry by the roads and through the valleys of the peninsula of Gennevilliers. The columns of these headed for Rueil, designed to coalesce with troops that had come out behind Valérien round its northern shoulder, and struck out for Bougival, their front covered by skirmishers, and the batteries firing furiously over their heads. The attack extended all the way round to Montretout and the park wall of St. Cloud, and on this flank the fighting was heaviest and the sortie assumed the most important dimensions. A contingent was detailed to threaten Chaton. On a splendid position in front of the carrières of St. Denis, the artillery of the 4th Army Corps took up its ground, and made brilliant practice in enfilading the French advance on Rueil, as well as in convincing the force that set its face towards Chaton that it was not wanted there, and that a strategical movement in the direction of its own rear was an advisable operation. I heard bickers of musketry fire from the direction of Bougival till nigh sundown, but about four o'clock the artillery made the only sound on our face.

The artillery of the 4th Army Corps lost four men and six horses. They were the targets, nevertheless, of a very furious fire; but the shells fell into the mud, which was nearly knee deep, and although they duly exploded, were muffled by the mire and did little damage. The feature of the sortie, as regarded the northern side, was the armoured railway train, which came out on the St. Germain line, considerably beyond Nanterre, and proceeded deliberately to exchange discharges with the German batteries. There were two gun-trucks in front of the protected locomotive; each truck mounting a long gun that worked on a pivot, and seemed at once a very handy implement, and one, from the protection the armour afforded, tolerably safe to work. The German artillerymen devoted themselves chiefly to efforts for

18*

hitting and disabling the locomotive, and succeeded so far as to damage the chimney—which was unprotected—whereupon the affair retired into the rear of Nanterre. It was Ducrot's command, marching from St. Denis, which our artillery enfiladed to so much purpose as to delay its progress till too late to take the share which had been assigned to it in the operations of the day.

The Germans were evidently not filled with deep apprehensions as to the last writhings of the captive in their grasp here. Artillery was held to form bonds quite as strong as the infantry grip which so long had held Paris down. In accordance with a policy which I have foreshadowed, portions of the besieging army were already being spared to co-operate in more active operations elsewhere. On the 18th the 16th Brigade of the 4th Army Corps was dispatched by railway from Gonesse to St. Quentin, to strengthen the hands of von Göben. In addition to this exodus, there was on the same day a general movement of the troops on the northern front. Details would be wearisome, but the general result was what might be termed a bracing up of the inner circle. The sortie of the 18th did not seem in the slightest degree to interrupt the relentless prosecution of the bombardment on the south and south-west. I judged as much by the evidences of firing which were audible to us on the north side in the intervals of the fog and rain. A German journalist, who was my temporary guest, employed one of those intervals on the 19th in earnestly contemplating Paris through a powerful field-glass, preserving meanwhile a rigid taciturnity. When the prospect once more became obscured, he turned to the fire with the sententious observation, "Dey are getting dare gruel." The phrase smacked of Jemmy Shaw's or Ben Caunt's, at which haunts, I understand, my guest had been a frequent visitor during his single short visit to England; but it was very expressive. They were "getting their gruel," those citizens and soldiers in the white city out there to the south; and the man who should refrain to bear testimony to the enduring constancy and valour with which they were taking the punishment, would have claim neither to the title of a truthful reporter, nor to a capacity for some appreciation of a spectacle and 'an event unique in modern times.

Military writers are busy just now in analysing the distinctions between an army of the people and a professional army. I saw an incident on the afternoon of the 19th, trivial in itself, but which to the comprehension of one familiar with the attributes of a professional army, and who had been also for some months studying the workings of a national military system, was not without its significance. In a field I passed a squad of young soldiers who were practising the bayonet exercise. Presently the drill instructor stood his pupils at ease, whereupon, instead of grounding arms and listlessly waiting for the next "Attention," the squad fell each man to practising industriously the lessons that had just been imparted. There was one young fellow lunging as if he would skewer the garrison of Paris; another preparing to receive cavalry with a pertinacity that must have struck terror into a brigade of horsemen. Then the men took to criticising each other's performances, not chaffingly, but quite seriously, and even anxiously, individual expressions of opinion being, so to speak, illustrated with cuts. Now, is there a drill-sergeant in the British army who can conscientiously assert he ever witnessed a similar "stand-at-ease" episode in any squad he has ever drilled? I have seen a good many squads drilled, but the chief occupations of such intervals I have ever noted to be chewing tobacco, surreptitious attempts at horse-play, and anxious glances at the barrack clock. There is a standing direction to cavalry recruits in our service that they shall take opportunities for practising the sword exercise in their leisure hours. Whoever saw a cavalry recruit fulfilling this injunction? In some barrack-rooms there are masks and single-sticks, but their use is confined to a few who have had some knowledge of cudgel play before enlisting. The Germans cannot touch the French as swordsmen, but both could walk round and laugh at us. An English Dragoon can cut the sword exercise without depriving his horse of its head, and about one in every three is tolerably dexterous at "heads and posts," but not one in twenty have any conception of utilising the sword exercise in actual self-defence. Yet the sword exercise is the mere means to a defensive and offensive end; it is what Euclid is to the practical utilisation of the science of geometry.

"Eight o'clock to-morrow morning, sharp to time, on the steps of the Schloss." These were the parting words to me on the night of the 20th, uttered by an officer of the Crown Prince's staff, to whom I was indebted for many kindnesses. "Sharp to time" I was, but the steps of the Schloss looked quite forlorn in their desolation. It was, in truth, a forlorn and disheartening morning. All the Maas Army, from the Prince to the private, wished for bright, clear weather, and you could not see twenty yards before you. Was this an omen? Did it signify that what the weather could do to throw obstacles in the way of bombarding Paris, it meant to do with persistence? If so, the weather must have owned that it reckoned for very little when the Germans had their minds made up on a line of action. The night before everything had been reported ready. Colonel Bartsch

was not the man to leave loose stitches in his work, and
the answering telegram came from Versailles, "Go ahead
at discretion." I ought by the way to give a brief detail
of what manner of work it was that Colonel Bartsch with
his coadjutors Colonels Himpe and Oppermann had done.
The armament of the new batteries consisted chiefly of
the siege-train employed in the reduction of Mézières,
and it had been brought down by the railway to Villers-
le-Bel, whence it had been brought, partly on the night
of the 19th and partly on that of the 20th, into the
emplacements which had been stealthily prepared for it
more than a week before. The batteries were ten in
number, mounting sixty-two guns, of which thirty-six
were ordinary 24-pounders, eight long 24-pounders, twelve
long 12-pounders, and six short 12-pounders. There
were also two mortars in position behind the Stains batteries. The guns might have been earlier pushed forward, but there was no occasion for hurry in this respect,
pending the accumulation of a sufficiency of ammunition.
Commencing on the right, there was no battery in the
neighbourhood of Epinay. The nimble gunboats might
have enfiladed batteries here. The field batteries on
Mont d'Orgimont could take care that they did not do
so as regards the other two in that neighbourhood, which
might otherwise have been affected by them. These
were—one battery (No. 30) of six 24-pounders behind
Ormesson on the left of the Rouen Railway, directed
against La Briche; one battery (No. 29) of short 12-pound-
ers at La Barre, a little nearer Montmorency. Between
Enghien and La Chevrette, almost directly in front of
Montmorency, there was a third battery (No. 28) of 24-
pounders. The battery of long 24-pounders (No. 27)
stood just in front of the terrace of Montmorency, with
a battery of short 24-pounders (No. 26) below it, above

Deuil.   The height known indifferently as Richebourg
or Pierrefitte (lying between the village of the latter name
and Montmagny) presents on its summit nearest St. Denis
a splendid offensive position for artillery, dominating
alike all the forts; but the position was so much exposed,
that it had been wisely avoided, without any detriment
to efficiency.   This long bluff, whose nose looks out
into St. Denis, contracts about its middle, so that its
promontorium throws forward, as it were, two sheltering
wings for batteries stationed in the narrow waist behind.
Its shape roughly resembles that of a wasp.   This configuration of ground had been admirably utilised.   The
summit had not been loaded with guns, but two batteries
(Nos. 25 and 24) had been, as it were, slung pannier-
wise across the narrow waist, one on either side, so that
they could throw a telling indirect and plunging fire
down into the forts, while the bastion-like bluff in front
of each was an effective screen against the French return-
fire.   No. 23 was just above Pierrefitte.   On the slope
behind the village of Stains (farther round to the east),
with the butt ends of the guns toward Garges, were four
batteries with the howitzers.   On an advantageous position between Pierrefitte and Stains were batteries Nos. 22
and 21, and the mortars.   Thus there was a converging
fire on the focus of the forts from the radius of very
nearly a semicircle.   Of course the fog mattered something.   True, the sights had been taken and distances
calculated over-night, but gunners, like other Christians,
have a natural pleasure in viewing the results of their
handiwork, and with a clear atmosphere openings may
present themselves that a mist effectually conceals.   To
give, then, the fog a chance to rise, the hour of commencing the bombardment had been altered from eight
to nine.   There was something melodramatic in the ex-

pectancy scene, and I wished that I were an artist.   The mist had partially lifted.   On the broad steps of the Schloss stood the Crown Prince, watch in hand, his handsome face bright with the excitement of expectancy. Behind him, in wistful silence, stood several members of the staff.   Saddled horses, fretting at the restraint, were being led up and down on the lawn.   At the gates were visible the watching faces of the straggling military and semi-military population of Margency—gendarmes, ordonanz-men, feld-postillions, the butcher, the Prince's grooms, and a representative of the marketender species. I once heard a travelling showman bawling in front of his booth, "Valk hup, ladies and gentlemen, and see the Hempror Solomon in hall his glory.   Vith vun heye he is a-kintemplatin' the Temple, vith t'other he is ogling the Kveen of Sheba."   As a feat of optics, this was a wonderful performance; but I would not be certain that our telegraph clerk did not match it this morning.   He stood just inside the door of the office, and it certainly seemed to me that he had one eye fixed on the Crown Prince's face and the other on his instrument.   A natural squint may have contributed to the facility of this dual vision.

The clock of the Mairie struck the first chime of nine; there came rolling up from Ormesson a dull muffled report; nearer in the wood behind the Schloss there was a clash, as a tree crashed down, that the woodsmen had kept upright by a single fibre in waiting for the event. Before nine had done striking the single report had swelled into a heavy diapason; the Crown Prince was in the saddle; the telegraph clerk hard at work with my message to England.   So began the bombardment of St. Denis.   Alas, for the short-lived lifting of the fog.   Everybody had fixed his own point, just as you see sportsmen branching off when the hounds give token that they have

found a fox in the cover. The quickest was not in time
to see so much as the smoke from a single canon. For
the firing drew down the heavy mantle again, and the
ears were the only organs called into exercise. The
Crown Prince, with General Schlotheim and an aide, sat
out the fog in his elevated eyry on Mont d'Orgimont,
and must have been rewarded by a partial glimpse of
what was going on between twelve and one, when the
fog again lifted, or rather grew thinner. I tried place
after place, but utterly in vain. Montmorency was blank,
save for a general and a doctor; the white house on the
crest above it had a balcony thronged with staff officers,
and a sea of dense mist surrounding it. Enghien was a
weariness of the flesh, and dangerously close quarters to
boot. So I came home to my interrupted breakfast, and
abode in hope that the mist might disappear later in the
afternoon. The hope was destined to be fallacious.
Although the mist did occasionally rise, just enough to
tantalise one with expectation, it regularly came down
again as heavily as ever. The Crown Prince, after three
hours' weary and bootless sojourn in the little room in
the observatorium, returned to lunch and discontent. Still
the guns kept thundering on steadily; now warming to
their work in the clearer intervals, then falling to the
minimum regulation number of shots as the mist wreathed
round them. Of results of my own knowledge I could
not speak, because I had not been able to see anything,
with the exception of a vague and dim attempt on the
part of the French heavily-armed batteries at St. Ouen
to enfilade our westmost one at Ormesson. This was
about four o'clock—I mean what I saw. The attempt
may have been going on before, and may have lasted
longer. I merely caught a casual glimpse through a
chink in the mist. It was respect for these batteries at

St. Ouen which had prevented the erection of any German battery nearer the Seine than Ormesson, and the contingency of a flanking fire from them had been carefully guarded against. The idea respecting the French fire impressed during the day on experienced artillery officers was that, although keen enough after noon, when the forts, and especially La Briche, pulled themselves together after the staggerer of the morning, the St. Denis forts were but weakly armed, and that with artillery of small calibre and short range; and the correctness of this estimate was vindicated on the surrender. One strong proof of this was that there seemed to be no attempt made to cope with the long 24-pounders on the brow of Montmorency, and the warmest French fire was directed against the heights of Richebourg, where the batteries were much nearer the fortresses. Of casualties on the German side the list for the day was trivial; one man was killed and three wounded (one an officer), belonging to the Guard Fusilier Regiment, quartered in Montmagny. This village was below the battery, and the damage must have been done by a blind shell fired from La Briche. I had expected a greater number of casualties, since the nature of the intermediate ground, well suited as it was for deployment under cover of mist or night, necessitated on the part of the Germans the retention of comparatively strong parties of troops in the villages and on the posts in front of the batteries. Even if the French did not fire into these intentionally, it is obvious that there was a likely billet for such projectiles as fell short. I thought this forenoon, as I looked out on the grey billows that filled the valley, what a chance there was for resolute men to make a spurt and give trouble and alarm at least, if they could do nothing else. And several times the rattling echoes of the big-gun reports sounded like the bicker of musketry; and once or twice I made sure the infantry were at it; but no, it was only the sharp reverberation of the reports in the hills and dells behind. The town of St. Denis was reported at nightfall to be burning. All Paris might have been in one blaze for aught we in Montmorency could have told. But adventurous patrols brought the news in from the precincts of Villanteneuse that a large fire was raging in one place and two smaller ones elsewhere. A bad hour for the ladies of St. Denis, who, daintily gloved and booted, had admired the stalwart limbs of the Prussian Guardsmen taken prisoners at Le Bourget, and likened the soldiers of their own garrison to dwarfs alongside of the big East Prussian men. There was a bitter flitting this bleak January night, I ween, along the straight road leading by the pretty suburb of St. Ouen into the already densely-packed Montmartre. And the citizens of Paris would meet the exiled ones of St. Denis, and asking them "What cheer?" would get for answer that the inexorable Prussian cannon were smashing and burning on the north as on the south. Would the strong hearts melt, we asked ourselves, the tension of the stern determination overstrain itself, and so relax into the conviction that enough had been done against fate, against possibility,—against the luck that every Frenchman strives to hope for in the future—to prove to the world that Paris was not a place of frivolous pleasure lovers only, but that the lovers of pleasure in the old luxurious peaceful city knew how to dare and to endure beyond all previous conception?

At night the German fire was allowed to drop away to one shot per hour from each gun—sixty per hour, or one shot per minute—mere snow-flake business in comparison with the day's cannonade; and that was said to have been comparatively mild on account of the fog.

Is the reader in a humour for a dose of statistics? If not he can skip this paragraph. There were, say, sixty German guns firing steadily all day at the St. Denis forts. Twice I timed the fire, and on one occasion made it twelve, on the other fourteen, shots per minute from the aggregated batteries. But there were periods of lull occasioned by fog, etc., and I have no doubt I am considerably within the mark when I say that six shots were fired per minute during the seven hours from nine a.m. till four p.m. This gives a gross total of 3,220 shots fired in that time. Of the batteries six were armed with 24-pounders, each throwing a shell of 52lbs. weight, four with 12-pounders, each gun throwing an elongated projectile of 26lbs. weight. It follows that the six 24-pound batteries threw in the time I have named 100,464lbs. weight, and the four 12-pound batteries 33,280lbs. weight of material; or, in other words, there were pitched into St. Denis during seven hours of this day very little under sixty tons of lead, iron, and powder. Fancy how the intermediate air must have been torn and vexed by 3,220 huge projectiles darting through it at an average velocity of 250 miles per minute. Fancy this pelting of colossal hailstones tumbling into so limited an area with a shower so profuse and yet so unremitting. Hailstones, say I? Why, hailstones are not full of powder, and do not explode, sending from half a dozen to a dozen massive, jagged, fanged fragments and splinters abroad centrifugally into upward space. There was used for each charge of a 24-pounder, six pounds of powder, therefore the firing off of the 1,932 shots fired by the guns of this calibre, used up 11,592lbs. of powder. For each charge of a 12-pounder was required a little over 4lbs. of powder —say 4lbs.; this gives the quantity used up by the 1,280 shots fired from guns of this calibre at about 5,120lbs.

Total quantity of powder used in charges 16,712lbs. Each shell fired from a 24-pounder gun contained four pounds of powder for explosive purposes—on the day's fire 7,728lbs. of powder fired away inside the larger shells. Each shell fired by a 12-pounder gun contains 2 1-10lbs. of powder—say 2lbs.—on the day's fire of this description of ammunition, 3,560lbs. of powder shot away inside shells. The consumption of powder in charges and for explosive purposes was, therefore, within a fraction of 22,000lbs., or, as nearly as may be, ten tons of powder alone consumed in a single day in one section of the bombardment. Remember they were at it on the east and on the south also, and one cannot be far wrong in estimating that in this one day there were close on 200 tons of projectile matter thrown upon the beleaguered forts and city out of the mouths of German cannon. The reckoning takes no account of the return fire, which was no trifle. Think of the labour and transport power involved in bringing to the front all the way from Germany 200 tons of material per diem for an indefinite number of days.

It seems to me that the whole war hardly afforded a more striking example of the military genius of von Moltke than the opportune railway trip he ordered for the 16th Brigade, forming part of the Maas army. Calculation had furnished him with evidence that von Göben would make his mark at St. Quentin all the deeper if he were strengthened by 4,000 or 5,000 men and a few guns; calculation and good information told him the hour at which this help would be good at need. The brigade quietly went away for the fight just as a lawyer goes down to Reading or Gloucester for the circuit; and the work done, it came back to its quarters before Paris just as the lawyer comes back to his cases in the Court of

Queen's Bench. This device simply for the time converted 5,000 men into 10,000 men. Napoleon I. was,
perhaps, the greatest utiliser of his soldiery by means of
rapid movements, of all von Moltke's predecessors; but
then Napoleon had not the locomitive and the *militär-
zug*.

I never knew a German officer or soldier who was a
family man that did not carry about with him photographs of the wife and the children. By this time the
cartes were getting dirty and thumb-marked, for they
were had out for inspection and admiration very often.
You would see a couple of officers in the casino or at
the mess table interchanging sights of photographs, and
then would come a gossip about the children's ages. I
watched the growth of a warm friendship between two
gentlemen of my acquaintance, the first link in which
was the discovery, at one of those quiet talks over the
pictures, that one had a boy and the other a girl, who
had been born on the very same day of the very same
year. I have seen two huge hairy sentinels at a double
post far to the front exhibiting one to the other the gallery of family portraits, fetched out of a sweat-besmirched
pocket in the breast of the tunic. On the afternoon of
the 21st I was standing by the white house on the hill
behind Andilly, trying with but little success to get a
glimpse of the firing through the fog bank, when there
joined me two or three men of the 26th Regiment, and
we naturally fell into conversation. Presently, as I turned
to go, one of them remarked in perfectly good English,
"Heigho! I wish this weary war was over, and I back in
New York." The man had been for some years earning
his two dollars a day as a house-painter in New York,
and had got married and begot sons and daughters.
When the war broke out he threw down his brush,

shipped himself, wife, and daughter—the boys were dead
—on board a North German Lloyd steamer and had
fallen into his place in the ranks with no more fuss or
consciousness of extra patriotism than if he had come
for a holiday.   It is the fact that men like this are in
the ranks of the former that makes the difference between
a national and a professional army.   Of course, out came
the photographs—he carried them, to be handy, inside
the folded cuff of his great coat.   "Ah! isn't she a fine
woman just, and isn't the girl a beauty?"   He was proud
of his belongings, and had no stuck-up reticence about
owning up to his pride.   As I walked home after leaving
him I fell a pondering on the differences in national
idiosyncrasies, and there came to my recollection the
pictorial contents of sundry French officers' knapsacks
that German officers spoke of after Sedan and Metz,
their noses in the air as if they inhaled a foul stink.
Also whether it were in the nature of things that boozy
old Tommy Tudor of the Royals should carry about
with him, if sent on foreign service, the photograph of
that slattern barrack-drudge, his wife Poll, whom human
eye never saw but with dirty face, toozled hair, and a
young one imbibing nutriment at a fount of nature extremely patent to the naked eye?

During the 22nd, 23rd and until four o'clock on the
afternoon of the 24th, the bombardment of the St. Denis
forts was conducted very languidly, the fog on the latter
day being even exceptionally dense.   At four there
sprung up a furious cannonade, which was obviously not
all one-sided.   The French had utilised the night and
the foggy day to repair the damages done to the forts by
the bombardment; to bring into du Nord heavier guns
than it had previously been manned with, and to throw
out a field artillery force backed by infantry and gun-

boats to threaten Epinay and Ormesson; and then they
assumed the offensive when the fog partly lifted at four
o'clock p.m.   Listening to it I thought I heard infantry
fire, but the echoes were so very deceptive, that I was
assured that I was mistaken.   There was a furious two-
handed cannonade, lasting for an hour and a half.   By
seven p.m. all was over, and our guns had dropped back
into the usual night average.

Two artillery officers, one a captain, were killed on
the 24th in one of the batteries.   On the previous night,
a reconnaissance accompanied by engineers, approached
close to the St. Denis glacis, and their report was that
great damage had been done to the fortifications.   In
consequence of an attack of fever, I was an invalid from
the 22nd to the 25th, and unable to gather information
at first hand—always infinitely the best method.

When my servant (who dwelt in Margency with my
horses) came for letters on the night of the 25th, he reported the probability of a sortie.   I asked him where?
He had no idea; his information was derived from an
orderly who was forbidden to speak plainly as to the
news he brought.   Morning, however, brought nothing
but the steadily remorseless fire from our batteries against
St. Denis.   There was no rattle of musketry borne rear-
ward on the light wind; no sharp crack of field artillery
filled up the brief pauses in the deep-throated noise of
the siege guns.   I found my way to the old haunt, the
emplacement in front of Montmorency.   Just below me
were two long 24-pounders trying their hardest to represent six.   By night there were to be six there in reality;
originally there had been eight in this battery.   Of these,
six the night before had gone down into the middle of
the plain, some eight hundred paces to the west of the
Château of Villanteneuse.   From the batteries in front of

Enghien the short 24-pounders had been moved forward
to a position between the railway and the hamlet of La
Barre, where the traveller by rail may no doubt still see
the remains of the emplacement. The short 12-pounders
from La Barre had been moved still farther forward, considerably in advance of the Epinay railway station, and
near the side road which quits the chaussée to diverge
into the village of La Briche. The French within about
1,200 paces of the glacis of Fort La Briche. The batteries
on the heights of Richebourg, repudiating all need for a
friendly screen, had come audaciously to the front, and
were now cocked one on either side of the slope of the
eminence.   The French continued to fire both from La
Briche and Du Nord, solely at the nearer batteries. Their
practice was utterly contemptible.   I saw shell after shell
fall and explode in the open plain quite six hundred
paces behind the battery at which it must have been
aimed—that is to say, no other rational aim was apparent.
Since the opening of the new and near batteries the
French had not succeeded in hitting them once.   It
seemed to me that their fire was quite thrown away for
want of system.   Now it was a shell which you might
guess aimed at Epinay; now one fell in Enghien—the
outside of their range; then two or three in succession
were let fly at the new batteries, all dropping wide.
Presently Du Nord would fulminate impotently and in-
termittently against Pierrefitte and Stains; and then the
gunners would take a rest.   With these tactics every shot
was thrown away.   They never got a reliable range of
any given point, and at the day's end must have been
worse off by damages and loss of ammunition than at the
beginning.   If the Fort gunners had deliberately taken
in hand a single battery, or two at the most, and concentrated a steady fire thereon, they might have had some

chance of dismounting a gun or two, and at all events
temporarily silencing one section of their tormentors.
As it was, like the skunk, they threw their virus miscellaneously, and did hardly any harm. The German losses
in the batteries had been ridiculously small.

The forts had been roughly dealt with beyond question. La Briche has two bastions, and the stone work
had been sorely pulverised in places. This I could
plainly discern with my glass. Some embrasures were
bunged up altogether, presumably on account of their
undue enlargement by the action of the German shells,
and the trim neatness of the whole aspect had changed
into a ruggedness for which I had almost written ragged-
ness. But the forts were far from shut up; that was
plain. Ordinarily they fired only slowly, but this was
apparently from choice, for presently, as if the humour
had bitten them, they would burst out into quite a re-
spectable cannonade, not however from very many guns.
The German artillerists and engineers asserted that the
curtain, which was known to have been thrown up between the forts, had been utterly beaten down and destroyed, and that the covered way no longer existed; so
that each fort had to depend on itself, or lean on supports from its direct rear. Covered ways, however, are
not crockery ware, and I took leave at the time to doubt
whether there yet existed any great difficulty or danger
in inter-communication between La Briche and Du Nord.

The night before I had thought I heard some chassepôt
firing, and it turned out I was not mistaken. The firing
had come from French marksmen potting at the German
gunners in the nearest battery over the ramparts of La
Briche. The range, as I have said, was about 1,200 paces,
far from an impossibility with the chassepôt, but not near
enough to do any serious damage. Some of the bullets,

however, I was told when I went forward into Villanteneuse, came pretty handy, and would have been bothersome if the German guns had been fired through embrasures. As they were not, but on the overbank system,
the gunners were fairly covered against anything but an
almost vertical fire. Of course, in front of and flanking
their batteries the Germans had infantry posts and rifle-
pits, and the Frenchmen were, I learned, to be introduced
on the coming night to the knowledge that chassepôt-
firing at gunners is a game at which more than one side
could play.

The town of St. Denis had not been seriously fired
since the first day of the bombardment. Especial orders
had been issued to aim clear of the venerable cathedral,
and every one hoped that, come what would, it might
escape unharmed. When the German gunners were told
to avoid hitting an object, their skill enabled them for
the most part to comply with the injunction; with French
gunners, from what I have seen of them, I think the
order would be waste of words, and it might be as wise
to let the thing take its chance. Was it possible that
there was not an adequate force of trained artillerymen
within Paris, when one came to think of the multitude of
troops there of all arms? From the briskness of practice
displayed from time to time, it was clear there was no
lack of men to serve and load the guns quickly; where
the fault lay was in bad training of the gun on to the
object intended to be aimed at. Now this is the duty of
but one man in a gun detachment; every gunner need
not be a good No. 1. If Paris, after four months of
siege, and after firing away so much powder and shot,
was now short of expert artillery marksmen, the fault lay
at the door of those chargeable with the conduct of the
siege operations. They could not ride off on the pretext

that they had found a scarcity of fitting men; they had time enough and practice enough to make a plethora.

One day, now more than a month previously, I had happened to be jogging along the road behind Pont Iblon, when a smart Vice-feldwebel accosted me with the somewhat startling question, "Do you know Gracechurch-street?" I owned, with the frank readiness of a Londoner, to a knowledge of Gracechurch-street. "Then, perhaps, you know Greenwich, too?" was the somewhat inconsequent second question. Vividly the memory of sundry dinners at the Trafalgar rose before me as I answered "Yes." My interrogator then told me that previous to the war he had been in business in Gracechurch-street, and had his private residence in Egerton-road, Greenwich, and after a pleasant conversation we parted. I learned afterwards that Mr. Hartwich had greatly distinguished himself by his conspicuous gallantry in the storm of Le Bourget, for which he had received the Iron Cross. Before the close of the siege, as a further reward for his valour on this occasion, he was promoted by the Emperor to a lieutenancy in the 4th (Queen's) Regiment of Guards. Thus, it seems, neither a desk in Gracechurch-street, nor family life in Greenwich, detracts from a good Prussian's willingness to fight for his Fatherland, or deteriorates the character of his valour. Speedy promotion, say I, to Lieutenant William Hartwich, of Gracechurch-street, City, and Egerton-road, Greenwich.

A little before this time I had the pleasure of a visit from Mr. W. H. Bullock, the able emissary of the *Daily News* Peasant Relief Fund; and was pleased to find that, after I had shown him several villages on this northern side of Paris, and after he had conversed with inhabitants whose testimony was to be considered trustworthy, he arrived at the same opinion which I had long held; that

while the active military operations in the neighbourhood
of Paris were pending, it would be both a present mistake and a weakening of subsequent potentiality for use-
fulness were any large sum expended in this quarter for
the relief of the poorer inhabitants. The vicinity of Paris
is very different from the vicinity of Metz. Around the
latter fortress the country is naturally poor, and it has no
great capital for its centre, the supply of which formed
the business and the study of the population. Long before the siege of Metz was over, the whole district had
been utterly exhausted of anything calculated to sustain
life in man or beast. There would have been real starvation—not starvation in that conventionally exaggerated
meaning of the word into which many are apt to be be-
trayed—but for the spare rations of the German soldiers.
Around Paris, on the north side at least, there was no
such utter depletion of the means of subsistence, or
rather, while it struck one that in the earlier days of the
siege such depletion really existed, a recuperative power
seemed to come into action afterwards, owing, as I reckon,
to easier and more assured communication with the country
farther back. About two-thirds of the population in most
of the villages had utterly vanished—clean gone away
out of ken. Some were inside Paris, no doubt; others
away into the background of the lurid scene. This exodus
was chiefly from the villages nearest the front. The people
who remained in these forepost villages were very few,
comparatively, and they were managing to live. They
might have had concealed stores of their own; what they
had not of their own, the Germans freely gave them according to ability; and the poor people kept alive, and
would continue to do so till the siege should be done, in
a precarious, unsatisfactory manner no doubt, but still
not starving. Were you to have poured out on them the

biggest till in the Bank of England while they were in
their then condition—hands compulsorily folded, houses
wrecked, fields untilled—I do not see in what important
particular you could have benefited that condition.   In
the villages farther to the rear, where the desolation was
less marked, there was little destitution; neither lack of
money, nor of the necessaries money will purchase. These
villages around Paris must have been very rich in a quiet
way.   And I have an idea that those who had remained
at home had made themselves heirs by a kind of natural
succession to the food-stores of those who ran away. Of
course everybody was living on his capital.   The poultry
woman, who used to send chickens and turkey eggs into
the Paris market, was killing her hens and her turkeys,
and selling them to the German officers.   If the hostile
occupation were to have lasted much longer, no doubt
stores would have come to an end, and the villagers
would have had to depend on the German troops, and
sometimes be very hungry.   But as yet there was no call
for laying out money among them for their sustenance;
and, as matters were, money expended for any other
purpose than just to tide them over the dismal hour would
have been wasted.

It was obvious, however, that there would come a time
when every penny that we could spare would be urgently
wanted.   The arrondissement mayors of Paris had plenty
of money, and that private enterprise was sure to bring
to market material on which it might be spent.   But it
was very different with the suburban villages. I am strongly
of opinion that in the warm flow of our sympathy we
rather overdid the relief of Paris.   We are a generous
nation when our hearts are stirred, and he would be a
churl indeed who should fail to appreciate the noble
promptitude with which Britain succoured Paris in her

extremity. But zealous and earnest as were the administrators of the English *don*, I am convinced that there was
a relative superfluity after the first absolute pinch had
been tided over, and that it helped to perpetuate that
self-helplessness among the poorer classes which the forced
inaction of the siege had made almost a second nature
to a population never averse to idleness. I say relative
superfluity, because, although it is obvious that the want,
poverty, and shiftlessness of any great city will always be
prepared to put forward claimants for relief in sufficient
numbers to admit of the distribution of any relief fund
however large, I think that the normal condition of the
east end of London is more wretched than was the state
of Paris after the strain had slackened and the revictualment
been fully effected. Not that I would counsel for Bethnal
Green a vast *don*, to be distributed with that perfunctoriness
of discrimination which inevitably in the nature of things
characterised the Paris distribution. Such a vast eleemosynary sowing of relief broadcast would but increase the
area of demand for aid, and intensify and prolong a
paralysis no inconsiderable proportion of which is already
ascribable to mal-administered and indiscriminate pseudo-
charity. But what we should judge it unwise to do as
regards our own fellow-countrymen and fellow-citizens, it
was surely *à fortiori* both unwise and unjust to do outside the bounds of Britain. I believe that the administrators, placed as they were in novel and arduous circumstances, acted as well and as wisely as it was possible for
any men to act in such circumstances. But this I have
not the smallest hesitation in affirming, that Britain, in
her impulsive overlavish contributions to this fund, swamped
Paris injuriously with eleemosynary succour, and, to square
her balance-sheet of charity, stinted her usual outflow towards many deserving internal institutions. But if it

seemed that wealthy Paris possessed within herself the
means of speedy self-recuperation, it was obvious that the
case was very different with the suburban villages. How
the position of those struck one who had been living
among them for over two months, it may not appear
wholly impertinent to show by an extract from a letter of
mine written shortly before the capitulation.

"To those villages hanging on to the fringe of the
capital will flock back their old inhabitants, the refugees
now in Paris, the waifs and strays now drifting about
the back country. The snug cottages that they left, with
the hectare or two of daintily-tilled garden ground and
the winter store of provisions and firewood, they will find
mere wrecked shells, incapable even of affording their
owners a barren shelter. There will be an interval of
syncope—that is inevitable—in which the mere keeping
to life, without giving a thought to retrieval, will be a
problem that many unaided may fail to solve. To face
and dissipate the abjectness of this syncope, to plough
up the dismal fallow waste of human misery that will be
soddening round Paris—that is the task for us. Bread
and meat will be wanted as the first requirement, but
food alone will not stimulate the people sufficiently to
shake off the apathy of despair their surroundings will so
inevitably engender. Put spades in their hands; send
them kitchen-garden seeds and young cabbage plants;
give them the chance to feel that they are once more
helping themselves, as they were wont to do before the
thundercloud of war burst over their heads. The genial
spring-time is not far off, and the tooth of Paris ever
watereth after its salad stuff. With judicious help, not
administered after a pauperising fashion—and pauperism
is far readier than jealousy to grow by what it feeds on
—the more humble inhabitants of the villages around

Paris might be on their legs again by midsummer. I do not see how, with decent justice to our home charities, we can deal with any other class. Our rôle is not surely to give compensation for ruined villas or the sack of detached family residences."

It is pleasant to know that not a little has been done in the direction indicated in these lines. The administrators of the Lord Mayor's Fund have most judiciously applied for such purposes a share of the money placed at their disposal, nor has active seconding been wanting on the part of those charged with the allocation of the French Farmers' Seed Fund, and the Peasant Relief Fund of the *Daily News*.

Great sensation was caused in the head-quarters of the Maas Army by a curt telegram from Versailles, which reached Margency about five o'clock on the afternoon of the 26th January, to the effect that the northern and eastern batteries were to hold their fire after twelve o'clock on that night, unless the French fire should be continued later, and that they were not to resume until further orders, unless in a similar contingency. Off galloped Ordonanz cuirassiers on their mighty horses; the news spread like wild-fire, and the word *"Friede"* was in every one's mouth. We were aware that Jules Favre had been in Versailles on the 24th, but had assumed that his visit was connected with his anticipated journey to England. But about seven o'clock there came a rather more detailed telegram, stating that the French minister had returned to Paris in the afternoon, after a second interview with Bismarck, and that the prospects of a speedy arbitrament were favourable. Meanwhile the cannonade was slowly, and, as it seemed, half reluctantly, dying out. I believe the Crown Prince of Saxony sent out orders that it should not be pitilessly persevered with till the last moment per-

mitted in the orders from Versailles.   By seven o'clock
it had fallen away to one-third of the ordinary night regulation; between eight and nine only two shots were
fired. The right to fire was, however, vindicated scrupulously till the very end.   As ten struck on the cracked
bell of the Margency Mairie, a single hoarse roar came
bellowing up the valley, at eleven there was the solitary
repetition; at the first stroke of twelve crashed out the
report of the last cannon-shot of the siege that was fired
on the north side.   It was morning ere its echoes had
ceased to reverberate in the glades of Montmorency and
the quarries of Sannois.

Not a few there were in Margency who refused to put
faith in the good tidings; cautious men who economised
emotion, knowing how poignant would be the revulsion
of the disappointment if no "*Friede*" should come of
it after all.   Everybody, however, remained up till after
twelve o'clock to listen whether the French would renew
their fire.   When they did not—at least on our side—
even the unbelieving Thomases began to let themselves
think there must be something in it, after all.   There
seemed to me so much in it that I thought it might be
possible to get into Paris by dint of a little unobtrusive
impudence.   Before daylight on the morning of the 27th
I struck down into Villanteneuse, the outposts of which
may be called quite close to St. Denis, and found there
an officer of my acquaintance belonging to the "Lady-
birds."   He laughed my desire to scorn, and his arguments, and others which were even more patent, convinced me how premature and how futile would be any
attempt of the kind.   So I returned to Margency, and
rode to Versailles instead.   All along the road there
was silence, although I was told that Valérien had fired
heavily on the previous night, and that there had been

firing that morning. The terrace of St. Germain was totally deserted; the first time during the siege I had ever
seen it without its groups of gossiping spectators.   Versailles was in a state of bewilderment, and, except the
astutest, who hardened their hearts and refused to believe
anything at all, the dwellers therein were wholly given
over to the dominion of chameleon-like canards of the
greatest magnitude and the strangest versatility.   From
one reliable source I learnt that there certainly had been
heavy firing in the direction of Sèvres in the morning.
Then came one who boldly affirmed that Paris was open.
He had not been in himself, nor had he seen anybody
who had come thence, but he had the fact on undeniable
authority.   A little later it was communicated unto me,
with much attention to detail, that the capitulation would
be signed at four o'clock to a minute, and that the terms
were very favourable for Paris.   Another report was that
there had been a revolution on the previous day when
Jules Favre went back into Paris, and that he would on
no account be allowed to come out again any more.   But
the *raconteur* of this collapsed when another interlocutor
struck in with the positive assurance that M. Favre with
two secretaries, and General Beaufort with two aides, had
really come out that morning, and that the former was
even then in close consultation with Bismarck.   "They
have been drinking champagne together," added another,
as confidently as if he had helped to finish the bottle.
Then came details as to the character of the negociations.   It seemed that M. Favre had come out intending
to ask terms for the city only, leaving the forts to be
dealt with separately.   Of this Bismarck would not hear;
and, on the other hand, refused to accede to a surrender
of Paris as a fortress apart from negociations for a general
cessation of hostilities.   He was, in fact, making the

misery of Paris the stick with which to beat France into yielding to her fate. M. Favre had represented what hard lines these were, and ultimately Bismarck had withdrawn this as an absolute postulate, on the understanding that the former was to use his best exertions with the other members of the Provisional Government to bring about the desired end. On this understanding he had gone into Paris, and returned to Versailles that morning, bringing with him General Beaufort, as the affair was the capitulation of a fortress, and therefore to be arranged by the military authorities. All this was explained with a detail that might have been expected had one been amanuensis to Count Bismarck, without any pledge to secrecy. "Then how about to-day's doings?" I asked. "Oh, I can tell you that too. The hitch is about Mont Valérien. It seems some 20,000 die-hards are determined to get up into that keep and hold out for a spell longer, and that the Germans are aware of this, and will not listen to any other arrangement except all or none. There is no regular armistice, but a cessation of hostilities up to six o'clock," and more detail equally reliable. That there was no firing for a number of hours, till six, is certain. Six came, and with it the information that the time for the suspension of the firing had been extended till nine. Men must dine, even in a state of excited suspense; for my part I always find such sensation stimulate appetite. Judging by appearances, the second "Staffel" in the Hôtel des Réservoirs did not find the edge of its hunger in the least taken off by sensational reports, and the bear-garden-like Babel was rather more noisy than usual. The *Moniteur Officiel* came out earlier than usual by a couple of hours, but was so great a sell, that one, I think, would have been justified in demanding his money back. "Nothing new before Paris." Thus

curtly was the situation dealt with in the official print.
An obese colonel was civil enough to announce to us,
as he left the dining-room, that negociations had been
"broken off" for the night; and then nine o'clock came.
It had hardly finished striking, when one side or the
other began to fire, and between nine and eleven several
reports of big guns were quite audible. I believe there
was silence during the night; and on the morning of the
28th there certainly was no renewal of the firing. I
quitted Versailles too early to hear any further intelligence; and as I rode to St. Germain met great droves
of lean cows, driven by Frenchmen, and frequent carts
laden with calves. All these were for Paris; the people
had heard of the *pourparlers*, and had rather taken time
by the forelock.

At nine o'clock on the evening of the 28th, while the
head-quarter staff of the Maas Army were assembled in
the drawing-rooms of the Crown Prince's château after
dinner, an orderly brought in a telegram to the Crown
Prince. His Royal Highness, having read it, handed it
to General von Schlotheim, the chief of the staff. That
officer perused it in his turn, and then rising, walked to
the door communicating between the billiard-room and
the saloon, and there read the telegram aloud. It was
from the Emperor, and it announced that two hours before Count Bismarck and M. Jules Favre had set their
hands to a convention in terms of which an armistice to
last for twenty-one days had already come into effect.
It was not easy to settle down to cards or billiards after
news like that.

PART IV.

THE CONQUERED AND THE CONQUERORS.

CHAPTER I.

The Conquered.

AT three o'clock on the morning of the 29th there came to Margency Major Krause from Versailles, with the detailed terms of the armistice and of the capitulation of the forts. No time was suffered to run to waste. In the early morning Major von Welck, of the Maas Army staff, rode into St. Denis to arrange with the commandant the details for the surrender of the surrounding forts. At ten a.m. the Crown Prince of Saxony and his staff were in the saddle, and the soldiers who had thronged into the street greeted his Royal Highness with hearty cheering as they set out for St. Denis. When we got to the outpost village of La Barre there was a halt, which turned out to be a long halt. Welck had not returned; the commandant (Admiral La Roncière) was understood to be sulky and impracticable, and the aspect of the French troops was threatening. While the staff waited, a rough lunch was eaten in a ruined house, for the delay was for hours. At last the Major returned, but not with tidings that all was settled. There was a hitch about something concerning which it was necessary to consult General Schlotheim. The Prince and his two officers went out into the battery at the back of the house and held an earnest conversation. Then von Welck went back, accompanied by Lieutenant von Hinüber, the latter to bring back word when all was settled.

Meanwhile the Crown Prince and his staff waited on still. A strong body of troops was marched forward in

anticipation.   The whole of the Ludwig Franz Regiment
and of the 27th, and four field batteries of the 4th Army
Corps, pushed on and halted on a little slope midway
between St. Denis and Enghien.   Before this a staff of
engineer officers had gone forward into the fort, accompanied by a detachment, to draw the charges from the
mines, and two companies of siege artillery were sent on
to take over the guns and magazines.

It was now nearly three o'clock, and, although
von Welck had neither sent nor come back, the Prince
started.   Von Welck met him at the half-way house, and
reported a conversation with the representative officer of
the French Etat Major, who had explained that the troops
had not all evacuated St. Denis, and that the population,
most of which was armed, looked somewhat threatening.
He had therefore counselled a strong body of occupation.
Welck and Hinüber had themselves been unmolested;
but testified to there having been much disorder, which,
however, was gradually dying out, as the inevitable came
to be accepted.

We rode on, with La Briche close on the right;
looking from the outside, it was not very seriously
damaged in essentials.   Its glacis was furrowed with
shells as with a plough, the massive stonework of its
scarp was pitted all over, and in places the coping
stones had been dislodged. The earthen ramp was rather
cavernous, especially about the angles; but there were no
signs of anything that the wildest imagination could con-
strue into a practicable breach.   There were only two
embrasures extant on one of the bastions; these from
their appearance had evidently required repeatedly making
good.   Guns showed through these.   All the other embrasures had been bunged up roughly, but seemingly
effectually, with fascines, &c. obviously a reason of the

adoption of the system of overbank firing. There· were the muzzles of guns visible sticking up over the parapet. Bending to the east we crossed the railway, and with another bend came to the northern entrance to Fort Du Nord. This fort had been served worse than La Briche. Its glacis was one series of shell pits. That, it is true, was nothing but evidence that many shells had fallen short. But great pieces of the earthwork were torn away, and the wall of the scarp had been shattered and penetrated in places. Here, too, the few embrasures left had been made good, but there was noticeable a paucity of guns. A terrible fire had converged on the gate; one draw-bridge was demolished, the other could not be raised. It struck me that in both forts the defences flanking the gates and intended to sweep the approaches at what are always weak points, were insufficiently provided for. Just inside the works and covering the gate there was a halt amidst a mass of German officers and soldiers. This was to permit the delegate from the Etat Major to make some explanations. He came forward—a wan, sad-faced young officer of Marine Artillery, with a grave dignity in the pale face and weary anxious eyes, that commanded re-spect and commiseration. He was quite alone, not even an orderly with him, and the solitary man looked for-lorn, yet full of a certain gallant pride, as he rode up to the Crown Prince with a high-bred greeting that was not, assuredly, of Republican France. His statement was that all the troops had evacuated St. Denis and gone into Paris; that the Mobiles, National Guard and Seden-taries who remained had been disarmed; and that the population had come to its senses. The whole of the supporting force being reported close up, the band of the 27th struck up the Paris March, and before it the staff, headed by the Crown Prince, marched up the principal

street, which was much cumbered with barricades, and
embarrassed by the conductors of undrawn mines, laid
down among gravel heaps in the road. The houses were
shattered into fragments as far as the great square before the Caserne. The whole town was a ruin. Civilians
swarmed on the side walks, men, women, and children;
none looking very like starvation. It seemed to me that
all the males over fourteen were in such uniform as a
pair of red trouser stripes represented. There was a
strange un-French silence, lowering brows, and many a
Sacré muttered between the teeth. That all the arms
had not been given up was very apparent. The staff had
quite an escort of chassepot-carrying individuals on the
side walks, not indeed of a very martial appearance, and
probably on their way to the depôt for the reception of
the firearms. It might have been the sight of the weapons
which prompted General Schlotheim, when the staff was
about half-way to the square, to order to the front the
detachment of Saxon Cuirassiers of the Guard which
formed the Crown Prince's escort. As the splendid
horsemen clattered forward at a furious gallop, the women
and children ran shrieking into the battered houses,
"The Uhlans!" "The Uhlans!" In the square before
the great barrack the Prince halted, wheeled on one side,
and the 14th Brigade of the 4th Army Corps, the brigade
that was detailed to garrison St. Denis, marched past
him, their bands playing the "Paris March" and "Ich
bin ein Preusse." Crowds of the French witnessed the
sight, and I could hear them gloomily owning to one
another their admiration of the physique and soldierly
bearing of the German troops. The interim Governor of
St. Denis was Brigadier-General Zychlinski. Before we
quitted it the provision-sellers were already crowding
into the place. The German forepost line was before

nightfall established all round 500 yards nearer Paris than the forts, and nobody was allowed to pass without a special permission. Strong patrols of occupation, composed of the first troops that entered the place, were at once marched into the forts. The Commandant of Fort de l'Est reported that there had fallen in it during one day of the bombardment no fewer than 1,200 shells. Prince George duly reported his successful occupation of the Eastern Forts.

When I rode into St. Denis on the forenoon of the 30th I found that it had in a measure recovered its tone since our hurried visit of the day before. It was true that it was as squalid and forlorn as then; that the men still clung to the red stripe on the trousers and the number on their cap, which with their wooden shoes and generally unwarlike *tout ensemble* rendered them somewhat incongruous-looking beings; but the shops had got their shutters down; the Germans had got themselves billeted; and the marketenders and provision-sellers were ready to present facilities to avert the imminence of starvation. One had to study the place with some care to comprehend thoroughly how devastating had been the nature of the bombardment. After passing the second big barricade, the houses on either side of the principal street had been spared by some casual luck, and I began to think that I had come through the zone of ruin, and had emerged into a territory comparatively unharmed. The aspect of the great barrack tended a good deal to undeceive me. A little farther on and I was again in the thick of the prints made by the bombs. The theatre had had its front utterly wrecked; through the great gaps you could see the painting on the roof and on the pillars flanking the stage. Turning off to the left I made in haste for the venerable cathedral, to discover what amount of damage it had sustained. The republicans who had painted *Liberté*, *Egalité*, *Fraternité* on its portals, had not allowed their republicanism to render them negligent of the historical monuments the edifice contains; all round it had been banked up high with sand-bags, which had caught and stopped several shells. The stained glass was intact, or all but intact. Only four shells had penetrated to the interior of the building. One of the elaborately carved crosses on the top of a buttress had been splintered off, and a coping stone had been shattered; this, I think, summed up the evil done to the cathedral by the shells of the enemy. The splendid carving on the arches around the great door had not been harmed in the least, although it must have had some very narrow escapes. Several houses in the neighbourhood had been utterly demolished, and others fired. The aspect of the cathedral inside was very strange; the tombs of the kings had all been protected by sand-bags; the interior might have been called one great sand-bag. The statues had been covered in with wooden frames, and the sand-bags laid over them. It is pleasant to be able to state that never a statue had so much as a nose knocked off. In fact, considering the weight and duration of the bombardment, the cathedral may be said to have escaped wonderfully well. The same cannot be said of the new church of St. Denis, which is just behind Fort La Briche. Its steeple was wrecked; its north side was stove in; and its interior was a chaos of mortar, stones, and smashed paraphernalia. The little Protestant chapel, however, had suffered worse than any other religious edifice in the place. One might almost fancy its pasteur trotting dolefully about picking up the pieces of his church from the open spaces in the vicinity. The pulpit and the door were intact; as for the rest, if you had had all

the bits collected, it would have been worse than any
Chinese puzzle to put them together again. The two
Protestant schoolrooms escaped the bombardment, with
the exception of having the windows broken; but in the
morning the German soldiers, hungry after wood, had
made a raid upon the desks and forms. Pasteur Saglier
thought it hard that when there were plenty of Roman
Catholic combustibles about the place, Protestants should
burn the furniture of the only Evangelical establishment in
the town; so he had paid a visit of remonstrance to
General Zychlinski, who sent his chaplain to exorcise the
evil spirits that were troubling the Evangelical woodwork.

It must have been verily the reign of the Prince of the
Power of Darkness, that period of five days during which
the bombardment lasted. While the shells were crashing
into the houses, they were ploughing up the streets as
with the deepest subsoil plough ever invented. There
was no safety for any but in the cold and dark cellars;
so heavy were the projectiles, that not always in the
cellars was there found safety. There were houses of
which garrets and cellars had been battered into a shapeless pile of stone and mortar. If you asked the loafing
bystanders whether any had been buried in the ruins,
they moodily muttered, "Qui sait?" shrugged their
shoulders, and turned away. For myself, I think there
must have been not a few underneath these jagged monu-
mental piles; but there was nobody who has interest or
energy to explore, and "Qui sait" might have been painted
up as the vague epitaph.

Before the commencement of the siege, the garrison of
each of the St. Denis forts had consisted of three artillerymen, a commandant, and a few military tailors and
shoemakers. When the siege began, St. Denis did not
share greatly in the tremors of her big sister; she was

girt by her forts, and she believed in them. Admiral
La Roncière was appointed to the command, and sailors
and artillerymen came and manned the forts. The population of St. Denis is peculiar. Its manufactures are
insalubrious, and it has the unenviable attribute of attracting all the worst workmen from other parts of
France, who can earn wages in St. Denis when they
would be laughed out of factories elsewhere. So it is a
chronically poor, shiftless, drunken place, with a population so floating that of the 30,000 the census gives it, it
is reported to change 15,000 every year. In the early
months of the siege St. Denis was tolerably quiet. Food
gradually got dearer. The people came to horseflesh
about two months before the surrender, and to reduced
bread rations ten days before it. The world is familiar
with the diet-throes of Paris—those of St. Denis had
been similar but more intense, because of the prevalent
poverty of the inhabitants. All the males had become
"soldiers," and earned their franc and a half a day;
which, as well as the 75 centime allowance for their
wives, most drank with regularity and thoroughness.
The wives and families, therefore, starved after they had
eaten everything on which money could be raised. There
had been in the place two ambulances, one a branch of
the International, another a military ambulance. The
bombardment had come on the town like a thunder-clap.
The corporation were fiercely abused for not having given
warning, which it was alleged it was in their power to
do. Whether this was the case I do not know, and as
far as the corporation goes it mattered very little, for its
members all ran away when the bombardment commenced. Nobody had any responsibility; with a few
noble exceptions, nobody had troubled himself except
about the wholeness of his own skin. The Admiral Com-

mandant concerned himself with his forts—the people might go hang for him. The members of the International Ambulance accepted the situation; took their lives in their hands, and went out to do what good they might. They dragged the maimed and shattered out of the ruined houses; they collected the corpses from the streets and the ruins, and buried them with some semblance of decency. They went round the town urging on the people that the women and children should go forth from the doomed town, and retire into Paris. The women and children had been huddled into the semi-security of the cellars. The shells were crashing into the streets, and avalanches of stone and brick were ever crashing upon the side-walks. The women peeping forth shudderingly declared that they would rather die where they were than incur a more certain and fearful death by sallying forth in that iron tempest. So they turned into the dank caverns to hunger and cold, and cuddling their children to their bosoms, utterly refused to budge. The Pasteur Saglier had gone to the Commandant and begged that he would allow him to go out as a parlementaire to the Germans, to ask for two hours' cessation of the bombardment, to give the women and children a chance to get away without being struck down as they went. The Admiral refused, and the ruthless devilry went on. Then the Pasteur sent an appeal to the Paris journals, begging all who possessed means of conveyance to send them into St. Denis to remove the perishing women and children. The response was but weak, and there appeared not a solitary representative of those ambulances whose members took delight in flags, and gave themselves to the vanities of buttons and uniforms. About half-a-dozen private vehicles turned up, and with the help of these the sick and wounded were got out of the hospitals in the

town, and located in two large factories on the plain
between St. Denis and Paris. Then children followed,
and women great with child such as cared to go, till the
plain-houses became like caravanserais. Meanwhile the
few vehicles belonging to this ambulance were toiling
assiduously in conveying to the rear the wounded struck
down at the guns; a few men, and a few only, so far as
I could learn, toiling with a zeal and energy that merited
better support. As for the bold National Guards, their
location was the wine shop. Therein they imbibed the
courage that prevented them from creeping into the cellars; and when their cups had made them reckless, they
sallied out into the streets, only to give the ambulance
more trouble with their worthless carcases. Not a few
were killed as they staggered about; others were brought
to the ambulance, wounded, indeed, but as drunk as
lords.

After a lengthened and searching peregrination of
St. Denis, I accompanied two German officers in a ride
beyond the foreposts toward the gate of La Chapelle.
In the course of the day the restrictions to passing out
had been materially relaxed, and the Avenue de Paris
was thronged with Parisians. It seemed to me that if
they could get out I might get in, and quitting my
friends I rode forward toward the gate. Before going
on a duty that seems likely to be hazardous, the wise
soldier overhauls his weapons, looks that his sword is
easy in the scabbard, and that his revolver is duly
capped. I was no soldier and carried no lethal weapons;
but before risking an entry into Paris, it seemed advisable to make sure that I had the important document
with me which vouched for my being a British subject
and a neutral. Alas, not anticipating the occurrence of
such an opportunity I had left my passport behind, and

there was nothing for it but to postpone my "invasion" of Paris until the morrow. On my way back to Margency, I must have met at least a third of the population of St. Denis returning from the fields in the plain, with barrow loads and armfuls of frosted half-rotten green stuff.

Next morning, that of the 31st of January, I left Margency better armed as to passports. Before essaying an entry into Paris,* I spent some time in investigating the condition of the St. Denis forts. Let me briefly describe the armament and condition of Fort la Briche. Its guns consisted mainly of long twelve and sixteen pounder muzzle-loaders, smooth-bores, and bearing dates from 1826 to 1841; and smooth-bore howitzers of antiquated construction. In each section of the banquette there was a gun and a howitzer. In most cases the ammunition by the guns was round, solid cannon-ball; the shells seemed to have been exhausted. It was interesting to notice how stress of events had driven the French from the embrasure to the overbank system, which is invariably used by the Germans. There were in La Briche fronting embrasures only the two guns I had

* I casually learnt since returning to England, there had been some controversy who was entitled to claim the priority of entrance into Paris. The matter is a bagatelle, but it seems fair that justice should be done. When I got in on the 31st, I went first to the American legation and afterwards to the British Embassy. At neither place had anything been seen of any prior correspondent. In the evening I visited a café, where I found the intra-Paris correspondents of the *Times, Daily News, Daily Telegraph,* and *Morning Advertiser,* none of whom had seen anyone from the outside before me. It was not until at least a fortnight after, that General Duff assured me of his own knowledge, that Mr. Coningsby, the representative, I believe, of the *Echo,* had entered Paris on the 30th. I have since had no communication with anyone who was personally cognisant of the circumstances, but of course General Duff's assurance sufficed to satisfy me of Mr. Coningsby's priority, which I now most cheerfully acknowledge. There is another aspect to the question. Of course, neither Mr. Coningsby nor I entered Paris as a mere personal adventure, but with a single eye to furnish the newspapers we respectively represented with the earliest possible tidings of the internal condition of the capital. To win a battle is one thing; to utilise promptly the victory is another.

noticed on the day of our first entrance. The other embrasures had been filled up, and the guns moved aside behind to overbank protections. Several, notwithstanding the change, had been dismounted. Still the fort, judging by such evidences of really serious damage, might, to all appearance, have held out longer; nothing was apparent to have made it untenable. The centre yard was full of pits for negativing explosions. No actual casemate had been penetrated. But my belief is, that there were not casemates enough for a sufficient garrison. Around the detached bombproofs in the area the blindages had been utilised as barrack-rooms, and protected on the roof with sand-bags, but the sides were left unprotected in a similar manner, and the erections were simply smashed into tinder. The barracks in the yard were both shattered and partially burnt. Perhaps Admiral La Roncière, taking everything into consideration, was justified in notifying that he could not face the enemy with guns and men two days longer.

In the hurry of evacuation the French had left in a casemate a quantity of biscuit and cognac, which the German troops were philosophically enjoying, as I went round. They wanted something to harden their stomachs before setting about cleansing the casemates, which were like hogsties. Cleanliness could not well have been insisted on under the circumstances.

Leaving St. Denis about two o'clock, I rode through the Prussian foreposts on to the neutral ground in company with two cuirassier officers, who turned back when we had got about two hundred paces up the Avenue de Paris. Had I accepted the well-intentioned advice of friends, I certainly would not have adventured on the expedition on which I was bound. A cool customer had sent his servant in the morning for a great-coat I had promised him when the war was over; his selfish reasoning being that the war was virtually over as regarded me, since, if I persisted in going into Paris, nobody would ever hear of me more than fragmentarily. The two cuirassier officers who rode with me into the neutral territory took leave of me quite pathetically, and when I said, "Au revoir," one of them shook his head significantly. It was rather nervous work riding along a road crowded with Frenchmen, not a friendly German uniform within sight, and one's self so dressed as to be easily enough mistaken for one of the hated race. The Porte de la Chapelle was closed and the drawbridge up, while sentries marched up and down inside the closed gates of the palisading. Nobody knew when the gates would open, but there was a general anticipation that they would open some time. I waited for a full half-hour, while a dense crowd collected with the desire to get inside, with whom I and my horse were the chief topics of observation. Men laid their heads together and discussed my personality. I was a Prussian, that was taken for granted. Had I countless cattle in reserve? or had I come to have speech with the authorities as to the further humiliation of Paris? I got into conversation in English with a man who had been in America, but this had no effect in leading my critics to suppose I was an Englishman. "These Prussians, *sacré*, they know every language under the sun;" sententiously remarked an elderly gentleman with a big cabbage under each arm, and a pair of red stripes down his legs. My horse shared with me the public interest. But it was not the interest usually attracted towards horses. There was no criticism as to her points, her probable action, or her soundness. No, "she was a fine fat animal; she must be succulent; how well she would eat; what would I not give for a slice of her?" When I saw a gentleman in a blouse produce a big knife in dangerous proximity to the mare, I had serious apprehensions that he was going to help himself to a buttock steak. It was very curious how horseflesh had come to be accepted as an ordinary viand, not to be noted as anything out of the common. On the previous day, when I had called on M. Saglier, the good pasteur of St. Denis, he hospitably asked me to have some dinner. I assenting, he told his servant to "bring in the meat," and I made an assault with vigour and perseverance on a rather ragged roast joint which was placed before me, the pastor looking on benignantly the while. I held my tongue till the edge was off my appetite, and then asked the minister what I was eating. "Well," said he, "of course you are eating horse, and a very choice joint it is. I knew the animal well. He was young and plump, and of a grey colour, which it is well known indicates tenderness." The pastor had been eating horse for the last four months; not because he was forced to do so so long, but because he had a numerous dependency of poor people, to aid whom he had to practise economy.

After waiting half-an-hour outside the barred La Chapelle gate, an officer appeared, and exclaimed, "A la Porte de St. Ouen." St. Ouen (or Clingiancourt) is the next gate to La Chapelle on the north, and we all therefore made to the right, I being mounted beating the others, who were all on foot. This gate was open, and a gendarme examining passes. I rode on slowly, looking straight between my horse's ears, and somehow nobody stopped me. When I had got just inside the gate I thought for certain my career was to be cut short. The Ceinture Railway runs close by the inside of the enceinte, and as I reached the bridge an officer came forward with

his hand raised. As luck would have it, a train came
puffing past at the moment. My mare thought proper
to go through a variety of fantastic gymnastic feats at
this apparition, the officer looking on admiringly. When
the train had passed, and she had condescended to come
down upon all fours again, the officer smiled and patted
her shoulder. I smiled and raised my hat, and somehow
I had slidden over the bridge before he had got the buck-
jumping idea out of his head and the interception idea
into it. As I rode down the Boulevard Ornano, I came
upon sundry groups of half-drunk National Guards. One
of these, as I passed him, raised the shout, "A bas le
Prussien!" further flattering me by calling me "cochon,"
and "assassin." Others took up the cry, and matters
were getting serious. The clamour was spreading, and
men tried to clutch hold of my bridle. I judged bold-
ness to be the wisest policy, so facing about, I pushed up
to the first man who had shouted, and proclaiming that
I was an Englishman come to do good if possible—not
harm—I reproached my denouncer for interfering with a
harmless and peaceable wayfarer. The demon of cowardly
and venomous suspicions had not yet been developed.
Ten or twenty days after, in such a dilemma, I should
have thought myself lucky to have got clear off after
being marched back to the guard-house, half-a-dozen
men at each bridle rein, as many more at each leg, and
forced to exhibit my passport to the officer on duty.
But hunger is a wonderful agent in making men mind
their own business, and in keeping truculence in a dor-
mant state. I cannot say, even after I had passed successfully the good fellow who had assailed me with the
cries of "cochon," that I liked the appearance of the
Boulevard Magenta. It was densely crowded with soldiers,
and some of them might be disagreeably patriotic. But

no, they were all too much busied with their own affairs,
getting their pay and discussing events.   The closed
shops appeared to me to be chiefly eating-houses; all the
other shops appeared to be open, although there did not
seem to be any trade doing.   The bouillon houses, however, at the street corners, were open, and I afterwards
gathered that Duval had had exceptional advantages extended to him.

Halting to go into a shop to make an inquiry—I was
not acquainted with the geography of Paris—I called a
soldier of the line who was strolling on the pavement to
hold my horse.   On coming out I had a little talk with
him.   Yes, he had had enough of it—*Sacré*.   They had
nearly killed him, these terrible Prussians, and he was
very hungry.   When would the gates open for food?
When I put my hand in my pocket to find something to
tip him wherewithal, I discovered that I had no other
but Prussian money.   Forgetting for the instant the
situation, I asked him whether he could do anything
with a ten-groschen piece.   Bless you;—it was silver,
and might have had the devil's pitchfork stamped upon
it instead of the split crow, for all that the hungry lines-
man cared.   Three weeks after it was not wise to carry,
much less to show, German money.

"Paris is utterly cowed; fairly beaten"—so said the
first Englishman I met; and his opinion was mine.   Yet
Paris was orderly and decent, and with a certain solemn
morose self-restraint mastering the tendency to demon-
strate.   The streets were crowded, almost wholly with
men in uniform.   Civilians were few and far between.
Many shops were open, but many also were closed.
There was no want of hardware in Paris.   You might
have bought enough and to spare of anything except
edibles.   Drink was plentiful enough, but except near

the gate I saw not a soul drunk. The food shops had
nothing to show. There were confitures and preserves,
jellies, &c.; but solid comestibles were conspicuous by
their absence. In one shop I saw several large shapes of
stuff that looked like lard. When I asked what it was,
I found it was horse fat. The bakers' shops were closed:
the grating down before the butchers'. And oh, the
number of funerals! One, two, three; I met six altogether in the course of my ride. Sad with an exceeding great sadness; such was what I found as regards
Paris long before I reached the American Legation; self-
respecting, too, in her misery; not blatant; not disposed
to collect in jabbering crowds. Each man went his way
with chastened face and listless gait.

After visiting the American Legation, where undis-
guised wonder was expressed at my appearance, I made
my way to the Hôtel de St. Honoré, to an old-fashioned
and well-known house kept by a worthy Briton of the
name of Unthank. I had nearly filled my wallet with
newspapers, and had only stowed away, for an exigency,
a few slices of ham. Did ever the rarest geological or
mineralogical specimen make such a sensation as these
slices of ham? When I reached my quarters the servant
women asked permission to take the meagre plateful out,
and show it as a curiosity to their companions; and
after the ham was eaten, stray visitors came in, attracted
by the tidings, and begged for a look at the unwonted
viands. Mr. Unthank had had for his boarder throughout the siege Dr. Gordon, our medical commissioner in
Paris, and he took pride in asserting, that the doctor,
under his auspices, had lived as well as any other man in
Paris. When dinner came it bore out Mr. Unthank's
boast. Positively there was a fowl—pretty well, I reckon,
the last fowl in Paris. Mr. Unthank had been offered

eighty francs for the biped while yet it had its feathers
on, but refused it, and so we had him for dinner with
my ham as an accompaniment, only I stood out of
participation in the ham, that the rarity might go the
further with the others.   There are advantages in being
a Scotsman.   One of these this siege had developed in a
curious way.   There was some store of oatmeal in Paris.
You can make porridge out of oatmeal; and Scotsmen
not only eat, but enjoy porridge.   Thus Dr. Gordon, a
Strathdon man, had supped his frugal bicker of porridge
every morning, while men not born to the manner of
porridge were giving themselves internal uneasiness by
eating the stuff which bears the conventional name of
bread.   Sharing the origin of Dr. Gordon, I shared with
him his bicker of porridge, and when I had scraped the
dish, came to the conclusion that the man who cannot
sup porridge deserves to starve.   Yet another national
dainty was Unthank equal to—a tumbler of such Scotch
whisky toddy as I had not tasted for months.

In the evening, after paying my respects to a coterie
of newspaper correspondents who had been trying to
dine at the Café Gaillot, in the Rue Neuve St. Augustine,
I there looked in on a party that had been experimenting
in dining.   They had eaten ostrich, cat, dog, rat, and
mice.   This seemed to me a hard-hearted mode of ex-
tracting a new sensation out of the pinch of the times.
Far better to have dined on horse, and given the fancy
price of more dainty viands,—is it not justifiable to
estimate the daintiness of a dish by its cost?—to put
bread into the mouths of the poor suffering women and
children.   For two days neither bread nor meat had been
distributed in the 8th arrondissement.   Those who had no
money simply had to hunger.   The sins for which Paris
had used to be famous, seemed all to belong to the past.

She had been half-starved, half-beaten into morality, or it might have been, I ventured to speculate, that other than physical influences had led her to wash and be clean. I saw some drunkenness, but far less than I had looked for among men whose clock, so to speak, had run down. A decent gloom was everywhere apparent. Some asserted that the gloom was as much theatrical and assumed as had been the previous valorous seeming. I tried not to think so—I fain thought that I could see the iron eating and burning into the hearts of those men— silent with unwonted silence; moody as they had never known how to be before; and as the downcast faces passed, I drew with a mistaken sanguineness for which I do not now reproach myself, a good augury from them for France and Paris.

The great and beautiful feature of the siege had been the absence of crime. No murders, no robberies, no social crimes, but a virtue in which, to me at least, there was something pathetic. I had intended to promenade Paris all night, to make the most of the time necessarily limited. But before ten o'clock the promenade had become almost a solitary one. By nine the dim lights were put out in the kiosks, and the petroleum was waning in the street lamps. By half-past the cafés were putting up their shutters; the red-striped waiters looking curiously nondescript. By ten the world of Paris was left to darkness and to me, and so I went to bed. The midnight air was not tortured by the sound of revellers, although there were no police to keep order. I woke up between twelve and one in the night, and the silence made me for the moment think myself back at Margency.

The whole city was haunted by the peculiar half-sweetish, half-fœtid odour which horseflesh gives out in cooking; an odour which I had learned to appreciate at

Metz. It permeated the deserted British Embassy, where, asserting my privileges as a Briton, I stabled my horse; it lingered in the corridors of the Grand Hotel, and fought with the taint from wounds in evil case. The Grand Hotel was one huge hospital. Half Paris seemed converted into hospitals, if one might judge by the flags. There had been more than were needed until the Southern bombardment began; and then when the hospitals, ambulances, orphanages, and madhouses on the South side had to be evacuated, there had been quite a squeeze on this side of the water. Very touching was the ignorance everywhere as to the outside world. "I have seen three English papers since September," said Dr. Gordon, our Medical Commissioner. "Is Ireland quiet? Is Mr. Gladstone still Prime Minister? Is the Princess Louise married?" Such were samples of the questions I had to answer. The ignorance as to the condition of the Prussians outside was equally dense. The day after negotiations began, Paris had been assured that the investing army had not eaten for three days; and that it was Paris which was granting terms rather than the other way. I was continually asked if the Prussians had not been half-starved all through? What they had done for quarters? Whether there were not 400,000 at the very least surrounding Paris? Whether they did not tremble in their boots at the name of the Francs-tireurs? Whether they were not half-devoured by vermin? Whether the king still resided in Versailles, they had not heard of his being emperor? and so on.

The pinch for food was worse than ever, pending the result of the negotiations for its supply. The day before but one the hungry populace had broken into the reserved store of potted provisions in the Halle, smashed all obstacles, and looted the place. From one who had paid the prices himself, and had the figures down in black and white without exaggeration, I got the following list:—2 francs for a small shrivelled cabbage; 1 franc for a leek; 45 franks for a fowl; 45 francs for a rabbit (which may be taken for granted as cat); 25 francs for a pigeon; 22 francs for a 2lb. chub; 14 francs per pound for stickleback; 2 francs per pound for potatoes; 40 francs per pound for butter; cheese, 25 francs a pound, when procurable. Meat other than horseflesh was absolutely not to be procured. I was assured that if I offered 50*l.* down in bright shining gold for a veritable beefsteak, I should have no claimant for the money! The last cow that had changed hands was for the use of an ambulance, and had fetched 80*l.* Those that were still left could not be bought for money. The bread was abominably bad, something between putty and chopped straw, bound together with farina starch; but its badness was not the worst thing about it, that was the difficulty to get it at all. Gentle and simple had to wait their turn outside the bakers' shops, and the same outside the butchers'. I saw huge throngs at both as I rode through Paris, chiefly women, waiting in silent shivering in the cold.

The trees on the Boulevards had suffered less than I had been given to expect. In the Champs Elysées likewise, there was little perceptible injury, but the gardens of the Tuileries, in which wooden barracks had been erected nearly all the length of the Rue Rivoli, had not escaped quite so well. The scarcity of wood was terrible in the latter days. People could not get their washing done for lack of wood to heat the copper. So far as I could gather the moral effect of the bombardment on the population was terrible, although unacknowledged definitely. After the first day of defiance the Government had felt the pressure. M. Jules Simon told a friend of

mine that the bombardment of St. Denis had shortened
the siege by a week. Competent authorities estimated
that Paris, had she been desperately obstinate, might
have gone on for another fortnight or three weeks, had
the pickles and preserves, and all the odds and ends now
sold at exorbitant prices, been taken and rationed. Certainly, the supply of horseflesh was far from exhausted.
It surprised me to see so many well-appointed vehicles
still in the streets of Paris, with well-conditioned horses.
Nor were the omnibuses either few or far between, and
their horses were in the best of condition, as were the
horses ridden at break-neck speed through the streets by
officers who looked, and who probably were, transmogrified
petits crevés.

I was inside Paris, but how was I to get out? It was
clear I was no use there, quite *de trop* in fact. People
who ought to know shook their heads. I must first get
my passport viséd at the Embassy. Then I must go to
the Prefecture of Police and get a permit, which would
probably be refused, and then there was after all the
Prussian lines to pass. I thought it wise to have the
passport viséd, in case of accidents. Who could visé
it? Oh, Mr. Blount, the banker, who had just been appointed British Consul. To Mr. Blount's I went. A
respectable man told me that was the wrong shop, I
must go to the Embassy and get my business done there.
To the Embassy I went accordingly. A porter, mopping
the stairs, was the sole representative visible of her
Britannic Majesty. He sent me into a room, and presently a little man in slippers arrived, who told me he
had been summoned from some cleaning operations upstairs, and was in a muddle. Inside his velveteen coat
was concentrated the representation of ambassador, attaché, consul, and the British flag generally, including

the lion and the unicorn. He produced the seal, and had to spit on the unused wad to get juice enough for the impression. With much mental perturbation, arising from thick ink and a seemingly defective acquaintance with the art of penmanship, he succeeded in achieving my skeleton credentials, and then said I must go to Mr. Blount and get his signature attached. Rather a scrappy way of getting accredited as a free-born British Christian, I thought, especially when I thought of the big house and the bigger item in the estimates. However, I went to Mr. Bount, who was remarkably civil for a consul, and owned, with ingenuous candour, to an utter ignorance of his new duties. He knew enough, however, to attach his name in the vicinity of the imposing stamp, and then advised me to go to the Prefecture.

I had had enough of gyrating among officialism, and determined to chance it. Trotting down the Rue Rivoli I met Dr. Cormac, who, as head of the English ambulance, supported by Mr. Wallace, had been doing very good work. On my right the gardens of the Tuileries were sadly desecrated, ploughed up with innumerable hoof-prints of cattle, scored with tracks of provision waggons. Wooden barracks had been built where dainty flower-pots once were. The Place du Trône had its eastern end blocked by a gigantic barricade, erected, as I supposed, *pour passer le temps;* for it was impossible that it could have been of any use for defensive purposes. Once outside this, the Vincennes gate stood before me. I pulled up into a walk, and tried to look as if I were doing the most ordinary thing in the world. There was a cordon of soldiers across the narrow passage just inside the gate. One made a half motion for me to halt. I began to whistle, and looked the other way. He forsook his purpose. In another minute I was in the

broad road outside the Vincennes gate, and was in full
trot through the suburb. A little beyond the fort I came
to the forepost line of the Würtembergers, and chancing
to meet an officer I knew, rode through without so much
as being challenged.

Except her forts, her garrison, and her *enceinte*, it was
curious to notice how much of an open camp Paris had
been all through the siege. The forepost defence line of
the French was hardly worth talking of as an obstruction.
Here and there, it is true, it was formidable. Around the
Château of Villanteneuse, for instance, there was a series
of works which were of a regular fortress character, and
of a construction which was creditable to those who had
made them; but there they stood all alone, unsupported,
as French soldiers as well as French works have been so
often during this war. So the German patrols had been
wont quietly to walk round these Villanteneuse works,
and do their business on the further side, utterly negativing them. Non-continuity was the striking feature
everywhere of the French line of defences. Fort Nogent,
close on the right of which I passed in my ride, had not
to all appearance suffered so much as the St. Denis
forts; but I had not time to enter it and make a minute
inspection. Up till the hour that I left Paris no provisions, otherwise than surreptitiously, had been introduced into Paris. The situation, indeed, until Colonel
Wortley and Mr. Moore's prompt and prudential arrival,
was hardly appreciably ameliorated as compared with the
siege times.

Lagny I reached about six at night, and slept, or
rather spent the night, in the guard-room, to ensure
priority in the inevitable squeeze for seats in the only
train for the frontier—a train leaving at the unholy hour
of half-past four in the morning. All day long we jogged

on, very slowly for a *Postzug*, through France, passed
shattered Strassburg about midnight, and reached Carlsruhe about two in the morning. Hurrying to the telegraph office, I spent the hours there till ten in the morning, superintending the doings of two very pleasant young
ladies who had the night shift at the wires, and was in
the return train for the front at half-past two in the afternoon (the 3rd).

Owing to an accident to the rails I did not reach
Lagny, on the return journey, till the afternoon of the
5th, to find that place (always crammed) now positively
overwhelmed by the flood-tide of those who had quitted
Paris. On the 6th I rode round the east and north from
Lagny to Margency. Every road was thronged with the
inhabitants of the country surrounding Paris, pouring out
of the city in which they had so long been immured. I
saw sad sights at every step; families gazing hopelessly
at their shattered homes, or women timidly asking permission of the Germans to be allowed a corner in their
own house wherein to shelter their children. I saw a
French nobleman visiting his own château, asked as a
guest by the German occupants to drink a glass of his
own wine, and proffered a shakedown in one of his own
bedrooms. I saw delicate ladies, with jewels on their
fingers, grubbing in the fields for frosted vegetables;
while the *bonne* stood in the road with the sobbing children, and the father mooned about picking up scraps of
firewood to warm the damp hearth in the wrecked château.
I saw the stupefied farmer gazing dreamily on the battery
emplacements cumbering his fields, and at the shell craters behind them, as if the solid works were spectral ap-
paritions, and would melt away and leave the easy furrows, if he only looked long enough. Faces passed me
not good to look upon. Dark faces of French ladies in-

side carriages, with tightened muscles, and eyes flashing
full of silent passion, as the German sentry stopped them
in the ruined village, and in the rough Teuton manner
demanded their papers. There were lurid faces of men,
too, with knitted brows and suppressed angry despair
working in each feature. Yet the picture had its other
side, thanks to French adaptability and light-heartedness.
A family finds its wine-shop empty, and the roof off. In
a couple of hours things are patched up somewhat; the
buried bottles are unearthed; and a brisk over-the-counter
trade is going on. Another family turns up in an omnibus, with impedimenta, including an assortment of babies
and green umbrellas, only to find its home tenanted by
Saxon soldiers. Pack closer, is the order with the Teutons.
Room is made for the new-comers. The corporal takes
the baby while the mother tries what erbswurst soup is
like; and the old household settles down into something
marvellously like content.

Bad times no doubt those in the environs of Paris,
when the starving beleagured came out to ruined homes
and to grub for food in the fields; yet times not without
some redeeming features. Separated families were re-
uniting, and the sight—albeit there was not a little pathos
in it—was cheerful. My village of Andilly had received
a great accession of kinsfolk—so much so, indeed, that
it was not able to contain itself, but habitually held its
coteries al fresco in the mud. When I had left for Paris
a week before the Frenchman who, in Madame Sapey's
absence, did me the honour to consider himself my most
obedient humble servant, had neither wife nor child in
his lodge; they were in the besieged city. When I came
back there was a homely air about the place it had never
worn before. The wife had come out, and brought the
bairns with her. They were rather a pallid crew, but

merry with the joy of being back again. When one called
there came a flaxen-haired child, with a "Plait-il, Monsieur?" instead of the unshorn porter, its father. When
the sun came out the flaxen hair and her brothers and
sisters fell a playing on the lawn. What a home-look the
little ones gave this war-devastated region! They made
it look so homely that one fell home-sick, and found
himself craving wistfully after the sight of his own flaxen-
haired ones.

For how many must it have been in those days a source of
congratulation that the plain of Montmagny is a series of
market-gardens! You have seen in winter weather a bevy
of crows following the plough. Like this was the swarm
of French, male and female, father and son, matron and
child, that I saw spread over the fields, grubbing for the
vegetables, as I rode toward St. Denis, on my way to
Paris, on the 7th. Some went in strongly for onions:
others for leeks, which they washed in the water by the
roadside; others again with stick or iron spike turned
over the potato drills to excavate the frosted tubers. Road
and railway track were alike thronged ever with quiet yet
seemingly cheerful journeyers. Cheerful, for they were
already out of captivity, and as yet had not come upon
the object of their visit in the shape of their homes.
When this stage should have been reached I trow the
blithe faces grew very long indeed. There is a time to
be glad and a time to mourn. The *émigrés* were glad
before they were warranted in being so; there was a bitter
time of mourning in store for them. Ah! this life is very
short! Too short, as I heard an utilitarian remark the
other day for a wise man to smoke bad cigars. Too short
also, it may be, for people to be sad before the inevitable
time comes. If that strange, half-frivolous half philoso-
phical French nonchalance permitted, why, in heaven's

name, should not these poor people be merry while they
might? It is only Teutons and that nondescript amal-
gamation of the breeds of the universe which we call
Anglo-Saxon, that pulls down the lower lip in anticipation.

It was a strange scene on the forepost line. The
hour was about half-past five when I reached it. As I
had understood, the nominal hour for closing intercom-
munication was six; but on the German side the living
barricade in the shape of a cordon of soldiers had been
put up at five instead of six. In consequence, a dense
mass of disappointed people had accumulated, complain-
ing bitterly. Behind the folks on foot were long lines of
carriages, and the number was being continually added
to. It was, indeed, an important question for many.
They lived in St. Denis; they had no place to go to if
they went back to Paris, and besides, by the time they
could get back the Paris gates would be closed. Were
they to pass the night on the plain? I thought the Germans were rather stern about the matter. Cavalrymen,
with horses that reared imposingly, rode continually across
the front in a succession of plunges, driving the people
back as I have seen a troop of dragoons clear Dame
Street, in Dublin, on "St. Patrick's day in the morning."
On behalf of a gentleman in charge of an International
Society's ambulance waggon, I appealed to the officer on
duty; but "I have my instructions" was the response,
which no one could challenge. One could not have got
into Paris now without a permission. There was a regular
and orderly system of examining passes, both on the
German side, and by the French at the point where the
road cuts into the glacis of the enceinte. There I found
an officer who spoke both German and English, and who
comically grumbled that his linguistic accomplishments
seemed to doom him to permanence in his present posi-

tion. A trying position truly. Had I not already seen
that everybody was trying to get out of Paris, I should
have certainly said that everybody was trying to get into
it. Verily civil was the polyglot officer, and I found myself inside La Chapelle ever so much sooner than I had
anticipated.

"Why, they have got over it already!" Such was
the remark I made to myself as I rode through Paris in
the dusk—a Paris no more like the Paris I had seen a
week before than is Niobe to a clown grinning through
a horse-collar. Paris had in a great measure recovered
her spirits, and with them her complacency. The
general population looked no more as if all were lost.
Groups formed and conversed—they even enlivened into
gesticulation. The wineshops got up quite a creditable
illumination, and they were the reverse of empty. But
they were not so full as were the public soup-kitchens,
from which as I rode past I reasoned that the contents of
the twenty-seven trains that had come in full of British
provisions could not have diffused themselves quite so
widely as to bring plenty into every household; and
there still were *cues* outside the bakers' shops, but there
was something better to wait for than in the old days.
True, the bread was still brown, but it was not like glue
jam, starch, molasses, brown paper, bill-sticker's paste,
and printer's ink, blocked together, as it had been the
other day. There was in it a goodly proportion of
wholesome British flour, and it was a toothsome morsel
compared to the stuff that I had loathed the other day.
There were many more shutters down from the shop
fronts than on the occasion of my first visit. It was
true there was not much food about yet, and prices were
"famine," but still the look ahead was toward a harbour
of plenty pretty soon, not to misery, cold, hunger, bomb-

shells, and despair. So Paris had got over the terrible twinge which the surrender gave her at first, and had owned to herself that things were looking up. "After all," I seemed to hear Paris say, "I do well to get rid of my moping humour, and to abjure my intention of jumping into the Seine and finding my way into the Morgue. It cut me very deeply, no doubt, to have to sign that convention, but only just think what I have braved, done, and suffered. You can't in common decency refuse to·own that I am at least something of a heroine; that I have deserved well of my country and of my traditional reputation. Well, *vive la gloire;* I have the glory if I have not the success, so let me smooth my face and pluck up my spirits a bit, and go out for a walk on the Boulevards, and once more assert the tongue-gift I am endowed with." Who could blame Paris if she reasoned thus, providing only that her tongue-gift, her *gloire*, and her shortness of memory should not combine to make her fortgetful of the terrible ordeal she had gone through? Keep that memory fresh in the mind of Paris—if it is possible to keep any memory fresh in such a mind, or if, indeed, she knows the meaning of mental freshness—and you may be easy about any more war on the part of France that Paris can help. Even now, while the last act of the tragedy seemed thickening, and there was the possibillty of a hitch and a postponement in the dropping of the courtain, Paris wanted peace at any price, and wished Gambetta dead. "No more fighting for · us, thank you." I do not believe, if the war had continued in the South, that half a hundred Frenchmen would have quitted Paris to take part in it. Over the Mairie of La Chapelle hung a white flag as I passed, blazoned with the inscription, "La Patrie est en danger; Formation des compagnies de marche; Appel aux voluntaires."

Bless you, it might have been a Hebrew text for all that
anybody regarded it. The patrie and the marching
regiments might go hang, if the provision trains would
only come in fast enough into the Terminus du Nord.
Their speedy advent was indeed still wanted badly.
There had been no bread distributed the day before in
the arrondissement of Passy, and a scant one in turbulent
Belleville. Dr. Innes had seen to the temporary relief
of the ambulances with a zeal and discretion that could
not be too highly commended. That omnibus of his,
which must have been like the wizard's inexhaustible
hat, was talked about everywhere. How he pulled out
of it first himself; then rabbits, turkeys, loaves, ham,
vegetables, four sheep (I don't know if they were alive),
and a quantity of little odds and ends, in the shape of
chests of Liebig and other small deer! How he con-
sorted with Dr. Gordon, and how the energetic pair
bustled out the good things all round the ambulances—
going the length, indeed, in their urgency, of requisitioning the carriage-horses of the Ambassador of a Foreign
Power!

What a contrast to the months of March and April
was February in Paris, especially the first half of the
month! Electioneering was going on most of the time;
but electioneering surely of a very quiet kind. I don't
doubt that one, had he known where to look for it,
might have found political excitement running high and
waxing warm; but I confess I felt more interest in the
hungry women and children than in politics. In indulging this interest I went about a good deal with Dr.
Gordon, our military medical commissioner, a man who,
while singularly modest and undemonstrative, was simply
working like a horse to alleviate the distress of this great
city. His knowledge, derived from a residence in Paris

during the siege, was now of the utmost value, and the circumstances called it almost continually into action. Our countrymen in Paris during the siege, although few in number, had no reason to be ashamed of their work. The expenditure of the British Charitable Fund for the last month had amounted to 18,000 francs, all contributed by British residents in Paris for the behoof of their poorer fellow-countrymen. Over 1,200 poverty-stricken British subjects were regularly fed by its machinery. There was another fund of a similar character, organised by the Rev. Dr. Smythe, for married women who themselves were English, although married to foreigners. Many of the husbands of these women had been serving as soldiers; the poor creatures had lost their own nationality, and therefore could not claim either for themselves or their children on the British Charitable Fund. Through this medium some thirty-five women and seventy-six children had been kept alive. This latter fund had also assisted a forlorn detachment of converted Jews, thrown over, of course, by the Jewish organisation. All those families, of which there were twenty-seven, were connected with England in some way or other.

Nobody could have been in Paris at this time a single day without hearing something of the noble work done by Mr. Richard Wallace during the siege. A rich man, he had not spared his wealth, nor had he spared personal exertions. At an expense of 12,000*l.* he had established an ambulance; he had paid down 2,000*l.* for the behoof of the victims of the bombardment; he had set up a hospital at his own expense; and another hospital for thirty patients he had established in his own house. The grateful people called him the Peabody of Paris. There are some practical people across the water

THE CONQUERED. 335

in our happy little island. Mr. Wallace's name for charitable actions had been celebrated by Paris correspondents during the siege. Another victim, thought the astute
begging-letter writers. The first letter that Mr. Wallace
opened on the resumption of postal communications was
a begging letter, asking for 50*l*. I am sorry to have to
add that the enterprising correspondent failed in his
laudable object. I much fear, however, after all, that the
good work that was being done—the hearty genial work
into which everybody seemed to enter with a pleasant
zest—missed a very important class. I refer to those
middle-class people, maiden ladies, widows with families,
&c., ordinarily fairly well-to-do, but whose means of
living the collapse of France had dried up. These people
did not and would not come a-begging. They suffered:
aye, good friends, and I fear they died of want, some of
them, rather than expose the nakedness of the land.
They were hard to get at. Much like the Scotch folk
before the Poor Law régime, they had an honest pride,
and they would, while they starved behind them, hang
clean starched curtains at their windows. One deeply
touching instance of privation among such people came
to my knowledge. On the 9th a gentleman was distributing bread in a certain quarter of Paris. He had a
slice in his pocket, scraps of which he was throwing to
a dog. It startled him when a woman ran out of a
doorway and begged him to give her for her child the
bread he was throwing to the dog. She was a lady,
God help her! the wife of a surgeon, who was in the
south with the army, and her infants were starving. Take
this fact home to ourselves—for that is the only way to
get at the conception of the position. Just fancy a London doctor's wife begging a bit of bread from a stranger!
You can't? No more can I; and yet here was the counter-

part of the incomprehensible.   We could not persuade the doctor's wife, and such like people, to come to the places of distribution.   We did not know where they lived.   Delicate work this, not fit for rough men, however big their hearts, in great boots, with loud voices, and big beards; the work was women's work.   We should have seen in Paris in those times some frank-faced British women with energy and discrimination, yet with soft voices and pleasant coaxing ways.   They could have done what with the best will in the world men could not do.

So far as I could learn, the French surgeons in the early days of the siege, when the conditions were favourable, were earnest in the pursuit of conservative surgery. One of the leading advocates for this system had been Dr. Mosetig, of Vienna, attached to the International Society's organisation, and he had great success, especially in the early days of the siege.   But as the siege progressed times changed.   Circumstances became unfavourable to the recovery of wounded men under any surgical conditions; wards became impregnated from long use with hospital taint; rations were bad; the men were physically "bad subjects."   True, it was possible still in some favoured lazarettes to pursue conservative surgery. There ventilation was good; patients were comparatively sparse; there was a large allowance of cubic space of air; and the attendants spared no pains to destroy any mysterious taint so noxious after operations.   A most favourable example of a pattern lazarette was that kept up by Mr. Wallace, and supervised by Dr. Cormac, where the sanitary conditions were maintained in thorough efficiency with hardly any regard to expense.   But all the receptacles for the wounded manifestly could not share this good fortune.   There were crowded and long occupied wards, generating pyæmia, gangrene, and erysipelas:

there were overworked orderlies; and there was food of
a character inevitably tending to the impoverishment and
vitiation of the blood. These conditions presented but
a poor field for the successful practice of conservative
surgery. Let me take two examples of conservative surgery, operations for success in which one of the most
distinguished of our British surgeons, Sir William Fergus-
son, is justly celebrated. I refer to the excision of the
knee and elbow joints, and the establishment of a juncture between the parts on either side of the excised joints.
The value of such an operation successfully consummated
is immense; and, under favourable conditions, with skill
in the operator, a fair bodily condition in the patient,
and sedulous after attention, such an operation is successful in most cases to a pitch of which our ancestors
did not dream. But when the ward is malarious with
those taints which poison raw flesh surfaces; when the
patient is low in habit at the time of the operation, and
good nourishment is not afterwards obtainable; and when
the dressing and attendance are not scrupulously careful,
it is obvious that the circumstances are altered. The
surgeon has to consider the practicability of diminishing
the risk to the lowest possible minimum. When he ex-
cises a joint and attempts a juncture, he has two flesh
surfaces patent to the taint; the dressing is complicated
and the demand on the vital energy that stimulates the
healing power is probably larger. On the other hand,
when he amputates he exposes but one surface, and the
other risks are smaller in every way. It was by argument
based on these facts that toward the end of the siege
conservative surgery was gradually abandoned, except in
very favoured localities. I fear the success of the operat-
ing surgeon had been in no case encouraging. It was
hardly in the nature of things that it should have been

so. When scientific men give to the world the results of their surgical experience of the siege of Paris, the communication cannot fail to be interesting and instructive. From all that I can learn, matters would have been worse than they were, had not all the victualling, medical, and surgical arrangements been in professional hands, instead of being left to the Intendance. Probably in the history of modern organisations there is no greater instance of stupendous and abject failure than the French Intendance. If it failed miserably in its obligations to the fighting men, it is not to be thought that its functions would have been more efficiently performed in attending to the sick and wounded. This war has snuffed out the French Intendance. If there are any adaptations or copies of it in other countries, let their administrators take warning by the abject collapse of their pattern.

The Paris elections of representatives to the National Assembly were atrociously tame. There are few who do not know what election times are in England. Beer, roughs, placards, speeches, men in the gutter, couriers, hustings, the man in the moon, and so forth. If one had come to Paris thinking to see anything of this kind, I can imagine his utter disappointment. Where are the hustings? in my innocence I asked a fellow countryman more conversant than myself with the ways of the natives. That was on the polling day. He laughed in my face and turned away. I found out that there were no nominations save in print, and so there was no use for any hustings. An economical arrangement this to dispense with the hustings; but, then, how about the speeches and the show of hands? Where was the influential manufacturer and large employer of labour, who rolls out his unctuous but slightly halting paragraphs concerning the merits of the gentleman who has found favour in his eyes? Where were the dead cats and the rotten eggs; the Brummagen pet and his corps; the tirailleurs instructed to cheer and groan at the right moment; the heavy metal in the rear to give weight to a moral conviction? Where were the poll sheriff and the nimble poll clerk; the important policeman who shows you the way in, and looks the other way when you come out after having voted the wrong way and are maltreated by the myrmidons of the other side? Where was the stately sheriff, big with the declaration of the poll-result known ever so long ago? Where were the candidates? Where was anybody?

I confess that as a Briton, wedded to time-honoured traditions and more or less fond of a quiet row, I was miserably disappointed with these Paris elections. Why, they had the impudence to be orderly even in Belleville. There was no nomination at all. Fancy the swindle for a man with a dint in his temple, got by a stone cast at him when "keeping the ground" at an Irish nomination. I should have been deeply gratified to have seen the whole of the 500 or 600 candidates, after a preliminary stumping of the arrondissements, give vent to their sentiments consecutively from the steps outside the Hôtel de Ville. The process might have been slightly tedious, but it could not have failed to be instructive. The only candidate I knowingly saw during the whole of the election times was M. Louis Blanc. He was not speaking when I saw him. He was eating his breakfast: and he seemed to enjoy it. I felt a craving come over me to demand, then and there, that he should get on the table and deliver an oration; but decency forbade the interruption of a man in the middle of a *plat*, and I forbore. Hustings! Polling booths! Why, the recreant and demoralised Parisians voted inside houses, and without rows of

22 *

policemen.   An election conducted in such a way was a
shock to one's system.   Belleville should have been good
for a row.   Belleville did not care twopence about the
elections, and wanted food and fuel very badly.   What
an opening for bribery and corruption!   I believe that
Dr. Innes, with that big omnibus of his full of "proviant,"
might have headed the poll in Belleville, had he cared,
and Mr. Richard Wallace might have been returned for
every one of the arrondissements.   It surprised one to
learn that so many people took the trouble to vote.   Who
did vote?   Who knew a man that voted?   I didn't.   I
asked many whether they voted.   One man told me his
boots were bad, and he did not care to go out in the
damp.   Another said that in the morning he had got
some fresh meat, and had spent the day in contemplation
of it, in preference to going to the Mairie.   But there
was no question about it, some people did vote.   I saw
them going in and coming out—quiet, orderly folk,
mostly inclined to melancholy, and suggesting by their
appearance that a pot of Liebig would have done them
much good; and yet such men as Gambetta, Garibaldi,
and Rochfort were near the top of the poll!   Were they
warlike, these sombre citizens, under their lugubrious
aspect, and did they crave war to the knife? or was voting for the Reds a kind of way they had of demonstrating their disgust that they didn't see it advisable to be
other than peaceable?   Were there half-a-dozen of them
that thought more of Gambetta than of a leg of mutton;
or who would have forfeited the offer of a turkey to save
Garibaldi from being "shooted"?   I candidly own I did
not know what to make of Paris in its present guise.   At
times I felt prompted to pull off my hat to it, and own
up to its magnanimity; at other times, I asked myself
whether this magnanimity was not a sham, and another

name for utter indifference. Magnanimity or indifference,
one might take his choice of terms; but the patience was
unquestionable. I wonder how an English constituency
would have relished being kept in suspense for five days
as to the result of an election. Paris stood the delay
like a lamb. I did not hear a grumble. The papers,
which gave the interim results, did not seem to sell with
exceptional briskness. There was no clamour for placards
outside the Hôtel de Ville. I went into the place where
the bewildered clerks were trying to make coherence out
of the medley of votes and candidates. I got in by
special favour. It struck me that if every arrondissement
worked as hard as the central bureau, the final result
might be known somewhere about the New Year. A
column at a time of addition was enough to exhaust one
of the gentlemen with red stripes down his breeches; and
he was a long time in recovering from his exhaustion. I
asked when the final result would be known. A shrug
of the shoulders was the reply. "Dangerous, turbulent
city!" said a member of the English ambulance to me,
who had never visited Paris before; "why, it is as docile
as my village, where there is a parson and one policeman." I did not at the time think the critic was far
wrong; how we were both deceived by appearances! The
noxious plant of turbulence was but stamped down, not
utterly eradicated. True, if one looked hard he might,
even in the times I speak of, come across mild instances
where the turbulence showed faintly above the ground.
I went to a red-hot Republican Club in Belleville, where
I heard some remarkably wild speaking. One of the
orators—from the conformation of his legs I inclined to
the opinion that he was a shoemaker—evolved out of the
fervour of his patriotic ardour a strategical scheme that
ought, had he only got an opening, to have made him

the saviour of France.   Here is the programme, much in
the speaker's own words.   "Ah, citizens, the hated men
of the thrice-accursed William are defiling the casemates
of that famous fortress to our west, that iron door which,
locked, would keep out for ever the brutal barbarian.
Valérien is dragged in the mire; her beauty ravished by
the vile Teutons.   And it was a Frenchman who deliberately handed over Valérien to the hateful embraces
of these heathen hounds.   Woe is me for France, that a
Frenchman could have dealt this great blow to *la Patrie*.
Before the shades of the mighty Republican dead I de-
nounce this sham Republican Jules Favre; this chicken-
hearted miserable pseudo-patriot; this vile panderer to
the passions of the conqueror.   Not now, it may be, is
the time for just retribution; but, *sacré*, away in the vista
of the future I see a guillotine and the heads of traitors!"
Wild cheering followed, led off by a little man so covered
with "fluff" that one would imagine he had been tarred
and feathered, or was developing an incipient feathered
state, but who, I was informed, was a journeyman flock-
bed maker.   I don't doubt but that he might have been
very terrible in his wrath—this little fluffy advocate for
the reign of terror, but when not in wrath he looked
rather insignificant, and had a look as if used to be
thrashed by his wife.   When the cheers had subsided the
bandy-legged orator went on in a practical vein.   "Well,
traitors have yielded Valérien; that dire fact confronts
us.   Is it to be said that the men of Paris are so nerve-
less as to sit still and look up, and see the wretched
Prussian flag flouting a French sky on the battlements of
Valérien?   Perish the thought.   No; let 20,000 patriots
come forward.   We shall select a leader, and he will
lead us in the dead of night up the side of Valérien, and
we shall fall upon the dogs, the thrice damnable Prussian

dogs, and butcher them as they snore their Teuton snore. *A bas les Prussiens! A Mont Valérien! A Mont Valérien!"* And the bandy legs jumped off the tribune with a tragic wave of his right arm over his head. His views as to the location of Mont Valérien were not apparently well defined; or if so, were erroneous. He got as far as the door and had a drink of water; then he came back. Perhaps the virtue went out of him, because those present, on whom he may have counted as the nucleus of his 20,000 recruits, confined themselves solely to cheering, and showed no anxiety to go out in the Mont Valérien direction in the damp night air.

On one of the early days of the armistice a friend of the English ambulance came in, and asked me whether I cared to accompany him on a journey round Paris, of a somewhat exceptional nature. For some two or three months he had been living in the neighbourhood of Lagny, and had made friends of many of his humble neighbours; when they heard that he was going into Paris, they had come to him, not a few of them, and begged him that he would carry a letter, it might be, or a few francs, or a piece of meat, find out their friends in Paris, and distribute unto them the tokens from outside. We started in a dog-cart, the well of which was full of provisions. Our first visit was to a lady in the Rue de Rome, a daughter of the Mayor of Lagny. For her Mr. Job had a letter. Although in such close proximity, there had been no communication between father and daughter for three months. It was pitiful to see the face grow pale, half in fear, half in hope, as the trembling hand went out for the letter; and then there was a burst of tears, and a sudden exit through a side door. Like an April morning presently came back the lady; the news was good, but, although the face was blithe, she had not quite conquered the tears and the twitching at the corners of the mouth.   There was another emotion expressed in the face of her little daughter, when Mr. Job, who had quietly disappeared for a minute, re-entered with a fine turkey.   The young fairy fell a-dancing round the re-spectable bird, clapping her hands and singing merrily. The breakfast stood on the table, the *pièce de résistance* being curried horseflesh—a dish I venture to recommend. This was a household in which money was plentiful, and distress had laid on its hand comparatively lightly.

Our next call was in a very different quarter, off northward and eastward into the dangerous Belleville. Belleville the dangerous was, however, as tame as if it had no savagery in its nature.   Up through the narrow streets of the Quartier du Temple we drove, between the tall houses, reminding one of the old town of Edinburgh, into the traditionally most turbulent and revolutionary part of Paris.   "Ah, here is a mob, at last," I remarked, as we wheeled into a narrow Rue, blocked at the upper end by a dense mass of people.   Now we shall see what we shall see.   What we did see was this.   Some two hundred and fifty poor wretches, men, women, and children, waiting in the slush outside a wood-yard, to get a chance of buying a few sticks at the price of twenty centimes per pound.   Bethnal-green the squalid never turned out pallider brats than those of Belleville; fear-some to look at were the creatures that ought to have shown chubby faces and plump cheeks, by reason of their great hollow hungry eyes and pinched wan faces. It fell out that the family of which we were in search dwelt opposite this same wood-yard, in a great old house that must have once belonged to a somebody.   What a noble trait is that French one of neatness unto the death! Here in this single room, most of the belongings of which

had gone to swell the height of the Mont de Piété, and
in the cupboard of which a mouse of the slenderest appetite could not have picked up a living, everything was
trim and tidy as if the times were good and the cupboard
shelves had been groaning. Look at the group which the
letter Mr. Job has brought draws together. A man in
uniform, a brother of Madame, reads the letter. Another
sister that has tried to listen for a while has broken down
utterly, and leans on the shoulder of the National Guardsman, both her hands covering her face. A child in bewilderment is pulling her skirts as she looks up; and
Madame herself is a study. A pretty little woman, with
a thin face and a neat figure, trying so hard to be civil
to the Messieurs, to thank them, and to appear as if, for
the moment, there was no other object in her life but to
show her gratitude. But, poor creature, the letter from
her husband—a husband in a Lagny lazarette, what of
him was left, for he had lost a leg since his wife had
bidden him good-bye in July—that letter is being read,
and she is only catching fitful ·scraps of sentences. I
notice her, as she talks with us, set her head to one side,
for all the world as you will notice a bird do, to catch a
word, and the eye wanders from Mr. Job to the fraternal
National Guardsman. Mr. Job has money for Madame.
Madame takes the big five-franc pieces, and tries to write
a receipt, but her hand will not steady itself somehow.
Although the face is tolerably calm in seeming, the
shaking hand betrays the hidden emotion. Not money
alone has Mr. Job; in the money part of the transaction
he acts only as a go-between; but it is his own act and
deed to have brought this fine leg of mutton. Is he going
to be mobbed as he lugs it out of the well of the dog-
cart? The haunters of the outside of the wood-yard crowd
around us densely; the wan-eyed children concentrate

their gaze on the succulent mutton, their mouths watering
visibly, so that you may see them actually slavering, as
dogs do when they smell cooking; the men and women
shoulder each other to get an eligible position for a view.
"Mon Dieu, all that meat for one family!—fortunate
family!" Madame suddenly becomes a personage. And
we, what are we? Englishmen! Ah! God bless England,
then! Has England any more legs of mutton to spare?
suggests a good lady with a dirty face and a practical
turn of mind. England, as presently represented, had
not; but England could spare a few cuts for the children
off a sausage coil; and so we drove away out of Belleville, not shot at, not jumped upon, our coats whole, and
no mud upon them but that thrown up by the wheels of
the dog-cart.

We wanted now to find a family at Ile St. Louis.
There was a child in the case, and Mr. Job had promised
some relative outside that for the behoof of the child he
would hand to the mother a couple of tins of concentrated milk. Want had driven the family from the Ile
St. Louis. They had flitted to Montrouge somewhere,
and we had to go find them. There was a chance, too,
of seeing what the bombardment had done. The first
trace of it we came to was a shattered and burned house
in the Avenue de la Conservatoire. The Rue d'Enfer
had probably attracted more than its proportion of shells
in consequence of its name, yet even here you had to
use your eyes very keenly to see much damage. There
was a hole in the side of the Hospice des Enfants Assistés,
and the "parochial" character of the Mairie had not availed
to avert the hole made in its gable. But the physical
effects of the southern bombardment, so far as my observation went, had been trivial. The head of the family
of which we were in search was an artilleryman of the

National Guard. We went to the house of his captain. Captain civil, but did not know in the least where any of the men of his company lived. He had a list of their names, that was all. The addresses were the adjutant's duty, and he gave us the adjutant's address. Him we routed up, only to find that in his opinion, if to have the addresses of the men was anybody's duty at all, it was the captain's. Certainly he had no addresses. "Curious state of things," I remarked; "suppose you wanted a man in an emergency, or suppose he did not turn up when wanted at the rendezvous, how could you lay salt on the tail of your bird?" Monsieur the adjutant shrugged his shoulders, and said he daresay the man would be got at somehow in such a case; if not, it was but one man, and one man mattered no great deal. "But you have no addresses at all," said I, "and one man may swell into your whole company." Another shrug, and a "Qui sait?" so the adjutant concluded the conversation. With infinite trouble we at last found the family; the father was on duty. The child had pulled through the privations of the siege, and was in a condition to appreciate the milk Mr. Job brought for it. We had still one other place to visit, a hospice for orphans in the Rue Bossuet. There was a letter in Mr. Job's pocket for the Sister Superior from her sister, who has been working among the wounded in Lagny; and there were sundry comestibles in the well of the dog-cart for the orphans. As we drove along the Boulevard Michel we passed great flocks of sheep being driven in, with a crowd of children following them, as at home you will see the young ones hanging round a Punch on its way to a good pitch. There was a man, too, leading a solitary cow. Whether he intended to exhibit the quadruped at so much per head, and therefore was desirous to conceal it as much as possible from the

public gaze, just as a showman makes the giant stop inside the caravan, I don't know; but he had covered up
the beast with a rug which hid all but legs, tail, and
head. The milky mother was a decided sensation in the
Boulevard Michel. When we reached the hospice, we
found the orphans at what I supposed was their supper
—horse broth and brown bread. The well of that dog-
cart was a phenomenon. White loaves, three legs of
mutton, a turkey, and half a cheese taken out at last
emptied it. We made a kind of trophy of them on the
table amid wondering half-timid joy on the part of the
orphans, and genially grave thanks from the sisters in
their white starched hoods. The well being empty, our
work was over for the day.

Paris had been kept wonderfully clean during the siege,
and that cleanliness had averted any raging epidemic,
such as was engendered by the foul squalor that con-
taminated the air and everything else around Metz. But
I saw during my drive an immense deal of a certain low,
sluggish type of fever, bearing a close resemblance to the
"famine-fever," of which during a day's walk with Mr.
Catlin, of the Cow Cross Mission I noticed so much in
London some eighteen months ago. The women and
children were the commonest victims. It does not force
you to bed, except in its last stages, this famine-fever;
but any one with eyes in his head can see its victims
dying as they trail their limbs listlessly about. The
skin is thin, dry, and tight, but has a dull opacity
that speaks of the liver action being deteriorated, and of
pores refusing to fulfil their duty; the eyes have a tired,
faded out-look; and the whole frame seems gradually
withering away. I think a full meal of victuals, granting
that it could be eaten, would kill one tolerably far gone
in this disorder. I wished that I were a man of leisure,

and had a big cellar of generous port wine, and a large consignment of quinine tincture.

Paris seemed different from Metz in one important and creditable particular; there had been no hoarding of secret stores of food on the part of "business" men, speculating on a market. In the interval between the signing of the Convention and the rolling in of provisions from outside, these hoards would have come to the front had there been any. But the shops were barer then than in the middle of January.

CHAPTER II.

The Conquerors.

IT was early stirring in the Reservoir on the morning of the 1st of March—of the eventful day of the German entry into Paris. By four o'clock its passages resounded to the clink of swords and spurs. Already by that hour the silence of the broad bare streets of Versailles was broken by the tramp of many horses, as the 14th Hussars rode out to keep the ground. When I started at six, day had already nearly broken—a morning cool and grey. We passed on the road a battalion of infantry—an "early bird;" it had halted and piled arms till comrades should turn out and come up. The long forest road was traversed by only an occasional orderly of the impatient 11th Corps Artillery. Ville d'Avery, once the home of the 6th Jägers, whenever that gallant regiment happened to be "at home" from forepost work, and whither many a gallant fellow had been carried back from the foreposts to die, seemed tenanted only by three old women and a grey terrier dog. Beyond lay the pretty little cemetery of the Jägers, decorated with its wreaths, and here had halted a solitary company of infantry. As the men stood gazing on the graves of their comrades, you might have taken them, in the dim grey morning, for phantom mourners over the gallant children of the Fatherland.

As from above St. Cloud we sighted the river, we became sensible of the magnitude of the general advance toward the common centre, the Bois de Boulogne. Long before, the barracks of Versailles, once the quarters of the soldiery that was the pomp and pride of the Empire, were pouring out their stalwart men in spiked helmets. To Neuilly, from the trim parterres of Nanterre and the river slopes of Courbevoie, the *pickelhaubes* were pressing forward. From the garrison-crater of Valérien ran down its grim sides lava streams of living armed men—men these of the mediatised provinces, Hesse, Weimar, Coburg-Gotha; men with memories of Courcelles, of the ravine of Gravelotte, of that deadly march up the Meuse from Donchery, and on to the plateau over against Sedan; with recollections of sorties, of typhus, of the knee-deep mud and the fearful mortality of the siege of Metz; yet brisk, healthy, and hearty now as if fresh from quarters at home. St. Cloud—burnt and shattered—had given up the men who may be said to have bivouacked in its roofless houses—the Sclave-faced Silesians of the Sixth Army Corps, who, disappointed of blood at Sedan, had led the still bloodless advance upon Paris, and were now to share the honours of the entry. From Sèvres the ghastly—a mild *souvenir* to them, it might be of Bazeilles—had marched out already the blue-clad Bavarians, glad as ever to stand in line alongside of the more lasting North Germans. Did they think, as they skirted the Seine, of the soil of Wörth, soaked inch deep with their south-land blood? Those who had seen the 1st Corps before von der Tann led it on the Orleans war path would have recognised, had they seen it now, but few familiar faces in the ranks. The bodies of the rest are mouldering under the damp sod of the south. But new stuff has replaced the staunch old "cannon-fodder." The Sixth Corps and the Bavarians fraternise warmly; Silesians and "Pandours" are kindred stuff. Assuredly neither corps deserves the biting sarcasm which Frederick the Great vented on his Pandours: "You dogs, do you wish to live for ever?"

They are over the river already, these ever-forward Uhlans! Lo, their pennons on the further side as they circle among the trees, and hark! from the village of Boulogne comes on the morning air the swell of martial music. It is German music, for the French do not play the "Pariser Einzugsmarsch." If the Germans ever want a new motto to stick under the eagle, I would fain recommend "Up in the morning early." Attention to it has won not a few of their victories; this musical corps over the water must have acted upon it "bright and spry" this morning. In twenty minutes more the slopes above the Longchamps race-course are chequered with dense masses of the dark-coated guardians of the Rhine. Hauptmann von Bock's pontoon bridge was already half bordered with wreaths of laurels; on the Bois de Boulogne side a triumphal arch had been erected. Look at the enthusiasm, and in truth taste, with which this rough-handed fatigue party are twining yet more wreaths and festoons. From the bridge of Neuilly—it was eight o'clock—the artillery of the 22nd Division is moving down the broad straight road through the Bois to form near the crest of the slope opposite the pavilion. Meanwhile, the infantry of the 6th Corps are streaming over the Sèvres pontoon bridge and forming in the glades and the open places on the bight of the loop. Staff officers, conspicuous among whom are now Bavarians in their blue uniforms, are galloping across the plain after

the reckless and slightly purposeless manner of staff
officers of every nationality.   Not an acre of the wood
but is sedulously patrolled by the Hussars; their bright
blue uniforms and red-bordered new shabracques glancing
between the trunks of the trees and through the denser
thickets.   Here comes the Gotha Regiment, not, however, headed by the Herzog.   From the other direction
comes at a crashing gallop, in squadrons, the 11th
Hussars, the Frankfurt Regiment; the squadrons get
to charging pace as they wheel round a clump, and are
steady in position before your admiration of their galloping has subsided.   By half-past nine the formation is
gradually taking shape.   Hark! there is a cannon shot,
and another.   Are they from Paris, or are the gunners
in Versailles fouling their tubes with the blank cartridge
of a Royal Salute as the Emperor leaves the Prefecture?
Crash! another kind of music.   With a quick bicker of
the drums, there strides through the trees of the south
and athwart the slope, a battalion of Bavarian infantry,
with the black shaving brushes crowning the helmets;
they wheel, form columns of companies, and take ground
with faces toward the Grand Stand.   There comes yet
another and another battalion of the blue Bavarians,
with Uhlans and Artillery following, till the whole of
the regiments representing the 1st Corps (Hartmann's) is
in position.

By ten o'clock, when the Bavarians were fairly in position in the centre, the infantrymen of the 6th Corps, who
had previously been lying down on the breast of the slope
on their left, had fallen in and moved out into the plain
in close columns of companies aligning on the Bavarians
on their right; the latter, again aligning on the division
of the 11th Corps forming the right of the line.   The
long line stretching from end to end of the racecourse

was everywhere four companies deep. It was broken by
narrow intervals marking the distances between the battalions—intervals that one unaccustomed to the aspect
of the formation of troops might hardly have discerned.
The second line—at a distance of four hundred paces in
rear of the first—was composed alternately of regiments
of cavalry and batteries of artillery. The intervals in the
second line are wider than in the first. The general
esplanade in front of the grand stand is kept clear, but
the "ring" before it is crowded with a brilliant and kalei-
doscopic throng of mounted officers—Uhlans, Dragoons,
Hussars, Cuirassiers, and Staff; the pride and pomp of
military Germany. It is swept away to the right, as if
some invisible besom were in action on it, leaving the
racecourse "finish" bare, and the level beyond, where so
often have stood the carriages of the *monde* and *demi-
monde* of Imperial Paris, without a living thing on it but
the inevitable dog. There is a sedulous dressing up of
the first line, till, standing by the side of the right-hand
man of the right-hand regiment, and resting the barrel of
a rifle across his chest, you might have sped the bullet
down the line and harmed never a man. Across the
extreme right behind the troops are drawn, in a wide
segment of a semicircle, and in clumps here and there,
the carriages of those who have the right of entry within
the cordon formed by the Hussars. Behind them, again,
is a lofty battlemented tower, sweeping from its summit
the whole line from the right to the left. Not a few
think the parapet surrounding the toy windmill, some
150 yards to the front, the most eligible point of view.
You may meet English and American ladies there, interspersed with doctors and journalists of all nations. I
think not a few of the smarter of the latter, and all the
artists, whose name is legion, would take in preference

to the battlements of the lofty tower, if they only knew what a coign of vantage they afford.

The front of the Prussian divisions on either wing is clear. Before the centre of the Bavarians in the middle stand two mounted men, the Imperial Crown Prince, the commander of the third army, and his *Flügeladjutant*. A few straggling horsemen saunter with seeming aimlessness about the grand stand, and the pause of expectancy becomes almost painful. The second line—the cavalry and artillery interspersed—turn the interval to account by perfecting the accuracy of its dressing. Each individual corps and battery was long ago dressed to death as regards itself, but it is now the somewhat defective alignment which is being seen to.

At ten minutes past eleven, without a moment's warning, a wild cheer of enthusiasm flashes along the line. A clash of music as the bands burst into "God Save the King." Half-a-dozen horsemen are galloping up from behind an angle of the stand, straight to the right of the line. The leader, an upright, broad-shouldered old man, with snow-white hair, half halts his horse with a handwave of salutation, as he reaches the Imperial Crown Prince, then gallops on with the latter hanging close on his flank. He pulls his horse on its haunches as he reaches the flank, and the "windmill battery" bursts out into a "hip, hip, hurrah," a waving of handkerchiefs, and a clapping of female hands. No need to tell England at this time of day that the white-haired soldier on the noble black horse is Kaiser Wilhelm of Germany. The densely packed staff that has been in waiting in front of the right come prancing up as the Emperor wheels his horse's head to the left, and commences his slow march along the front. Two horsemen are before him. An interval, and then the grand old man proceeds

alone, the solitary focus of the splendid picture. This
great day for the Empire of which he is the ruler seems
to have cured him of his ailments. Where is the lumbago,
the gradual decay, the breaking up about this fresh-
coloured old chieftain, with the eye like a hawk? His
crest is as erect, his back as straight, his seat as firm, his
bridle-hand as light on the black horse, as those of his
gallant son, who seems so proud of his father. Verily he
reneweth his youth as doth the eagle, this stalwart, sem-
pervirent Monarch of the Teutons. His son follows him
half a horse's length behind him, and then, princes,
powers, and potentates—half the Gotha Almanack. Great
heavens! are these deep-throated men of the mediatised
provinces under the belief that if they but cheer loud
enough, the roar of their glad clamour will echo in billows of sound across that Rhine which so well they have
helped to keep? Sharper and shriller, but to the full as
loud, and with a hot ring in it as when steel, not iron,
is struck by the hammer, bursts out the cheer of the children of King Ludwig. Germans, allies of Prussia not in
name alone, but in heart, the alliance sealed loyally by a
deluge of Bavarian blood, they have earned good right
and title to stand here in line to-day, and to claim the
low bend of appreciation that the Emperor of Germany
accords them. But although the Bavarian troops cheer the
Emperor of Germany and King of Prussia, the Bavarian
bands will by no means strike up the Prussian National
Hymn. For has not Bavaria a national *Lied* of her own,
a wild fanciful air, befitting the Landsleute to whom it
appertains?

The Kaiser is not well among the Bavarians till the
22nd division is bodily out into the plain in dense
masses; having left-wheeled, they stand looking at the
Emperor's back. The distant, and yet more distant roar

23 *

of cheering comes to us on the right from the far away
left flank formed by the 6th Corps, and then, as the
Emperor turns the left flank, and comes towards us again
along the front of the second rank—the cavalry and
artillery—the cheering draws nearer and nearer. As its
right flank, in its turn, is gained, and the head of the
staff turns away toward the pavilion, men notice, and the
kindly German hearts swell at the sight, that Royal
father and Royal son have drawn together—horse head
to horse head. Etiquette is potent, but more potent still
is love; and surely if ever there was love between father
and son, it is between these two. See; the proud father
lays his hand on the neck of his son's horse, and the
staff fall back in delicacy as the two converse. Then
spurs go into the horses' sides, the raking black goes to
the front again, followed by the white-heeled chesnut.
The staff dash through an interval of the 22nd division,
and the Emperor takes up his position in front of the
east end of the pavilion.

The drums crash out, and the marching past has
begun with the infantry, the 83rd Regiment leading. The
formation is close columns of companies. The Prussian
marching is very fine, but the infantry men hardly show
so well in columns of companies as when marching in
fours. Let the civilian onlooker regard the sloped arms
—indication that this is a display in time of war, and not
a bath-brick and pipe-clay review in the piping times of
peace. Before night it was not utterly impossible that
these now sparkling bayonets might have their sheen
smirched with blood. To my thinking the triumph of
the Prussian marching past was reserved for their Artillery,
which went past in a manner simply perfect. No dress
parade on Woolwich Common, after a month's preliminary
battery drill, ever surpassed it. In a military experience

of not a short duration, I never saw finer dressing than
that displayed by the companies of the Bavarian battalions,
as they stood waiting on the racecourse for the word to
march. Away goes their general staff in advance, the
white cocks' feathers of the chiefs floating out in the air
like handfuls of snow-flakes. The leading battalion
follows, at a short, jerky quick step, to the music of a
curious breakdown jig, such as I have often heard in
pantomimes. It made a tidy marching step, and the
Bavarians did their best; but a martinet would have
thought more of them had he never seen them in motion.
As with the Prussians, their Artillery excelled their infantry in marching past. But writing of marching past,
what shall one say of a detachment—a column—a what
shall I call it?—of half-a-dozen ambulance waggons in
line dressing as true as the smartest horse artillery in the
world? What a gallant show make the light blue and
white pennons of the Bavarian Uhlans as they sweep
down the slope in quarter squadron formation to take up
their station in the marching-past order! The flashing
lance-heads seem dressed as smartly up in the air there
as the noses of the horses are in the ranks. Truly a
gallant and chivalric sight these brilliant lancers of the
Pfalz, sharing, to the mind of an old cavalry man, with
the Dragoons and Hussars the chief honours of the day.
Out rings the clarion of the trumpets, clash goes the
silver music of the kettledrums, tempered by the deep
notes of the ophicleide. The horses, ever lovers of sweet
sounds, arch their necks, champ the bits, and toss flecks
of foam back on the polished leathers of the riders. They
are as proud as if they realised the meaning and the
glory of the day.

But enough, surely, of marching past. Getting tedious
is the spectacle, and à fortiori its relation must do after

a short time. Yet it is not fair to quit the subject without one word. These troops, reader, passing there daintily clean in serried files that would have rejoiced the heart of an adjutant of the Guards, these troops have had other work for the last six months than to study the trimness of drill and dressing. Fighting, falling, bivouacking, earthworking, marching for hours, weeks, months at a stretch, there are few soldiers, according to the rules of the old school, whose parade neatness would not have deteriorated. The secret lies here, that in the thick of the fighting, marching, and bivouacking, time was found in these German ranks for such *divertissement* as the goose-step.

For the march-past spectators had mostly forsaken other points and converged on the neighbourhood of the shattered Grand Stand. A strange scene it was to be sure—ladies, correspondents, artists, royal servants, field postmen, aye, marketenders even, male and female, packing pretty closely here within the odour of royalty. I have a fancy that that black servant of Prince Carl is a cynic, standing there showing his big white teeth, and looking for all the world like a Zouave that has seen the error of his way and adopted the Fatherland and a costume with buttons. When the heads of the 11th Corps column and of that of the Bavarians showed themselves conspicuously on the road toward Paris, having wheeled left-about after marching past, and strode away toward Paris, I fear the stalwart Silesians got scant recognition of their smart marching past. There was a general rush Parisward of the non-officials, eager to conquer even the victors in celerity. But those who waited saw a right genial and soldier-like sight after the last of the 6th Corps had filed past. The Kaiser turned his horse and met his son face to face. Hand went out to hand, and the grip

was given of love and mutual appreciation. Then the
Staff came forward—the Princes, Poins, and "Lairdies"
—and they had doffed bonnets and congratulatory words
for their monarch. It was truly the right time for congratulation—the morning of the consummation of triumph.
You were saying in England the triumph was remorseless
and over stern. Look for the refutation of this inside
Paris; on the day when what I am writing of was being
transacted;—inside Paris, where the cowardly yelpers of
the canaille were impotently hauling about their pitiful
field-pieces in quarters you might be sure enough would
not be visited by the German men-at-arms; throwing up
trumpery barricades, from which, as ever, they would run
like hounded foxes, yelling *trahison;* assailing with their
venomous rancour honest neutrals who meant them no
evil; and clamouring that, because Paris was not wholly
occupied, Paris was not utterly at the feet of the conqueror. Say, I pray you, did such a citizenhood deserve—had they earned the Quixotic consideration that
would tempt soldiers in war time to yield the price of
their victories and of their losses? Say you not rather,
now that prejudice has cooled, that it might have been
the best thing that could have befallen this impotently
truculent populace that they should have been made to
pass through the burning fiery furnace of the uttermost
degradation of humiliation?

The heads of columns took two ways through the Bois,
the Prussians all but skirting the *enceinte,* the Bavarian
Uhlans adventurously plunging into the bosky dells of
the wood—wherein indeed these slashing soldiers lost
themselves, and threatened to become Teutonic babes of
the wood, but for certain awe-stricken Frenchmen, who
put the advance guard right at least half-a-dozen times.
The ignorance on the part of the Bavarians of the topo-

graphy of the Bois de Boulogne lost them the priority. When we gained the open, lo! on our left front was Rittmeister von Jachmann's squadron of the 13th Hussars, followed by the staff of the 22nd Division. It was too aggravating to see in the near foreground the grizzled grey whisker of General von Schachtmeyer, commander of the 11th Corps, and not to see the full face of him. Five minutes' gallop sufficed for this. The Porte Maillot was reached; there was a brief parley about a certain gate which had been walled up, a move forward, and we were in l'Etoile that spreads its rays inside the gate. A few forlorn, but self-respecting douaniers kept over it a nominal guard; farther inside were some green-coated gendarmes, and von Jachmann's Hussars held the gorge of the Avenue Beaugar. In the centre sat grey von Schachtmeyer, pulling his grizzled moustache; he had his dispositions to make, and these were seemingly aided by capillary exercitation. A man of prompt action is von Schachtmeyer. "The 22nd Division will march on to the Place du Roi de Rome, and there pile arms; the Bavarians will march by the Arch of Triumph, down the Champs Elysées, on to the Place de la Concorde; the 6th Corps will follow, and occupy the Place de l'Etoile and the Champs Elysées themselves—and now *Vorwärts!*"

At the word the cavalry trumpets ring out, and the officers shout "March!" On they go up the deserted Avenue, followed by the 80th Regiment playing lustily the Paris March. On, through the appalling solitude of the Avenue Beaugar, across the Place d'Eylau, where stood a solitary horseman, and up the Avenue de Malakoff to the Place du Roi de Rome. There were those among the on-lookers who had seen the French soldiers march with their English allies into the grim fortress from

which this avenue takes its name. Where were the men
who stormed the Mamelon, the dauntless and crafty campaigners of the Crimea? Alas! their courage sapped,
their craft gone, they, and men who should have been
such as they, were languishing in the German prisons,
and the conquerors of the new era of warfare were marching in triumph over them up the Avenue named after one
of their deeds of prowess. The head of the long snaky
column marches steadily on through curious groups—for
the Avenue de Malakoff is densely populated, and its inhabitants cannot resist the humiliating fascination—till at
length it reaches the Trocadero. Lo! before the Teuton
host lies Paris as in a panorama. Over against rises the
gilded dome of the Invalides. Are the ashes of the First
Napoleon quiescent in the sarcophagus to-day? Behind,
the grand pile of the Arch of Triumph rears its head.
In the distance rise the towers of St. Sulpice, the Pan-
theon, and Notre Dame. At our feet winds the Seine,
striped out with its beautiful quays, esplanade, and bridges;
beyond the Champs de Mars, clad with the white tents
of the French. On the Field of the God of War a dense
mass has collected of French soldiers, no longer warriors.
And what effect has this rich and varied panorama on
the German soldiery? Business first of course. They
tramp on with the stolidity of perfect discipline, form
companies on the grassy slope leading down to the river,
and pile arms with mathematical precision. And then
they are free to stare and wonder. It is blank wonderment at first; then the gradual dawn of profound silent
admiration. The wistfulness of that concentrated fixture
of the multitudinous eyes! And then a man with a deep
sigh, such as a man heaves after a long pull at a beer
flask, gasps out the single word, "Wunderschön!" He
breaks the ice. There is a chorus of "wunderschöns,"

and the Teutons, with that love of pure beauty which is
one of their best attributes, fall to quiet, thoughtful comment on the glories of Paris. They lie down on the
grass, and drink their fill of the sight; they roll it like a
sweet morsel under their tongue; they lave themselves, so
to speak, in the beauties of the beautiful city. The Pont
du Champs de Mars down below has its German end still
held by a Zouave guard, and they have run a rude barricade across it, consisting of a mule cart and a few baskets.
A company is marched down; it halts, and the hauptmann rides out and parleys with the Zouave officer amid
the intense interest, not unmingled with hooting, of the
densely lined quay on the opposite side. The fezzes
cross the bridge, and the spiked helmets occupy the
hither end; straightway the two sentries of the "double
post" are stalking to and fro as if they had held the
ground from beyond the memory of man. Up on the
brow of the slope his Reverence, the division chaplain,
on a white horse, is gazing open-mouthed on the scene;
but never mind him, let us push now to the Arch of
Triumph. As we walk along the Rue du Roi de Rome,
we see the chalk marks of the *Quartiermeister* already
on the doors, and the German flag is floating from the
conciergerie window of the Commandant. The neighbourhood of the Arch of Triumph is densely crowded
with the infantry of the 6th Army Corps halted, with
portly old von Tümpling sitting in his saddle at their
head. Thickly interspersed with them were Parisians,
chiefly of the lower order. Boys, tatterdemalion gamins,
were in wild profusion—young rascals of wonderful pan-
tomimic ability, with a concerted shrill whistle that drowned
or discorded the music of the bands. Already the ver-
satile rogues had learned to mimic the harsh words of
command and the somewhat clumsy gestures of the men.

Impudent varlets they were, and they had apparently already gauged the good temper of the Hussars who kept the ground, for they mocked without ceasing, in apparent certainty of impunity. But clear the way, ye gamins! At a lumbering canter come some gigantic cuirassiers of the Guard Corps, and then the general staff. No, good friends with the broad Sclave-features, ye stout Kinder of von Tümpling, you need not glance so keenly up at the arch there. For the Emperor comes not, neither comes his son, yet the blood royal of Prussia is not unrepresented. For there is Prince Albrecht, of the cavalry, and burly Admiral Adalbert, looking uncommonly like the late Sir Charles Napier, and as bad a rider as are most sailors. And here is a face familiar to and honoured by me, by reason of sincere respect and many kindnesses—the face of the Heir Apparent to the throne of Saxony, at once a Prince and a soldier. And he of Saxe Coburg Gotha, and Luitpold of Bavaria, and Leopold of Hohenzollern, and, not to waste the readers' time and my own ink, the whole ruck of the "*Zweite Staffel*," the blue-blooded band of "wee German lairdies," not a few of them very big in bodily bulk and in their own conceit.

Following the general staff come the Bavarian troops, marching still to the breakdown in half-company columns. The men of the 6th Army Corps follow them towards the Place de la Concorde, and we fall into the tide on the broad side-walk. The soldiers already billeted are staring out of window or loitering by the doorways. I ask a Hessian dragoon what he thinks of Paris. "Oh, it's very fine," he replies, much in the tone of the Scotch baillie who thought Edinburgh could not hold a candle to Peebles. "But"—there was a "but" in every fibre of the tone—"but he had got nothing to eat yet, and there was no straw for his own or his horse's bed." Not

surely a fierce requisitionist this man, whose *summum bo-
num* in the bed line lies in a lock of straw. Wood was
another want which the occupants of the little theatres
on the Champs Elysées were fast repairing by dragging
out and chopping up the chairs and benches, with which
they lit their *al fresco* fires in the garden plots. The
22nd Division men on the Trocadero had been able to
stack arms and lie down. Not so their comrades on the
Place de la Concorde. There were too many disturbant
elements simmering in the vicinity. It is true that single
officers walked unmolested through the crowds on the
side-walks, that the Princes rode leisurely to and fro, the
cynosures of all eyes. But there was an ugly yeasty
throng, not so much in the Champs Elysées as in the
Place de la Concorde. Here the Bavarians stood to their
positions looking up at the statues of the chief French
cities, the faces of which were each veiled in crape.
Through the film of black, German Strassburg looked
down dimly upon the German soldiers, her pedestal still
bedight with the wreaths and garlands which grateful
Paris had affixed thereunto. Down the vista of each
entering street was apparent first a thin and vacillating
line of red-breeched troops of the French line, nearer
now to the Germans than ever they had dared to come
before. Behind this line again a densely-packed crowd
of angry, truculent faces, with a dash of the wolf about
the eyes of them, bloodthirsty, yet cowards the whole
pack. Looking at them is one man by the statue of
Rouen here, whom not to name would be to leave my
description very incomplete—a tall strong man, in a
Cuirassier uniform without the cuirass, but with the helmet.
Paris looks at the keen eyes, the *brusque* moustache, and
the square lower jaw, as if it ought to know them, yet is
not quite sure about it. Take your helmet off, Otto

von Bismarck-Schönhausen, and let the gazers have the worth of their money in a long stare.

And this allusion to the impotently furious population leads up to a narrative of the aspect which Paris presented when the German occupation began. I had striven exceedingly hard to think well of Paris under this tribulation of hers. Nor had I been altogether without justification. Only on the 28th of January, when everybody was talking of revolution and anarchy, I had made a perambulation of the quarters whence were reported the chief disturbances, and had come back unmolested; and after what I had seen, with the word "calumniation" ready on my lips. The silence and solitude of the Avenue Beaugar, by which we had entered Paris, had seemed very pathetic. The proud beauty, I said to myself, is veiling her eyes from her humiliation. The Avenue de Malakoff took the edge off the sentiment, and it vanished utterly when a little woman who kept an auberge, where I quenched my thirst in beer, importuned me to bring her as many Prussian customers as possible, and did not hesitate to designate them as bons garçons. She might have been an isolated case; but the aspect of the Champs Elysées clenched the nail. All Paris was there, as you may have seen on a day when there was a grand Imperial pageant. Ladies in dainty dresses and high-heeled boots tripped about; chevaliers of France, with the ribbons in their button-holes, gratified their curiosity at the expense of their honour. The windows were so full that I imagine some of them must have been let for money. But it was the conduct of what may be designated the mob, that disgusted me most. Touch a German soldier they dared not. They cowered—half a hundred of the white-blooded hounds—before a solitary Uhlan strolling his horse listlessly about. But let them only catch an

unfortunate civilian, and then just mark their valour.
Fortunately they were too limp and vague to know how
to take life adroitly, else many a murder might have been
done in Paris this afternoon.   Say you I speak from
prejudice?   My prejudice, if I had any, was fain to lie
the other way.   I speak from sore-boned experience.   As
I walked down the Champs Elysées, the Crown Prince of
Saxony with his staff rode by.   His guest for many a
week before, I would have eaten dirt had I not raised
my hat to his Royal Highness.   He returned my salute,
and, beckoning to me, shook hands, and a short conversation ensued.   After I had taken my leave, Count
Vitzthum, his aide-de-camp, rode after me to communicate from the Prince a piece of information which he was
kind enough to think would be of interest to me.   My
companion and myself soon found that this episode had
gained us the marked attention of about a hundred of
the hungry prowlers after heroic seizures on which no
risk was attendant.   We thought little of the demonstration at first, and tried to lose our suite by turning back
in the rear of the Bavarians, and halting there, but our
unconcern seemed but to aggravate the patriots.   After
much consultation a little party came forward and civilly
requested us to accompany them to a certain post.
Although apprehensive of the consequences, we were
unwilling to appeal to the Bavarian officers, and so be
the possible means of precipitating a fracas; we therefore complied.   No sooner were we outside the German
quarter than the tactics were changed.   My friend was
torn away from me, and for many hours I saw no more
of him.   Cries of "Mouchard," "Sacré Prussien," "Cochon,"
assailed me.   Somebody hit me over the head with a
stick; another kicked me from behind; yet another
tripped me up.   I went down, and the patriots jumped

on me with sabots. I struggled up, and hitting out right
and left, made my way to an officer of the National
Guard. He laughed and turned away. Then they got
me down again, striking each other in their eagerness to
have a blow at me. Some clamoured, "To the Seine
with him," but others, the majority, were for the police
station. Thither, accordingly, I was conducted in a novel
fashion, on my back and dragged by the legs, a distance
of some 300 yards. Needless to say that my coat was
in ribbons, my head was cut, my back bumped into
bruises, my legs torn nearly out of the sockets. Great
powers! how I longed, as they dragged me along, for a
single section of the old Royal Dragoons, or that I might
have a chance at but three of the cowards at a time!
Chucked inside the police station like a bale of goods, I
was conveyed by a back door, and in the pleasing com-
panionship of a drunken woman, a blouse who had
stolen a lump of putty, and a tatterdemalion who had
been seen selling a couple of cigars to a German, to a
certain prefect, a venerable gentleman in a white tie. I
sent a note to the British Embassy, whence emanated
with creditable alacrity the porter, an official whom I had
learnt to look upon as the British Embassy incarnate.
The benevolent prefect released me, and I was glad to
slink home in my soiled and tattered clothes. I paid
another visit, however, to the Place de la Concorde.
There I noticed what seemed threatening symptoms. The
French mob was sorely taxing the patience of the Bavarians, whose blood was beginning evidently to rise. I
should in no wise have wondered, I said to myself, as I
turned away, if there were wild work before morning;
and it struck me with surprise that the Germans had not
cleared their quarter and held it militarily. But it was
not for me to stay and watch what might befall. There

was other work before me. It was past five o'clock, and
I had to be outside the *enceinte* by six. A dog-cart, with
a stout horse, was waiting for me by the Madeleine.
Bruised, sore, with the blood and mud yet unwashed
from the back of my head, I had still my programme to
fulfil. Up the Rue de Lavalette, almost deserted; along
the flank of the Terminus du Nord, and so into the Rue
de La Chapelle at a smart trot. La Chapelle was up,
and its truculent dwellers scowled and muttered at us as
we passed. My driver, a Frenchman, lost his nerve, and
began to tremble. I made him change places, and got
hold of the reins myself. A long look ahead showed me
no babies and no barricades, so I dropped the whip over
the good horse's flank, and let him have his head. Before
we got to the Porte they were yelling after us like a
pack of mongrels, "Prussien!" "Prussien!" "A bas le
Prussien!" Only once through the gate, and they might
yell till they burst. But, lo! the drawbridge was up.
There faced me, as I drove up, the grim faces of a couple
of mitrailleuses, pointed down the Rue. And the pursuers
were hot on our heels. Away to the left, clear and deserted ran the intra-enceinte road leading to the gate of
St. Ouen. I turned the horse's head down this and
sprung him into a gallop. I had sunk my tail before I
reached the gate of St. Ouen, which was open, and
through which I drove without interruption. Then there
was the ten miles' trot out to Margency, where General
von Schlotheim had kindly given me permission to use
the head-quarter telegraph wire, and then, without a moment to spare, another drive back to St. Denis, to catch
there the train leaving Paris at nine p.m. for Calais. I
reached England at six the following evening, handed in
the "copy" I had written on the way, and was on the
way back in the mail train by nine o'clock the same night.

When I got back to Paris on the forenoon of the 4th, I found that the Germans had cleared out that morning, and that Paris was in ecstasies over her triumph. Lives there the man who understands Paris and the rationale of its shifting moods? Man, say I! He must be something more than man—a creature gifted with the powers of penetration of an augur, and with a variety of other all but impossible qualifications. I could not, for the life of me, understand Paris. I could not, being as I hope a reasonable man paying poor-rates, and having a respect for constituted authorities, get any further insight into the inscrutable mystery of Paris than the acknowledgment that she "is a thing which no fellow can understand." She has as many notes as an Æolian harp. In the beginning of February she had been in abject despair. She was decent then, and I had felt bound to respect the dignity with which her quiet despair manifested itself. On the 1st of March she had been rabid yet cowardly; sublimely foolish; utterly lost to a sense of dignity or even of shame; truculent where she dared to be so; utterly contemptible in every respect in the eyes of those who would fain have respected her most. By the 4th of March the wheel had come round full circle. The Germans were gone. "Richard is himself again." Paris was full of complacency, the logic of which was not easy to understand. Here, so far as I could make out, was the process of reasoning:—"The hated intruders have gone away after a very brief stay. They meant to stop ever so much longer. The Prussian Guards made sure they were coming in. The Saxons were dying to do the same, and are dying now with disappointment. But the aspect of Paris struck terror into the Teuton soul. The foe bundled out in hot haste, awed by the black thunder-cloud of the impending storm. On the whole their evacuation is rather more creditable to Paris than victory gained in a set fight. They have practically run away. We are free from the incubus; let us be ourselves again. We have, so to speak, scowled them out; now let us smile at the success of our scowl."

"Smile" is hardly the word; it seemed to me Paris was to-day positively on the broad grin of complacency. She had legitimately earned her triumph. With the stern rigour befitting the circumstances, she had actively discountenanced anybody holding communication with the foe. She had jumped upon men unfortunate enough to know any member of a confraternity of nations numbering some forty millions of souls; she had stripped women naked who had dared to smile upon the Teuton satyrs. Let me not malign Paris. In some cases she had not stripped the women naked; I had heard of instances in which bonnets, stockings, and boots had been left. She had sacked a café where a few German officers took supper, thereby *pro tanto* purging herself of the unclean thing. I believe an extensive use was being made of Condy's disinfecting fluid and chloride of lime in the Palais de l'Industrie, the theatres on the Champs Elysées, and other public buildings occupied by the Germans. Deodorisers had been largely strewn over the thoroughfares used by them, and the chain of the enclosure around the Arc de Triomphe, over which the young hussar lieutenant jumped his horse, had been removed and replaced. The original chain was no doubt being melted down into axles for dung-carts.

The foes having recoiled in rapid panic from the consequences which they had so rashly and unthinkingly braved, Paris remained the virtual mistress of the field. Why should she not enjoy her triumph? She was doing so. Her valiant soldiery, now that peace was signed, looked and spoke as if it were by a crowning and special exercise of their mercy that the Germans were allowed to exist in the neighbourhood, and as good as intimated that they only did so on sufferance, and to give them time to pack up their portmanteaus without undue bustle and haste. The streets had burst out into sudden liveliness. All the shops were open. It was a beautiful day, and everybody was out walking and enjoying the triumph. It was a singular evidence of the moderation of the Parisians that there was at night no movement in favour of a general illumination. Cynics may say that a lack of gas prevented this demonstration, but I for my part am inclined to believe that the reason was based upon much higher grounds. Since I had been in Paris, I had observed how much the Parisians had before now held aloof from their favourite exercise of sitting in front of the cafés. Those few who dared to be *outré* and to break the rule sat as if they had the stringhalt, with their legs ignobly tucked under them. Mark the contrast to-day. Everyone was sitting in the sunshine outside the cafés, and everybody was stretching his legs as well out before him as their natural configuration and the condition of his boots would legitimately permit. There was a method in this seeming trifle. The straddle of the Parisian legs intimated the rehabilitation of the self-complacency.

In one of Mr. Dickens's novels, somebody calls attention to the mystery attending the disappearance of dead donkeys and old postboys. Had the sagacious observer in question been in Paris at this period, I think he might have added a third wonderment to his list. What on earth had become of the crowd—crowd is too good a word—of the scum of wretches that had inundated the German quarter and its environs on the 1st?

24*

Where were the stunted, thin-faced, evil-eyed, scraggy-
necked, knob-jointed, white-livered horde of miscreants
that had yelled and whistled and swore and shrunk into
their clumsy sabots or rotten high-lows when a German
looked their way? Where the noble bands of patriots
that had stripped wretched women and painted the German
colours on their naked flesh? Where the three hundred
heroes, none above five feet three inches in height, who
had achieved the gallant exploit of my capture, and, with
such Herculean exertions for the behoof of *la patrie*,
dragged me along in the gutter? I protest I could not
find a trace of them, nor could I find anybody who knew
anything as to their whereabouts. Certainly they were
not myths. My knuckles demonstrated unto me the
certainty that they were not "trifles light as air," even if
my back and ribs had not been confirmatory. And I
think I should have known some of my more particular
friends again if I could only see them. My supply of
cartes de visite was unfortunately short, but I took the
liberty of distributing a few souvenirs, which were not so
graciously received as might have been, but yet might
have served for purposes of identification. But the whole
horde had utterly vanished—faded clean out of sight.
People told me I could find a large proportion of its
members in Belleville. I went to Belleville in the afternoon, but saw nobody I knew, and not many of the pattern of my friends. Did they live habitually in the cellars, these interesting contributions to the aggregate of
the population of Paris, and never came up but when
there was some work to be done that was after their own
hearts? There are roughs in London. These I know
where to find. They are something like roughs, too.
The K division of police runs small, and a good Shore-
ditch or Whitechapel rough has no objection, when oc-

casion demands, to cope singly with any member of that
respected force. But the Paris rough, as he demonstrated himself on the 1st of March, is individually a
contemptible creature. Physically he is a cross between
a cat and a rabbit. His lust for blood beats that of a
stoat—and it is here wherein he differs from your British
rough, who hates blood except under the skin in the
shape of extravasation—but his cowardice interferes with
his realisation of the treat. Where he gets to when times
are not favourable for the free development of his idiosyn-
crasy was to me one of the chiefest of the many puzzles
which this strange city afforded.

Quiet head-quarters ordinarily were those of Prince
George at Le Vert Galant. But on the night before the
review at Villiers, on the 7th of March, there were no
cards, and the bureau was full of the staff immediately
after coffee-time. For any quantity of organization had
to be perfected for the morrow, and then there was after
to-morrow also to be seen to. For in a day or two the
Saxons were to quit the face of Paris to occupy the Ardennes, with head-quarters at Rethel.

There was not a little disappointment in the Maas
Army that it had not fallen to its lot to see the inside of
Paris. But the reparation for the disappointment was
thorough. To whatever quarter others might point as
the scene of their exploits, they were reviewed far away
therefrom. Even the Guards—forming as they did a
portion of the Maas army—were brought to Longchamps
to be reviewed, away from Le Bourget, so wedded to
their name, from Pierrefitte and Stains, the gallantly held
forepost villages, in order that there might be no Prussian element in the force which the Emperor reviewed on
the scene of a victory won by Saxon and Würtemberger
arms. It is not easy to conceive of a greater compliment

paid to soldiery than that which the Emperor paid in
this review to the fighting men of his allies. Located as
he was at Versailles, he did not see the deadly struggles
of the 30th November and 2nd of December. But on
the ground where the review of the 7th of March was
held it scarcely lay with any one to ask for corroborative
proof of the narrative given by the despatches. The
Saxons and Würtembergers might have said to any one
asking for a sign and token, "Si monumentum quæris,
circumspice." For the review was held at Villiers, the
key of the position in the desperate fights of the 30th
November and 2nd December. Monuments of valour were
everywhere around; honour was done to men on the very
spot where they had gained and maintained their fighting fame. Look up and around, O Emperor-King! and
realise what these troops battled against in the days I
speak of. See how close is Avron, its bluff then crowned
with the big naval guns that helped to shatter Brie, and
made this Villiers here a place to wonder at and shudder at, till such time as the masons shall have made
good the damages. Frowns out upon the Horseshoe that
grim Fort Nogent there, that could throw shells even into
Champs, and lower down the batteries of Faisanderie and
Gravelle contributed to the dominance now happily de-
parted. From the south-west, Charenton casts a baleful
side-look on Champigny and Chenevières; its squint is
ugly now, even when we know it is harmless. Monuments
of Saxon and Würtemberger valour! I have named some,
for they have had to be valorous men that stood up
against the impact of the projectiles cast by these now
harmless forts. Other monuments were there, too, in
abundance. Kaiser, you can look no whither but you
look on graves of brave men who died for you and the
Fatherland! From where we stood as the Emperor rode

on to the field, we could see many of the mounds over
the trenches which served as graves. We were standing
within view of the spot where I shook hands with the
two Saxons, boy-lieutenants of the 108th, as the regiment
went out to close quarters, and when it came back it had
left the lads needing nothing but the grave a little way to
the front yonder. Monuments for Saxon braves! Surely
the laurels were already growing thick over the dead
brows, for they must have been well watered. Aye,
watered by the tears of women in the quiet villages of
the Saxon Switzerland. Watered by the tears of such as
the lone mother, who wanted to know about her boy who
"has blue eyes, flaxen hair, and a green stone ring on
one of the fingers of the right hand." Watered by the
tears of the woman of Kamenz, one of whose sons lies
two hundred yards nearer Brie than where we stood; the
other had by this time begun to limp on one leg about
the lazarette. Monuments—aye, if of loss, also of valour.
There is Brie below us, held by a single regiment for
hours against an army. To the left is Champigny, to
hold and to retake which the Würtembergers poured out
their blood as if it had been water, and counted their
lives but as dross. On this peninsula was enacted the
turning-point scene of the siege of Paris. Had these
25,000 men not been staunch, 100,000 Frenchmen would
have been outside the ring of environment. Let Deutschland never forget, while grateful memory is left her, what
she owes for these two momentous days to the Saxons
and Würtembergers. But for them it might have been
that Kaiser Wilhelm would have been in other plight than
reviewing troops here to-day in peace.

As we left Le Vert Galant early in the morning, and
took the pleasant winding road through the forest of
Bondy, one would have been puzzled what to say of the

weather. Now it smiled, now it looked uncommonly like
weeping; yet still there was no rain. Around Chelles
were halted the cavalry and artillery of the 23rd division
(Montbé's), and over the pontoon bridge at Cournay, and
so along the south bank to Neuilly. The last time I had
passed this way the riding was hardly so pleasant, as
those great shell holes gave evidence. Then up on to
the broad flat upland between Neuilly and Villiers, with
Brie on its right front—the very tract for which the
French fought so fiercely on the 2nd. It was fringed
with battery emplacements. The most reckless aide-de-
camp dared not gallop over it, for there were shell holes
at every second horse length over the whole surface. The
ground did not admit of such a formation as that which
was effected at Longchamps. Somebody had to stand
out and go to the rear, and as the commander of the
Maas Army was a Saxon, he chivalrously ruled that his
countrymen should give the *pas*. On the right of the
first line stood the Würtembergers, with their artillery
and cavalry in another line behind them; on their left
the Bavarians, with their artillery and cavalry arranged
similarly. At a considerable distance in the rear, and
rather behind the Bavarians than the Würtembergers, was
the Saxon infantry, with its cavalry and artillery in its
rear. There was no selection here of one battalion of
each regiment, as at the review in the Bois de Boulogne.
Each battalion was represented, but its number was restricted to 500 men. Judging from appearances, several
of the battalions, particularly among the Bavarians, hardly
knew how to complete even this muster, notwithstanding
the recent reinforcements. The troops on the parade
were as follows:—The Würtemberger Division, consisting
of twelve infantry regiments, of one battalion each (the
Würtembergers have not yet adopted the Prussian ar-

rangement of three battalions in a regiment), four cavalry regiments, and proportional field artillery, the whole under the command of General von Obernitz; the 1st Bavarian Army Corps, under the command of General von der Tann, and the 12th (Royal Saxon) Army Corps, commanded by Prince George of Saxony. The latter corps comprised the 23rd division, commanded by General von Montbé, the youngest divisional general in the German armies, and contained the 101st, 102nd, and 103rd regiments, and the gallant Schützen regiment; and the 24th division, commanded by General von Nehrhoff, containing the 105th, 106th, and 107th regiments, and the Saxon Jägers. There were but two regiments of Saxon cavalry on the field; the rest, quartered at Compiègne, after taking part in the campaign of the North, were too far off to be present at a review ordered on so short a notice. All the artillery of the 12th Corps was on the field.

By half-past ten all were in position. Most of the troops had come long distances to the field, and the contents of haversacks were being investigated. Quick-sighted men those Saxons in the rear; they saw the eldest son of their king coming up from Noisy le Grand, and burst into a hearty cheer. The Prince had a detachment of Cuirassiers for his escort, and was accompanied by his staff. One word with his brother, and then he rode on to the right of the first line, and met General von Obernitz, of the Würtembergers. After a short conversation, he started for a tour of the lines. Before half-past eleven he was back, and everything was ready. But the videttes of the staff on the brow of the hill, among the flags and the triumphal arches, and the artificially-planted fir trees, and the rows of graves, were still motionless. The Emperor was late. Half-past eleven had been his set time, and he came not for another hour. The sky became overcast; rain began to fall just as we heard the sound of distant cheering. The Emperor's road lay right athwart the forefront of the battlefields of the 30th November and 2nd of December. He had crossed the Marne at Joinville under a triumphal arch. Before he came to the railway arches he had passed the spot where 800 French dead are buried in one little field; his road was lined with graves right up to the big mounds under the park walls. This park—the mansion in which had been inhabited by a French lady, its courageous owner, right through the siege—he entered, and exchanged his travelling carriage for the back of a light chestnut horse. The Imperial Crown Prince, who accompanied him, rode to-day the same dark chestnut that had been his mount on the 1st. And then the Imperial party topped the rising ground between the flags, and the bands struck up. There was a little cheering, but not much. The Emperor rode to the front, and was met by the Crown Prince of Saxony. The meeting was very cordial. Then the parade inspection at once began, the Emperor, the Crown Prince of Saxony, and the Crown Prince of Prussia riding side by side. The Würtemberger infantry cheered moderately; the Bavarians were altogether silent. The Emperor playfully buckets his horse over the shell holes, and when the end of the first line was reached gave the staff a stretcher over some very rough country to the head of the second. There was more cheering among the artillery and cavalry, both Bavarian and Würtemberger. From the end of this line to the Saxons was quite a long canter. Some dodged it, and turned up in a good place when the "check" came before the Saxon Guards; but the Emperor sent his horse gaily over big ridges and furrows, and through vineyards and battery emplacements, only turning aside when graves

came in the way. The Saxons were not enthusiastic.
They were mad to be home, and they had just been
ordered to march into "other catonments in the Ardennes."
But presently they got over the sulks and cheered a little,
especially the cavalry and artillery in the second line.
Then the Emperor diverged to look into a siege battery
on the Saxon left flank, and then there was a gallop back
to a flagstaff in front of another battery, and the march
past began—the Würtembergers first.

Right well do the Würtembergers march, with a long
and yet decided step, and differing from us as regards
their marching in this—that they swing in cadence the
disengaged arm. Here comes Colonel von Brandenstein
of the black whiskers, he who headed the assault which
retook Champigny. Behind the infantry are the cavalry,
and I notice Rittmeister Count Kronsfeld, who headed
the only cavalry charge in the history of the siege of
Paris. Of the Bavarians, but that they marched past
splendidly, I have nothing to say, because I was not of
their exploits the eye-witness. But here comes our own
kindly Saxons, Prince George at their head. Here is
Colonel Abendroth, who had three horses shot under him
over the way there, and never a hair of his head singed.
Jog on there, good old Oberst Hausen of the Schützen
Regiment; Kaiser Wilhelm never looked on a better
soldier than thee—and that regiment of thine, what
valour it displayed, and what losses it sustained, following thee! There is "little Hammerstein," now a
captain, but only a lieutenant on the 2nd of December,
who though but a lieutenant yet commanded his battalion
as it marched out of the fray, so deadly had been the
slaughter of the officers. With a long English seat in the
saddle comes General von Montbé, by whom I stood on
the 21st of December, when the shells tumbled on to his

château in Clichy. And here comes Colonel Dietrich, of the 103rd, whom I have not seen since he turned aside from his dead Landwehrman in the park of Raincy. Behind him is a face I know well. Aha! Major von Schön-berg, you may now soon see Frau Majorin, and I hope it may be my lot to drink one day with you a glass of beer in Kamenz; and here is Hammerstein and Kirchbach, and the adjutant and the doctor, the staunch fellows with whom I spent Christmas night under the lee of Avron. I wonder, von Zanthier, if that is the saddle you found on Avron? *Gott in Himmel!* Here comes Under-officer Schultz, as wooden as ever, yet with a kindly side glance for his Crown Prince, as he goes · past pointing his toes as if for a wager.

The pageant is over; the last of our friends are past. The Emperor King makes off for Ferrières, the Crown Prince of Saxony going with him. Soon the environs of Paris will know no longer the Maas army. In two days the head-quarters were off to Compiègne, and all would set their faces homeward. Their home lies to-wards another point of the compass from mine, and so I take my leave of my comrades of two eventful months —comrades from whom I received kindnesses never to be forgotten. From prince to private I have experienced hearty Kameradschaft. The obligations I rest under to his Royal Highness the Crown Prince, General Schlot-heim, and other members of the staff, are greater than I can describe. But the feeling of the staff permeated right down. I do not think there is a man in the Maas army who did not know me by sight, and was not aware of my avocation. We had been together in fair weather and in foul. We had made merry together. I had stood by and seen them fight; my hand had been pressed by the dying among them. I had looked down upon not a few of them in the trench that did service for a grave. So let me take my hat off to the Maas army, in kindly and fraternal adieu, wishing well right heartily to every man in its ranks.

With the departure of the Emperor, the disruption of the armies, and the ratification of the peace preliminaries, the German position in the neighbourhood of Paris assumed a new phase, the unexpected prolongation of which must be inexpressibly wearisome to the homesick troops. The events referred to, to speak of small things after great, set at liberty the newspaper correspondents who had been with the German armies before Paris—more fortunate the correspondents than the soldiers, in that it was free to them to return home when they listed. I did not immediately avail myself of my privileges in this way. Ever since Sedan a change in the state of feeling between England and Germany had been observable, as expressed in the press of both countries. With an army in the field as far away from Germany as from England, it is obvious that the medium referred to was the only one at one's command through which to discern the nature of the relations between the two nations. But, in common as I dare say with many, I had learned to recognise the fact that the tone of a press is not always to be relied on as a wise and correct enunciation of the *vox populi*. The press of England evinced a jealousy lest German successes, followed by German unity, should stimulate Germany to a new *rôle* of general aggressiveness. The press of Germany, whether actuated by a spirit of irritated defiance, thrown off its balance by the flush of triumph, or accurately reflecting the tone of the nation which was its constituent, I could not tell, was characterised by an arrogant arbitrariness which seemed in a great measure to justify the expression of feeling on

the part of our own journalists. A short visit to Germany
occurred to me as the readiest way of arriving at some
estimate of German citizenhood as regards the alleged
aggressive tendency of Germany superinduced by her
acknowledged military supremacy and her successes in
the war which has just terminated. It was obvious that
a flying visit—and that was all that was in my power—
did not admit of one hearing and seeing sufficient to
enable him to speak with any great weight or assurance
on a subject covering so wide a field; but, as feathers
show which way the wind blows, *indicia* showing how the
current of popular opinion sets will ever present themselves, unless a man goes about with his eyes and ears
hermetically sealed. I desired also to see something of
the manner in which the Germans should welcome home
the first fruits of the victorious army, and also to witness
the arrival of the Emperor in his capital after so long an
absence. Before going to Berlin I spent a short time in
Cologne and Bonn.

Before speaking of the feeling and temper of the
German civilian citizenhood as to the future policy of
Germany, let me first say a word as to the army. You
don't keep men in the field for some eight months, and
win ever so many battles, without making professional
fighting animals of at least some of them. Officers, for
instance, to whom piping times of peace would bring
monotony, sluggish promotion, and the routine of garrison duty, lusted for continuous war with somebody, no,
matter whom. I venture to say that if England declared
war to-morrow with any state in the known world, without the semblance of a provocation, the officers of the
British army would hail the announcement with joy.
Wherefore, when I heard in the Officer-Casino in Gonesse
just before the armistice, a knot of young guardsmen

praying for more fighting; and when one lad turned to
me, and, clinking glasses, benignantly announced that
the Queen Elizabeth Regiment would before two years
were over be besieging Windsor Castle (which he evidently took to be our strongest fortress), I did not conclude that the German army was eager for a quarrel with
England; but only asked my young friend whether he
had learnt to swim. I had only to go outside into the
road or up to the battery, or on to the outposts to find
how the men of the army were sighing and longing for
peace. They would do their duty to the last; would have
followed my fire-eating youngster to the cannon's mouth;
but they were hungry for home with an exceeding great
hunger, and candidly owned that they wanted no more
war in this their generation. For whereas young von
Fähnrich was a professional soldier, they were citizens
made soldiers by force of circumstances, and longing to
return to their citizenhood. Depend upon it that so long
as Germany wishes for peace she will never be embarrassed by the clamours of her army for war.

What said the citizens then: the *patres conscripti* who
sat at home when the young men went to the war; the
women of the nation, who in a free and cultivated people,
such as the Germans, exercise so great an influence over
the national bias and impulses? There seemed to me a
surprisingly universal unanimity of conviction that Germany must be peaceful in the future, come what may,
save absolute loss of honour. Flags were flying, crowds
were cheering as the military train went by; but the
people was shuddering and quivering again under the
price of the victory. Wherever I went, I found under the
pride and the bursts of gladness, stimulated by such a
sight, a deep feeling of melancholy. The mourning ware-
houses in Cologne and Bonn must have driven a fine trade

this winter. The streets swarmed with men on crutches.
I met a pleasant group in the Rheingasse of Bonn one
forenoon—four of them—and there were three capable
legs among the four. They bore the number of a regiment
that I knew before Metz, and which afterwards went to
the north; and we had a little chat together. Private
soldiers all the four, mark you; but let me give their
professions, because it is of importance to my argument.
One was the son of a master tailor; the second was the
tenter of a steam-engine in a factory; the third had been
the apprentice of an emigration agent; and the fourth
had had a shop of his own which his absence at the war
had ruined and shut up. Hard, was it not, to lose a leg
and your living at one *coup*, even if it be for the Fatherland? It is owing to the presence—and, according to her
military constitution, the inevitable presence—of such men
in her ranks that Germany is perforce a country averse
from war. It is because so many of this class are now
no longer in her ranks, because they are rotting under
the soil of French battle-fields, that she shudders and
blenches at the name of war, even while she cheers her
heroes. It is because she feels that the war has cost her
so much of her lifeblood, of the real bone and sinew of
her stirring business population, not of mere waste cannon fodder, that she has exacted terms so hard from
France—terms that, as she reckons, make it impossible
that France in sanity will ever again disturb the peace of
the Fatherland.

Statistics of relative losses in such a war as that just
over, I take to be of little value. In any war it seems to
me that you must regard, not so much the quantity as
the quality of the losses, if you wish accurately to gauge
the virtual depletion of either contending nationality.
So far as I was able to learn, the French loss lay for by

far the most part at either end of the social string. The
old maxim of *noblesse oblige* held good at all events to
an extent which was not discreditable. Then there was
a great gulf, for the bourgeoisie had an intense respect
for their skins. The Frenchmen of the rank and file who
have fallen victims in this war may be said, and that
without any intention to impugn the value of their sacri-
fice, to represent quantity rather than quality. They
were rank and file, and their best friends could say little
more of them. The army never was able to claim to
be a national one in the highest sense. What sort of
an army is that of Germany as to its rank and file has
never been rightly appreciated, spite of explanations, however long and lucid, as to its character as a distinctively
national army. Those familiar with German newspapers
know the death notices surviving relatives and friends
are fond of inserting to commemorate their deceased
kinsfolk. The idea occurred to me to go through a file
of the *Cologne Gazette* for a month, and extract the professions of such deceased private soldiers and non-commissioned officers of the German armies as were commemorated therein in this way. I made no selection,
but took name after name, wherever I found the profession designated. Here, copied from my notebook as I
took them out, is the list of professions, rigidly restricted
to private soldiers and non-commissioned officers:—
Tavern-keeper, medical student, merchant, clothier,
cabinetmaker, son of a public accountant, master mo-
deller, steamship superintendent, upholsterer, barrister,
schoolmaster, lecturer in a public school, head forester,
medical student, engineer, post-office clerk, son of chief
administrator of mines, academy student, son of a superintendent, brewer, the Count of Salm Hoogstraeten, medical student. Of course many hundreds died uncom-

memorated, who were not, in the sense to which I am referring, such valuable members of society. But then, when the dead list of the rank and file of an army must perforce, from the constitution of that army, comprehend men so valuable as the above in a politico-economical sense, who will have hardihood enough to say that the nation owning that army dare crave for war, or indeed have any other feeling thereanent but that of horror—a horror only to be overridden by the strongest necessity?

Experience has convinced me of the inutility of "interviewing." You set a man at once to weighing his words, and he either gammons you intentionally, buncomises, or is reticent, so as to be of no service. Everybody who knows Bonn knows the Rheinecke, and everybody who knows the Rheinecke knows the nightly meeting of responsible citizens over the bottle of Rhine wine. The night of my arrival I sat down at the end of the long table, with the *Cologne Gazette* in my hand as a make-belief, and, keeping my mouth shut, kept my ears open. Of course there was not a word save about the war and matters thereanent. A corpulent gentleman was great on tactics, and while he was rather depreciatory of the Duke of Mecklenburg, expressed profound admiration of von Werder. But what chiefly struck me was the conversation as to the terms of the peace. A quiet, sagacious person said plainly he thought the money indemnity was too great. It was not an indemnity he said, it was a premium on war. Another struck in with the rejoinder that the indemnity was exacted, not alone for the money charges which the war had cost the Germans, but for the cost of life and blood, as well as the stagnation of profitable industry which it had caused. The quiet man sighed as he replied that there were losses for which no money indemnity could compensate. "Do you think," said he, "I reckoned my poor dead Carl by the milliard?" On the territorial annexation all were united. It was a necessary preservative ot peace for Germany. But for this necessity, Metz was a nuisance rather than otherwise. One gentleman was not contradicted when he alleged that if Germany could have got a guarantee against any future aggressiveness on the part of France, she would not have demanded an inch of territory—not even Alsace. "What do you mean by a guarantee though?" asked his neighbour;—"A French guarantee?" "*Gott bewahr!*" was the emphatic response—"Thiers' guarantee to-day might be kicked to the devil in two years by an Orleanist, the weak President of a red-hot Republic; no, I mean an European guarantee." Then a Professor of the University made an observation which I quote simply as an indication of the horror with which the possibility of a future war is regarded. "Sooner," said he, "than in ten or twelve years' time my sons should run the chance of being maimed and killed in a war with France, I would gladly see now every village in France burnt, every deed done against her, even to actual extermination of her population, that would guarantee us against the possibility of our peace ever again being disturbed by her." It is strange how intense can be a craving for peace that can prompt to a contingent blood-thirstiness so uncompromising as this.

It was quite in consonance with the German character that there should not be any manifestation of cock-a-whoop exultation among the people by reason of the victorious campaign just concluded. The feeling of sedate satisfaction seemed to find vent chiefly in flags and universal good humour. You might jostle anybody you liked; and whereas he might under normal conditions growl not a little, now he turned unto you a smiling face

25*

as if to say you might do it again and he would not
quarrel with you, so complaisant was he in his quiet realisation of what the Americans call a "good time." It
seemed as if in those first weeks of peace most people
were celebrating the event by refraining from doing any
work; and stationing themselves from day to day in
great groups in the neighbourhood of the railway sta-
tions, to watch their fighting brethren pass through on
their way home. A considerable proportion of the population of Bonn had apparently permanently bivouacked
in the avenue adjoining the railway station. Hour after
hour they stood there—men, women, and children, as if
they could never have enough of gazing. They stood
under a perfect forest of flags, and they had made a kind
of bower with evergreen branches, which was turned to
the practical use of a depôt for refreshments, to be served
to the occupants of the passing trains. On an average
there was one of these about every hour, and a curious
sight the military train was. For the two days of my
stay in Bonn the passing troops chiefly consisted of
Westphalian Hussars, and those bold warriors took huge
delight in mounting upon the tops of the carriages, and
from this elevated position waving hand flags while they
cheered vehemently. A vocal contingent inside sang
without intermission the "Wacht am Rhein." At the
sight of the train the waiting crowd would waken up
and burst into reciprocal cheering. The sedate satisfaction for the time gave place to a modified ecstasy. The
boys clambered up beside the Hussars and gave the tenor
to the bass cheering of the soldiers. The women pushed
to the front regardless of the squeeze. A blousy frau is
in the first rank, baby in arms, shouting an inquiry, addressed. miscellaneously, about a certain Johann, who,
probably enough, occupies the position of male parent to

the embryo Hussar in her arms. A hairy Hussar leans over a truck, deftly kisses the frau, and annexes feloniously the baby, which he elevates triumphantly into mid-air, the young Teuton crowing and kicking in huge enjoyment. A baby in a military train, full of Landwehrmen coming home from the war! Here is a prize, indeed. The frau seems half pleased, half inclined to be frightened, as her urchin is passed hand over hand along the roofs of the carriages, each temporary possessor of the living morsel giving it a kiss and a cunning tickle that speaks of paternal habit before he parts with it. Curious how a baby may dispel the grave forebodings of a pacific professor. Such a grave and reverend seignor stood beside me as the train came up with its cheering freight. "Alas!" quoth he, "for the evil influences of war. I recognise in these faces a savagery that was not to be seen when the fellows passed through, six months ago, on their way to the war. They have tasted blood, and the fell meal shows itself in their faces." Truly, in a sense, the Professor was right. The faces had got bronzed and hair matted. There was a truculency in their aspect, and a buccaneering air discernible, that might be taken as a memento of high-handed requisitioning and long chases after Francs-tireurs. I think the air was in a great measure assumed for the occasion, for we know the weakness of human nature. But the baby drove the savagery out of the faces, and stamped out the buccaneering swagger, so that Herr Professor owned himself satisfied, with the reservation that he hoped all the Hussars were married men with families.

None of the Bonn Johnnies coming marching home arrived in this particular train I am speaking of, with the exception of a single Landwehrman. I saw this Landwehrman disembark. He was a living proof that

fluids of an inebriating character exist on the road
traversed by the train previous to its arrival in Bonn.
In point of fact, our Bonn Landwehrman was pretty
considerably drunk. But drunk as he was, it was plain
that he realised the fact that he had his character to
maintain in his native place. It was with portentous
solemnity that he emerged from the station, inadver-
tently carrying his arms reversed. A porter followed
bearing his knapsack. Another brought his havresack,
his drinking flask with the cork out and plainly empty,
and a few other trifles. Once outside, our Landwehrman halted and blandly surveyed his fellow-townsmen.
It seemed as if he was about to give them his blessing.
But he had forgotten to report himself at the Etappen
Commando. You should have seen the effort he made
to straighten himself up, and go right about into a creditable manner. While he is complying with the demands
of discipline, there is a stir in the throng, which results
in the advent of the identical frau, whose baby the
Hussar had looted. She has recovered said baby, severely
tousled. It appears that the solemnly inebriated is
Johann, the lawful spouse of the frau, and parent of the
baby, as well as of a ladder-like assortment of elder
hopes. The frau, it is clear, admits the prior claims of
the Etappen Commando, nor seeks to intrude on the
interval sacred to duty. She compensates herself for
the self-restraint by tumbling bodily, baby and all, upon
Johann the moment he gets outside. There is a curious
miscellaneous group, in the posturing of which baby
gets squeezed and begins to squall, Johann's face appearing at intervals from behind his wife. In the glimpses
it is apparent that Johann is blubbering. The frau un-
locks herself, and presents unto her husband their family
member by member, till the top step of the ladder is

reached, and then a sort of informal procession is formed
for the homeward route. Johann is visibly limper under
the influence of family emotion, yet he straightens himself up every now and then, and throws out his shoulders
as he glances down at the iron cross in his button-hole.
He is denuded of every impediment. A mob of children
surround him and the frau, contending for the honour
of carrying something belonging to the hero. A neighbour has the baby, so that the frau may devote herself
exclusively to Johann. Probably enough on the morrow
you might have met that honest fellow in his civilian
clothes going about the avocation he had relinquished
when called on to go and fight for the Fatherland.

In the throng continually by the railway station one
could not but be sensible of a certain sombreness in the
dress of the women. Likely enough at first one did not
come to draw any inference from this. There was the
sombreness, just as when a cloud comes between the sun
and a landscape, a mere fleeting accident. But the
sombreness of colour in this throng was no fleeting accident. You came to realise that before you were a
strange number of women dressed in black, in which
crape profusely showed itself. Crape and cheering!
Mourning and the joyous reunion of husband and wife,
father and children! Were these kill-joys of malice
prepense who came out among us with their weepers and
weeds to dull with their trappings of woe the gladness
and the triumph? Ah, for these crape-wearers—and
they are many this day all over the Fatherland—there
was no joy, no gladsome reunion. Your triumph! What
was your triumph on this pale woman with the drawn
face and haggard eyes, and with the three children, who
now looked wonderingly into their mother's face, and
now joined, unwitting of their bereavement, in the fun

of their young comrades, to whom the war had left
fathers? One asked himself why they came here? Why
does the moth come to the candle? There must, I suppose, be a kind of pleasurable torture in a fresh pang,
a kind of exquisite poignancy not to be resisted. One
saw but little manifestation of acute emotion among
those sable-clad spectators. Surely in most cases the
bitterness of death must have been past.

The train rolled on with its buzzaing freight, and
the bustle in the crowd lapsed for a while. But not
for long. Here comes an hospital train, its engines
decorated with evergreens. If you look at the windows
of the long carriages, built on the American model, you
may see the poor wounded fellows raising themselves on
their elbows in their narrow cots, to look out upon their
countryfolk. It is only for privileged people that there
is admission to the platform of the station while the
ambulance train is drawn up there; sympathisers, however warm, are in the way when delicate work has to be
done systematically. On the platform one sees ready
a number of mattressed stretchers, for Bonn has no fewer
than fourteen lazarettes, and in addition numerous private families have virtually turned their houses into
hospitals. Members of the committee come out of their
store-room, and take each so many carriages to supply
with such refreshments as the inmates may be allowed
to receive. Here is the head doctor, a tough old boy to
be sure. The first time I saw him was in the château at
Amelange, on the 7th October, a suture-needle behind
his ear, and his hands in such a state that I respectfully
declined to shake them. Since then he has been all
through the northern campaign, and is doing good work
right to his own door. An upright man and a just, he
candidly owns he has not time to gossip, and must go

see to the disembarkation of such of his patients as are
to be left in Bonn. Here is one of them, a hollow-eyed
under-officer, on this stretcher, with his coat thrown
over him. He seems all but comatose, yet see how he
manages feebly to disengage a hand to turn out the
breast of his coat, so as not to hide the iron cross hanging there. By the look of him, I fear it will task the
Bonn surgeons to bring him round. Here is the head
doctor in a passion, and bullying quite vehemently.
Well, after all, doctor, it is natural enough. He is a
Bonn man, it seems, this hussar Wachtmeister, and these
are Bonn-folk that are crowding about him. But the
doctor is right; you must let the air in about him, good
people, and so give ground. The Wachtmeister seems a
philosopher, lying there with one of his legs the Lord
knows where. There is a quiet, amused smile on his
handsome face, and he seems to be relishing his cigar.
It is clear the Wachtmeister does not quite belong to
himself. A strapping, good-looking girl has quietly but
potently taken possession of him, and none challenge her
title. She stands fast by the head of the stretcher, while
the rest give ground at the mandate of the surgeon, and
there is the air of conscious property in the business-like
manner in which she gives her directions as to lifting
and moving her complaisant goods and chattel. A brave
girl truly—fit to be a soldier's wife of the Mrs. Colonel
O'Dowd stamp. If the doctor cared to lay his finger on
her pulse this minute; I'd bet a good deal he'd find it
over a hundred! How near she is to hysterics those
tell-tale twitchings about the corners of the mouth and
swellings of the throat give evidence, yet gallantly she
maintains her composure, and gives her instructions as
if she were telling the people how to boil a potato or
scrub a floor.

It froze hard in Berlin during the night preceding
March the 17th, the day of the Emperor's home-coming;
and morning brought bright sun and cloudless sky.   It
brought also an universal ebullition of bunting.   A crowd
had collected in the morning under the statue of the
Great Fritz opposite the Imperial Schloss.   The crowd
was drawn by a banner which floated from the pedestal,
having a long poem stamped on the black and white
linen.   "Hail Kaiser Wilhelm, hail to thee and to the
brave German host thou leadest back from victory, ghost-
like from afar.   Like the clash of distant bells sounds
the glad cheering of the conquerors.   Old Fritz looks
down with proud glance upon his descendants, approv-
ing greatly their valour."   So opened the poem which
struck home to the sympathies of the crowd so heartily
that a policeman relaxed into rubbing his hands.   Mean-
time an adventurous youth, with a flag in his hand, had
climbed up, and sat astraddle of Old Fritz's helmet,
waving his banner proudly.   All the forenoon the preparations in the way of decorations and for the illumination steadily went on.   The lazarettes were not behind-
hand in an humble way, and it was touching to see the
poor broken fellows elaborating their simple decorations.
At one o'clock came guard-mounting.   On this important
day the guard was found by the 2nd Guard and the
Kaiser Franz Regiments, and consisted wholly of soldiers
who had come back from the war.   I recognised among
the stalwart fellows, marching to the strains of the Paris
March, not a few old familiar faces that brought to mind
Le Bourget, Stains, Pierrefitte, and Le Blanc Mesnil.
Long before four o'clock every street was crowded, the
throng being specially dense by the station, where the
great people had begun to arrive to await the Royal
arrival.   The Princess Frederick Charles, Queen Elizabeth,

and the Baden family were among the earliest arrivals. A great cheer rang out as Count Bismarck, bluff and smiling, drove up with his wife in an open carriage. In the reserved portion of the platform all were in uniform or court dresses. Here was staunch old Marshal von Wrangel in the uniform of a White Cuirassier, rather bandy, but good seemingly for another twenty years. Here was Prince George, more familiar with the pen—a bad one—than the sword, wrapped in a large cloak, with an attendant bearing his helmet of state. He had a chat with a Jäger private with one leg, who had got somehow in the forefront. Here too was General Vogel von Falkenstein, grey and grim; and von Steinmetz, all the way from his Posen governorship. But the list was too long for enumeration. Every pillar of the long station was in a flutter of flags; on those on either side of the royal passage were blazoned the words Metz and Strassburg, while over the statues of Victory behind were Sedan and Paris. Was it by accident or design that opposite the platform on a siding an ambulance train had been halted, from the windows of which pallid faces looked out with hollow eyes on the brilliant scene? Its roof was clustered with convalescents, and a little squad of men maimed at Spicheren and Courcelles gave Steinmetz a cheer—old "Immer Vorwärts," as they lovingly styled him—and so with gossip and endless kindly salutations the moments of expectancy fleeted by.

Twenty minutes later, at the sound of a shrill distant whistle, out of the waiting-room stalked Count Bismarck in full war paint; Wrangel doffed his plumed helmet; a stream of ladies and children followed Bismarck's stalwart form; in three minutes more a near rumble, and the train, bedizened with flags, rolled into the siding. Three carriages passed a flight of steps, and the fourth came into sight; there rose a mighty cheer, and at the window stood the Emperor Wilhelm, framed as in a picture. The old man's face was working as the cheers rang in his ears. He was down the steps and kissing the Dowager Queen Elizabeth. What! would the women of his family mob him, then, as they crowded round him for his kisses, while grandchildren hung about his knees? No wonder that he had to brush his eyes with the back of his hand as he struggled through the women folk before him. In his path stood the white figure of Wrangel, the rays of the setting sun flashing on his snow-white hair. The soldier-patriarch raised his hand, and tried to lead off a cheer, but his voice failed him, and the tears rolled down his face. His master, not less moved, kissed his servant on either cheek. The two old soldier comrades embraced, while one of Steinmetz's wounded fellows headed, from the top of the carriage, a real rousing cheer. Then the Emperor grasped Bismarck by the hand, and kissed him too. He served von Steinmetz in the same manner with special cordiality, as if to refute the calumnies anent that gallant soldier. He kissed his way right through out of sight into the waiting-room, the Empress following him with a look of conscious ownership; and so exit Kaiser Wilhelm.

Behind him as he came from the carriage was a younger face, that of his son. I wondered the Princess was not jealous to see all these pretty girls, princesses, grand duchesses, and what not, hugging her husband "with effusion." But not she. She had fast hold of his right arm, and she looked about so proudly and gladly, the light of love in every feature. Her back hair had come down and it streamed over her shoulders in beautiful confusion. It was comical to see how she gently extricated "Our Fritz" from the press, when it seemed as if there had been enough of the kissing. But, then, the Prince had hairier faces to kiss, and more stalwart forms to embrace ere he reached the haven of the saloon. Von Roon, von Meydam, all the well-known Versailles faces followed, and then the women burst into the reserved space, and hugged and kissed the staff men who belonged to them as they came out of the carriages. The scene was like an April day, showers and sunshine, tears and smiles in about equal proportions—all state and ceremony went down before the gush of homely affection. The Emperor almost at once passed to his carriage, and drove off unescorted at a trot, followed by carriages containing the Royal Family and the other personages, along the Thier Garten, through the Brandenburg gate, and down Unter den Linden to the Palace, amidst immense cheering. As he passed under the arch the Imperial flag was run up on the palace. The cheering continued after he alighted. His Majesty lingered on the threshold, and at length went in; but his subjects were not to be denied, and he had to appear again on the balcony, helmet in hand and the Empress on his arm. His last appearance was at the window of the corner room where he showed himself on the declaration of the war, and here he listened to the Wacht am Rhein, sung by the crowd. The Imperial Crown Prince had also to come repeatedly to an open window of his palace, accompanied by his wife and their children; the eldest boy, dressed in full Uhlan uniform, especially delighting the people. The Princess, with her eldest son, had accompanied the Empress to Wildpark.

On the morning of the 22nd March, the Emperor's birthday, Berlin received her first regular consignment of home-coming warriors, in the shape of the 1st Battalion of the 2nd Guard Landwehr Regiment. The battalion

had gone out over 1,000 strong; I do not care to estimate how far beneath that number it mustered as it
marched down the Linden on the bright March morning.
It was never my fortune to see the Guard Landwehr men
fight, but Versailles correspondents have told Britain in
graphic language how they held the park-wall of St. Cloud
against all comers in the fierce fight of the 19th of
January.   It was no child's play that day, as this battalion gave proofs in its shortened column of fours as it
strode along behind the band of the 3rd Guard Regiment,
who played their comrades in.   Nearly all the men had
bound green wreaths round their helmets.   Some had
stuck nosegays in the muzzle of their needle-guns; others
carried chaplets on their bayonets.   Big muscular fellows
all of them, of set frames and mature years, hair to the
eyes, and clumsy rather of build and gait, but of rare
weight and toughness—troops that evidently knew the
meaning of fighting, and had good fight in them as a
matter of course and quite in the way of business.

After their Kaiser had had a look at them, and they
had marched past the palace, the battalion broke into
companies, each company taking a different direction to
a halting point.   I accompanied the 2nd company through
the Friedrich Strasse to the top of the Jäger Strasse.
While it was in the Linden rigorous discipline was the
order of the day.   But it relaxed somewhat in the Friedrich
Strasse, and the people got among their martial fellow-
citizens.   It made one laugh, though mirth was not the
sole emotion, to see the women claim their husbands,
throw arms round their necks and kiss them heartily;
while the honest fellows, fain to reciprocate, had still to
keep step and not materially lose their dressing.   Once
the women-folk got possession of the men that belonged
to them, there was no parting these twain of one flesh,

and so the fours became eights in many cases; in yet
others an indefinite number, as when the women had
babes in their arms and when elder children got a hold
of their father somewhere, and objected to leave go of
him. One woman I saw with two babes, plainly twins.
She wanted to hug her husband; but if she did she must
drop one of the babies. A comrade, whom no wife
claimed, and who was, I suppose, a sort of Landwehr
Brother Cheeryble, genially relieved her of one baby,
which he carried with singular address on his left shoulder.
The young one pulled the nosegay out of the muzzle of
his needle-gun carried on the other shoulder. And so
the company struggled on under difficulties, striving to
be martial to the last, but visibly embarrassed by family
considerations, till they reached the top of the Jäger
Strasse, where they halted. "Front," was the sergeant's
word of command; but with nominal intervals and doubled
files, how to perform it was rather a puzzle. Somehow
a double line did get formed; but the sizing was queer,
resulting from the fact that it was partially composed of
women, who, clinging fast to their husbands' arms, came
"Front" along with them. With the "Stand at ease"
came unreserved intercourse. Friends trooped around,
handshaking was incessant, the hairy Landwehrmen
grinned and perspired with exuberant joy. The lieutenant-colonel rode by, waving his kindly adieu to the men
who had so staunchly stood by him when he led them to
victory; they fell in and carried arms to the bluff old soldier, responding to his "Adieu" with a hearty cheer.
Then the captain, who had been transacting a little
family recognition on his own account on the pavement,
strode out among his men, and they formed a circle
about him as he began to speak. Orders as to disposal
of arms and accoutrements, rendezvous for pay, &c.,

were the matters with which he had first to deal; then his voice changed, as, after a little pause, he addressed his command as "comrades." "We have been together, men," said he, "through the campaign. I marched you out of Berlin, and now I march you back again. Not all indeed that went out with us have come back with us. God so willed it that some should have fallen in the war, but they died for King and Fatherland. You have done your duty, men, as good Prussians, and so now adieu!" "Adieu!" came back from every throat in answer, and with the response the company was disbanded. The men were free to kiss wives, hug bairns, and shake hands with friends. Surely no better finis can I hope to find for my book than the captain's little speech, the men's hearty respectful adieu, and then—wives, children, and friends.

THE END.

www.ingramcontent.com/pod-product-compliance
Lightning Source LLC
Chambersburg PA
CBHW022257280326
41932CB00010B/892